PROPHETS,
PUBLICISTS, AND
PARASITES

PROPHETS, PUBLICISTS, AND PARASITES

Antebellum Print Culture
and the Rise of the Critic

ADAM GORDON

University of Massachusetts Press
AMHERST AND BOSTON

ISBN 978-1-62534-453-3 (paper); 452-6 (hardcover)

Designed by Sally Nichols
Set in Palatino
Printed and bound by Maple Press, Inc.

Cover design by Frank Gutbrod
Cover illustration: "The Massacre of the Innocents," *Young Sam* (April 1, 1855), 49.
Courtesy of the American Antiquarian Society, Worcester, Massachusetts.

Library of Congress Cataloging-in-Publication Data

Names: Gordon, Adam, 1981– author.
Title: Prophets, publicists, and parasites : antebellum print culture and
the rise of the critic / Adam Gordon.
Description: Amherst : University of Masschusetts Press, 2020. | Includes
bibliographical references and index.
Identifiers: LCCN 2019020027 | ISBN 9781625344526 (hardcover) | ISBN
9781625344533 (paperback) | ISBN 9781613766972 (ebook) | ISBN
9781613766965 (ebook)
Subjects: LCSH: Criticism—United States—History—19th century. | American
literature—19th century—History and criticism. | Book industries and
trade—United States—History—19th century. | Publishers and
publishing—United States—History—19th century. | Books and
reading—United States—History—19th century.
Classification: LCC PS74 .G67 2020 | DDC 810.9/003—dc23
LC record available at https://lccn.loc.gov/2019020027

British Library Cataloguing-in-Publication Data
A catalog record for this book is available from the British Library

Parts of chapter 3 and chapter 5 appeared in slightly different forms, respectively,
as "'A Condition to Be Criticized': Edgar Allan Poe and the Vocation of Antebellum
Criticism" in *Arizona Quarterly* 68, no. 2 (Summer 2012) and "Beyond the
'Proper Notice': Frederick Douglass, *Uncle Tom's Cabin,* and the Politics of Critical
Reprinting" in *American Literature* 91, no. 1 (March 2019).

CONTENTS

ACKNOWLEDGMENTS

At each stage of writing this book, I've been supported by communities that affirm literary criticism's value as a communal endeavor above all else. The ideas in these chapters were born in classrooms and conference panels; advisers' offices and fellows' talks; over dinner conversations and in intellectual exchanges with editors, colleagues, and peer reviewers. The seed of this project was planted in college at the University of Pennsylvania. There, Colin Dayan sparked my fascination with Poe and set me on the path to graduate school; Max Cavitch helped turn that passion into an undergraduate thesis; Susan Stewart showed me the creative potential of criticism; Nancy Bentley affirmed my love for nineteenth-century American literature; and Peter Stallybrass made sure I never strayed too far from the material text. Joe Dimuro's blend of humor, thoughtful inquiry, and concern for student growth has been one that I've worked to emulate throughout my teaching career.

In graduate school at UCLA, Chris Looby was tireless in providing intellectual guidance, editorial supervision, and personal encouragement from this project's earliest stages to its final drafts as a dissertation. Then as now, he stands as my aspirational model for scholarly community, whether in the classroom, at meetings of the Americanist Research Colloquium and C19, or in more office meetings than I can count. Michael Colacurcio was as generous with his emotional support as he was exacting in his high standard of scholarship, showing me not just how to read early American literature but how to teach it, and reminding me to always have fun in the process. Eric Sundquist encouraged me to think big and advised me from Los Angeles and Baltimore. Barbara Packer has been, and will continue to be, a model of elegant scholarship, whose grace, clarity, and intellectual command in print and in person have left their imprint throughout these chapters.

Cindy Weinstein was charitable with her time and suggestions in serving as an outside reader while shaping my approach to Stowe.

The book would also not have been possible without generous support from a number of different institutions. The UCLA English Department and the UCLA Graduate Division gave me time away from teaching to write through multiple year-long fellowships. And while the conception for the project took place at UCLA, the book took the course it did through support from three research libraries. James Green and the staff of the Library Company of Philadelphia encouraged the project through the Albert M. Greenfield Dissertation Fellowship, which provided an archival foundation, clarity of focus, and a renewed sense of energy and excitement in the final year of graduate school. I am grateful, too, to the Huntington Library for two summer fellowships in which the chapters came together as a whole and for the wonderful community of staff and fellows that made my time there as fun as it was productive—Diann Benti and Juan Gomez in particular.

Above all, this book would not exist without the support of the American Antiquarian Society. It was during my year as the 2011–2012 John B. Hench Post-Dissertation Fellow that an unwieldy dissertation began to take shape as a book. I'm particularly thankful to Paul Erickson, who has supported this book in countless large and small ways while cultivating the thriving intellectual community that is the AAS Fellows Program. During my year at the American Antiquarian Society, I benefitted from the intellectual feedback, support, and friendship of my cohort of fellows—Lara Cohen, John Demos, Yvette Piggush, Jack Larkin, Caroline Eastman, and Joe Adelman—and from the productive conversations we had as we challenged each other to develop our ideas. The staff at AAS now feels like a family, and I want to thank, in particular, Ashley Cataldo, Elizabeth Pope, Caroline Sloat, Laura Wasowicz, Lauren Hewes, Vince Golden, Tom Knoles, Marie Lamoureux, Jacky Penny, as well as Ellen Dunlap for skillfully steering the ship. One of the most remarkable components of the Hench fellowship was the opportunity I had to invite three scholars to read my dissertation and to offer advice as I revised it toward publication. Robert Levine, Leon Jackson, and Meredith McGill proved more generous than I ever could have hoped, offering invaluable guidance on how to turn the dissertation into a book. And while the influence of their scholarship on the chapters to follow is plainly evident, I also couldn't have predicted how far their generosity would extend over the years.

I am thankful, too, for the support of my colleagues at Whitman College. Chris Leise has been a constant source of friendship and encouragement; Mary Raschko and Kisha Schlegel have been cheerful fellow travelers on the road toward tenure; while my colleagues Theresa DiPasquale, Sharon Alker, Gaurav Majumdar, Scott Elliott, and Katrina Roberts have guided me with grace and good humor through my first few years as an assistant professor. I'm thankful as well to Whitman College and the Office of the Provost for the support provided by two sabbaticals. I'm grateful also to the many students who tested out ideas with me in the classroom while serving as constant reminders that literary criticism is not dead letters but a living enterprise, a way of making sense of the world and transforming literature into tools for living thoughtful, productive, and compassionate lives.

I'd have been lost, too, without my friends. Austin Graham, Erin Suzuki, and Maureen Shay brightened the path through graduate school with constant advice, friendship, and lots of trips to Amoeba Records. Winston Pear and Alison Pear have endured my neuroses for almost two decades, giving me endless encouragement as well as much needed distraction, whether in Philadelphia, Los Angeles, or the Pacific Northwest. Laura Ferguson listened patiently as I worked through ideas, gave feedback on chapters, and provided emotional support. Lisa Uddin, Alissa Cordner, Lucy Schwallie, Matt deTar, Melissa Salrin, Jamie Warren, Josh Slepin, Ben Murphy, Antonia Keithahn, Lily Seaman, and Jack Jackson have filled my time in Walla Walla with laughter and comradery. Sarah Wagner-McCoy gave me helpful feedback as well during my sabbatical in Portland. Thanks especially to Molly Phillips, who cheered me on in the final stretch, offering love, advice, and every manner of support and encouragement as this project finally emerged into the daylight of print..

I am grateful as well to Brian Halley, Rachael DeShano, and the University of Massachusetts Press, who transformed this project from a manuscript into an actual book. Two anonymous readers helped crystallize this project in its late stages, lending precision and clarity to its final shape. Michael Winship also provided useful suggestions for revision. Parts of chapter 3 and chapter 5 appeared in slightly different forms, respectively, as "'A Condition to Be Criticized': Edgar Allan Poe and the Vocation of Antebellum Criticism" in *Arizona Quarterly* 68, no. 2 (Summer 2012) and "Beyond the 'Proper Notice': Frederick Douglass, *Uncle Tom's Cabin*, and the Politics of Critical Reprinting" in *American Literature* 91, no. 1 (March 2019). I'm thankful for the helpful feedback from anonymous readers at each journal and to the editors for the permission to reprint material from those articles here. Thanks also to Heather Dubnick for compiling the index.

Finally, this book wouldn't exist without the unwavering support of my family. My sister, Leah Gordon, has been encouraging me for as long as I can remember, modeling the academic path for me, while her family—Adam, Miriam, and Elijah—have brought cheer to my life. Lastly, my parents, Clifford and Linda Gordon, have provided constant support while imparting to me a love of books, a passion for ideas, and the means to pursue them as a vocation. This book is dedicated to them.

PROPHETS,
PUBLICISTS, AND
PARASITES

THE CRITIC IN THE AGE OF INDUSTRIAL PRINT

"THE PRESENT CENTURY has been eminently characterized by its critical spirit," Edwin Percy Whipple observed in 1846. "Institutions and opinions, men, manners and literature, have all been subjected to the most exhausting analysis. The moment a thing becomes a fixed fact in the community, criticism breaks it to pieces, curious to scan its elements. It is not content to admire the man until satisfied with his appearance as a skeleton." This critical zeal can come to no good, Whipple warns, and "the science of criticism is thus in danger of becoming a kind of intellectual anatomy. The dead and not the living body of a poem or institution is dissected, and its principle of life sought in a process which annihilates life at its first step." Though Whipple was a critic himself—indeed, one of America's best—he insisted that criticism's purpose was to enter sympathetically into the spirit of a work, clarifying the author's design for readers rather than judging based on fixed standards. What he saw around him, however, were displays of vivisection rather than elucidation, as critics probed a poem or novel with cold, critical detachment the way a medical student might a corpse.[1]

While this disconcerting preponderance of what Whipple called "the critical spirit" is perhaps familiar to us in our self-characterized information age, it carried an air of novelty for inhabitants of the 1840s, many of whom could recall childhoods in which household reading matter frequently consisted of little more than a Bible, a primer, an almanac, and perhaps a novel or two. The period saw the rise of a new sort of cultural figure, moreover—the professional literary critic—along with the consolidation of a mature American critical establishment. Between 1820 and 1861, a series of technological innovations within print production, coupled with improvements to internal transportation and growing literacy rates, decreased the price of reading material while increasing the number of readers. With a market flooded by print and an enlarged reading public, the role of the critic took on newfound importance. And yet the precise nature of this role was a matter of continuous debate, a debate that played itself out through the proliferating forms of antebellum critical culture.

The following chapters reconstruct these debates over the role of the critic in the first age of industrial print, a period in which books and literary criticism became more abundant within American society and a more ingrained part of everyday literary culture. Moving beyond traditional scholarly accounts that view the period's criticism instrumentally as storehouses of aesthetic principles, part of a narrative of US literary emergence, or for what they tell us about the developing genres of poetry or the novel, I ask instead what other more practical tasks criticism performed within the expanding print culture of antebellum America.[2] In the following pages, that is, I work to bridge the fields of book history and critical history, arguing that a material approach to critical theory and practice empowers our understanding of the critical institution by showing the range of cultural functions criticism serves.

In developing this broader methodological intervention, I assert four central claims. First, I argue that in approaching critical history, we need to read literary criticism in light of the critical forms through which it circulated, contexts that reveal criticism's varied applications within US culture. Second, I argue that nineteenth-century critics understood their critical affiliations as much along lines of critical form as political party, literary nationalism, or aesthetic movement, frameworks that have long dominated scholarly accounts of the period's criticism. These critical forms shaped critical arguments, which shifted as critics plied their trade across different critical genres and print media, a versatility that was typical of critical careers in the antebellum period.

Third, I argue that debates over criticism in the mid-nineteenth century anchored themselves in conversations about the relative capabilities and risks of specific critical forms. As antebellum print culture grew, and as new print forms entered the literary marketplace, observers debated the critic's role in society in relation to their disseminating print media, from quarterly reviews and popular monthly magazines to lavish anthologies and penny newspapers. Just as we worry today about the democratization or debasement of critical judgment in Amazon reviews and book blogs; lament the constriction of academic publishing and the shuttering of newspaper book review sections; and debate the perils and potentials of literary scholarship in the digital age, so too, antebellum critics debated the nature of literary criticism in terms of its emerging print media.

To read criticism with a sensitivity to its constitutive forms, finally, revises entrenched narratives of American literary and critical development; complicates naturalized definitions of literary criticism; and expands our sense of how criticism was put to use in the nineteenth century. Specifically, an attention to critical form tempers a long-standing overemphasis on literary nationalism, feuding Whigs and Democrats, and a bifurcated view of literary and critical theory split between romantic and neoclassical camps or between sympathetic and judicial schools of criticism. To be sure, nationalism and aesthetics were of concern to the period's critics, but they weren't the *only* concerns. Here I join a number of scholars who over the past decade have worked to decenter the paradigm of nationalism from narratives of early American literary culture, whether expressed in classic exceptionalist accounts of US literary emergence or more recent re-inscriptions via post-national, transnational, or hemispheric revisions.[3] This is not to deny the political valences of criticism or its investment in aesthetics or literary nationalism; yet these concerns have obscured the other sorts of work that criticism carried out within US society in an era of proliferating print forms. When nationalism did emerge as a topic of conversation, moreover, as it occasionally will in the following pages, it was frequently tied to discussions of specific print media, from quarterly reviews and anthologies to mammoth reprint weeklies, forms that gave material shape to otherwise abstract political contests and in ways that complicated the very positions being debated.

The largest claim of this book, accordingly, is that scholars need to broaden their definition of literary criticism to reflect the diversity of

critical forms and practices that collectively made up antebellum critical culture. The first challenge in writing about literary criticism is,
indeed, to settle upon a definition of it. Within critical histories, definitions range from narrow nineteenth-century neoclassical under-
standings like Noah Webster's "the art of judging with propriety of
the beauties and faults of a literary performance," appearing in his
landmark *American Dictionary of the English Language* (1828), to broad
twentieth-century definitions such as René Wellek's "any discourse
on literature," which framed his monumental eight-volume *History
of Modern Criticism* (1955–1992).[4] Not surprisingly, definitions tend to
reflect scholars' periods of study and methodological investments. In
his account of the origins of criticism in classical Greece, for instance,
Andrew Ford defines criticism as "any public act of praise or blame
upon a performance or song," a conception rooted in the oral culture
of early classical Greece and that distinguishes judgment from interpretation. Michael Gavin, by contrast, whose work treats seventeenth
and eighteenth-century British criticism from a book history perspective, distinguishes "critical writing," defined as "the generically heter-
ogenous mix of texts that engage arguments about poetry, plays, and
prose fiction," from "criticism," defined more broadly as *"the socially
realized exercise of judgment."*[5] A surprising number of studies don't
define criticism at all.

    If the definition of literary criticism in the antebellum period is par-
ticularly difficult to pin down, part of the reason is that critics in the
nineteenth century struggled to define it too. While Webster identified
the critic's primary task as evaluating beauties and faults, a definition
dating back to the word's classical origins in the Greek *kritikos*, or one
capable of judging, that view was undercut by romantic critical theory, which insisted that the critic's job was to appreciate and explain
works of genius for readers rather than judge based on fixed standards
of taste. The distinction between "critic" and "literary critic" was similarly blurry. "Literature" in the antebellum period still retained its
eighteenth-century sense of polite letters and learned writing, while
the average literary critic reviewed books far beyond the domains of
fiction and poetry. Since literary critics focused on but seldom confined themselves to "literary" works in the modern sense of the term,
to exclude non-literary works would be to ignore much of their critical

output. More importantly, it would provide a skewed sense of the critical vocation in an era when the idea of specialized expertise was only just coming into being, ignoring the reality that critics like Whipple, Margaret Fuller, and William A. Jones viewed themselves as perfectly able to review a work on the treatment of prisoners or Arctic exploring expeditions, touring violinists, as well as the latest novel by Dickens.

For Wellek, one of the most influential figures in the field of critical history, literary criticism is broadly divisible into three main subgenres of literary theory, literary criticism, and literary history, though each inevitably informs the other. In differentiating the subdisciplines, Wellek argues that there are two main distinctions: first, the view of literature as synchronic or diachronic, part of an isolated simultaneous order or as works arranged chronologically across time and in relation to history; and second, the study of principles and criteria of literature as opposed to the study of specific literary works. With these distinctions in mind, Wellek asserts that, "'literary theory' is the study of the principles of literature, its categories, criteria, and the like, while the studies of concrete works of art are either 'literary criticism' (primarily static in approach) or 'literary history.'"[6]

Though there is slippage in the terminology ("literary theory" versus "science of criticism" versus "literary scholarship," for instance) and though in English, "literary criticism" has come to be the umbrella term for most other critical genres, nonetheless, the fracturing of literary criticism into hierarchical subdisciplines can, for Wellek, be traced to the early nineteenth century when the German university, and in particular the disciplines of philosophy and scholastic historiography as influenced by Kant and Hegel, began to take an interest in art and literature. The prestige associated with these fields established philosophical aesthetics and poetics, on the one hand, and historically rigorous literary scholarship, on the other, as endeavors above and apart from the practically and temporally oriented mode of journalistic criticism that, with the progress of print production and the growth of the reading public, had come to dominate everyday literary culture in the early nineteenth century. In other words, we see the splintering of the concept of criticism from the unifying figure of Samuel Johnson in the eighteenth century into the diverse fields of philosophical aesthetics, historical scholarship, and literary journalism in the nineteenth century.[7]

Throughout the twentieth century, scholars would continue to map, categorize, and subdivide critical practice, while others like Terry Eagleton and Jonathan Culler worked to interrogate criticism's underlying ideologies and institutional bearings. Yet as different as these inquiries are, as Ford and Gavin both observe, such studies generally approach critical practice through a history-of-ideas framework, slighting the material dimensions of criticism and collapsing the history of criticism into a history of literary theory.[8] Resisting this abstracting slant, in the following pages I suggest that the definition of literary criticism is tied to the forms through which it circulated. At its most general level, literary criticism is writing about books, a field of discourse that takes as its jumping off point other works. Depending on where a piece of criticism appeared, the nature and character of these responses could vary widely from the brief abstracts of literary notices to surveys of entire intellectual fields; from blunt evaluations of quality to sensitive explorations of authorial intent; from practical reviews to meta-discursive discussions of the nature of criticism itself. Sometimes criticism hewed closely to the work under review; at other times the critic barely mentioned the book. And while both Ford and Gavin affirm classical definitions of criticism as judgment, literary criticism in the antebellum period frequently subsumed evaluation to other tasks. Criticism was often less concerned with judgment than entertainment, education, or polemic, while reviews routinely consisted primarily of lengthy excerpts from the book with hardly a judgment to be found. In such cases, criticism functioned more as previews of the work than as critical evaluations of it. Judgment was one task of criticism, that is, but it wasn't the sole task.

Just as my understanding of "literary criticism" requires explanation, my use of "critical form" does as well. By "critical form," I mean two intertwined and overlapping structures: the print media through which criticism circulated (monthly magazines, daily newspapers, anthology, pamphlet, etc.) and the critical genres through which it expressed itself (brief notice, lengthy review essay, tabloid literary gossip, etc.). A critical form accordingly encompasses both print media and critical genre: the periodical the *Dial* and the genre of the Literary Notices section at the back of the *Dial*; a literary anthology and an authorial headnote. Different print media have their own distinctive qualities (quarterly versus anthology; newspaper versus magazine), while each individual print medium often includes within its pages more than one critical genre (notices, reviews, gossip). The differences between critical forms—both print media and critical genres—I argue, had a profound impact on critical theories broadly and judgments of individual texts specifically, providing molds for critical arguments while shaping criticism's applications within the culture. What I am calling critical form thus becomes an effective way to organize the diversity of critical practices and debates at any one moment of US literary history and to do so using the categorical framework that antebellum critics most often invoked themselves in accounting for differences among critical practices.

Rather than suggesting that forms correlated reductively to a single set of critical conventions, however, in the following five chapters each form becomes a site of conflict, a battleground for competing conceptions of the critical office in which theory and practice, critical ideals and material realities, clashed with one another. In employing form in this way, I join scholars like Caroline Levine who see form not as a singular, delimiting category correlating to one meaning or application but as a productive staging ground for the clash between competing ordering principles, whether social, political, material, or aesthetic. For Levine, as for myself, moreover, form encompasses both genre and materiality, each of which possesses its own affordances, which Levine, drawing on Don Norman and design theory, describes as "potential uses or actions latent in materials and designs," signaling constraints and potential uses.[9] If the term "critical form" risks vagueness, it also has the advantage of inclusiveness, expansive enough to include a wide range of critical venues and practices, while countering a tendency to box critics into one category or another or to impose a strained unity based on political, religious, or aesthetic affiliations.

To understand critics only according to the philosophers they read, the church they attended, the social class of their parents, or their political affiliation assumes authors' rigid adherence to prescribed ideological systems while denying them intellectual flexibility or an ability to think above and beyond a given creed. Even more important than the question of authorial autonomy is the practical consideration that as criticism expanded as an occupation in the mid-nineteenth century,

critics came to depend for their livelihood on an intellectual, if not ideological, flexibility. With the rise of mainstream magazines like *Graham's*
and *Godey's*, which adopted the innovative practice of paying contributors well, criticism evolved from an amateur pursuit to a paying trade,
such that by the 1840s critics were minor and sometimes major literary celebrities. Yet the precarity of the vocation's financial bases also
required critics to be adaptable, a reality that, as Leon Jackson argues,
complicates the dominant professionalization paradigm promoted by
William Charvat and others in studies of antebellum authorship.[10]

Within the expanding critical culture of antebellum America, literary criticism took a variety of forms, and any practicing critic would
have engaged many if not most of them throughout his or her career.
In 1850, for instance, a consumer with a literary bent could read Edwin
Percy Whipple's review of *The Scarlet Letter* in the popular *Graham's
Magazine* with its circulation of 40,000 for pleasure, insight, or purchasing advice; buy one of several volumes of Whipple's collected
reviews published by Ticknor and Fields; see him deliver a lecture on
the lyceum circuit; or read excerpts of his writing in Rufus Griswold's
anthology, *The Prose Writers of America* (1847). This multiplication of
critical forms across diverse media and genres for an individual critic
was typical rather than exceptional, constituting what Paul Fussell in
his study of Samuel Johnson calls "the life of writing."[11] The critical
careers of Poe, Emerson, Fuller, James Russell Lowell, W. A. Jones, or
any other prominent critic were equally diverse such that to reduce
any one of their critical corpuses to a single mode—aesthetics or puffs,
ars poetica or literary gossip—is inevitably to exclude or mischarac-
terize much of his or her critical output. The homogenization of volumes like *The Norton Anthology of Theory and Criticism* in turn flattens
the multiple historical dimensions of critical practice by marginalizing,
if not ignoring completely, the print contexts of criticism and the cultural applications and entanglements that such contexts suggest.[12] To
understand Poe or Emerson as critics, rather, requires an understanding of literary criticism as a lived cultural practice as well as a sensitivity to the diversity of printed forms that criticism took in antebellum
America.

If studies of antebellum critical culture betray a certain tunnel vision
when it comes to the critical concerns represented, this limited scope

results in part from the print archives privileged in scholarly accounts, with journals like *Graham's*, the *Dial*, the *North American Review*, and the *Knickerbocker* occupying outsized roles in the constructed narratives.[13] To see the critical vocation in its more expansive cultural purview, rather, requires a commensurately expansive sense of critical print culture. Within the past thirty years, literary scholarship, influenced by the New Historicist turn within the academy, has increasingly sought to situate the literature of the period within the cultural and material contexts that mediated its production, circulation, and reception, whether through periodical studies, book history, reader-response criticism, or studies of oral or manuscript traditions. Since the pioneering work of Elizabeth Eisenstein in the 1970s, the field of print culture studies, in particular, has charted the impact of print technologies on the cultural, social, and political landscape. Building upon the ideological work of New Historicism, the best recent practitioners of a print culture approach within American literary studies—scholars like Meredith McGill, Leon Jackson, Trish Loughran, and Lara Langer Cohen—have employed a renewed archival vigor to unsettle the ossified narratives of American literary history.[14]

While increasing numbers of scholars are flocking to research archives and scrutinizing literary artifacts in the forms in which they originally circulated, large-scale digitization campaigns funded by Google Books, subscription databases like EBSCO, or undertaken by individual libraries have made once inaccessible materials not only digitally available but keyword searchable and PDF exportable for scholars in even the most remote locations. These developments within our own twenty-first century scholarly print culture, spurred on by cultural, material, and revisionist methodological approaches to literary history, have collectively reshaped our understanding of nineteenth-century print culture, invigorating a new generation of literary scholars for whom the return to the archives has been aided by both novel theoretical orientations and new digital technologies.

Despite the vitality of book history and print culture studies, however, scholars have been slow to apply these methodologies to literary criticism itself. While book history and critical history have much to contribute to one another, as Gavin observes, "when marshaled as evidence in the history of media, criticism fades from view as an object of study in its own right." Though literary criticism has been a key source of evidence in reading and reception studies, "an important if never perfectly reliable index of reading practices and mentalities," criticism remains largely insulated from treatments as a material text, produced, circulated, and received in ways that shape its meaning. From the vantage of periodical studies, Joanne Shattock, following Laurel Brake, warns similarly of the widespread tendency to divorce criticism from its original periodical context, "a context that reveals much about the nature of the criticism, and indeed did much to shape it."[15]

In returning literary criticism to its multiple sites of production, dissemination, and reception, we gain not only a clearer sense of critical history and the uses it served but a new perspective into current debates over the value of criticism. If poststructuralists in the 1970s and '80s emphasized the constructed-ness of historical narratives, the contingency of critical value, and the inseparability of literary history from our own ideological investments, such insights risk replacing unreliable narratives with no narrative at all.[16] More recently, proponents of the post-critical turn have worked to move past the hermeneutics of suspicion to discover a wider range of critical postures and applications. Registering fatigue with the now predictable moves of critique—of exposure, defamiliarization, debunking, and subversion—and with the questionable political payoff of such approaches, critics like Rita Felski, Elizabeth Anker, Bruno Latour, and Christopher Castiglia have begun to ask what other more affirmative work literary criticism might do.[17]

A print culture approach to criticism helps address these concerns, resisting the over-privileging of a single synthetic narrative without giving way to critical nihilism, allowing us to see the range of uses criticism serves and the variety of critical conversations occurring at any one moment in history. It provides a material basis for such theoretical concerns, moreover, grounding the abstractions of contingency or competing styles of critical affect in the practical affordances of specific print forms. Pierre Bourdieu's "position-takings" within the field of cultural production or Barbara Herrnstein Smith's "variable constancies" among broader contingencies of value take material shape through the diverse critical forms that constitute the day-to-day practice of the critical profession. The multiplicity of these forms, meanwhile, answers Felski's call for a greater sensitivity to the range of sensibilities, constituencies, and uses criticism serves beyond suspicion. "Reining in critique is not a matter of trying to impose a single mood upon the critic," Felski notes, "but of striving for a greater receptivity to the multifarious and many-shaded moods of texts . . . Rather than looking behind the text—for its hidden causes, determining conditions, and noxious motives—we might place ourselves in front of the text, reflecting on what it unfurls, calls forth, makes possible."[18] A sensitivity to the diversity of critical forms takes up the challenge posed by Felski to move beyond suspicion and to seek out the range of possibilities, affects, and applications that criticism "unfurls" at any one moment in time.

Critical Forms, Critical Norms

If this sense of literary criticism as a materially embedded cultural practice with a range of applications is increasingly visible to twenty-first century scholars, it was plainly evident to nineteenth-century observers. In an address entitled "Forms of Criticism," delivered to the seniors of Harvard College and published posthumously in 1856, for instance, the late Boylston Professor of Rhetoric and Oratory Edward Tyrrel Channing differentiated five main types of criticism: private, "friendly" criticism; critical editions by "annotators"; literary histories; philosophical aesthetics; and book reviews. While each form has its particular uses and characteristic traits, Channing notes, it is the literary reviews of monthly and quarterly magazines that constitute the "distinction of the age," having risen to an importance never known before. "Instead of short analyses, summaries of literary news and slight strictures," Channing observes, "reviews now contain elaborate investigations of the subjects of works, of the genius of authors, the principles of criticism, the faults and beauties of the style of language." Not only do reviews contain the work of "the profoundest and best-informed minds," they provide readers with a cheap and comprehensive education on all matters of contemporary concern. It is this elevated cultural role of reviews that makes them an indispensable feature of the age. They are now "a part of our most popular, fashionable and instructive reading, and fill a large place in public and private libraries," Channing notes. "Subjects of all sorts, of local and temporary, or general and permanent interest . . . are placed within the reach of everybody."[19]

For Channing, a rhetorician by training, critical forms correlate to different applications, each of which attests to the centrality of criticism within antebellum cultural life. For William A. Jones, by contrast, it is the differences between types of periodicals specifically that establish the most significant fault lines within critical practice. Magazines are more refined in audience and subject matter, Jones observes, while quarterlies are more scholarly, the quality of their contents improved by their less frequent publication and greater length of treatments. When Jones's two-part survey of contemporary criticism appeared in the *United States Magazine and Democratic Review* in August and September 1844, he could add that the newspaper now comprises "a chief, if not the most important educational element in our national civilization, and forms the staple reading of our people." "For our own part, we love each and all of these," Jones avers, "from the paragraph in the daily journal up to the elaborate and exhaustive analysis of the Quarterlies." Though, to be sure, Jones praises his own preferred medium of the magazine review most enthusiastically, presenting it as more flexible, accessible, and entertaining than quarterly reviews and more respectable than newspaper reviews.[20]

In article after article, antebellum critics categorized and evaluated critical practice in relation to its critical forms. That is to say, nineteenth-century critics were as attuned to the practical affordances of criticism's print contexts as twenty-first century scholars, invoking critical form as a way to understand their own critical practices. Nor should this surprise us: Beyond being participants in a rapidly transforming print culture that was plainly visible to observers, developments that brought the material production and dissemination of print media to center stage, nineteenth-century criticism also grew out of and assimilated the methodological investments of philology and rhetoric, traditions attuned to textual scholarship and cultural use, respectively. "To the philologian, all possible meanings are a function of their historical emergence as material artifacts," Jerome McGann observes, while "the investigation of those artifacts is the foundation of literary and cultural studies."[21] In their sensitivity to the material bases of textual meaning, to the ways texts circulate and how this corresponds to their cultural roles, nineteenth-century intellectual preoccupations intersect with our own twenty-first century methodological investments, particularly the return to the material text. In short, critical theorists of the 1840s had a bibliographic bent long before book history and focused on print culture long before print culture studies.

Not all critical forms were created equal, moreover. Since the early decades of the nineteenth century, the standard bearers of critical authority in the United States were the lengthy essays published in the quarterly reviews, journals drawing on the influential British model of the *Edinburgh Review* such as the *North American Review*, the *American Whig Review*, the *Dial*, and the *Christian Examiner*. Quarterly essays signaled seriousness of purpose through their length, their intellectually rigorous engagements with the subjects under review, and the cultural authority of their critics, who employed the books under review as occasions to sermonize liberally on the topics at hand. Second in prestige to quarterlies were book reviews in popular monthly magazines—journals like *Graham's*, *Godey's*, or Lewis Gaylord Clark's *Knickerbocker*—wide-circulation magazines that turned authorship into a professional trade by paying writers well, and that raised subscription numbers to unprecedented levels through fashionable, entertaining fare by popular contributors.

This increasing reliance by publishers like George Graham and Louis Godey on a growing cadre of critics of established reputation—figures such as Poe, Lowell, Fuller, Whipple, or Jones—was reinforced by the growing popular taste for literary gossip, "personality" criticism, and by the construction of critics as minor celebrities in a number of series, including *Graham's* "Our Contributors," Poe's "Literati of New York City" in *Godey's*, and Clark's popular "Editor's Chair" column in the *Knickerbocker*, in which, as Perry Miller notes, the comings and goings of critics became entertainment in its own right.[22] Margaret Fuller's career move from editor of the *Dial* to contributing literary editor of the *New-York Tribune* gestures at a third critical context, meanwhile, as reviews and notices became prominent features in wide-circulation daily and weekly newspapers, a placement that even more than with quarterlies and monthly magazines blurred the line between politics and literary criticism, both ideologically and in the material intermingling of their diverse contents, as literary events became front-page stories instead of belletristic affairs relegated to the Literary Notices section.

Literary weeklies like the *New-York Mirror*, Greeley's *New-Yorker*, and

Poe's own *Broadway Journal* comprised another prominent outlet for criticism, occupying a hybrid position between the fashionable literary content of magazines and the local reporting of weekly newspapers. Their form blended the two periodical formats as well, with editors exploiting the lower postage rate for newspapers by printing what was essentially magazine content in the guise of a newspaper at a cheaper cost, a factor that proved attractive to readers, particularly in the depressed economic conditions following the Panic of 1837. In "mammoth weeklies" like the *Boston Notion, Brother Jonathan,* and the *New World,* meanwhile, Rufus Griswold, Park Benjamin, and other editors exploited not only the novelty of their large format but the lack of an international copyright, reprinting serialized novels by Charles Dickens, Eugène Sue, and other popular foreign authors at cheap rates to large audiences.

As individual critics built reputations for themselves using the expanded platform of periodicals, they increasingly reprinted their reviews and essays in bound collections, a phenomenon that Shattock argues contributed to the emergence of criticism as a profession.[23] Such collections not only implied a catholic, humanistic appeal that went beyond evaluation of the book under review but the popularity of literary criticism as a genre in its own right as well as the growing tendency toward the individuation of specific critics with distinct styles and personalities from the general mass of anonymous reviewers. If reviews in the early republic were typically unsigned or written under a pen name, by the 1830s, critics like Poe or Nathaniel Parker Willis went to great lengths to extend their authorial reputations through the cultivation of highly fashioned critical personae.

Once a critic's reputation was established, critical collections gathered together reviews conceived of by the author as having some sort of lasting worth or entertainment value beyond the act of critical judgment, while excluding reviews of a purely evaluative or perfunctory nature. Critical volumes of this sort were ubiquitous in the 1840s and '50s, issued by just about every critic of note and frequently going into multiple editions, a genre that included Fuller's *Papers on Literature and Art* (1846), Jones's *Literary Studies* (1847), Whipple's *Essays and Reviews* (1848), and Horace Binney Wallace's *Literary Criticisms and Other Papers* (published posthumously in 1856), to say nothing of their British counterparts, which remained popular reading in America. Indeed, it was a collection of literary studies that Poe was working on when he died unexpectedly in 1849.

Beyond original reviews and essays in these four prominent peri- odical contexts—quarterlies, monthly magazines, daily/weekly news- papers, and literary weeklies—as well as the critical volumes that col- lected them, criticism also circulated through a range of other less frequently discussed forms. These contexts that shaped a piece of criti- cism's argument, orientation, and sense of cultural purpose—from lit- erary lectures, introductions to anthologies, and prefaces to novels and poetry volumes, on the one hand, to blurbs, advertisements, brief liter- ary notices, and excerpted, fragmentary, unattributed, and reprinted notices, on the other. If published critical collections consolidated crit- ical reputations and raised the profile of literary criticism as a popular genre in its own right, critical culture also entailed a number of criti- cal forms that effaced critical authorship and were less readily identifi- able as criticism: diffuse, fragmentary, and generically eclectic critical forms whose critical legitimacy was undermined by brevity, anonym- ity, unoriginality, and generic hybridity.

If scholars like Nina Baym have privileged original reviews in presti- gious or high circulation journals like the *North American Review* or *Gra- ham's* in their critical studies, reprinting critical reviews was also a com- mon editorial practice in the antebellum period, with editors frequently drawing from obscure, local newspapers while citing only the source journal rather than any named critic.[24] It was also common for reviews on contentious subjects to be reprinted as pamphlets, a practice that, while prevalent in accounts of early British criticism, has been all but ignored within American critical history. And while criticism often took the standard form of a book review, at other times it adopted less pre- dictable forms, with critical responses to literature expressing them- selves in editorials, published letters from correspondents, minutes from literary or political gatherings, and through a range of other dis- cursive genres that, while not explicitly literary criticism, contained crit- ical reactions to literature, contexts that signaled criticism's proximity to other socio-political discourses and concerns. These various liminal and hybrid forms, frequently ignored in critical histories, provide a more comprehensive sense of the uses of literary criticism in nineteenth- century US culture.

Antebellum Print Culture and the Critical Vocation

Literary criticism of course dates back much further than nineteenth-century America. The earliest literary criticism, as Ford notes, began appearing in ancient Greece in the fourth century BCE. The modern critical institution, meanwhile, as Derek Roper observes, first took shape in Paris in the abstract-journals of the late seventeenth century and with the expansion of the literary marketplace in late seventeenth and early eighteenth-century England, a development that produced the distinguished critical careers of John Dryden, Joseph Addison, Richard Steele, and Samuel Johnson, not to mention critical spoofs, such as Alexander Pope's *An Essay on Criticism* (1711).[25]

In the United States, while literary criticism in the republican and national periods was robust in its own right, it had different economic and ideological groundings from the criticism that emerged with the growth of the literary marketplace. Criticism in the new nation, as Michael Gilmore observes, situated within an agrarian preindustrial economy, was rooted in ideologies of republicanism, civic humanism, and a communalist understanding of literature and authorship oriented toward the public good. For Federalist critics like Joseph Buckminster and William Tudor, as Lewis P. Simpson notes, literature was inseparable from moral guidance, with reviewing employed in the service of protecting a social order that was slowly slipping away amid the transformations of liberal democracy and industrial capitalism.[26]

Criticism in the early republic was primarily an amateur endeavor, a pastime of professional men rather than a profession in its own right, published anonymously or under pseudonyms as contributions to an Enlightenment public sphere. Paying their authors poorly or not at all, periodicals like the *Monthly Anthology* or Brown's *Monthly Magazine, and American Review* relied on contributions from members of literary coteries like the Boston Anthology Club and New York Friendly Club, respectively, and on the money received from subscribers. Securing both contributions and subscription payments could be challenging, however, as Frank Luther Mott notes, accounting for the high failure rate and short life span of early American magazines.[27] In the transatlantic republic of letters, meanwhile, books and periodicals were still largely imported from abroad, rendering the necessity of critical evaluations, particularly ones concerned with promoting a national literature, less urgent and frequently redundant since Americans were reading the British quarterlies just as devotedly as the British books they reviewed.

While eighteenth-century newspapers carried literary content and the occasional book review, it was not until the 1780s and '90s with growth of the American book trade that a more developed critical establishment emerged in the magazines, which began appearing in increasing numbers, frequently bearing close ties to publishers and booksellers. While magazines like the *Columbian Magazine* (1786–1792), Mathew Carey's *American Museum* (1787–1792), Isaiah Thomas's *Massachusetts Magazine* (1789–1796), and the *New-York Magazine* (1790–1797) included reviews (generally made up largely of extracts) as well as literary essays and criticism on the model of Addison and Steele, it was in the quarterly reviews and monthly magazines of the early 1800s, following the model of the *Edinburgh Review,* that criticism began to find firmer cultural grounding, promoting a Federalist social vision, a transatlantic knowledge culture, and an incipient nationalism to an intellectually acquisitive professional class.

Once glossed over or ignored completely in surveys of American literature, dismissed as the retrograde effusions of a conservative cultural elite working fruitlessly to stem the tide of a democratic market economy, the criticism of the Federalist period has begun to garner more careful attention in recent years. Drawing on the foundational work of Simpson and Charvat, scholars such as Catherine O'Donnell Kaplan, Jared Gardner, Bryan Waterman, and Edward Cahill have differentiated the critical styles, aesthetic orientations, and ideological commitments of magazines like the *Medical Repository* (1797–1824), Brown's *Monthly Magazine* (1799–1800), the *Monthly Anthology* (1803–1811), Joseph Dennie's *Port Folio* (1801–1827), the *Analectic Magazine* (1813–1814), and the Baltimore *Portico* (1816–1818). Looking beneath guises of anonymity and disinterestedness, these scholars have taken stock of the critical productions of an expanding roster of critics, including not just Brown and Buckminster, but Dennie, Fisher Ames, Elihu Hubbard Smith, Samuel Miller, and Judith Sargent Murray, as well as the diverse social and intellectual interests these critics represented.[28]

Nor was criticism limited to periodicals, or to print for that matter. Rather, as David Shields has shown, literary criticism was a staple of eighteenth-century social life, circulated not just through printed books and periodicals but through a vibrant manuscript culture, and expressing itself in the diverse institutions of belletristic culture, from literary clubs and salons, taverns and coffeehouses, to college societies and circulating libraries. Just as citizens of the new republic were invested in the world of polite letters, they were equally engaged in the demanding discourse of philosophical aesthetics, which, as Cahill argues, became a language for exploring the political bearings of the new nation through a range of literary forms, print genres, and aesthetic concerns. The rhetorical traditions of Scottish Common Sense philosophy, of Lord Kames and Hugh Blair, meanwhile, as Jay Fliegelman and Robert Ferguson record, were a fixture of the standard educational curriculum for young men, eroding the distance between the realms of criticism and politics while orienting literary criticism toward practical uses beyond the world of literature.[29]

In the early decades of the century, however, as Gilmore observes, criticism began to reorient itself to the demands of an emerging print-capitalist marketplace and to new conceptions of literary property, authorship, and literature itself, a term that increasingly came to signify imaginative works rather than learned writing. The main limitation with Charvat's formative study, rather, which traces the origins of American critical thought from 1810 to 1835, is that it concludes with the year 1835, or the moment when the American literary marketplace was in the midst of a wide-ranging transformation and reorientation as a result of the tandem communication and transportation revolutions, changes that rendered Charvat's essentially Federalist literary-critical aesthetics obsolete. If critics of the republican and national periods drew their authority in part from their social ranks and primary professional occupations, the professionalization of criticism in the 1830s, along with the institution's increasingly cozy relationship to the publishing industry, prompted a public backlash as well as a challenge to critical authority as authors and readers began to wonder: what exactly qualified a critic to judge the works of others?

Within a forty-year period, American print culture was transformed from a network of local artisan printers and publishers to an increasingly connected national market. Between 1820 and 1861, when the Civil War disrupted infrastructure building, Americans saw the introduction of steam-powered ships and railroads, accompanied by hundreds of thousands of miles of tracks and new canals. Steam-powered cylinder presses upped the number of newspaper impressions from 250 per hour to 12,000, while advances in papermaking and plate stereotyping drove manufacturing costs down. Telegraph wires, trains, and ships cut the time of both communication and travel, which combined with huge land annexations to open up a vast continent that by 1848 stretched all the way to the Pacific. The sum of these technological innovations was that publishers could produce printed matter in higher quantities and at lower costs, and then distribute it quickly and relatively inexpensively to huge areas of the country that had before been landlocked, inaccessible, and in a very literal sense, foreign. These factors were capitalized on by a consolidating publishing industry, as within this same forty-year period America witnessed the rise of many of its greatest publishing houses: Putnam's, Harper's, Ticknor and Fields.[30]

These developments, as Ronald Zboray reminds us, were, of course, neither instant, all-encompassing, nor equally distributed across all segments of the population, with exaggerated talk of "cheap print revolutions" promoted by the publishing industry itself. Nor did an increasingly connected nation necessarily mean a more unified one. Rather, as Trish Loughran argues, the increased intercourse between north and south produced by improved infrastructure paradoxically produced not union but disunion, fanning the flames of sectional crisis and hurtling the nation toward war.[31] Though the results were complex and frequently paradoxical, however, the changes wrought to nineteenth-century print culture were impossible to ignore, as a range of developments large and small transformed the way Americans consumed literature.

This growth in book publishing was fueled not just by new technologies and infrastructure but by shifting reading practices and an expanding readership, as a Jeffersonian legacy that emphasized education combined with more available reading material produced increases in literacy across all strata of the American population. Throughout the western world, "the reading public . . . achieved mass literacy," Martyn Lyons observes, as the shift from agrarian to urban-industrial life saw the emergence of expanding reading demographics among women, children, and the working classes. Though even many farm laborers in late eighteenth-century America were literate, pleasure reading nevertheless remained the practice of expanding middle and upper classes with the requisite time and disposable income to invest in books and magazines. This changed in the early decades of the nineteenth century when, as William Gilmore notes, reading became a necessary component of everyday life. This expansion of literacy occurred even as the gap between rich and poor widened and the displacement of agricultural life by factory life changed the social implications of reading. Reading was no longer just culture, but *self-culture*, a tool of social uplift and the key to the Franklinian American dream of the self-made man.[32]

The manner in which people read changed too, shifting from intensive to extensive reading practices, as consumers began purchasing a greater number of books and magazines that they read just once, rather than closely rereading a carefully culled handful of texts. More modest technological innovations like cheaper eyeglasses and improved lighting let readers read for longer, meanwhile, and with less strain to their eyes. Collectively, these changes amounted to a "reading revolution," as scholars term it, making reading a more central facet of US cultural life and driving the growth of the critical enterprise. It did so as the modern mass media first began to take shape, moreover, developments that, as James Machor notes, render the study of criticism in antebellum America particularly significant.[33]

While the growth of book publishing and an expanding reading public gave the critic an enlarged cultural function, the parallel growth of periodicals gave the critic an expanded platform to ply his or her trade as well as an enlarged source of income. Though the first American magazines began appearing in the 1740s, and with them book reviews, the rise of industrial print ushered in what Mott has described as the "golden age of periodicals." While in 1825 there were fewer than one hundred non-newspaper periodicals, by 1850, there were approximately six hundred.[34] Thus, while for Whipple the 1840s were the age of criticism, for John Inman, editor of the *Columbian Lady's and Gentleman's Magazine*, the present was "decidedly . . . the age of the magazine, as well as of railroads, Ericson propellers, miracle-working pills, and medicated candy."[35] If the price of books and magazines still made them luxuries for most Americans, the same could not be said of newspapers. With the emergence of the penny press in the 1830s, newspapers made the frequently touted epithet of "reading for the masses" not just rhetoric but reality. Besides their cheaper price, newspapers included more engaging material aimed at attracting a wider and more diverse audience, advertising themselves as required reading for anyone who hoped to rise in the world. The new model succeeded. While there were approximately 1,200 newspapers in 1833, three times as many as in England or France, by 1860 that number increased to 3,000, not including the thousands of short-lived papers that came and went during the same period.[36]

With an expanded audience of readers and more venues to publish their writings, critics appointed themselves cultural watchdogs, moral guardians of an impressionable public continuously hungry for amusement. Not surprisingly, as Charvat notes, this protective moral stance made sense when you considered that many critics of the national period were lawyers, doctors, or clergymen.[37] By 1840, however, literary authorship had become a vocation, albeit a risky one, not just for a lucky few, as was the case twenty years earlier with the frequently cited first professional American authors Washington Irving and James Fenimore Cooper, but for anyone foolish enough to trade financial security for the title "man of letters." As Edgar Allan Poe's difficult life suggests, by the mid-1830s one could survive by writing alone with or without recognition, though it was hardly an easy life. Still, others such as Horace Greeley, Rufus Griswold, William Cullen Bryant, and Nathaniel Parker Willis managed to have a slightly easier time of it, largely through their occupations as editors at successful periodicals. Female authors and editors like Fuller, Fanny Fern, and Sarah Josepha Hale gained a foothold as professional writers as well, overcoming even greater obstacles than their male counterparts.

With the proliferation of periodicals, there was a proliferation of critical reviews while a growing anxiety over the perceived overabundance of books caused readers to turn increasingly to critics to help them navigate the crowded literary marketplace. Even as early as 1819, when Washington Irving surveyed the current state of society through his persona Geoffrey Crayon, he saw a world flooded by an impossible surfeit of books, a situation that would only grow worse in the decades to follow. As Crayon wanders among the dusty, neglected volumes of Westminster Abbey, his concern is that the natural balance of literature has been disturbed; for it used to be that "the works of genius and learning decline and make way for subsequent productions. Language gradually varies, and with it fade away the writings of authors who have flourished their allotted time; otherwise the creative powers of genius would overstock the world, and the mind would be completely bewildered in the endless mazes of literature." As Irving saw it, the improving technologies of print and paper production had flooded society with print and made everyone a writer such that the world was overburdened by an untenable excess of literature, in which oracles and luminaries were lost among the throngs of amateurs. This perceived overabundance of print demanded new strategies of reading if one was to entertain the least hope of keeping pace with the literature of the day.

It was for this reason that Crayon supported the expanding vocation of criticism as a necessary arm of the literary industry, one that separated the wheat from the chaff. Critics were not to be derided but hailed as the promoting agents of a literary meritocracy, Crayon insisted, sifting through the dross of new literature and selecting that which deserved to see the light of day for an increasingly befuddled and helpless reading audience. In helping to negotiate the surplus of literature, Crayon assents that "criticism may do much," for "it increases with the increase of literature, and resembles one of those salutary checks on population spoken of by economists. All possible encouragement, therefore, should be given to the growth of critics, good or bad." Despite critics' best attempts to narrow the ever more expansive field of literature, however, Crayon resigns himself to the fact that, "I fear all will be in vain; let criticism do what it may, writers will write, printers will print, and the world will inevitably be overstocked with good books."[38] Even with greater amounts of criticism, the glut of books was such that as Crayon complains, "It will soon be the employment of a lifetime merely to learn their names. Many a man of passable information at the present day reads scarce any thing but reviews, and before long a man of erudition will be little better than a mere walking catalogue." For Irving, that is, literary criticism was both a symptom of and an antidote to the seemingly unstoppable growth of antebellum print culture.[39]

To be sure, such anxieties over information overload were hardly unique to the United States or to the nineteenth century. Rather, "every age was an age of information, each in its own way," Robert Darnton reminds us. As early as the sixteenth century, monastic scholars expressed anxiety about there being "too much to know," Ann Blair observes, concerns that stretched from Europe to China and that predated but were intensified by the invention of print. Worries over information overload were not only perennial, James Gleick and Alex Wright separately note, they shaped the cognitive pathways of human consciousness through society's repeated attempts to contain and master the glut of information through newly devised information systems, from alphabets, encyclopedias, and library classification systems to computers and the internet.[40] Criticism was one such system, devised to help readers navigate the world of print, as abstract-journals like Paris's *Journal des Sçavans* (f. 1665) or Ralph Griffith's British *Monthly Review* (f. 1749) took on the formidable task of noticing, if not reviewing, all new works, keeping readers informed of the progress of human knowledge, an enterprise that by the early nineteenth century American publishing required as well.[41]

The increasing cultural importance of criticism wasn't simply utilitarian, however. In the same decades, the role of the critic in relation to literature went through an epistemological reconfiguration as well. As Jacques Rancière observes, around 1800 the hermeneutic enterprise experienced a paradigm shift. Throughout the neoclassical period, the aesthetic orientation of literature was primarily mimetic, and the role of the critic was accordingly to evaluate based on fixed standards of literary value and aesthetic judgment. In the early decades of the nineteenth century, however, the orientation of literature shifted from mimetic to expressive. Romantic theory emphasized the subjective nature of truth and perception, and tasked art with representing the artist's organic vision rather than a fixed record of nature. In M. H. Abrams's classic figuration, artistic theory underwent a shift from that of the mirror to the lamp, as literature was now understood to project an artist's perceptive truth rather than serve as a mirror to nature.

With representation unhinged from any set moorings in objective nature, the critical office changed as well. While critics in the eighteenth century served as articulate curators of established standards of taste and judgment, the subjective turn in art empowered critics to give voice to the "mute speech" of the artwork itself, as Rancière terms it. It was no longer the critic's job merely to say whether a piece of artwork

had succeeded or failed in its representation or to point out its "beauties," as neoclassical critics ubiquitously termed them. Nor was the mea-
sure of literary value any longer whether, in Samuel Johnson's formulation, a work stood the test of time as a result of inherent, immutable
qualities. Rather, the critic was now the arbiter of interpretive meaning
and, with it, critical value.[42]

This reconfiguration of the critical office had far-reaching implications for the relationship between art and interpretive meaning. Critics weren't necessary merely to tell readers what to read in an over-
crowded literary market or to note whether a work succeeded or
failed in representing the world according to the established rules of
art; increasingly, readers looked to critics to tell them what a work
meant and why it was significant. Not surprisingly, the new hermeneutic authority of the critic, coupled with his or her power to make or
break a book or authorial reputation, caused authors no small amount
of concern. While scholars of antebellum criticism have focused primarily on partisan feuding and debates over literary nationalism,
on Whigs versus Knickerbockers and the Anglo-American paper
wars, the more fundamental question asked of criticism in the mid-
nineteenth century was not whether it over- or underestimated American literature but whether it served any necessary function at all.
Throughout the nineteenth century, a chorus of commentators repeatedly asked, what was criticism for? Was it necessary? And if so, who
was qualified to judge?

Much as John Guillory has argued that the cultural prestige of literature suffered a devaluation in the late twentieth century, prompting both the canon wars and the rise of literary theory, the rising cultural status of literature in the early nineteenth century set off a series
of debates over the role served by that group who presumed to speak
on behalf of literature.[43] The rise of literary nationalism was in this view
symptomatic of the new authority of the critic, an answer to those who
questioned his or her right to hold forth on a literary work that was the
product of another's labor. Critics like Poe and James Russell Lowell
responded to this widespread questioning of critical authority with the
most ambitious defense they could muster: that, as Lowell famously
put it, "before we have an American literature, we must have an American criticism."[44] Critics didn't merely judge an individual work, they

were responsible for the fate of the national letters, which was increasingly tied to the prospects of the nation as a whole.

Such grand claims met with their fair share of skepticism. Observers were wary of the rhetoric of literary nationalism long before Benedict Anderson, Lara Langer Cohen reminds us, comparing nationalist puffing of a fledgling American literature to currency inflation and land bubbles, and figuring it through images of balloons filled with hot air.[45] This suspicion regarding hyperbolic nationalist rhetoric was, I would add, one expression of a deeper cultural suspicion of the office of criticism in the era of its cultural ascendancy and hermeneutic empowerment. This suspicion emerged not from crisis and diminished cultural power, as in the late twentieth century, paradoxically, but from its newfound institutional authority and enlarged hermeneutic scope. Even the hyped-up insistence that a national criticism was the necessary precondition for a national literature was itself a defensive justification by critics of the cultural utility of criticism itself, fueled by culturally pervasive attacks on criticism as both institution and practice. Thus, while a critic like Poe insisted on the need for a national criticism, as I'll argue, he was also deeply ambivalent as to whether criticism was necessary to the individual experience of art. Lowell is perhaps best remembered today, meanwhile, not for his celebrations of a national criticism but for his satire of American criticism, *A Fable for Critics* (1848).

If early-twentieth-century studies of US criticism emphasized the critic's role in fostering a national literature, more recent studies of the critical institution in the nineteenth century have shifted focus to the professionalization of literary judgment, the split between academic criticism and literary journalism, and the emerging concept of specialization and disciplinary expertise.[46] Over the course of the nineteenth century, the basis of critical authority shifted from the patrician authority of amateur critics in the republican and national periods—rooted in their social status and the prestige of their primary occupations—to the emergence of the literary vocation as a paid profession in its own right in the mid-nineteenth century, a shift supported by expansion of the book and periodical industry.

The same economic developments that made authorship a viable, if precarious, livelihood paradoxically became a centerpiece in attacks on critical legitimacy. Just as the purity of republican criticism was ensured by its anonymous and unpaid status as part of a disinterested public sphere (or so republican critics claimed), getting paid for writing turned literary journalists into "hirelings" or "hacks," as they were ubiquitously derided, terms that Roper notes signified little more than being paid writers. Money, the very thing that enabled the emergence of authorship as a profession, delegitimized the validity of critical judgment, substituting vulgar financial gain, as detractors insisted, for the purer motives of truth, justice, or morality, while installing a host of inept journalists as the arbiters of literary value and the judges of artistic genius. Such charges, Roper notes, were typically overstated and hollow, with the term "hack" directed at unnamed reviewers in contrast to the extensive roster of known and respected critics whose critical legitimacy was widely accepted. "The notion that these Reviews were simply puffing-machines," Roper notes, "must therefore be discarded, and unsupported charges of commercial bias should be treated with great caution, even when found in the gossip of the period."[47]

Though broad attacks on critical practice were exaggerated, rooted in anxieties over the commodification of literature and literary judgment as well as persistent resentment by social elites displaced from their former seats of authority, they also foreshadowed the widening rift between two emerging forms of professional criticism: literary journalism and academic scholarship; generalists and specialists; paid writers and credentialed experts. Such developments, as numerous scholars suggest, extended beyond the realm of literary criticism to all segments of American professional life, marking a broader cultural and epistemological shift toward disciplinary specialization and professional expertise as new strategies for managing knowledge production by subdividing and focusing it.[48] The same anxieties over mastering increasing amounts of information driving the rise of disciplinary specialization also drove the growth of reviewing, helping readers keep pace with literary production while paradoxically adding to that glut of reading matter.

These parallel developments regarding critical authority—its institutionalization, professionalization, hermeneutic empowerment, and pragmatic exigency within an expanding print culture—help explain the simultaneous proliferation of ennobling and disparaging portraits of critics within the antebellum popular imagination: the critic as hero

and the critic as parasite, a guiding prophet in the age of print overproduction and glorified publicist for the publishing industry. Nineteenth-
century periodicals printed as many essays about the plague of puffing
as the need for an American criticism to support a national literature, as
many screeds against the legitimacy of magazine and newspaper critics as paeans to the heroic man of letters. Nowhere are these two competing narratives more evident than in accounts of Poe himself. Though
Lowell in a sketch for *Graham's* "Our Contributors" series lauded Poe
for promoting America's literary interests through his fiercely honest criticism, Poe was far more notorious as the "Tomahawk," a critic
feared and reviled for the venom of his critical attacks. While *Graham's*
accompanied Lowell's biographical account of Poe with a flattering
portrait of the author—sober, distinguished, book in hand (figure 1)—
the cheap, entertainment weekly *Holden's Dollar Magazine* in the same
year embellished A. J. H. Duganne's verse satire *A Mirror for Authors*
with a comical image of Poe wielding a tomahawk, by the popular
illustrator F. O. C. Darley. As the accompanying verse mocked: "With
tomahawk upraised for deadly blow, / Behold our literary Mohawk,
Poe! / Sworn tyrant he o'er all who sin in verse— / His own the standard, damns he all that's worse."[49] (See figure 2.)

These competing conceptions of the critical enterprise extended
beyond individual critics. While a widely circulated engraving such as
Thomas Hicks's *Authors of the United States* presented a fanciful image
of a coherent, unified American literature (figure 3), such an image was
a fantasy, a rhetorical construction that belied the anxieties of American
authors and critics and the disorder of the US literary sphere, to say
nothing of the nation itself, which in 1866, when the image appeared,
was anything but united.[50] In contrast to this representation, we get a
more accurate reflection of popular perceptions of the critical establishment in a satirical portrait from two years earlier appearing in the
comic paper *Funniest of Awl*, entitled "The New York Bohemians, or the
Literary Critics Amusing Themselves at Piff Paff Puff," depicting the
bacchanalian revels of America's literary critics, debauching themselves in the notorious New York literary hangout Pfaff's Cellar (figure
4). We see an even more straightforward expression of Americans'
mixed feelings toward critics, meanwhile, in an illustration for the periodical *Young Sam* from ten years earlier entitled "The Massacre of the

Edgar A. Poe.

FIGURE 1. A. C. Smith, "Our Contributors. Edgar Allan Poe," *Graham's Magazine* 26, no. 2 (February 1845): 48. Courtesy of the American Antiquarian Society, Worcester, Massachusetts.

FIGURE 2. F. O. C. Darley, Illustration for A. J. H. Duganne's "Mirror for Authors," from *Holden's Dollar Magazine* (January 1849): 22. Courtesy of the American Antiquarian Society, Worcester, Massachusetts.

With tomahawk upraised for deadly blow,
Behold our literary Mohawk, POE !
Sworn tyrant he o'er all who sin in verse—
His own the standard, damns he all that's worse ;
And surely not for this shall he be blamed—
For worse than his deserves that it be damned !

Who can so well detect the plagiary's flaw ?
"Set thief to catch thief" is an ancient saw :
Who can so scourge a fool to shreds and slivers ?

Innocents," in which two critics terrorize three innocent books, spearing one through the heart with a quill as two others beg for their lives, desperately attempting to purchase their salvation with a bribe (figure 5). That is to say, though Lowell insisted that "Before we have an American literature, we must have an American criticism," not everyone was so sure American critics were up to the task.

Rather than privileging one narrative or the other, in the chapters to follow I focus on the clash between these competing images: on flattering critical self-conceptions of critics as agents of cultural progress versus the disparaging portrait of critics as corrupt, venal, self-serving, and driven by their own interests or those of the publishing industry; on the trumped-up rhetoric of nationalist print-emergence and

FIGURE 3. Thomas Hicks, painter, A. H. Ritchie, engraver, *Authors of the United States,* New York, 1866. Courtesy of the American Antiquarian Society, Worcester, Massachusetts.

FIGURE 4. "The New York Bohemians, or the Literary Critics Among Themselves," *Funniest of Awl the Phunnyest Sort of Phun* (December 1864): 12. Courtesy of the American Antiquarian Society, Worcester, Massachusetts.

FIGURE 5. "The Massacre of the Innocents," *Young Sam* (April 1, 1855): 49.
Courtesy of the American Antiquarian Society, Worcester, Massachusetts.

romantic literary genius versus the more skeptical counter-narrative of the growth of print capitalism with the critic as exploited functionary, dueling conceptions that Sandra Tomc argues were inextricably linked.[51] In reconstructing these conflicting accounts, I draw on an extensive, understudied body of criticism that worried about criticism itself, critiques of critique that were frequently written by unknown authors, published in obscure periodicals, and in critical forms that fail to align with twentieth-century notions of critical authority. That is to say, like other recent contributions to the field of print culture studies, I draw from an expanded print culture archive that serves to decenter long privileged accounts in American literary history, here specifically the triumphalist account of the critic's contribution to national literary emergence.

Indeed, the structure of this book deliberately resists the primacy of the single narrative, instead foregrounding simultaneous competing narratives given material shape through the various print forms that served as both catalyst and focal point for debates over criticism. In organizing the following five chapters, while most scholars of criticism from Wellek to Eagleton structure their studies by critical schools and movements arranged chronologically, the present study takes a different course by sorting criticism according to its print forms, from quarterlies, anthologies, and monthly magazines to newspapers and reprinted pamphlet reviews. Though scholars have produced valuable work on non-print expressions of criticism, from literary societies and lyceum lectures to the private responses of everyday readers, in the following chapters—with the exception of a discussion of Emerson's lectures in chapter 1—I limit myself to public, printed criticism since it was here that criticism reached its largest audience, intersecting with and responding to the transformations of antebellum print culture.[52]

I focus on a deliberately short span of time, moreover, beginning with the accelerated growth of periodical publishing in the 1830s and concluding with the critical response to *Uncle Tom's Cabin* in the 1850s, tracing not the linear progress of a single critical narrative but the overlapping concerns associated with five common critical forms during a thirty-year interval in the history of American criticism. I ground each chapter, finally, in case studies of authors whose reputations were tied to particular critical forms, embedding my treatment of each author (Emerson, Griswold, Poe, Fuller, Douglass) within broader discussions of the critical forms with which they're most closely associated (lectures/essays, anthologies, magazine reviews, newspaper criticism, reprinted reviews).

In chapter 1, "Cutting Corners with Emerson," I begin with Emerson's use of quarterly reviews in the 1830s as a heuristic device within an expanding transatlantic intellectual culture. Quarterly reviews, and book reviews more generally, were formative to both Emerson's lecturing career and to the emergence of the Transcendental movement, I argue, facilitating the introduction of invigorating strains of foreign thought while helping public intellectuals like Emerson keep pace with the accelerating output of industrial print culture. Yet while Emerson relied on criticism for his lecturing career, his critical ideas also adapted themselves to his critical venues, shifting according to the forms they took and the occasions they addressed as they moved from the podium to print and from one type of journal to another. Emerson's anxiety over the overwhelming abundance of books in an expanding print culture, finally, shaped not just his use of book reviews but key tenets of his critical philosophy, in particular, his theory of intellectual self-reliance with his advice to young men to unburden themselves of tradition and think their own new thoughts. In opening with Emerson's relation to criticism, then, I explore two central and recurring questions of the book: What cultural functions does criticism serve? And how do critical contexts shape critical theories?

In chapter 2, "Anthology Wars," I turn from lectures and quarterly reviews to literary compilations, as I examine a series of debates over the project of a national anthology, a contest that constituted the forgotten literary culture wars of the 1840s. In volumes such as the best-selling *Poets and Poetry of America* (1842) and *The Prose Writers of America* (1847), America's first professional anthologist, Rufus Wilmot Griswold, gave material shape to the dream of a national literature through the physical form of the literary compilation. Yet his efforts also provoked a heated debate between Griswold and his editorial rivals, Evert and George Duyckinck, over the relationship between literary history and the material text, between literature as a symbolic, national endeavor and literature as a commodity, as the American canon took shape within the multiple constraints of the book as physical object.

In chapter 3, "Reviewers Reviewed," I proceed from the macro-lens of the anthology and the concerns of literary history that the form represents to the micro-lens of the magazine review as expressed in the 1840s by the form's most notorious practitioner, Edgar Allan Poe. While critics attacked Poe for his cruel brand of slashing criticism, Poe insisted that American literature could not improve if it did not have a severe, honest criticism. Yet Poe's own medium of the magazine review, appearing in the new and transformative venue of wide-circulation popular monthly magazines like *Graham's* and *Godey's*, also proved deeply unsettling to Poe, who worried that the emergence of criticism as a popular genre of writing in its own right threatened to corrupt the true critical vocation.

In chapter 4, "Black, White, and Read All Over," I explore Margaret Fuller's career as newspaper critic. While Fuller made a name for herself as editor of the Transcendentalist *Dial*, in 1844 she left New England to take a position as literary editor of Horace Greeley's *New-York Tribune*. In the eighteen months that Fuller occupied that post, she turned the genre of the newspaper book review, long disparaged as the lowest form of criticism, into a respected medium for literary criticism, inaugurating the tradition of the newspaper book review section in the United States and deploying it in the service of social reform. If newspapers empowered the critical office by expanding its audience and the demographic range of its readership, however, the ephemerality of the material form also limited the temporal reach of her writings. As a result, though the newspaper medium made Fuller the most widely read American critic of her day, it also proved debilitating to her critical legacy.

Finally, in chapter 5, "Slavery Reviewed," I trace the critical response to *Uncle Tom's Cabin* in three critical forms that have been largely ignored in critical history: pamphlet reviews, critical companion volumes, and reprinted reviews in periodicals. In the 1850s, the escalat-ing slavery crisis taxed the conventions of reviewing, pushing critics to devise new critical strategies, as commentators employed criticism of *Uncle Tom's Cabin* to promote arguments for and against slavery through the accessible form of the review. This political appropriation of criticism through reprinting is seen not only in pamphlet reviews of *Uncle Tom's Cabin,* in which southern critics sought to overcome the constraints of periodical reviews, but in the early black press. In antislavery journals like *Frederick Douglass' Paper,* editors such as Douglass employed reprinted reviews as a powerful weapon in the war against slavery, enlisting a variety of genres (editorials, correspondent letters, sales blurbs, antislavery meeting minutes) in the service of a critical enterprise oriented toward social change rather than aesthetic evaluation. In closing the study with critical forms that carry low critical authority—unsigned, unoriginal criticism circulated as pamphlets, reprinted reviews, or in generically hybrid forms—we see, paradoxically, the degree to which a dematerialized approach to criticism limits our scholarly sense of the scope of criticism within antebellum cultural life. For in the volatile response to *Uncle Tom's Cabin,* I argue, it was precisely liminal critical forms such as pamphlets and reprinted reviews that displayed most clearly the centrality of criticism to the social and political life of the nation.

As a coda, I turn briefly to the current state of American criticism in the wake of the digital revolution. Where many twenty-first century critics see rupture, however, I see continuity, as technological changes once again prompt an examination of critical principles. By approaching criticism from a print culture perspective and with attention to the multiplicity of its forms, we see the degree to which criticism served, and continues to serve, a variety of uses crucial to the cultural life of the nation, uses that are bound up with its material bearings. This approach reaffirms my overriding argument, finally, that to understand criticism, then as now, we need to pay attention to the material form it takes. Today, in this new age of critical instability, amid the often-proclaimed crisis of the humanities, on the one hand, and the reconfigurations of the digital revolution, on the other, the book serves as a reminder that literary criticism is, and always has been, vital not only to the development of American culture but to the most pressing concerns of the nation.

CHAPTER 1

CUTTING CORNERS WITH EMERSON

Quarterly Reviews and
Intellectual Culture

SINCE ITS BEGINNINGS, early American literary criticism has expressed itself through a range of cultural forms, bridged intellectual traditions, and traversed national boundaries. With a culture rooted in the scriptural word, the Puritan colonists of the seventeenth century made exegesis and biblical interpretation a central part of their daily lives. In the eighteenth century, "the centrality of private judgment to Protestant republicanism," Jay Fliegelman argues, "made criticism not merely an emergent professional activity but the essence and science of one's moral and social existence."[1] The Enlightenment ethos of rational enquiry extended the high value placed on books, writing, and reasoned argument into civic culture, as the ideal of a disinterested public sphere, theorized most famously by Jürgen Habermas, united the polite letters of literary culture to the political values of the young republic. For citizens of the early republic, as Michael Warner suggests, print was more than a communication medium; it was a governing metaphor for their ideal society, a "republic of letters," of civic participation through a print public sphere, and a constitutive part of their political vision as within republican ideology, printed documents came to represent "the material reality of an abstract public."[2]

These ideals extended beyond print. Literary culture of the eighteenth century, as David Shields describes, expressed itself equally through a vibrant manuscript culture, in salons and coffeehouses, in colleges, clubs, and learned societies, as well as through a developing transatlantic book and periodical trade.[3] The concepts at the heart of eighteenth-century literary culture—sensibility, wit, didacticism, propriety, judgment—like the books and magazines themselves were imported from abroad but slowly began to blend into something self-consciously "American." What precisely that designation entailed, however, was a matter of continuous debate that spanned decades from the first years of independence through the Civil War.

These various threads—religious, political, and literary; print and oral; amateur and professional; imported and homegrown—combined to produce a literary criticism more properly defined. To speak of criticism in the eighteenth century, as in the nineteenth century, is to invoke a range of intellectual fields and print genres: Scottish Common Sense philosophy; Enlightenment aesthetics; philology and hermeneutics; and the rhetorical manuals of Kames and Blair. In its more popular literary forms, literary criticism entailed the neoclassical productions of Pope, Swift, and Addison, as well as the essays that filled *The Spectator*, *The Tatler*, and *The Gentleman's Magazine*. Critics reflected on poetry, drama, and the rising form of the novel; their writings emanated not just from the academy but from Grub Street.

In its most common expression, however, literary criticism took the form of the periodical book review. While a number of studies trace the intellectual sources of American critical tradition and its developing moral, aesthetic, and political concerns, criticism also served an essential practical function within an expanding transatlantic print culture. In the following chapter, I develop several argumentative threads, tracing the ways in which critical uses and critical theories, print forms and print anxieties became entangled with one another. First, I explore the cultural work that literary criticism performed within a transatlantic knowledge economy, its role as a conduit for foreign strains of thought that helped overcome geographical and linguistic divides for a developing culture. This work of cultural transmission and mediation was national and transnational; it introduced foreign authors who contributed to the growth of a domestic literary tradition. And nowhere is this more evident than in the foundational role of quarterly reviews in promoting an incipient Transcendentalist movement.

Second, while reviews served the crucial function of diffusing new ideas, as print production increased in the early nineteenth century, reviews also helped writers like Ralph Waldo Emerson get a foothold on an expanding print culture that could often feel overwhelming. In Emerson's career as lecturer and essayist, we see how critical arguments both adapted themselves to these proliferating critical media and reflected the anxieties of industrializing print culture. His critical views shifted to suit audience, critical venue, and critical genre, while his broader critical philosophy of intellectual self-reliance, of unburdening oneself of tradition, confronting nature directly, and thinking new thoughts, can be seen as a theoretical solution for the challenges of industrial print culture, one that aided Emerson in much the same way that book reviews did. In short, book reviews were at the center of American intellectual culture, simultaneously spreading knowledge and providing a check on it.

The Quarterlies and Knowledge Management

While criticism in the republican and national periods expressed a vocal strain of literary nationalism that twentieth-century historians have seized upon in accounts of the period, most periodicals revealed a far more complex and deferential relationship toward transatlantic culture. Indeed, the rise of quarterly reviews signaled a crucial secondary function of literary criticism beyond previewing and evaluating new works: the transmission and management of knowledge within the world republic of letters. Though American periodicals insisted upon the need for critical and literary independence, they simultaneously employed reviews to support the growth of intellectual disciplines by introducing foreign ideas to American readers. While nationalist rhetoric proclaimed critical independence, these same critics relied heavily upon foreign theoretical models circulated through British and American quarterly magazines. Nowhere is this dependence more evident than in the intellectual origins of Transcendentalism, when, in the early decades of the century, new theories spilling out of Germany in the field of philology excited the imaginations of a young group of Boston scholars. Yet the books that contained these field-transforming theories were as difficult to acquire as they were intellectually invigorating.

Beyond the language barrier and the challenge of acquiring books from abroad, there was also the more basic difficulty of knowing about new foreign works in the first place. In this sense the importance of the emergence and growth of scholarly periodicals like the *Edinburgh Review* or the *North American Review*, as well as the literary coteries that gave birth to them, cannot be overstated. Since scholarship and periodical culture were closely intertwined in the nineteenth century, it should come as little surprise that Joseph Stevens Buckminster, the talented young minister at the heart of Boston's Unitarian movement, was actively involved in the Anthology Club and in the periodical venture it spawned, the *Monthly Anthology, and Boston Review* (1803–1811), edited by Ralph Waldo Emerson's father.[4] Though William Emerson oversaw the founding of the Anthology Club and with it the heyday of the magazine, the province of the review transformed dramatically by the time his son, Waldo, founded the *Dial*.

The *Monthly Anthology* was belletristic in taste, liberal in religion, and conservative in politics. It revered classical and neoclassical texts, aped Addison and Steele, and condemned Byron and Wordsworth. The magazine's topical scope was catholic and in the prospectus to the first volume, taking up the conceit of an adopted child, as the magazine had been from its founding editor, Phineas Adams, William Emerson observes that, "it is our intention to have him instructed in several ancient and modern languages, matriculated in two or three universities, and versed in almost every art and science." That its contributors included ministers, lawyers, and doctors, and even a future president, for whom literature was an amateur interest and a diverting excuse for frequent dinners, suited it particularly well to the task of critical judgment. In carrying out this duty, "as his very liberal education will peculiarly fit him for the task, he shall read and review the most important literary productions of our country, and candidly give his opinion of their worth." Accordingly, the reviews evaluated works according to adopted neoclassical aesthetic standards, guarded the public taste, and casually promoted liberal religion. And though not shying away from candid judgments, the editors promised that the tenor of the journal would remain always genteel, for "though we have principally in view his literary and scientific attainments, we purpose that he shall not be destitute of the manners of a gentleman, nor a stranger to genteel amusements."[5]

Though the *Monthly Anthology* was more genteel and neoclassical in orientation than its successors and issued monthly as was the habit of broader appeal monthly magazines, its existence signaled the rise of the quarterly review in the United States as a new mode for managing intellectual culture. Specifically, the quarterly reviews kept readers informed of new works, provided summaries of hard-to-find books, and distilled diverse fields of inquiry into accessible surveys perfectly suited to the leisure hours of a busy, though intellectually acquisitive professional class. The *Monthly Anthology* thus marked an important juncture in the development of American periodicals, as William Emerson enlisted the talents of a coterie of Boston's professional elite in the service of American letters. Though the *Anthology* died in 1811 within eight years of its founding (a respectable lifespan for a magazine at the time), it gave rise to a second generation of quarterly reviews that would prove both more enduring and more aggressive in their ideological affiliation: namely, Andrews Norton's *General Repository and Review* (f. 1812), Noah Worcester's *Christian Disciple* (later the *Christian Examiner*) (f. 1813), as well as William Tudor's *North American Review* (f. 1815).[6]

It was through the quarterly reviews that Americans not only learned about new works but also received distillations of their central arguments and overall significance to contemporary intellectual culture. Such concerns over keeping up with new discoveries in a range of disciplines, while not new, were exacerbated in the early nineteenth century as the pace of print production increased. For young divinity students in the early decades of the century, the new interest in German scholarship only compounded what was already a crushing intellectual load. Students were already responsible for Greek and Latin while many undertook Hebrew and French as well. Now enterprising students were learning German too. Indeed, considering the tremendous amount that students were already responsible for under the Harvard curriculum of the 1820s and '30s, it is hardly surprising that German was slow to be adopted as a further course of study.[7] As a result, any form of digest or gloss served an important heuristic function: anthologies, series with attached prefaces, biographical dictionaries, essays and reviews, and even sermons, which by their form were necessarily short and often summarized longer material, became essential to the scholarly enterprise. For a nation situated on the cusp of a curricular shift and isolated from the European centers of scholarship, biblical study, and elite literary culture, the review was fast becoming an increasingly important site for the management, dissemination, and transmission of knowledge.

It was precisely the simultaneous interest in and lack of access to German scholarship that made reviews such an important part of the literary landscape in the national and antebellum periods since they redressed the scarcity of new foreign works in America while easing the intellectual burden on scholars. After winning the influential Eichhorn New Testament, one of the founding texts of modern biblical criticism, at the auction of Buckminster's library following the young scholar's death, for instance, Moses Stuart agreed to provide Edward Everett access to the work. Though conscientious on Stuart's part, however, such arrangements did little to spread Eichhorn's methods beyond a small circle. Rather, it was not any single text but Buckminster's reviews of Griesbach's Greek New Testament, written in the years before his death in a series of articles for the *Monthly Anthology* and Norton's *General Repository*, that gave broader dissemination to both the methods and intellectual significance of philology and biblical criticism. Soon after the reviews began establishing the importance of textual criticism in 1807, Harvard issued in 1809 a one-volume edition of Griesbach's text for use in the divinity school.[8] It was through these practices of issuing American editions and writing lengthy reviews that German ideas reached a larger audience, though of the two practices, reviews were both more widespread and more intellectually accessible. The speed with which Harvard produced an American imprint of Griesbach was indeed not typical but rather occurred because of Buckminster's high regard within the Cambridge community.

Far more representative was the temporal lapse occasioned by the appearance of Johann Gottfried Herder's *Spirit of Hebrew Poetry*. Though Herder published *Vom Geist der Ebraischen Poesie* in 1782–1783, it was not until fifty years later in 1833 that James Marsh, president of the University of Vermont, finally produced an American edition of the work. Though influential for Unitarian theology and later a catalyst for the Transcendentalist movement, the book's history testifies to the challenges of material transmission that worked to delay the movement's development. Though Stuart and Everett had battled over Buckminster's copy of Eichhorn, soon after the auction, Stuart solicited Everett to produce a translation of Herder's *Spirit of Hebrew Poetry*. Busy with other responsibilities, Everett declined, and it was not until 1826 that Marsh took it upon himself to begin translating the work, publishing sections of it in the *Biblical Repository* before issuing a complete American edition in 1833.

As much as the translated book itself, however, it was the series of articles reviewing Marsh's edition in the *Christian Examiner*, a Boston Unitarian quarterly review, in 1834 and 1835, first by Elizabeth Palmer Peabody and then by George Ripley, that gave a broader platform to Herder's philology with its ennobling conception of the poet as inspired translator of spiritual ideas instead of a mere passive medium to divine revelation.[9] While the earliest scholars exposed to Herder in Göttingen such as Everett, Buckminster, or Ticknor had employed the work's insights to bolster Unitarian arguments in its theological quarrel with Calvinist orthodoxy, Peabody's articles broadened its appeal beyond a theological context to promote a vision of Scripture as creative translation by primitive people of the divinity omnipresent in the world of nature. The Hebrew poets were not merely amanuenses to God's divine decree but rather they perceived God's divinity in the world around them and gave it creative articulation through poetical form.[10]

Though Peabody's article proved influential to the incipient Transcendentalist movement, however, the review itself had little to do with either Marsh's edition or Herder's original text. Indeed, in a note attached to the final page of the third installment of the review, Peabody admits that in truth, "these Essays were written before I had any knowledge of Herder." In making such an admission, Peabody's concern was not that the essays should be viewed as tangential to the work supposedly under review but rather that upon reading the book alongside the review she should be accused of plagiarism. As Peabody avers, "When preparing them for the press, there happened to fall into my hands a manuscript translation of the first chapter of Herder's work, and I therefore took the advantage of his name as giving authority to the speculations with which the first Essay began. But the Essays, with the exception of that one passage, retain the form into which they were put when they were first written, several years since."[11]

Peabody admits that the essays have little bearing upon the work being reviewed, instead merely taking "the advantage of his name as giving authority to the speculations" put forth in her articles. It is only in the opening paragraphs of the first article that Peabody addresses Herder at all. Rather, the articles were an occasion to assert her own theological speculations, speculations that Andrews Norton cut short after the third installment for fear of apostasy. The reading that resulted, instead of merely refracting Herder, spanned five months, extended to three articles, and ran to sixty pages, as Peabody enlisted Hebrew scripture in the service of an increasingly radical Unitarian Christianity. Peabody's review was indeed not so much a review of Herder as a manifesto for a still nascent Transcendentalism, disseminated through the form of a review and taking Herder's subject of the Old Testament as a platform upon which to give a Transcendentalist reading of Genesis.

While Peabody's outright neglect of the book under review was admittedly atypical, her employment of the critical genre as a medium for the promotion of her own intellectual agenda was increasingly common within the quarterly reviews. As the vision of reviewer as journalistic hack gave way to that of the more elevated man of letters, aided by the efforts of Francis Jeffrey, Thomas Carlyle and others, the province of the review expanded along with it. In some reviews, as with Peabody's review of Herder, the title attached was little more than a pretense to launch into a discussion of the reviewer's own views on a subject, often motivated by the text at hand though frequently not. And like Peabody, from time to time the reviewer even admitted this fact freely, as when William Ellery Channing in his influential "Remarks on a National Literature," appearing originally in the January 1830 issue of the *Christian Examiner* as a review of a published oration by C. J. Ingersoll on *The Influence of America on the Mind*, notes that, "We shall use the work prefixed to this article, as ministers are sometimes said to use their texts. We shall make it a point to start from, not the subject of our remarks." Rather, "our purpose is to treat of the importance and means of a National Literature," a topic that "seems to us a great one, and to have intimate connexions with morals and religion, as well as with all our public interests." Of Ingersoll's original text, meanwhile, Channing makes not even passing mention throughout the entirety of the review.[12]

Though Peabody's idealist extrapolations of the book of Genesis startled Norton sufficiently to put a halt to the series of articles, far more often reviews took up the cause of the periodical in which they appeared—political, nationalistic, religious, or otherwise—while fashioning their rhetorical register to suit the character and audience of the magazine. As a later anonymous commentator for the *Christian Examiner* noted at the conclusion of a review of a volume of Philip James Bailey's poetry, for instance, "Here we might end, but for remembering that this is a 'Christian Examiner,' and that therefore there is a further duty to be discharged towards the public,—a much more important duty than belongs to mere literary criticism."[13] Specifically, the reviewer proceeds from observations of a literary nature to attacks on Bailey's religious beliefs. Such ideologically prescriptive criticism was ubiquitous. Rather than "mere literary criticism," as Bailey qualified it, reviews offered opportunities for editors or critics to promote an ideological agenda, putting works of literature and culture through a critical gauntlet or enlisting them to the particular cause of the periodical in question.

In sum, reviews performed a variety of services beyond straightforward evaluation or book promotion crucial to the development of American literature and to the maintenance of nineteenth-century intellectual life more generally. First, they provided knowledge of and access to new works both domestic and foreign, helping to make up for material obstacles limiting availability. Second, they offered a broad public platform for scholars to assert views upon specific topics through a discursive medium that was less intellectually demanding and time consuming than writing a book and reached a far larger audience. Third, reviews performed a crucial service to readers by delivering condensed summaries of arguments, works, and, on occasion, surveys of entire fields. The significance of this heuristic function in an age when knowledge production was heading toward specialization but which also placed a high cultural premium on knowledge acquisition, not just for the highest stratums of society but for everyone, cannot be overstated. As Barbara Packer observes, "This impression of intellectual mastery combined with vigorous expression of opinion gave the reviews an air of authority that could make each essay seem like an education in itself, a quality particularly valuable in the United States, where foreign books were difficult to obtain. The high caliber of the reviewers and their practice of quoting copiously from the books they reviewed gave readers a sense of contact with an intellectual world they might never otherwise approach."[14] Reviews provided a cheap and quick education, in other words, or at the very least an opportunity to fake familiarity with a wide range of subjects in a society that placed a high value on such shows of intellectual refinement.

Ralph Waldo Emerson and the Occasion of Criticism

It was not merely the unscrupulous that took recourse to such time-saving expedients. In the 1830s and '40s, Ralph Waldo Emerson checked out volumes of more than twenty different periodicals from the Boston Athenaeum. It seems no coincidence, moreover, that in the early 1830s, when Emerson was changing vocations and writing his first few series of lectures, he borrowed numerous volumes of the *Westminster Review*, the *Edinburgh Review*, *Blackwood's*, the *Foreign Quarterly Review*, the *New Monthly Magazine*, as well as the local *North American Review* and the international *Revue des Deux Mondes*. Of *Fraser's Magazine* alone, in which Carlyle published his essays on German writers, Emerson checked out volumes one through four in October/November of 1832 and an additional eight volumes from 1838 to 1839 when he was working on an edition of Carlyle's critical writings.[15] In his personal library, meanwhile, Emerson owned the first five bound volumes of the *Christian Examiner*.[16]

These magazines were the front line of exposure to foreign ideas while their format made entire authorial corpuses, disciplines, or philosophical traditions both intellectually and materially accessible. Such reviews worked alongside and frequently as complements to other dedicated works of cultural mediation by the likes of Coleridge, Madame de Staël, and Carlyle by providing distilling reviews of what were in themselves distilling surveys of German philosophy and culture. Similarly, reviews of American editions of foreign works offered culturally assimilating mediations of what were themselves cultural translations, not only bringing new and invigorating ideas to American readers but sifting them through different ideological lenses.

As critical culture expanded in the 1820s and 1830s, criticism not only helped scholars manage print culture, increasingly critical ideas were shaped by this culture as well. Nowhere is this fact more evident than in Emerson's writings, in which critical arguments adapted themselves to suit their venue. In July of 1838, for instance, Emerson's essay on "The Poetical Works of John Milton" appeared in the pages of the *North American Review*. Though the essay was unsigned in keeping with the standard practice of the journal, readers may have guessed the author's identity since its contents were drawn from a series of six lectures on the theme of biography that Emerson delivered at the Boston Masonic Temple in the winter of 1835. Beginning with an introductory lecture on the "Tests of Great Men," Emerson proceeded to treatments of Michelangelo, Milton, Luther, Edmund Burke, and George Fox.[17]

Besides exploring the careers of several notable men of history, the series also confirmed a new vocational direction for Emerson. As has commonly been noted, the early 1830s marked a turning point in Emerson's life. In February of 1831, his young wife Ellen Tucker Emerson, to whom he had been married for less than two years, died of tuberculosis. The following year, a controversy between Emerson and his congregation over the sacrament of the Lord's Supper prompted him to resign his pulpit at the Second Church in Boston, confirming a spiritual break with organized religion that had been years in the making. Personally and vocationally adrift and in poor health, Emerson used the inheritance from his wife's family to embark upon a prolonged trip to Europe, a trip which proved to be transformative, amounting to what Robert Richardson Jr. has termed "his second birth."[18]

When he returned from Europe, Emerson was a changed man. His visit to the Jardin des Plantes in July 1833 affected him so deeply that he declared himself a naturalist while his budding friendship with Thomas Carlyle excited a new sense of secular vocation as writer and lecturer. Three years later, after lecturing first on natural history and then on biography and English literature, Emerson issued a thin book entitled *Nature* that excited murmuring among a small audience of liberal Bostonians. The murmuring became more pronounced the following year when Emerson delivered the well-received Phi Beta Kappa commencement address to the graduating class of Harvard College accompanied by an array of Boston notables. It was in July of 1838, however, the same month that his essay on Milton appeared in the *North American Review,* that Emerson captured the public's attention once and for all with his Divinity School Address. The talk scandalized Boston's religious establishment, both liberal and conservative, earning Andrews Norton's derisive label as the "latest form of infidelity."[19] It also sealed Emerson's break with the church while informally installing him at the head of a new movement that was only just then beginning to understand itself as such. Yet if the Divinity School Address was meant to ruffle feathers, the essay on Milton that appeared the same month was decidedly more restrained, even compared to the commencement address he gave a few days later to the literary societies of Dartmouth College.

Though appearing the same month, the Milton essay and the Dartmouth literary address approach literary tradition from opposite vantage points, betray contrasting methodological orientations, and employ dramatically different stylistic modes. In assessing Milton's prose writings in the *North American Review,* Emerson assumes a reverential stance toward cultural tradition and the great figures of English literary history. With this reverence as a given, however, he is not shy with his evaluative judgments: *The Defence of the People of England* is the worst of Milton's prose works, Emerson asserts, while his defense of free speech in *Areopagitica* is his best. In general, Milton's prose tracts, which his contemporaries read with avidity, "are earnest, spiritual, rich with allusion, sparkling with innumerable ornaments; but, as writings designed to gain a practical point, they fail. They are not effective, like similar productions of Swift and Burke."[20] In their rhetorical construction, meanwhile, they have "no perfectness," the "whole is sacrificed to the particular."

At times we might even mistake Emerson's review of Milton for a piece of neoclassical criticism, or better yet for a slashing review by Poe. And though Richardson suggests that Emerson's essay on Milton prefigures many of the central ideas of "The Poet," there seems to be little in the essay to bear out this assertion.[21] In it, poetry is not a transcription of divine utterance but rather a worldly activity. Drawn from the earlier topical lecture series, Emerson's treatment of Milton accordingly revolves around his interest in biography, as he treats Milton not as a prophet or as a "liberating god" but as a man, discussing at length his physical aspect, his endowments, and his character, qualities that he generally dismissed as opposed to the true office of the poet as translator of natural correspondence.

Whereas the figure of the poet as presented in *Essays: Second Series* (1844) is an inspired channel through which divine truth flows, reconciling the appearance of the material world with the higher truth of ideas, the figure of Milton as formulated in the lecture series on biography and reconstituted for the staid *North American Review* is the worldly poet, the poet incarnate, whose strength and talent come not from the suppression of personality but from the strength of his principles, the purity of his character, and his power to inspire. He is not divested of the world or of personal concerns as Emerson insists is necessary in his sketch of Shakespeare as ideal poet in *Representative Men* (1850), but rather his personal qualities become the driving force of his poetry: conviction, sincerity, moral virtue are the true poetic principles, evident in all aspects of his poetry, rather than meter or rhyme. While "Shakespeare is a voice merely," Emerson proclaims, "Milton stands erect, commanding, still visible as a man among men."[22]

Just as Emerson substitutes the embodied Milton for the transparent eyeball of *Nature*, the clearly reasoned and orderly argumentative style of the review was also a marked departure from the dense oracular style for which Emerson was known, speech that was "Emersonially Emersonian" as Oliver Wendell Holmes termed it.[23] Rather, the essay was uncharacteristically focused, following the central idea of Milton's poetic accomplishments as rooted in the endowments of the man himself and hewing closely to that organizing theme. Such focus was rare for Emerson. Indeed, in reviewing Emerson's Dartmouth oration from the same month, Orestes Brownson interrupts his review and exclaims with exasperation, "But we give it up. We cannot analyze one of Mr. Emerson's discourses. He hardly ever has a leading thought, to which all the parts of his discourse are subordinate, which is clearly stated, systematically drawn out, and logically enforced. He is a poet rather than a philosopher,—and not always true even to the laws of poetry."[24]

The same could hardly be said of Emerson's review of Milton, however. The argument develops in an orderly fashion with a defined structure and strong topic sentences. The progression of the essay is signposted still more explicitly in header glosses that walk readers through the essay's arguments, describing the topic of each page with descriptions such as: "His Contemporaneous Fame," "His Natural Endowments," "His Moral Greatness," "His Love of Liberty," "Relation of his Poetry to his Character," etc. At the same time, Emerson abandons the techniques necessary for keeping the attention of a live audience: he restrains his tendency to jump abruptly from idea to idea or image to image as he does in his lectures and essays; he refrains from presenting a string of rhetorical aphorisms or metaphors drawn from nature; he even manages not to contradict himself, perhaps for the simple reason that he expresses his ideas with precision and understatement rather than in overblown rhetorical pronouncements. This is not to say that he abandons his core beliefs. Emerson still expresses ideas consistent with his literary philosophy (a definition of poetry as reconciling the real with the ideal, the poet as a revealer of divine truth, insistence on sincerity, etc.), but he does so with more rhetorical moderation.

Whether the context of the *North American Review*, for which Emerson had contributed another article on Michelangelo the previous year, proved liberating or constraining is uncertain, though within months of the Milton piece's appearance, Emerson went out of his way to note in his journal that, "When I read the North American Review, or the London Quarterly, I seem to hear the snore of the muses, not their . . . waking voice."[25] Despite his lack of enthusiasm for the journal, however, his publication there nonetheless lent his writing a clear, grounded quality absent from many of his more famous essays and addresses. Such stylistic qualities are, of course, partly a matter of the reader's taste, and as commentators have noted, Emerson designed the rhetorical form of his essays strategically to achieve certain effects with his audience while his unpredictable prose style doubled as a protest against the tyranny of the "understanding," as Coleridge termed it.[26]

The larger significance of the uncharacteristic straightforwardness of the Milton review, however, is that both the rhetorical delivery and thematic content of Emerson's criticism adapted themselves to the conventions of the *North American Review*, where the excesses and eccentricities of Emerson's style were tempered by the moderate tenor of its sober periodical context. Nor was this an isolated phenomenon. Rather, Emerson crafted all of his works to suit their cultural and material contexts, despite his expressed concern regarding this adulterating tendency. Indeed, though Emerson vowed in his journal soon after taking up lecturing as a vocation that, "I will say at Public Lectures & the like, those things which I have meditated for their own sake & not for the first time with a view to that occasion," such an idealistic pledge proved difficult to uphold. The frequency with which Emerson privately invoked this vow of "self-reliant originality," as Merton Sealts Jr. calls it, only emphasized the extent to which Emerson worried that the occasional nature of his discourses, their adaptation to local and material circumstances, violated his inveterate preaching of intellectual autonomy.[27]

Resist as he might, circumstance could not help but impact thought. As Emerson asserts in the Milton essay's opening paragraphs, literary criticism constructs authorial reputations to suit the cultural demands of present-day readers; yet as the chaste tenor of those very reflections suggest, criticism is shaped by its own cultural contexts as well. Accordingly, in the pages of the scholarly *North American Review*, Emerson produced a restrained appreciation of the great poet of the seventeenth century, a treatment devoid of nationalist rhetoric, iconoclastic dismissals of tradition, or mystical conceptions of the poet as the inspired interpreter of nature's symbols. In other contexts, however, his critical theory would take on different dimensions, speak in other registers, and often contradict earlier—or even contemporaneous— critical positions.

In the commencement address Emerson delivered later that month to the literary societies of Dartmouth College, for instance, the views he expressed about authorship and literary tradition were different altogether. Nor should this surprise us given the context. While the Milton piece was a popular lecture delivered as part of a series on biography and revised for Boston's most respectable quarterly review, "Literary Ethics," as it came to be called, was a commencement oration geared toward a graduating class of seniors. As a result, the address is simultaneously more oriented toward vocational guidance, more motivational in tone, more iconoclastic toward the cultural monuments of the past, and more rhetorically hyperbolic as such occasions demanded. "I am to harangue the Dartmouth College boys on the last Tuesday of July," Emerson jocularly quipped to his brother, William.[28] While the Milton piece was scholarly and reflective, wearing its erudition on its sleeve, there is a practical logic to the Dartmouth oration in its context as an address delivered to outward-bound college seniors. In organization it divides itself into treatments of the resources and subjects available to the scholar as well as to the discipline necessary to succeed. The term "ethics" itself denotes right principles of conduct for the scholarly profession, which Emerson here conflates with the literary vocation.

Throughout the address, meanwhile, Emerson provides consoling advice constructed specifically to ease the anxieties of young scholars. They need not feel overwhelmed by what has already been done and said, Emerson assures his audience; nature provides fresh truths when you engage it directly. Nor should they worry about the past or that there's nothing new to say. Instead, follow your ambition, look to nature, seek truth in solitude, and trust the emanations of your soul. In a sort of cultural Jeffersonianism, Emerson insists that the intellectual debts of one generation must not be passed on to the next. "The new man must feel that he is new, and has not come into the world mortgaged to the opinions and usages of Europe, and Asia, and Egypt." As Emerson's rhetorical momentum builds, his metaphors accrue as the image of a mortgage transforms into that of a coffin: "Now our day is come; we have been born out of the eternal silence; and now will we live,—live for ourselves,—and not as the pall-bearers of a funeral, but as the upholders and creators of our age; and neither Greece nor Rome, nor the three Unities of Aristotle, nor the three Kings of Cologne, nor the College of Sorbonne, nor the Edinburgh Review, is to command any longer. Now we are come, and will put our own interpretation on things, and, moreover, our own things for interpretation."[29] It was precisely sentiments such as these that Christopher Pearse Cranch mocked a year earlier with his affectionate caricature of Emerson's Phi Beta Kappa address to Harvard seniors, portraying Emerson bowed under the weight of books, crying "They pin me down!" with the Harvard Library in the background, perched precariously above the River of Time on a foundation of Shakespeare and Virgil (figure 6).[30]

To be sure, in his Dartmouth address, Emerson does not renounce tradition altogether. Rather, he insists that tradition must be in the service of new thoughts; it must inspire young men in their own fresh exertions and not hold them in thrall to the past. Similarly, within Emerson's

FIGURE 6. Christopher Pearse Cranch, "River of Time," Illustrations of the New Philosophy: Drawings. Ca. 1837–1839. MS Am 1506. Houghton Library, Harvard University, Cambridge, Massachusetts.

humanistic conception of the past, biography inspires contemporary readers with visions of their own human potential. As Emerson asserts, "The whole value of history, of biography, is to increase my self-trust, by demonstrating what man can be and do." And yet despite such disclaimers, there is a clear difference in the way Emerson conceives of tradition here as opposed to in his Milton essay of the same month. The reverence for history and for the great works of the past that Emerson capitalizes upon in his lecture series on biography, English literature, or the philosophy of history is replaced by a sharp iconoclasm, delivered with hyperbolic relish to a graduating class of seniors anxious to make their own mark. Discounting the burden of tradition, Emerson now insists that, "The inundation of the spirit sweeps away before it all our little architecture of wit and memory, as straws and straw-huts before the torrent."

Emerson knows his audience. While the Milton review presupposes a high regard for tradition, in his address to the Dartmouth literary societies, as with his Phi Beta Kappa address to Harvard the year before, Emerson groups Milton with those imposing figures of literary history who now threaten to suffocate the creative energies of new generations. Emerson even names Milton specifically. "Whilst I read the poets, I think that nothing new can be said about morning and evening," Emerson reflects. "But when I see the daybreak, I am not reminded of these Homeric, or Shakspearian [sic], or Miltonic, or Chaucerian pictures. No; but I feel perhaps the pain of an alien world; a world not yet subdued by the thought; or, I am cheered by the moist, warm glittering, budding, melodious hour, that takes down the narrow walls of my soul, and extends its life and pulsation to the very horizon." As with Plato's critique of art, Milton's poetic depiction of daybreak here stands for a copy of nature that gets in the way of immediate experience. Rather, the young scholar needs to put down *Paradise Lost*, confront nature directly, and trust in his own abilities.[31]

Emerson concludes by noting that the work of scholarship is its own reward, that the scholar must "embrace solitude as a bride" and not pander to the public. "Let him know, that, though the success of the market is in the reward, true success is the doing; that, in the private obedience to his mind; in the sedulous inquiry, day after day, year after year, to know how the thing stands . . . in a contempt for the gabble of to-day's opinions, the secret of the world is to be learned, and the skill truly to unfold it is acquired." Emerson quickly qualifies this remark, however: the scholar cannot ignore the public completely, rather it is his task to communicate the truth of nature to the mass of men, a conception that follows Coleridge's call for a cultural clerisy.

> The man of genius should occupy the whole space between God or pure mind, and the multitude of uneducated men. He must draw from the infinite Reason, on one side; and he must penetrate into the heart and sense of the crowd, on the other. From one, he must draw his strength; to the other, he must owe his aim. The one yokes him to the real; the other, to the apparent. At one pole, is Reason; at the other, Common Sense. If he be defective at either extreme of the scale, his philosophy

will seem low and utilitarian; or it will appear too vague and indefinite for the uses of life.

This contest between ideas and audience, between pure expression and the cultural contexts of this expression, is a fundamental tension of Emerson's career. In the above example, we see it play out in the difference between his essay on Milton for the *North American Review* and his address to the Dartmouth graduating class, where one capitalizes upon tradition and the other dismisses it like "straw-huts before the torrent." As Emerson suggests, the scholar needs to balance a sense of one's audience with a fidelity to truth in order to avoid being "low and utilitarian," on the one hand, and "vague and indefinite," on the other. And though Emerson did his best to achieve this balance, in practice every work of his career reflected the material and cultural circumstances of its production and dissemination.[32]

The material forms that Emerson's critical writings took shaped both their content and their legacy. The Emerson we are most familiar with is that of *Nature* and of his major essays, most of which were condensed distillations of his lectures. As scholars have observed, the lyceum context as well as the exacting process of revision his lectures went through to become essays had a profound impact on the style of Emerson's major collections.[33] Yet not all of Emerson's works were created through this refining process. Indeed, many of Emerson's critical works were commissioned for specific occasions that determined the nature of their content and delivery. These works range from canonical texts such as "The American Scholar" and "The Divinity School Address" to obscure works relegated to late miscellany volumes of Emerson's collected writings, such as his remarks at commemorative celebrations of Scott or Burns, or uncollected works, such as the introduction to his poetry anthology, *Parnassus*.

Though poems are frequently labeled "occasional," as Emerson's corpus suggests, all literary criticism is in a sense occasional as well. It appears in cultural and material contexts that influence its arguments as well as its presentation. To understand a work of criticism, accordingly, we need to recuperate the material circumstances of the critical performance. This is in fact the same point Emerson makes at the beginning of his remarks on Milton when he observes that, "The fame of a great man is not rigid and stony like his bust. It changes with time."[34]

To this I would add that not just literary reputations but the critical estimations that shape them change with the context as well. While Milton
is an icon and a source of inspiration in the *North American Review*, he is
a dusty relic in "Literary Ethics."

Modes of critical dissemination matter, in other words, since different formats carry with them specific conventions that influence
the message, content, and style of the thoughts expressed. Scholars
are quick to account for Emerson's tendency to contradict himself by
pointing to his aversion to restrictive systematic thinking, to the inevitable evolution of his thought over time, and to his famous assertion in "Self-Reliance" that "a foolish consistency is the hobgoblin
of little minds."[35] But Emerson's shifting opinions on the same literary figures or topics was also a product of the diverse material and
cultural forms in which Emerson worked as well as of his composition process, which recycled and repurposed material from earlier lectures and essays. As a result, Emerson's treatment of a topic
adapted both substantively and stylistically to suit the material context or oratorical occasion. As Emerson himself acknowledged in his
essay, "Intellect," — "To genius must always go two gifts, the thought
and the publication. The first is revelation . . . But to make it available,
it needs a vehicle or art by which it is conveyed to men. To be commu-
nicable, it must become picture or sensible object."[36] Even revelation
of spirit needs a material form. If Emerson was an idealist in philosophy, he could not help but be a materialist in practice since thought
could not communicate itself without form.

It was ironically in the "Prospectus" to the *Dial*, a magazine rich in
talent but beset by numerous material challenges, that Emerson set
out his vision of criticism in its most idealized form. Though Emerson
describes ideal criticism as a "protest against usage, and a search for
principles," in practice, principles and usage proved difficult to disentangle. As with all of his philosophy, Emerson's abstracted critical theory in the *Dial* formed itself in accordance with its material and cultural contexts. "Editors to the Reader" is a magazine prospectus: it
generalizes, speaks from the perspective of editor (though Emerson
was not technically that), and views criticism metonymically as an
expression of the journal's larger cultural endeavor. Yet in actuality,
Emerson's criticism frequently departed from the sort of abstracted,

affirming criticism he described in the *Dial*'s prospectus. As he noted half-jocularly in a letter to Christopher Pearse Cranch, "I am a vigorous, cruel critic, and demand in the poet a devotion that seems hardly possible in our hasty, facile America." Though John Anderson brushes this comment aside as facetious, Emerson could be a tough audience.[37] Despite his critical legacy as the great promoter of American literature, his actual evaluations of literature were far more frequently harsh and dismissive than they were sympathetic and encouraging. He had a generally low estimation of America's literary accomplishments, panned the entirety of British literary tradition in *English Traits*, and maintained a cold, critical detachment even to his favorite authors in *Representative Men*, to the point that it can often be difficult to discern whether he likes Plato, Goethe, and Shakespeare at all.

Within the pages of the *Dial*, meanwhile, under the ennobled heading of *criticism* broadly conceived we find all sorts of lesser, subsidiary *criticisms* directed toward pointed ends. As Margaret Fuller notes in "A Short Essay on Critics," the problem with the current state of criticism is that it has no fixed standard or defined parameters: "An essay on Criticism were a serious matter," Fuller asserts, "for, though this age be emphatically critical, the writer would still find it necessary to investigate the laws of criticism as a science, to settle its conditions as an art." On the one hand, "essays entitled critical are epistles addressed to the public through which the mind of the recluse relieves itself of its impressions," and of which "the only law is 'Speak the best word that is in thee.'" On the other hand, "they are regular articles, got up to order by the literary hack writer, for the literary mart, and the only law is to make them plausible."[38] Criticism was no one thing but rather divided between different conceptions and applications, nor was the *Dial* exempt from this multiplicity of uses.

The varied critical contents, indeed, the very existence of the *Dial*, bear out Fuller's sense that the republic of letters lacked a set standard of criticism. The very first issue of the magazine contained an editorial prospectus, Fuller's "Short Essay on Critics," critical reflections culled from the personal journal of Emerson's recently deceased brother, Charles Emerson, Fuller's critical observations upon an exhibit of Washington Allston's paintings, a twenty-five-page review of Orestes Brownson's writings by George Ripley, and a young Henry David

Thoreau's critical review of Aulus Persius Flaccus. In the journal's second issue, the editors opened with Emerson's "Thoughts on Modern Literature," which surveys the current state of literature, its prevailing character and tendencies, but also appended a "Record of the Months" section as a new segment of the magazine, including within it a "Select List of Recent Publications," which takes not nature and truth as its object but rather abbreviated notices of recently published books.

Instead of expansive treatments of subjects or disciplines or occasions to explore specific topics as was typical of the essays of the main body of the *Dial*, the criticisms contained within "Record of the Months" were book reviews in the more utilitarian sense of the term: pointed evaluative summaries of recent works ranging anywhere from one to four pages that hewed closely to the volumes under review and gave readers a sense of whether the book was worth purchasing. Those notices included under "Recent Publications," meanwhile, were even shorter (sometimes no more than a paragraph or two), brusquely judgmental, and frequently contained large block quotations from the text under review. Though Emerson suggested that criticism in the *Dial* would be "poetic, unpredictable," taking life as its subject and "making new light on the world," in practice, the journal included all scales of criticism from philosophy to puff, as many critical styles as there were contributors, and a hybrid critical format that fell somewhere between the general monthly magazine with its poetry and prose sketches and the quarterly review with its lengthy critical essays by ministers and scholars.[39]

While Edgar Allan Poe, as I'll suggest, epitomized one form of criticism (the popular magazine review) and Rufus Griswold another (the anthology), Emerson has typically been taken as representative of the long-standing tradition of criticism as philosophy. But aesthetics was only one strain of Emerson's extensive corpus of literary criticism. Emerson's career also signaled the more recent emergence of criticism as a popular form, tethered to the new universal figure of the "man of letters," or what Emerson himself called the "scholar." He belonged to the tradition of Samuel Johnson and Samuel Taylor Coleridge and of Victorian sages like Thomas Carlyle, Matthew Arnold, and John Ruskin who made literature a central front in the battle to uphold culture against the forces of degradation. He wrote the manifesto *Nature* but was also a fixture of the lecture circuit. And while Emerson merged philosophy with the popular lecture, he explored other forms as well. His writings spread out through countless journals, letters, essays, pamphlets, collected volumes, miscellanies, editorial projects, and magazines, to say nothing of non-print forms. Much of the difficulty we confront in contemplating his authorial corpus is in fact a direct product of the multiplicity of forms that Emerson's thought took and the impact that shifting from one form to another had on the coherence of his works both individually and collectively. As a result, Transcendentalism is a perfect case study for the way that literary criticism in the antebellum period cannot be fully understood divorced from the material practices of its dissemination.

The fertile contradictoriness of Emerson's life and art, in other words, was partly a result of diversifying material practices within antebellum print culture as well as of a historical shift in the conception of criticism itself, changes of which Emerson was both aware and took full advantage. Though Emerson's philosophy was idealist, his intellectual heritage emphasized the contingency—historical, linguistic, epistemological, or otherwise—of interpretation. Emerson was an heir to the philology of Wolf, Eichhorn, and Herder and the hermeneutics of Kant and Schleiermacher. The historical methods of the Schlegel brothers and Hegel stressed the material significance of history upon interpretation while Lessing's *Laocoön* grounded the aesthetic effect within different material mediums in the arts. As Emerson himself acknowledged, even revelation of spirit needs a material form. And so Emerson preached; he lectured; he gave addresses that circulated as pamphlets, and wrote magazine articles that reappeared in essay collections. The source material for these lectures and essays he culled from his extensive journals, which he in turn gleaned from his extensive reading. And while these dimensions of his career have been noted individually by scholars, what I want to call attention to here is the diversity and fluidity of these material practices, the shifting from one to another, and the cultural implications carried not only by individual mediums but by the proliferation of critical forms as a cultural phenomenon in its own right.[40]

The "Vast Carcass of Tradition":
Information Overload and Critical Theory

As critical culture expanded alongside a diversifying print culture in the 1820s and '30s, this proliferation began to have a formative impact not just on individual critical works, but on the orientation of American critical theory as a whole. Nowhere is this constitutive relationship between critical theory and an expanding print culture more evident than in Emerson's evolving sense of the scholar's relation to literary tradition. Though the *Dial*'s prospectus promised a criticism directed toward principles, in surveying the current state of the art in "Thoughts on Modern Literature," it was not principles but rather the material practices of antebellum print culture to which Emerson kept returning. The age is obsessed with information, he observes; it wants facts and knowledge; its appetite for information is voracious such that, as Emerson avers, all "Christendom has become a great reading-room." The publishing industry has not been lax in responding to this demand, moreover, spewing from its ever more efficient presses books of all sorts, with the result that the bookstores now present an "immense miscellany," every species of book, "for every opinion old and new, every hope and fear, every whim and folly has an organ."

The age prints not just new books but those of the past as well, ushering from the press with gathering momentum countless reprints of old works. "Our presses groan every year with new editions of all the select pieces of the first of mankind," Emerson notes, "—meditations, history, classifications, opinions, epics, lyrics, which the age adopts by quoting them."[41] It examines these books with a new spirit of critical inquiry, moreover, as conscious of its own operations as it is of the text in front of it. Emerson is careful to withhold explicit judgment in recording these characterizations, contenting himself with their observation. And yet the essay is no celebration while the language betrays more than a little ambivalence. Reprints of older works present a "vast carcass of tradition," readers demand not insight into nature but "the superficial exactness of information," while the new spirit of subjectivity divides between critical self-awareness and egotism.[42] The knowledge that results is in turn superficial, providing mere information rather than wisdom, while what matters for Emerson are principles, the truth of reason rather than the facts of the understanding.

More than a little of this concern was an expression of Emerson's own anxiety as a writer and lecturer upon an eclectic range of topics. Though Emerson claimed criticism should seek truth, in essays such as "Thoughts on Modern Literature" we see the degree to which Emerson's critical theory had roots in the material practices of antebellum print culture. Indeed, many of Emerson's most famous proclamations on the need for a national literature, the throwing off of dependency on foreign books and models, and a direct relationship with nature masked a deep anxiety regarding the demands of the scholarly vocation as it was taking shape in the 1830s and '40s.[43] Specifically, Emerson worried that antebellum culture was in a state of overproduction, that it was generating more books than it could handle and was thus becoming superficial in the knowledge it possessed. And though Emerson incessantly blurred the titles he gave to men of intellectual and artistic aspiration—"scholar," "man of letters," "poet," "critic"—it was increasingly the critical vocation that for Emerson made the scholar's vocation feasible by providing digests of new works and concise surveys of entire fields.

Given the range of services that by the 1830s reviews provided— some high, others low—the critic is a difficult figure to pinpoint in Emerson's writings, occupying a middle ground between poet and scholar, nature and the marketplace, original thinker and cultural mediator. As the number of colleges grew, moreover, the knowledge industry began to splinter between scholars, occupying university chairs and claiming extensive knowledge of specific fields, and journalists who lacked expertise but made up for it in the service they provided by charting the publication of new books and promoting the acquisition of knowledge more generally.[44] In between these two poles of scholar and critic, there emerged the new figure of the man of letters, defined by Emerson as one who made a living by his pen and who, according to both Emerson and Carlyle, was the representative man of the new era, typified by figures like Goethe and Coleridge as well as by Emerson and Carlyle themselves.

The man of letters was a jack-of-all-trades—and, indeed, this was the problem. The man of letters fashioned himself as the new Renaissance man, positioned between the esoteric world of specialized knowledge typical of the academy and the ever-expanding popular audiences of the lecture circuit, who desired an acquaintance with diverse fields of knowledge presented in engaging and accessible form. In practice, however, this proffered claim to both broad and thorough knowledge within a host of disciplines put heavy demands on men like Emerson, who, as Lawrence Buell suggests, were early precursors to the modern public intellectual.[45] While Emerson could certainly hold his own within the intellectual circles of his day, he was also no prodigy. His time at Harvard was undistinguished, and he experienced continued self-doubt throughout his career. Yet his career as preacher, public lecturer, and essayist forced him to maintain the image of a man of comprehensive knowledge, an image which the demands of constant lectures, editorial work, duties to friends and family, and other everyday concerns did much to strain.

It is this anxiety of intellectual competence, driven by a populace hungry for knowledge, a perceived surplus of both old and new books, as well as the pressure produced by the image of the man of letters as master of all fields that, beyond the frequently cited sources of Unitarianism and German idealism, proved formative to Emerson's literary and critical philosophy. It is also within this context of the pressures of antebellum print culture, intensified for figures caught between the realms of academic and popular knowledge production, that we can best understand Emerson's sense of the critical vocation as well as his major statements regarding literary culture. It was this anxiety in the face of what Emerson perceived as an untenable overabundance of books and information, moreover, that made Goethe such a seductive figure for Emerson, prompting Emerson's extended treatment of him in *Representative Men* as the consummate figure of the writer.[46]

Goethe was a man at home in the eighteenth and early nineteenth centuries, Emerson notes, a period of polite society, cultural refinement, and extensive but superficial knowledge across a diverse range of disciplines. "We conceive Greek or Roman life, life in the Middle Ages, to be a simple and comprehensible affair," Emerson muses, "but modern life to respect a multitude of things which is distracting." But "Goethe was the philosopher of this multiplicity, hundred-handed, Argus-eyed, able and happy to cope with this rolling miscellany of facts and

sciences, and, by his own versatility, to dispose of them with ease." As
Emerson observes, the second part of *Faust* is "a philosophy of literature set in poetry; the work of one who found himself the master of histories, mythologies, philosophies, sciences, and national literatures, in
the encyclopædical manner in which modern erudition with its international intercourse of the whole earth's population, researches into
Indian, Etruscan and all Cyclopean arts, geology, chemistry, astron-
omy; and every one of these kingdoms assuming a certain aerial and
poetic character, by reason of the multitude." Goethe is a figure who
incorporated the overwhelming mass of information that confronted
the scholar in the Age of Enlightenment and yet reconciled it with a
countervailing spirit of romanticism.[47]

Completed upon the year of Goethe's death in 1832, *Faust*, like T. S.
Eliot's *Waste Land* just under a century later, assembled the fragments
of culture, the panoply of traditions and disciplines and information, into a coherent vision of the present. Goethe masters and assimilates a multiplicity of knowledge, distilling truth from a glut of facts,
for which Emerson views him with reverence. The sense of information overload was a cultural phenomenon that not just Emerson but all
aspiring writers and scholars of the era had to reconcile in their own
way. As Emerson observed in his earlier lecture "Literature," Goethe
was a new type of the "universal man," a figure that "is now coming to
be a real being in the individual mind as the devil was then."[48] For the
more cynical Melville, this type would take the form of the confidence
man. Poe responded to the glut of information, meanwhile, through
the fantasy figure of C. Auguste Dupin, a man of pure intellect with
scarcely any physical characteristics who solves crimes that confound
the police through a combination of impossibly wide reading, an encyclopedic knowledge of obscure facts, and the process of what Poe calls
"ratiocination," giving birth to the detective genre in the process.

Just as with Poe's Dupin, Emerson's Goethe has mastered the panoply of human intellectual accomplishment. Speaking again of *Faust*,
Emerson notes that, "The wonder of the book is its superior intelli-
gence. In the menstruum of this man's wit, the past and present ages
and their religions, politics, and modes of thinking are dissolved into
archetypes and ideas." It doesn't matter what topic he treats: "He sees
at every pore, and has a certain gravitation towards truth. He will real-

ize what you say." As Emerson concludes, "Goethe, coming into an overcivilized time and country, when original talent was oppressed under the load of books and mechanical auxiliaries and the distracting variety of claims, taught men how to dispose of this mountainous miscellany, and make it subservient." In doing so, "he was the soul of his century . . . cloth[ing] our modern existence with poetry."[49]

It was this "mountainous miscellany" that Emerson struggled himself to subdue throughout his own career. If Goethe is a fantasy image of the writer as "universal man," however, Emerson constructs a more practical vision of knowledge management in an age of print abundance in his essay "Books," which provides readers with a handy list of tricks, shortcuts, and reading aids for handling the seemingly endless extent of books confronting the contemporary scholar. While Emerson gestured at this anxiety of information overload in "Thoughts on Modern Literature," it is all but explicit in "Books," which, though written during the early part of his second trip to England in 1847–1848 and a staple of his future lecturing, didn't appear in print until January 1858 when published in the *Atlantic Monthly* before finally being collected in *Society and Solitude* in 1870. In its treatment of literary tradition, the essay offers a striking contrast to the high rhetoric of "The American Scholar," the romantic aesthetics of "The Poet," or the idealist philosophy of *Nature*. Rather, "Books" is a practical manual for managing the daunting surplus of reading material that confronts modern readers as well as a candid airing of the various tricks Emerson employed throughout his career to navigate centuries of accumulated knowledge.

Decades earlier at the end of "Literary Ethics," Emerson closed his address to the Dartmouth undergraduates with an injunction not to students but to professors. Ardent students inevitably look for wisdom from their teachers, Emerson observes, half-expecting them to unmask the secrets of the world. Upon seeking this insight, however, "they find that he is a poor, ignorant man, in a white-seamed, rusty coat, like themselves, no wise emitting a continuous stream of light, but now and then a jet of luminous thought, followed by total darkness." It is this self-aware poverty of true insight on the teacher's part (as well as a deep insecurity on Emerson's) that prompts "the temptation to the scholar to mystify; to hear the question; to sit upon it; to make an answer of words, in lack of the oracle of things." Yet there is no need to hide one's ignorance or uncertainty, Emerson insists. "Always truth is policy enough for him." Instead, let the scholar "open his breast to all honest inquiry, and be an artist superior to tricks of art," Emerson advises. "Show frankly as a saint would do, all your experience, your methods, tools, and means. Welcome all comers to the freest use of the same. And out of this superior frankness and charity, you shall learn higher secrets of your nature, which gods will bend and aid you to communicate." It is this "superior frankness," this free and self-assured revelation of the "tricks of art," the "experience, methods, tools, and means" at the scholar's disposal that Emerson provides with unsurpassed candor in his lecture-turned-essay "Books."[50]

If "Literary Ethics" and "The American Scholar" provide a respectable, if politely iconoclastic treatment of the resources available to the scholar, delivered to the undergraduates and faculty of Dartmouth and Harvard respectively, "Books" is the nineteenth-century version of Cliffs Notes. While in "The American Scholar" and "Literary Ethics," Emerson famously instructs young scholars to unburden themselves of the oppressive weight of tradition, to read what books they will and ignore the rest, in "Books" he is far more precise in advising his readers on which books to disregard. Specifically, Emerson asserts three steadfast, clearly enumerated rules for deciding what to read: "1. Never read any book that is not a year old. 2. Never read any but famed books. 3. Never read any but what you like."

Like all of Emerson's essays, "Books" prevaricates in its stance toward tradition, alternating between outright dismissal of books as limiting to new thought and loving encomiums to the wisdom they contain: books "work no redemption in us," Emerson asserts, they are like worthless stocks, while a paragraph later he proclaims that books "take rank in our life with parents and lovers and passionate experiences," bestowing upon us "the perception of immortality." Yet the prevailing note of the essay is practicality. Without wide reading, a scholar won't be taken seriously, Emerson observes. "If you know that,—for instance, in geometry, if you have read Euclid and Laplace,—your opinion has some value; if you do not know these, you are not entitled to give any opinion on the subject." Books are the price of admission into learned conversation. This is as it should be, moreover, since most topics cannot be discussed productively without a common foundation in certain canonical texts.[51]

This reflection immediately gives way to anxiety, however, as Emerson's mind wanders to the sheer number of books contained in the great libraries of the world. As he ponders the subject, his thoughts turn to calculations:

> We look over with a sigh the monumental libraries of Paris, of the Vatican, and the British Museum. In 1858, the number of printed books in the Imperial Library at Paris was estimated at eight hundred thousand volumes, with an annual increase of twelve thousand volumes; so that the number of printed books extant to-day may easily exceed a million. It is easy to count the number of pages which a diligent man can read in a day, and the number of years which human life in favorable circumstances allows to reading; and to demonstrate, that, though he should read from dawn till dark, for sixty years, he must die in the first alcoves.

The specific choice of sixty years does not seem incidental since as of 1858, when "Books" appeared in the *Atlantic*, Emerson was fifty-five. With well over half his life behind him, Emerson knew only too well how little one could read in a lifetime. The saving grace is that most books are not worth one's time, while the best books are already on the shelves of most home libraries. Such essential books are few, while by and large, as Emerson insists, "the crowds and centuries of books are only commentary and elucidation, echoes and weakeners of these few great voices of Time."[52]

As a result, readers require not an infinitude of time to cloister themselves in dimly lit libraries and reading rooms so much as a knowledgeable guide to lead them through the overstocked annals of history and culture, a figure whom Emerson deems a "professor of books." "No chair is so much wanted," Emerson adds, for, "In a library we are surrounded by many hundreds of dear friends, but they are imprisoned by an enchanter in these paper and leathern boxes." They are lost to their uniform materiality, rendered indistinguishable since "the enchanter has dressed them like battalions of infantry in coat and jacket of one cut," has hidden their riches in uniform caskets, except unlike *The Merchant of Venice* there are not merely three caskets to choose from but "half a million caskets, all alike." For this reason, the scholar requires the assistance of one of "those great masters of books who from time to time appear,—the Fabricii, the Seldens, Magliabecchis, Scaligers, Mirandolas, Bayles, Johnsons—whose eyes sweep the whole horizon of learning." Such a service should not be left only to the great librarians, pedants, and polymaths of history, moreover; rather, it is the office of every scholar to share those books that have eased his laborious task. For as Emerson reflects, "it seems, then, as if some charitable soul, after losing a great deal of time among false books, and alighting upon a few true ones which made him happy and wise, would do a right act in naming those which have been bridges or ships to carry him safely over dark morasses and barren oceans, into the heart of sacred cities, into palaces and temples."[53]

It is precisely these "bridges and ships" on the sea of knowledge that Emerson spends the rest of the essay enumerating. If "Books" is not frequently read today, it is in part because the majority of the essay consists of a condensed reading list surveying thousands of years of recorded history from the Bible and the ancient Greeks to George Sand and Charlotte Brontë. It is a distilling catalogue of those books that have proved invaluable to Emerson, much as with Thomas Jefferson's well-known letter to his brother-in-law, Robert Skipwith, listing those books indispensable to a gentleman's library.[54] In providing his own list, we get a strong sense of the scholarly shortcuts Emerson relied upon throughout his career: his reliance upon compendiums and accessible surveys of historical periods; his preference for English translations whenever available; and his enumeration of secondary works that have proven helpful guides (despite his insistence that most secondary works could be safely ignored).

More than a few of these suggestions are surprising. Emerson asserts that a translation is always preferable to reading the work in its original language, for instance, adding that, "the respectable and sometimes excellent translations of Bohn's Library have done for literature what railroads have done for internal intercourse." "I do not hesitate to read all the books I have named, and all good books, in translations," Emerson admits. In fact, "I rarely read any Latin, Greek, German, Italian, sometimes not a French book in the original, which I can procure in a good version . . . I should as soon think of swimming across Charles River when I wish to go to Boston, as of reading all my books in originals, when I have them rendered for me in my mother-tongue."[55]

As with his singling out of Bohn's Library editions, much of Emerson's advice is rooted in the innovations of nineteenth-century print culture and in works aimed at making knowledge more accessible. As he notes in suggesting Plutarch's *Lives,* for instance, "But this book has taken care of itself, and the opinion of the world is expressed in the innumerable cheap editions, which make it as accessible as a newspaper." In keeping with his directive to teachers in "Literary Ethics," Emerson does not hide behind a pose of impossible erudition. Rather, in speaking of Greek writers he notes that, "of course a certain outline should be obtained of Greek history, in which the important moments and persons can be rightly set down; but the shortest is the best, and, if one lacks stomach for Mr. Grote's voluminous annals, the old slight and popular summary of Goldsmith or of Gillies will serve."

The entire essay is full of such tips as Emerson catalogues those indispensable volumes that serve as quick tours through centuries of history and literature, drawn from diverse languages and traditions, and spread out across continents. Each discipline, each nation, has its compendiums and accessible surveys, its critics and historians, who ease the scholar's path by way of their engaging narratives and time-saving summaries, furnishing "superficial, yet readable and conceivable outlines," as he notes of Hallam's *View of the State of Europe in the Middle Ages* (1818). Each period has its guide: Hallam for The Middle Ages; Sismondi for the Italian Renaissance; Hume for the Elizabethan Era; and so on and so forth. Even these aids Emerson is not above skimming, as in navigating Italian literature Emerson notes that, "to help us, perhaps a volume or two of M. Sismondi's 'Italian Republics' will be as good as the entire sixteen."[56]

To say that such admissions are uncommon among scholars is an understatement. Indeed, "Books" is in some ways far more remarkable than more famous works like "The American Scholar" or "The Poet" since it gives us a rare behind-the-scenes look at how Emerson survived as a scholar. While *Nature* presents an idealized critical theory, "Books" shows us how scholarship really gets made. What interests me finally about the essay is that it is the practical correlative to Emerson's famous dismissal of books and tradition. In addresses like "The American Scholar" or "Literary Ethics," Emerson insists that young scholars must not stifle their own genius and imagination under the weight of accumulated tradition, that they abandon libraries for the solitude of their own thoughts and for the original text of nature, though always with the accompanying disclaimer that he would not

dispense with books completely, that they have their use in moderation, provided one maintains a healthy perspective. It was this sort of
invigorating iconoclasm, moreover, for which Emerson was, and still
is, famous, and which Cranch recorded in his caricature of "The American Scholar" address with Emerson pinned down by the crushing burden of tradition.

In contrast, "Books" is an actual field guide for how readers are to
navigate the abundance of printed materials, full of tips, tricks, heuris-
tics, shortcuts, and candid scholarly admissions. What the essay helps
us see, moreover, is that like quarterly reviews and the book reviews
they contained, which assisted nineteenth-century readers in keeping
up with the endless stream of books, Emerson's philosophy of intellectual self-reliance and his iconoclastic stance toward literary tradition and acquired knowledge are also ways of responding to a stultify-
ing sense of the untenable overabundance of reading material. It is not
just Harold Bloom's anxiety of influence but the anxiety of intellectual
competence, the anxiety of print surplus and the feeling that we have
not and *cannot* read everything that we are expected to read. And while
reviews provide glosses of books or condensed surveys of fields, Emerson's philosophy allows us to dismiss all that we haven't read as unim-
portant, to ignore the specter of endless, cavernous libraries with a free
conscience, and, indeed, to feel empowered in our ignorance.

In this sense, "Books" provides a candid acknowledgement of the
ways nineteenth-century authors responded to information overload.
While reviews were one practical response, a technology for dealing
with print surplus, Emerson devised an intellectual philosophy that
compensated for this perceived overabundance by denying literary tradition the authority books held in the Enlightenment. Such a philosophy was personal as well as cultural, as Emerson struggled to reconcile
his own ambitions and anxieties with the natural limits that confronted
scholars in the mid-nineteenth century. Academic specialization was
only just beginning while Emerson, in his profession as general lecturer
and eclectic essayist, claimed to be knowledgeable about any number
of fields. Yet breadth of knowledge frequently came at the expense of
depth. It does not seem coincidental that Emerson's final book-length
work was *A Natural History of the Intellect* since not only epistemology
and ontology but also the practical functioning of the intellect were life-

long preoccupations for Emerson from his earliest journal entries to his final posthumous works. One way to approach Emerson's critical philosophy, then, is from within the context of the management of knowledge, or more simply, as a way of responding to the overabundance of books and an expression of Emerson's anxiety that there is too much to know, as Ann Blair puts it.[57]

While Emerson created a critical theory that responded to an overabundance of books by alternately dismissing tradition or instructing readers on ways of managing it, however, and though he complemented this vision with an ennobled portrait of Goethe as representative man of letters, imbued with a preternatural power to assimilate the innumerable fragments of a culture obsessed with information, Emerson nonetheless also contributed to this cultural clutter. The extent of Emerson's full corpus presents a striking contrast to the succinctness of his essays viewed individually or as collections. The concision of an essay such as "Experience" or "The Poet" hides the extensive material prehistory that preceded each essay. While Goethe assimilates fragments of culture into a coherent vision of unity, Emerson's compositional practice was to assemble fragments of his own earlier journals and lectures into new pieces. And though Emerson's critical theory founded itself on a proliferation of both books and material forms, modern studies of Emerson tend to focus on the idealized critical theory rather than the splintering nexus of contradictory ideas expressed across a variety of material texts. It is the latter rather than the former, however, that more accurately represents the multifarious, culturally contingent nature of Emerson's critical views.

That central tenet of Emerson's critical theory, meanwhile, that we must cast off tradition, must "live for ourselves,—and not as the pallbearers of a funeral," developed not above or apart from but as a compensatory response to the state of print culture in antebellum society. Indeed, Emerson's critical theory was a way to free men from the thrall of retrospect. For other observers, however, discarding the past was neither possible nor desirable. Rather, if Emerson's critical theory sought to unburden Americans from the weight of tradition, for Rufus Griswold, America's first professional anthologist, the question was not how to overcome the past but how best to harness it for the needs of the present.

CHAPTER 2

ANTHOLOGY WARS

Rufus Griswold and the
Compilation as Literary History

WHILE EMERSON WORRIED about the stifling burden of tradition and devised a critical theory that worked to overcome it,
for antebellum America's foremost anthologist, Rufus Wilmot Griswold, what the current generation needed was not to escape the past
but to face it head on. "The question between us and other nations,"
Griswold declared in the introduction to *The Prose Writers of America* (1847), "is not who shall most completely discard the Past, but
who shall make the best use of it. The Past belongs not to one people
but to those who best understand it." As such, "it cannot be studied
too deeply, for unless men know what has been accomplished, they
will exhaust themselves in unfolding enigmas that have been solved,
or in pursuing *ignes fatui* that have already disappointed a thousand expectations."[1] Even more clearly than in his earlier compilation, *The Poets and Poetry of America* (1842), Griswold's practical vision
for *The Prose Writers* was as a cultural catalyst, a volume designed to
bring together a representative sampling of America's past cultural
achievements for the present generation to use toward the creation of
new literary productions.

For American literature to improve, new generations of writers
needed to contemplate, comprehend, and build upon the past—a view
that contrasted sharply with that of Emerson, who maintained that for

American literature to be original and organic it needed to unburden itself of the past. While F. O. Matthiessen would later expand upon Emerson's organic nativism in his positing of a period of American renaissance, Griswold's anthologies gave bodily shape to a competing theory of literary influence, one that embraced the past rather than discounting it. And while Griswold admired Emerson, giving him central billing in *The Prose Writers*, he nonetheless rejected the idea that American writers must throw off all foreign influences as well as the "absurd notion that we are to create an entirely new literature," a plan that was in his mind neither possible nor desirable.[2]

It is here, in the belief that the fragments of past cultural accomplishment must be succinctly synthesized so that contemporary authors may survey their nation's literary heritage before progressing onward to greater levels of achievement, that we see the role of the literary anthology in contributing to the advancement of American literary culture. Griswold's anthologies assembled the gleanings of centuries into a usable past, promoting new creative activity in the process. They were collections of the best of what the national culture had already produced, arranged so that young writers might better know how and where to leave their own mark. Like a happy version of Eliot's *Waste Land*, Griswold shored the fragments of culture not against ruin but as spur to production, a cultural base on which to erect something new. With this in mind, he ended his introduction not with the now familiar vision of renaissance, but with the motif of the *Translatio studii*, of the westward march of learning and culture, which though not yet ascendant was both immanent and inevitable in the days to come.

This sense of the anthology's practical vocation was only one aspect of Griswold's larger theory of cultural promotion, which, at its most general level, gestured outward toward a comprehensive political economy of literary development. Griswold was no sentimentalist; rhetoric alone could do only so much for the cause of American literature. Real change, Griswold maintained, came from the substantive domains of legislation, tariffs, and the support provided by national infrastructure, by bills mandating the creation of railroads, canals, and cheap postage, forces that Paul Starr terms "constitutive choices," political decisions that "create the material and institutional framework of

fields of human activity," and which Starr argues have underwritten
the evolution of the media in America since the upheavals of the American Revolution.[3]

For though few would deny that the general state of a nation's
authors and artists, the bearers of its cultural and intellectual flame,
is a barometer of the nation's overall health and well-being, still, as
Griswold complains, "our legislators . . . choose to consider them of
no consequence, and while the states are convulsed by claims from
the loom and the furnace for protection, the demands of the parents
of freedom, the preservation of the arts, the dispenser of civility, are
treated with silence." In arguing his point, Griswold's diction moves
from the domain of international trade—whereby the effusions of
American genius are seen as valuable national commodities, natural resources requiring protection like any other gross domestic product—to that of the divine right of intellectual property, a position to
which he had been converted since the pirating days of his mammoth
literary weekly *Brother Jonathan*, as he usurped Young America's central platform only to emerge as the copyright cause's most ardent pros-
elytizer. "That property which is most actual," Griswold deplores, "the
only property to which a man's right is positive, unquestionable, inde-
feasible, exclusive—his genius, conferred as by letters patent from the
Almighty—is held to be not his, but the public's, and therefore is not
brought into use."[4]

Genius was not enough by itself, while an international copyright
was only the first step toward its cultivation. To flourish, American
literature needed the support of an extensive national infrastructure;
it needed universities, libraries, and an educated public receptive to
works of genius, as well as a class of men to instruct and guide such
a public—"a class, the end of whose lives shall be to search after and
reveal beauty and truth, a class acting upon the nation, but acted upon
both by it and by all nations and ages."[5] The latter assertion situates
Griswold within a long-standing critical tradition of the critic as cultural guardian, with contemporary echoes of Carlyle's heroic man of
letters and Coleridge's cultural clerisy as well as verbal traces pointing
back to Samuel Johnson and ahead to Matthew Arnold in his confident
belief that critics elucidate the truth and beauty inherent in literature
and in so doing, promote the stability of the polity. Yet more so than

Carlyle or Arnold, Griswold's critical vision carried a decidedly material emphasis rooted in the workings of contemporary print culture
with copyright reform and the literary anthology occupying two ends
of a materialist continuum devoted to the encouragement of American
authors.

So too, Griswold's remarks point more generally to the anthology as
a powerful expression of the critical impulse, as central to the nation's
literary development as Emerson's orations or Poe's reviews. Yet while
Poe theorized that only a serious, scientific American criticism could
bring about a general improvement in the overall state of the national
literature, his critical corpus taken as a whole failed to produce practical, quantifiable results — at least during his own lifetime. Rather, it was
in Griswold's catholic approach to the critical art that we find a literally
constructive criticism, conceived on a grand scale, that approached the
belletristic field from the macroscopic perspective of literary history.
For, as Griswold maintained, only when aspiring American authors
could survey comprehensively the accomplishments and deficiencies
of American letters would they progress to greater levels of achievement. While others preached or prognosticated, Griswold gave material shape to the desire for a national literature through his investment
in the critical genre of the literary compilation, a form that began the
task of canon formation through its material codification of an American literary past.

In contrast to the book review, the anthology as a critical genre took
on the national literature collectively rather than piecemeal, naturalized critical judgment through its paratextual apparatuses, masked
its biases through the invisible rule of selection and omission, and
promoted a specific vision of literature's social vocation through the
physical aspects of the volume itself. In a practical sense, constructing anthologies meant bridging the divides within America's literary landscape and assimilating a jumble of cultural fragments into a
coherent narrative. This metaphoric correlation between the text and
nation expressed by the titles of Griswold's anthologies—*The Poets
and Poetry of America,* for example—though a common feature of the
early republic when the founders literally wrote the country into existence through documents declaring independence, confederation, and
finally constitution, became more strained as industrial modernity

moved the nation toward increasing diversity along class, racial, and sectional lines. While *E Pluribus Unum* was a handy epithet with the nation unified against Great Britain, it carried increasing dissonance as the nation's newly sewn seams slowly began to unravel in the years leading up to the Civil War.[6]

Anthologies were not merely cousins to the culture of criticism; they were, and still are, a second incarnation of that same enterprise. Both criticism and anthologies attempted to make order out of disorder, to construct a narrative out of the scattered literary gleanings of two hundred years of history. To be a judicious critic when approaching literature on a national scale, moreover, meant striving for a fair estimation of the strengths and weaknesses of America's literary accomplishments, reining in both subservience to foreign opinion and overzealous nationalism. As the uproar inevitably caused by each of Griswold's anthologies suggests, the task of the anthologizer was not an easy one: it was impossible to please everyone, and though Griswold was never lacking for censure, the critical consensus was that he had done about as well as anyone in undertaking the treacherous chore of a national anthology, certainly better than any of his anthologizing predecessors had done before him. For though Griswold holds the dubious distinction of being America's "first professional anthologist," he was not the first editor to take on the treacherous task of producing an American anthology.[7]

From Miscellany to Literary History:
The Rise of the American Anthology

Born in 1815, Griswold came of age during a transitional period of book history as printing transformed from an artisan trade carried out by local printers and booksellers to a centralized industry dominated by major publishing houses that competed against one another using new business strategies of advertising, marketing innovation, and calculated management of risk.[8] Griswold was a product of his times: born in a rural Vermont town, the son of a farmer and tanner, Griswold attended the local schoolhouse until age fourteen, at which point he set off on his own to learn the printing trade. Throughout the early years of his life, he earned a scanty living first as a journeyman printer and then as an itinerant editor, going wherever his services could profitably be employed. And in the 1830s, with the growth of the book and periodical industries, there was no lack of editorial work, as innovations in print technology, coupled with an expanding readership, lowered the price while increasing the demand for print publications of all sorts. Between his first apprenticeship at a Rutland County newspaper and his sudden emergence onto the national stage with the success of his literary weekly *Brother Jonathan* in 1839, Griswold built up his editorial resume at such obscure ventures as the Syracuse *Constitutionalist*, Fredonia's *Western Democrat and Literary Inquirer*, the *Olean Advocate*, and the Whig affiliated *Vergennes Vermonter*.[9]

In 1837, with the encouragement of his friend and fellow Vermonter Horace Greeley, Griswold settled in New York City where he announced plans for a journal of his own—titled the *American Antho-logy*—plans which were promptly dashed by the financial panic of 1837. It was paradoxically the financial collapse that set the stage for *Brother Jonathan*, in which Griswold and his partner, Park Benjamin, capitalized upon the lean times by offering large quantities of reprinted literature at low prices. While the large publishing firms raced to reorient themselves to the depressed economic conditions, the clever editors stayed several steps ahead by repeatedly devising competitive advantages. At a time when most periodicals failed within a year or two, Griswold and Benjamin succeeded with not one, but two periodicals. In 1839, the two men launched the trendsetting weekly *Brother Jonathan*, but after a disagreement with their publisher, they split from the magazine hoping to replicate their former success with a second journalistic attempt. Having departed from the old, they appropriately named their second endeavor the *New World*, and though its title stressed novelty, its strategy followed the winning model of *Jonathan*. Riding the wave of the cheap print revolution, Griswold and Benjamin harnessed the marketability of the penny newspaper for a literary weekly. Their ingenuity was visibly displayed in the physical materiality of the journal; for though a magazine in content, both *Brother Jonathan* and the *New World* were newspapers in appearance. Though an issue sometimes consisted of as few as four pages, the sheets were huge, four columns across and two feet high, and the two periodicals quickly found themselves popularly referred to as the "leviathan" or "mammoth."[10]

The plan's cleverness lay in its simplicity. Since the days of Jefferson, the government had tried to foster the creation and maintenance of an educated electorate by subsidizing the distribution of newspapers through the postal system. Because a functioning democracy required a well-informed populace, newspapers cost only a cent or two to mail. Griswold and Benjamin capitalized upon this loophole to distribute their periodical at near negligible rates. They saved money too by filling most of their journals' pages with reprinted British material, which cost them nothing but was in high demand by readers. To be sure, unauthorized reprints were the rule rather than exception in antebellum America with an international copyright law still a half century away, but the two editors managed to edge out their competition by publishing the newest work by fashionable authors like Dickens, Bulwer, and Ainsworth before anyone else had a chance. The various strategies worked; the combination of fashionable literature with a cheap price made first *Brother Jonathan* and then the *New World* instantly popular.[11]

Griswold and Benjamin made literature accessible to a steadily increasing mass readership even more dramatically through their invention of what was essentially a crude prototype of the paperback novel. Much of the success of *Brother Jonathan* was the talent of the two editors in acquiring new British novels fresh off the boat from Liverpool, but a perhaps obvious difficulty that they quickly encountered was that many readers impatient for further serialized installments of some compelling fiction by Frederick Marryat or G. P. R. James could simply go out and buy the book, immediately gratifying their curiosity. So Griswold and Benjamin came up with a solution: the "supplement." Twice a month, they would sell an entire fictional work as a so-called supplement to the magazine. It was inexpensively printed and bound in brightly colored paper, but it was cheap—a mere ten or twenty cents—and it provided instant gratification. The paperback was born. Though some may have criticized *Brother Jonathan* and the *New World* as trash, its supplements, later renamed "extras," carried much of the same literature that respectable members of bourgeois society were reading, just much more cheaply. Whereas mainstream publishers like Harper and Brothers would sell two-volume novels for between one and two dollars—still a sizable sum for working class readers—*New*

World extras could cost as little as twelve and a half cents. Now even the poorest could afford new novels by names they recognized. Newsboys started selling them in the streets, at train stations and port terminals. Soon it wasn't just new novels but classics of drama and nonfiction prose: Shakespeare, Gibbon, Johnson.[12]

In an unexpected turn of events, the mammoths proved so profitable that Benjamin maneuvered to seize complete control of the *New World* within months of its inception, forcing Griswold out of the very venture that he had helped conceive. As a result, by 1840, though both *Brother Jonathan* and the *New World* continued to increase in circulation and notoriety, Griswold no longer had a hand in either, having moved on to pursue other endeavors, including preliminary researches into an anthology of American poetry. Griswold's forced occupational change paradoxically proved to his ultimate advantage since the success of the mammoths had largely been a result of the depressed economic conditions of the late 1830s, the novelty of the huge format, and a profit structure based on small returns for large print runs, conditions that were all rapidly disappearing by the early years of the 1840s, as prosperity began to return to the nation's markets. As James Barnes suggests, when economic conditions began improving in 1842, "a shift in income elasticity of demand took place: people began to find more employment, to feel they had more disposable income, and to prefer better looking books and magazines to the cheapest editions possible," such that for the mammoth weeklies, "prosperity proved to be their final undoing."[13] As with his investment in cheap reprints years earlier, Griswold's ability to gauge the demands of the market was precocious—indeed, much better than his former partner's—and his reinvestment in the more refined avenue of literary anthologies proved timely, if not prescient.

Though Griswold was the first to make a career of editing anthologies, the origins of the literary anthology in the United States date back much further. While there was no lack of anthologies prior to 1800, few of them correlate to our modern sense of the anthology as a work both historical and comprehensive in scope and ambition. Rather, selections of poetry in eighteenth-century compilations were generally tethered to some more practical usage. As early as 1729, for instance, Philadelphia printer Samuel Keimer issued an American imprint of

Mary Mollineux's *Fruits of Retirement; or Miscellaneous Poems, Moral and Divine,* a collection of mostly religious poetic fragments designed to facilitate divine contemplation. Similarly, numerous anthologies such as *The Young Gentleman and Lady's Monitor* (1787), *The Moralist* (1791), and Berquin's *Friend of Youth* (1789) were targeted directly at children and doubled as both literary anthology and conduct book. Other collections such as *Miscellanies, Moral and Instructive . . . for the Use of Schools* (1787) or *Lessons in Elocution* (1788) catered toward educational use, the latter billing itself as "a selection of pieces in prose and verse for the improvement of youth in reading and speaking."[14]

It was only after independence that American publishers began printing anthologies divorced from some more pragmatic usage, or rather whose utility resided primarily in their cultural and national claims. This nationalist agenda confronted a second challenge, however, as both colonial and republican readers preferred British poets to their American counterparts. The 1789 catalogue for the Library Company of Philadelphia, for example, established by Benjamin Franklin in 1731 as the first circulating library in the country, lists as part of its holdings compilations of British poetry such as *Poems upon Several Occasions* (1716), *Poetical Miscellanies* (1727), *The British Muse* (1738), *A Collection of Poems, by Several Hands* (1758), and *A Poetical Dictionary; or the Beauties of the English Poets* (1761).[15]

When America's first national anthologies began appearing in the 1790s, editors were tasked not only with collecting the scattered productions of native poets but, perhaps more dauntingly, with convincing readers on both sides of the Atlantic that a national poetry existed in the first place. In Elihu Hubbard Smith's *American Poems* (1793), generally held to be the first dedicated anthology of American verse printed in the United States, the editor asserts that his objective was to collect fugitive pieces by esteemed American poets under one roof, to rescue scattered verse from the ephemeral materiality of newspapers and magazines, and to provide a forum in which to view and compare verse effusions from various states and regions, such that "a more certain estimation can be made of the comparative merit of their various writers." In doing so, Smith aimed to present a more just representation of the "state of the belles-lettres in the individual parts of the Union."[16]

Two years before Smith's volume, the savvy Philadelphia publisher Mathew Carey articulated a similar goal in *The Beauties of Poetry, British and American* (1791), which contained selections by the likes of not only Goldsmith, Burns, and Gray, but also Dwight, Hopkinson, Freneau, and other native versifiers. While Carey's primary purpose was to provide an "elegant fund of rational and innocent entertainment, to fix upon such pieces of poetry as have a tendency to enlarge the understanding, and refine the heart," before concluding, he also added his hopes "that to Americans this work will be more acceptable than those on the same plan from Great Britain as, besides the . . . pieces of British poetry, they will here find copious extracts from the most celebrated American bards."[17]

In Carey's equal split between British and American poets, as well as his understated suggestion that Americans might approve of seeing some native poets in a selection of this sort, Carey balanced a nascent national pride and gentle Anglo-American competitiveness with a perhaps practical concession to the fact that, for American readers in 1791, the familiar authors were inevitably British. While national sympathy may have leaned toward American poets, American poetic taste still gravitated back to Goldsmith's "Deserted Village" and Thomson's *The Seasons*. For those who wanted a division more generous to American poets, Carey's appended list of available volumes advertised another of his compilations entitled simply *Select Poems, Chiefly American*, while three years later, Carey published a third verse compilation entitled *The Columbian Muse: A Selection of American Poetry, From Various Authors of Established Reputation* (1794). The subheading spoke directly to the visible reluctance to present American poets on their own in the 1791 volume, for though Carey did so now, he also prominently asserted their status as vetted versifiers by adding their qualified characterization as authors of "established reputation." The apprehension seemed to be that, while irrefutably American, the native authors selected may be little more in the way of poets, a possibility that Carey anticipated with his own endorsement.

Though Smith intended his *American Poems* to be the first installment of many, he never issued any subsequent volumes, and for reasons we can probably infer since Smith hinted at the challenges faced by early American anthologies among his enumerated motivations for

producing his compilation in the first place. The nation in the early
republic was disconnected, spread out over a vast territory with only
the rudiments of a transportation infrastructure. The printing industry was decentralized and locally based as well, clustering around
urban centers. Publishers tended to invest in sure-sellers, and it is
likely that in Litchfield, Connecticut, where Smith published his collection, demand was not sufficient to warrant a second volume. If
Mathew Carey's compilations sold tolerably better, one could in part
attribute it to the fact that he was selling his wares in Philadelphia and
was years ahead of his competition in having established primitive
distribution networks and effective methods of book promotion. Fur-
thermore, books produced by artisan handpresses in 1793 were still
relatively expensive, and *American Poems*, a slim volume of largely
recycled poetry selling for one dollar, would most likely have seemed
a luxury to all but the wealthiest of consumers.[18] In short, the age of
the anthology had not yet arrived. Before it could, printing had to get
cheaper and the national readership much larger.

By the time Samuel Kettell issued *Specimens of American Poetry* in
1829, these contingencies had begun to fall into place. As Michael Gilmore observes, Kettell's *Specimens* "ushered out the formative period and
inaugurated the reign of the anthology in American verse," which, by
the time of Griswold's appearance on the anthology scene in 1842, had
come "to dominate the consumption of poetry in the United States."[19]
While Smith's *American Poems* was an amateur affair—a belles lettres
side project with vague intentions to collect, preserve, and cross-
fertilize the fields of American poetry—Kettell's *Specimens* was the first
anthology to fit modern conceptions of the term: a comprehensive, historically based survey of American poetry from 1640 to 1829 that balanced a temperate nationalism with a scientific ideal of objectivity. In
it, Kettell reconciles an Enlightenment taxonomic impulse to categorize
and record the representative "specimens" of native poetic production
with the Romantic interest in national cultures and sensitivity to historical relativism.

This was the period that saw the arrival of philology, of the Higher
Criticism in biblical studies, of Schlegel's historical rigor in treatments
of Shakespeare. Literary criticism was emerging as a historical science rather than a belletristic hobby for lawyers and doctors. Kettell

suggests as much in his preface when he bypasses neoclassical standards of taste, proportion, and beauty for a historian's appreciation of the non-aesthetic value of even the homeliest pieces of verse: "What though our early literature cannot boast of a Dante or a Chaucer," Kettell avers, still, "it can furnish such testimonials of talent and mental cultivation as are highly creditable to the country, and of sufficient interest to call upon the attention of those who are desirous of tracing the general history of letters, and their connexion with the development of the moral and intellectual character of a people." As Kettell insists, "everything published among us must have some value, if not on account of its intrinsic merits, at least as affording some insight into the spirit and temper of the times."[20]

The result was a prodigious achievement: Kettell blazed a trail through almost two centuries of uncharted American literary history with few precursors to serve as either sources or models. While Smith's compilation collected sixty-five poems by twenty-five different poets, six of them anonymous, Kettell's includes 189 poets in three volumes of over four hundred pages each, answering for the necessity of omission by appending to the final volume a chronologically arranged catalogue of every work of American verse which he had come across in his researches. In addition, Kettell introduced each poet, from the authors of the *Bay Psalm Book* to John Greenleaf Whittier, with a detailed biographical sketch and restrained critical estimation, attaching to the whole a thorough historical introduction.

Though Kettell pioneered the historical anthology in America, the model itself he imported from his British contemporaries. Though anthologies as a literary form had been around for hundreds if not thousands of years, with the term dating back to Meleager of Gadara's *Anthologia* (or "Garland"), a collection of epigrams by forty-six Greek poets drawn from diverse periods of classical poetry and assembled by the compiler around 60 BCE, its evolution in the eighteenth and early nineteenth centuries corresponded largely with parallel developments in the field of literary history.[21] While René Wellek traces the earliest antecedents of English literary history back to the bibliographic catalogues assembled by medieval monks, marking its apotheosis by the appearance of the first volume of Thomas Warton's *History of English Poetry* (3 vols., 1774–1781), ultimately, as David Perkins concludes, it was the Romantic period that truly gave birth to the discipline.[22] In Wellek's account, the genre that emerged was not a new practice so much as a combination of a number of older scholarly approaches that had traditionally been carried out independently of one another. Specifically, as Wellek writes, "literary history as a distinct discipline arose only when biography and criticism coalesced and when, under the influence of political historiography, the narrative form began to be used," a process that, as Wellek notes, "took almost two centuries."[23]

These developments had a direct impact on the construction of anthologies. Since the genre's inception, anthologies were defined primarily by their gathering function as heuristic repositories for material that was traditionally scattered or ephemeral, and as Barbara Benedict suggests, during the Renaissance the metaphor that anthology editors most often employed was that of the cornucopia or feast, "a collation of fruits, gathered in one banquet to suit a variety of tastes."[24] Though early modern and neoclassical collections were often delimited by author, genre, or topic, applied to some practical usage (education, moral improvement, religious meditation), or simply allowed to exist as unspecified "beauties," in the mid-eighteenth century, anthologies began adopting some of the trappings of history. This shift did not occur all at once, nor did it fully replace the other more haphazard sorts of literary compilation. Gradually over the course of the eighteenth century, however, more and more anthologies began adding biographical material, employing periodization as a structuring principle, attaching critical introductions, and emphasizing connections between literature and history.

These dimensions began to coalesce in the latter decades of the century when, as Julia Wright contends, the broad periodization employed by Thomas Percy's influential *Reliques of Ancient English Poetry* (1765) eventually gave way to Warton's integrated arrangement of poetry into a progressive Whig historical narrative before finally settling into the habit of precise chronological arrangement employed by the Romantic anthologists—a mode that persists to this day. The early stages of canon formation may have predated the neoclassical age, but as Wright insists, "the crucial innovation in the late eighteenth century . . . [was] the genealogical arrangement of that canon into a history of the national literature."[25] It was Romantic anthologies such as George

Ellis's *Specimens of the Early English Poets* (1790), Robert Southey's *Specimens of the Later English Poets* (1807), Thomas Campbell's *Specimens of the British Poets* (1819), and William Hazlitt's *Select Poets of Great Britain* (1831), with their progressive historical narratives and chronological organization, that served as the immediate precursors for first Kettell's and later Griswold's anthologies.

As Kettell modestly asserts in the Preface to his 1829 *Specimens*, his overriding motive for compiling the anthology was "to do something for the cause of American literature, by calling into notice and preserving a portion of what is valuable and characteristic in the writings of our native poets." For as the editor muses, "when we take into view the influence which an endeavor like this, to rescue from oblivion the efforts of native genius, must necessarily have upon the state of letters among us, we shall have occasion to wonder that an undertaking of this kind was not sooner entered upon." Like Smith before him, Kettell wants to preserve America's poetic accomplishments, to "rescue from oblivion" interesting relics of America's cultural past.[26]

When Kettell's anthology appeared, however, reception, to the extent that there was any, was largely negative. The opinion of the *North American Review* was that America's obscure poetic forefathers were not worth the saving and that, paradoxically, Kettell's compilation would, if anything, prove injurious rather than beneficial to America's cultural reputation. To the notion that historical value matters as much as intrinsic merit for the glimpse it provides into the intellectual spirit of the times, the anonymous reviewer flatly retorts that, "it is a doctrine we cannot agree to"; rather, "it matters very little at what period, or by whom bad poetry was written, and we should hope that it would be set down as characteristic of nothing but the individual taste and skill of the author." Bad poetry is bad poetry, and "it is in vain to endeavor to give dignity and value to these by calling them characteristic of the age, or the people, among whom they appeared."[27]

The matter soon becomes clear enough. Though Kettell's intentions were noble, his all-inclusive survey, the reviewer fears, will inevitably give fodder to those English critics determined to prove America's cultural inferiority. The reviewer concedes that while in Kettell's collection "there is a great deal which is certainly not poetry . . . there is also a large proportion, which displays that brilliancy of imagination, fervor

of feeling, delicacy of sentiment, and power of expression, which are
essential ingredients in the first, and indeed in every class of poetry."
With this in mind, the commentator laments that, "We wish the collection had been confined to those pieces, which discovered one or more
of these characteristics. It would have been smaller, to be sure, but we
should have been much more proud of a single volume, containing
only good poetry, than of this miscellaneous assortment of three volumes. Our American claims to the reputation of having written good
poetry, would likewise have been less contested and less disputable,
if that which is really valuable had been selected and separated with a
more careful discrimination."[28] According to the reviewer, Kettell had
unwittingly done more harm than good to America's literary reputation by allowing such a wide berth for poets of differing abilities. He
was making it far too easy for belligerent foreign critics.

As the years drew on, it became virtually impossible to dissociate
anthologies of the national and antebellum periods from America's cultural feud with Britain. By 1830, a class of anthologies presenting themselves as staging grounds for the nation's cultural achievements had
appeared, provoking critiques that treated them as such. While anthologies of the early republic followed the original "garland" model, offering
up a non-representative selection of individual flowers or gems of poetic
achievement—in some cases thematically delimited by nationality—
anthologies in the antebellum period began to present themselves as,
if not comprehensive surveys of a nation's cultural achievements, then
at least as culturally representative selections. Yet despite the strain of
Anglo-American competitiveness in the quarterly reviews, as Leonard
Tennenhouse and Elisa Tamarkin have shown, Americans in the 1830s
and '40s were also ardent consumers of British literature.[29] Indeed, it
was the British anthologies that Americans were buying rather than
Kettell's, which sold poorly and never warranted a second edition.

Much of Griswold's success was due precisely to his ability to walk
a middle line with the tempered nationalist posture of his anthologies,
refusing the jingoistic rhetoric of Young America while maintaining
due reverence for the British models that naturally influenced American writers. Griswold's *Poets and Poetry of America*, like Kettell's *Specimens*, reflected the historical turn of Romantic anthologies as modeled
first by Percy and Warton and later by Southey, Hazlitt, and Campbell.

Yet Griswold was more forthright in acknowledging America's debt to British literary tradition. In his capacities as anthology editor, Thomas Campbell was a personal hero to Griswold, who owned a portrait of Campbell as part of his private collection—"the last, I believe, ever painted from life," as Griswold notes in his will—which he bequeathed to the New-York Historical Society upon his death. The auction catalogue for Griswold's personal library, sold shortly after his death, lists not one, but two copies of Campbell's seven volume *Specimens of the British Poets*, moreover, noting that the earlier of the two copies, suffering from heavy use, was in "imperfect" condition. This same catalogue includes other influential volumes like Percy's *Reliques*, Southey's *Select Works of the British Poets*, and Chambers' *Cyclopaedia of English Literature*, not to mention Kettell's own *Specimens*.[30] These volumes record the fact that Griswold and Kettell were heirs to the Romantic anthology tradition with its historical rigor, chronological arrangement, and progressive nationalist narratives of literary and cultural development. Yet Griswold, while clearly indebted to Kettell as well and sharing many of his critical affinities, also seems to have understood much better than his predecessor the numerous interests that a national anthology had to balance if it was to succeed on a large scale.

When Griswold took up the task of compiling a national anthology in the early 1840s, he did so with the fate of Kettell's volumes in mind. Like Kettell's *Specimens*, Griswold's *Poets and Poetry of America* was historical in scope and ambition, including in its initial 1842 edition works by ninety-one poets introduced by biographical sketches with some critical estimation of each. Following a preface and a lengthy historical introduction, Griswold commenced the compilation with Philip Freneau's "The Dying Indian" and proceeded chronologically, concluding with selected poems of Lucretia and Margaret Davidson, followed by an "Appendix" of various poets too minor to warrant inclusion in the main body of the text. Given the space constraints of the anthology form, Griswold's principle of selection favored the lyric, while in choice of subjects he was eclectic, balancing patriotic, moralistic, or naturalist themes featuring American characters and locales, as with James Kirke Paulding's "Ode to Jamestown" or Richard Henry Dana's "The Buccaneer," with poems celebrating foreign subjects such as Charles Sprague's "Shakespeare Ode" or Edward Pinkney's "Italy."

In estimating poetic longevity, Griswold included soon-to-be classics of a nascent nineteenth-century canon—works like Joel Barlow's "The Hasty Pudding," William Cullen Bryant's "To a Waterfowl," Henry Wadsworth Longfellow's "The Village Blacksmith," and Poe's "The Haunted Palace"—and popular poems by then fashionable writers like James Gates Percival and Nathaniel Parker Willis, not to mention liberal selections by personal friends like Charles Fenno Hoffman. And though the volume contained more poetry by men than women, Griswold nonetheless provided extensive selections by female poets of the period, from Hannah Gould and Maria Brooks to Lydia Sigourney and Elizabeth Ellett, redressing the gender imbalance still further in 1848 with a volume devoted exclusively to *The Female Poets of America*. With each round of critical reception, meanwhile, Griswold worked to address criticism, as in revised editions of 1847, 1849, and 1855, he expanded the roster of poets and poems, answered accusations of regional bias, and assimilated poets from the ill-conceived appendix into the main body of the text.

By and large, it was what Griswold left out of the volumes, however, rather than what he added that revealed the most about the shifting sands of antebellum literary culture. Specifically, Griswold omitted all American poets prior to Philip Freneau, a decision which, while unthinkable by modern standards for a work claiming to provide a historical survey of American poetry, made sense in light of the *North American Review*'s attack upon Kettell's *Specimens of American Poetry*. In opening his historical introduction, which spanned the century and a half from the Pilgrims' landing to the Revolution, Griswold admitted that the introduction was strategically positioned so as to preclude the need to include poems from this period. On this point Griswold does not mince words: before the Revolutionary period, "but little poetry was written in this country, although from the landing of the pilgrims at Plymouth there was at no period a lack of candidates for the poetic laurel." Though "many of the early colonists were men of erudition, deeply versed in scholastic theology, and familiar with the best ancient literature," as Griswold demurs, "they possessed neither the taste, the fancy, nor the feeling of the poet, and their elaborate metrical compositions are forgotten by all save the antiquary, and by him are regarded as the least valuable of the relics of the first era

of civilization in America."[31] Griswold had learned his lesson from
Kettell: not everything that rhymes could be considered poetry. Historical value was all well and good, but what American critics and audiences wanted most in a national anthology were displays of cultural
refinement. With this in mind, Griswold returned to a less controversial, more aesthetically grounded definition of poetry as "the creation
of beauty, the manifestation of the real by the ideal, in 'words that
move in metrical array,'" a broad definition that walked a careful line
between Romantic idealism and neoclassical formalism.[32]

Much in the volume's conception, in fact, seemed intentionally
designed to anticipate and preemptively address objections by foreign
critics. In the introduction, Griswold steered away from Kettell's blun-
der by omitting what one reviewer referred to as the "antiquated dog-
gerel" of America's earliest poets.[33] And though the appendix didn't
go over well, Griswold seems to have intended it as a strategic way
to include mediocre writers of prominent social standing while tacitly
acknowledging their deficiencies as poets. Above all, this strategic pre-
emption was the task of Griswold's preface. Amid the transatlantic culture wars of the 1830s and '40s, the two critical positions were generally
held to be either subservience to British opinion or overzealous nationalism, and in a book entitled *The Poets and Poetry of America*, a work
that explicitly asserts in its opening pages that its design is "to exhibit
the progress and condition of Poetry in the United States," we might
reasonably expect the editor to lean more toward patriotism than deference. This was decidedly not the case, however.

Rather, Griswold's preface was a tour de force of national self-
deprecation, as instead of encomium and panegyric, it delivered a full-
fledged apology for and justification of America's deficiencies in the
field of poetry. America's poets, Griswold tells us, are not so by profession; they are doctors, lawyers, clergymen, wives and mothers, who
pursue poetry as an amateur side-project, and considered as such, they
display a precocious ability. So too does the landscape pose practical
impediments to a national poetry, both in demanding the attention
of American citizens and keeping them dispersed. Griswold makes
no hyperbolic claims for America's poetic achievements; instead he
admits that America can as yet claim no Shakespeare or Milton.

Of those poetic talents the nation can boast, internationally respected authors like Longfellow, Bryant, or Dana, "too few of them, it must be confessed, are free from that vassalage of opinion and style which is produced by a constant study of the Literature of the country from which we inherit our language, our tastes, our manners." Griswold is calmly resigned to this fact, nor does he mean to belittle America's accomplishments by his acceptance of it. Rather, American literature is in its infancy, and as such shows great promise for the days to come, though it is still far from reaching its full potential. In surveying the impression left by the poems in the volume, Griswold concludes that, "considering the youth of the country, and the many circumstances which have had a tendency to retard the advancement of letters here, it speaks well for the past and present, and cheeringly for the future."[34] He then closes his preface with a vigorous championing of the need for an international copyright, the cause most dear to British authors and critics and one that reached a fever pitch in 1842 amid Charles Dickens's celebrated tour of America.

When it first appeared in 1842, critics were generally pleased with Griswold's volume, commending his return to a more rigorously aesthetic standard of poetry, praising his judicious decision to omit poets of the seventeenth and eighteenth centuries as well as the historical introduction, which critics agreed did an admirable job of sketching that terrain without forcing readers to endure too much of the ungainly poetry itself. The most frequent complaint, in fact, was that, in treating the contemporary poetic scene, Griswold was perhaps too generous in his indiscriminate bestowal of the poetic laurel. The *Democratic Review* summed up this opinion with its pithy suggestion that Griswold might more accurately have titled the volume "The Poets, Poetry, and *Poetasters* of America."[35]

Beyond this objection, however, the most frequent complaints were that Griswold had underrepresented southern poets, overrepresented his friends (a fault most reviewers deemed natural and forgivable), and that, even despite his expansive roster of names, he had nonetheless failed to include one or two deserving bards whom the reviewer then proceeded to name. Reviewers also thought that the appendix was a misstep, for as one critic noted, it was better to be left out completely than insulted by inclusion in that poetic purgatory: "None of those thus distinguished, if possessed of the slightest degree of sensibility and pride, would not have greatly preferred to be excluded from his book altogether, than to be thus seated down at the second table to partake of the leavings of the feast of fame."[36] Yet if Griswold garnered criticism for his regional bias and his ill-conceived appendix, the compilation nonetheless managed to avoid the pitfalls of Kettell's earlier volume, passing muster with both American and British critics as a fair and balanced estimation of America's accomplishments in the field of poetry.

Finally, if Griswold proved adept at espousing a middle-of-the road nationalism, part of his success with *The Poets* must also be attributed to his ability to gauge the changing tastes of the time and to shape his anthologies accordingly. Specifically, Griswold's *Poets* registered a shift toward early Victorian sensibilities in both taste and book production. Its nationalistic claims are sublimated to its more pervasive self-presentation as culture, if not high culture. Here we see the beginnings of a move from a conception of the anthology as reflective of nationalist ideology, typical of the first half of the century, to a view of anthologies as reinforcing social distinctions, or what Pierre Bourdieu terms "cultural capital," a phenomenon typical of the latter half of the century. And though the split between highbrow and lowbrow culture culminates in the 1880s and '90s, as Lawrence Levine suggests, the process of cultural bifurcation began early in the antebellum period.[37]

Just as cheap weeklies and paperback reprints suited the depressed economic conditions of the late 1830s, the more refined mode of the anthology adjusted to the renewed prosperity of the 1840s while capitalizing upon a variety of cultural needs and preoccupations, including the push for literary nationalism, anxiety over an untenable surplus of print, and a desire for social refinement and cultural distinction that emerged as part of an expanding Victorian commodity culture. In just about every review of *The Poets*, the commentator was quick to commend the publishers, Carey and Hart, for sparing no expense with the elegant volume. In contradistinction to the mammoth weeklies, which advertised their cheapness as a democratic virtue, reviewers interpreted the expense of *The Poets* as evidence of the cultural distinction of those who bought it. As one literary notice on the occasion of the anthology's third edition put it: "We believe that no other book of so expensive a character has passed to a second edition in the United

States during the year. The fact that this has reached a *third* edition in six months seems to indicate that our poetical literature is properly appreciated, in our own country, at least."[38] The high price paradoxically became a selling point rather than a sales hurdle since it was construed as reflecting the refinement of the purchasers as well as his or her commitment, financial or otherwise, to the cause of an American poetry.

The production value of the volume itself betrays Griswold's intentions. It is an elegant, expensively produced octavo volume with attractive boards decorated with gilt ornamental designs, while for those who so desired, it could be purchased in morocco half-calf leather binding at an additional charge. Inside, the title page displays an expensively designed illustration depicting an idyllic lakeside scene, while across from it, on the adjacent page, we see engravings of America's poetic luminaries—Dana, Bryant, Sprague, Longfellow, and Halleck— framed by parted curtains at the sides, an American crest at the bottom, and an eagle perched above the words *E Pluribus Unum* at the top, a motto particularly well suited to the gathering work of the anthology (figure 8). Illustrations are also interspersed throughout the volume as adornments to poems such as Washington Allston's "The Spanish Maid," Edward Pinckney's "The Indian Bride," and Longfellow's "Maidenhood." The elegant volume provided a striking contrast to Kettell's 1829 *Specimens of American Poetry,* moreover: a sober affair, published in three quarto volumes with gray cardboard binding and intended, from the look of it, more for the antiquarian's shelf than for fashionable drawing rooms (figure 7). Judged by their covers, there is no contest, and at least part of Griswold's success with *The Poets* must be credited to his sharp eye for presentation and keen awareness of the social significance of high production value.

The Nation in Fragments:
Evert Duyckinck, William A. Jones, and the Anthological Theory of History

The success of Griswold's *Poets and Poetry of America* ushered in a new age of the anthology in the United States. In a century that was soon to abound in compilations of both verse and prose, in no little part because of Griswold's success in the field, Griswold's compilation

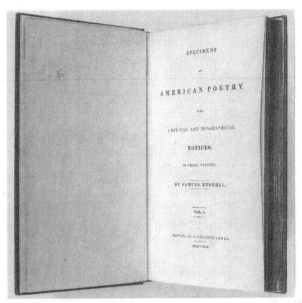

FIGURE 7. Title page, Samuel Kettell, ed., *Specimens of American Poetry*, vol. 1 (Boston: S. G. Goodrich and Co., 1829). Courtesy of the American Antiquarian Society, Worcester, Massachusetts.

FIGURE 8. Title page, Rufus Griswold, ed., *The Poets and Poetry of America* (Philadelphia: Carey and Hart, 1842). Courtesy of the American Antiquarian Society, Worcester, Massachusetts.

was the century's most popular anthology of native verse, selling close to three hundred thousand copies at the original cost of three dollars apiece.[39] Even at this high price, the handsome, 468-page volume was an immediate success. Issued by Philadelphia publishers Carey and Hart on April 18, 1842, the first run of a thousand copies sold out within three months, while the second more conservative printing of five hundred copies again sold out by the end of the year, prompting a third edition of five hundred more copies in December. For the remaining years of Griswold's life, the volume was a steady seller, reprinted at least once a year, often twice, in runs of varying number. For fourteen years, *The Poets and Poetry of America* was the unquestioned leader in the anthology field with no serious challenger until Griswold's rivals, the Duyckinck brothers, deliberately set out to upset Griswold's reign as America's premier anthologist in 1856 with their *Cyclopaedia of American Literature,* an event that deeply affected Griswold and which his biographer, Joy Bayless, credits with speeding the physical decline that culminated in his death from tuberculosis in 1857. Even after his death, however, and even with fierce competition from the Young America compilation, Griswold's *Poets* continued to sell, finally appearing in a twentieth edition.[40]

In the introduction to *The Prose Writers of America,* published five years later in 1847, while looking back on his first national anthology from the standpoint of his second, Griswold reiterated the unsentimental view of the national literature that he had expressed years before: "Not all the specimens in that book are fruits of genius or high cultivation," Griswold admits; rather "it was designed to show what had been accomplished in the most difficult field of intellectual exertion in the first half century of our national existence. With much of the highest excellence it includes nothing inferior to some of the contents of the most celebrated anthologies of other countries; and while the whole showed a remarkable diffusion of taste and refinement of feeling, we could point to Mrs. Brooks, Mr. Bryant, Mr. Dana, Mr. Halleck, Mr. Longfellow, and others, as poets of whom any people would be proud."[41] American poetry could claim for itself a handful of luminaries and a generous sampling of poets of taste and refinement, but to carry praise much further would be to mislead the public. To acknowledge the poetic field as it was, free of hyperbole or distortion, was for Griswold the necessary first step for a nation desirous of greater achievements. And while *The Poets and Poetry of America* exemplified Griswold's promotion of the national literature through an honest presentation of its attainments, *The Prose Writers of America* expanded his sense of the anthology's social vocation still further.

The success of *The Poets* immediately established Griswold's reputation as a man of influence and ability within the American literary scene, and in the months and years after its publication, he didn't hesitate to capitalize upon his newfound prominence. Amid the renewed prosperity of the 1840s, Griswold ushered from the press a steady stream of hastily produced volumes such as the small format *Gems from Female Poets* (1842), the textbook *Readings in American Poetry* (1843), *The Cypress Wreath: A Book of Consolation for those who Mourn* (1844), and *The Poetry of Flowers* (1844). The success of the latter, a contribution to the popular flower book genre, prompted Griswold to follow up the volume with a series of similarly conceived gift books— *The Poetry of Love* (1844), *The Poetry of the Passions* (1845), *The Poetry of the Sentiments* (1845)—as well as gift books of a loftier nature as with his *Illustrated Book of Christian Ballads and Other Poems* (1844) and *Scenes in the Life of the Savior, by the Poets and Painters* (1846).

Griswold's middle-of-the-road nationalism found material form, meanwhile, in the time he devoted to anthologies of British poetry such as *The Poets and Poetry of England in the Nineteenth Century* (1844) and to overseeing American editions of a range of foreign authors from Pierre-Jean de Béranger, Felicia Hemans, and the "Corn Law rhymer" Ebenezer Elliott, to Caroline Norton and Walter Scott. He even tested his expertise on one of the pillars of English literary history when he edited an American edition of *The Prose Works of John Milton* (1845). In these "jobbing" endeavors, as Griswold termed them, he seemed content to take a break after the exertion of his first major national anthology, a respite further necessitated by the personal tragedy of the death of his beloved first wife. Eventually, however, he returned his sights to the more ambitious editorial vision promoted by *The Poets and Poetry of America*, resuming the project of a representative survey of American literary accomplishments by extending his scope from poetry to prose.

Seeing no reason to tamper with the proven formula of the earlier compilation, publishers Carey and Hart adhered to the design and scale of *The Poets* in putting together *The Prose Writers*, issuing an elegant octavo volume of 552 pages that New York bookseller Charles S. Francis and Co. advertised for sale at the price of $3.75.[42] The volume's contents chronologically spanned seventy writers from Jonathan Edwards and Benjamin Franklin to Edwin Percy Whipple, all but two of whom Griswold accompanied with prose excerpts of widely varying length. The selected passages reflected a diverse range of prose genres from history, theology, political oratory, juridical writing, natural philosophy, and ethnography to lighter belletristic modes such as short stories, descriptive sketches, travel writing, correspondence, literary criticism, as well as an occasional passage or two from a novel.

Each author Griswold in turn prefaced with a lengthy biographical sketch as well as some critical estimation, usually including observations upon the writer's contribution to the general store of knowledge, his strengths and deficiencies, as well as his critical reputation and rhetorical style. In these assessments, Griswold promised to carry out his duty with more equanimity than in his earlier volume, vowing "to be accurate in statement, liberal in principle, and just in criticism; to select and arrange materials with taste, and to form and express opinions with candour," while by way of general introduction, he preceded the compiled material with both a short preface and an expansive forty-page survey of "The Intellectual History, Condition and Prospects of the Country."[43]

Though more than one reviewer accused the collection of lacking a governing principle of selection, Griswold's guiding criteria throughout, as with his previous volume, was to provide a fair sampling of America's intellectual and cultural achievements across a diverse range of disciplines, a task that Griswold admits proved easier than in the preceding poetry collection since America's ingrained ethos of industry found more natural expression through the utilitarian genre of prose writing. As a result, *The Prose Writers* was more confident and less self-deprecating than *The Poets* in its assertion of American literary ability, in part because Griswold, in drawing from a wide variety of intellectual disciplines, only had to select a few preeminent spokesmen from each. The result was more wheat and less chaff. In selecting authors and passages, Griswold's choices followed the neoclassical injunction that literature serve a practical purpose, with the editor favoring so-called "serious" genres like history and theology over more purely entertaining modes like fiction. That fiction which did make it in, meanwhile, tended to come from approved sub-genres such as historical romance, to depict characters possessing estimable virtues, or to display stylistic virtuosity that reflected well on the country while refuting charges of cultural inferiority.

While Griswold has been frequently dismissed by twentieth-century scholarship on account of his conservative Whig affinities, these political sympathies manifested themselves more through avoidance than provocation as when in selecting writers and passages he steered clear of inflammatory figures like Thomas Paine, avoided contentious topics like slavery or expansionism, or excerpted heavily from uncontroversial patriotic addresses by prominent national figures like Daniel Webster and William Ellery Channing. Griswold knew only too well that his audience extended to both sides of the political spectrum, and he had no desire to alienate either Whigs or Democrats. Rather, his governing principle throughout was simply to promote the national literature, an apolitical objective that expressed itself not only through his prefatory championing of an international copyright, but through the specific content of the passages he selected and implicitly through the constructive potential of the cultural digest enacted by the physical volume itself.

Yet such an ambitious, ennobling conception of the anthology's cultural vocation inevitably clashed with the limitations of the form's material dimensions. Poetry lent itself naturally to anthologizing while prose was prolix and diffuse. To be sure, this was hardly a new problem. Rather, as Leah Price documents, the challenge of excerpting prose had troubled anthology editors ever since novels entered the literary domain in the mid-eighteenth century.[44] While 468 pages was ample space for a survey of the young nation's poetry, the decision to design the new compilation as a companion volume to the earlier poetry anthology, thereby limiting him to roughly the same number of pages, presented Griswold with a distinct challenge given the expansive nature of prose writing. Even with these preliminary restrictions, however, Griswold exacerbated his space constraints still further by reducing *The Poets'* original ninety-one authors to an only slightly more manageable seventy.

Nor did he drastically limit the number of excerpts accompanying each author. Rather, of the volume's 552 total pages, Griswold represented the seventy authors by 306 excerpts, making the average length of a passage only half a page, concision which strikes us even more forcibly when we consider that the average length of a biographical head-note was approximately two-and-a-half pages, or five times the length of the average excerpt. The excerpts taken together, meanwhile, comprised only 62 percent of the total volume, the other 38 percent consisting of critical commentary, biographical introductions, and other bibliographic apparatuses. That is to say, Griswold added to the publishers' bibliographic strictures through his own editorial privileging of both variety among author selections and an elaborate critical apparatus.

As a result, in selecting passages Griswold only very rarely excerpted works in their entirety, indulging in this luxury only occasionally with such pieces as Richard Henry Dana's criticism on "Kean's Acting," Irving's "Rip Van Winkle" and "The Wife," Poe's "The Fall of the House of Usher," Hawthorne's sketch "A Rill from the Town Pump" and his Bunyanesque allegory "The Celestial Railroad," as well as with a handful of other less enduring short works. In the case of William Gilmore Simms, Griswold went so far as to include the first five chapters of his novel *Grayling*, though this proved the exception rather than the rule. Far more often he pulled a page or two from a longer work, as for instance with Charles Brockden Brown's *Edgar Huntly*, James Fenimore Cooper's *The Prairie*, or Catharine Maria Sedgwick's *Hope Leslie*. Even more frequently, he mined authorial corpora for paragraph-length chunks containing sound moral or practical advice, churning out edifying aphorisms or uplifting patriotic affirmations from the works of Benjamin Franklin, William Ellery Channing, or John Calhoun, or bits of wholesome nature description from Theodore Dwight's *Travels* or Henry Rowe Schoolcraft's Native American ethnographies. One excerpt culled from Washington Allston's letters reads only: "Such a sunrise! The giant Alps seemed literally to rise from their purple beds, and putting on their crowns of gold, to send up hallelujahs almost audible!"[45]

In making his editorial selections, it is at times difficult to discern just what for Griswold conveyed the most honor upon an author: the inclusion of a lengthy passage, the aggregate number of pages, or the final tally of excerpts. Several of the most eminent authors listed in the table of contents—Jonathan Edwards and John Marshall, for example— received no excerpts at all. Griswold bestowed the highest number of passages, meanwhile, to Daniel Webster (19), Channing (15), and Irving (14); the highest aggregate number of pages to Irving (22), Cooper (21), Simms (15), and Franklin (14); and assigns engraved portraits in a manner that bears little correlation to either of the above two considerations.[46] The result, as reviewers pointed out, was that the volume's organizing assumptions got lost among a distinguished though dizzying cacophony of voices and messages.

One persistent motif that did manage to rise above the discursive din, however, was the subject of history itself. As Griswold asserts, "there are few if any kinds of composition requiring a higher order of genius or more profound and varied acquirements than History."[47] It was a testament to the nation's intellectual vitality that despite its relative youth, it had produced historians of such high rank as William Prescott, George Bancroft, and Jared Sparks, and Griswold betrayed his historical predilection still further through his tendency to select historically oriented passages from authors whose renown lay in other areas. Though the majority of these excerpts presented exemplary specimens of historical writing, others approached the discipline more abstractly by offering meta-historical reflections on the role historians were to play in the new nation, reflections that invariably coincided with Griswold's own sense of the historical vocation.

In an essay entitled "American History," for instance, one of only a handful of pieces that Griswold excerpted in its entirety, Jared Sparks calls on Americans to undertake the important task of writing their nation's history, an endeavor which as yet proved lacking. "If we have a few compilations of merit, embracing detached portions and limited periods," Sparks observes, "there is yet wanting a work, the writer of which shall undertake the task of plodding his way through all the materials, printed and in manuscript, and digesting them into a united, continuous, lucid and philosophical whole, bearing the shape, and containing the substance of genuine history." Rather, as Sparks laments, "The public taste has run in other directions, and no man of genius and industry has been found so courageous in his resolves, or

prodigal of his labour, as to waste his life in digging into mines for treasures, which would cost him much, and avail him little." Still, "symp-
toms of a change are beginning to appear, which it may be hoped will
ere long be realized."[48]

Griswold's own anthologizing efforts were both a sign of this change
and a contribution to that history, one that gave form to the national
spirit and allowed the nation to know itself better. As William Ellery
Channing notes in another passage excerpted by Griswold, "The glory
of an age is often hidden from itself. Perhaps some word has been spoken in our day which we have not deigned to hear, but which is to
grow clearer and louder through all ages." Griswold took it upon himself to make sure such words *were* heard, however, and in volumes
such as *The Prose Writers*, he gave material support to Channing's confident prophesy that, "We are to survive our age, to comprehend it, and
to pronounce its sentence."[49]

When reviews of *The Prose Writers* began appearing in the spring of
1847, reactions were, like the volume's contents, decidedly mixed. Positive reviews invariably commended Griswold for the valuable service
his book provided in displaying in accessible form a diverse survey
of America's intellectual accomplishments and for freeing the nation
from vassalage to British critical opinion.[50] More contentious reviews,
meanwhile, divided their attention to censure on personal grounds,
attacking Griswold for his harsh handling of Cornelius Mathews and
Margaret Fuller; on ideological grounds, as when Young America complained that Griswold favored writers like Prescott and Irving whose
careers rested largely on foreign subjects; and on material grounds, as
reviewers pointed to the practical difficulties of excerpting prose.

Among the chorus of reviewers, Griswold's most enthusiastic support came from his friends at the New York *Knickerbocker*, where, in
the first of two reviews to appear there, Horace Binney Wallace, a
longtime supporter of Griswold and the man to whom *The Prose Writers* was dedicated, focused on the important function served by such
compilations while steering clear of issues regarding the structural
challenges of the prose anthology. As Wallace asserted with echoes
of Griswold's own prefatory sentiments, "It is then of the first consequence that everyone interested in associating his name with his
land's language should apprehend correctly the tendencies of the lit-

erary spirit of the country, in order that he may divine the nature of that literature in its perfect development; for it is only as his productions embody and represent that native spirit of art, that they will have a permanent life." To do so, Wallace notes, "He must look backward, and catch a prophecy of the future from the performances of the past. He must listen to the various notes that have been struck; observe which sound falsely, which have died away and become inaudible, and which rise and flow and swell upon the ear, the true key-notes of the symphony."

To progress beyond its current stage of development, American authors must fairly apprehend their literary heritage, Wallace insists, both that which is best and that which has failed or been forgotten. We err if we neglect our failures and instead focus narrowly on our achievements, Wallace maintains. Rather, "an honorable self-dependence, a manly self-reliance, can be inspired only by contemplating, as external, the monuments of one's own character and ability, or by seeing that others regard them with esteem and deference and admiration. For either purpose, of enabling the literary genius of the country to know itself, objectively, or of causing other countries to receive the complete impression of its power, we hold such efforts as have been made by Mr. Griswold to be of great value." As Wallace concludes: "He has done a useful work, and he has done it well."[51]

The *Knickerbocker* was on its own in choosing to skirt the technical problems associated with anthologizing prose, however. In most other notices, even commendatory ones, reviewers inevitably followed up their praise with polite admissions of certain generic difficulties posed by prose compilations. The reviewer for *Godey's Lady's Book*, for instance, after praising the volume by noting that "we have turned over these pages with mingled pride and pleasure, delighted to meet in one group so many intellectual friends and names endeared by patriotism and fame," still cannot help but marvel at what must have been the prodigious difficulty of Griswold's task. For "the field presented in this last undertaking was so large and various, that we conceive, in view of the limits prescribed by a single volume, the task of selection must have been one of extreme difficulty." To do true justice to the nation's intellectual achievements in prose, admittedly, "a library instead of a volume would have been requisite."[52]

Other reviews were far less diplomatic. In his review for the *Literary World*, the most Evert Duyckinck was willing to concede was that several of the book's failures emanated from generic difficulties rather than to missteps solely blamable to the editor, admitting that, "unsatisfactory as *The Poets of America* was pronounced in this form, it is much easier to make a collection of poems than of prose specimens." Poetry lent itself to the format of the anthology-piece, all the more so as Romantic taste veered toward the eminently quotable form of the lyric. This was not the case for prose, however, for as Duyckinck suggests,

> Even brilliant writers, cut into little squares, are defrauded of their crystalline proportions: and Willis looks dull, Webster scrappy, and Neal common-place, in these paltry six to twelve inch specimens . . . But what oration of Webster's can be judged of by extracts? What is a passage of Cooper or Brockden Brown worth, taken from its original framework? . . . Extracts of this kind may do for reading books in schools, but they will be of little value otherwise.

A paragraph divorced from the unity of the whole, from the phenomenology of reading or hearing a work in its entirety, Duyckinck observes, sacrifices both the pleasure and edification produced by prose literature in the first place. A book is not the sum of its *sententiae* but rather, "we value it from the journey we have performed in reaching it; from the pleasure it gives us to glance back upon it." And though the problem is in part "an essential difficulty," still, Griswold might have adopted several simple practical measures to alleviate his editorial burden. Duyckinck finds it difficult to comprehend, for instance, why when space is already limited, Griswold would begin each new author with a new page; or, similarly, he might have integrated text and commentary together rather than segregating them, thereby overcoming "the difficulty of stiffness and formality" by endeavoring "to quote the passage in connexion with the text, to mix the plums with the pudding."[53]

The weaknesses of the book rankled Duyckinck still further since the imposing form of the anthology necessarily conveyed an authority that belied the genre's structural incompatibility with prose. In short, a material contradiction existed between the anthology's cultural connotations and its restricted literal denotations, between its stately outward form and the practical limitations of its physical dimensions, a contradiction originating from the fact that "the composition of a book or history is essentially different from any contributions to reviews or periodicals." As Duyckinck explains, "A review is rarely taken as conclusive authority on the merits of an author: it may be revised or superseded: it is frequently nothing more than the view of but part of a great whole, or perhaps a convenient abridgement: it is published to-day and succeeded to-morrow. But the book is stereotyped: it has the authority of a book: it is preserved: it goes abroad, and gives color to opinion for perhaps an entire generation. How important, then, that it should be wisely and honestly written." A review is transitory; it is written and soon forgotten, the slightness of its intellectual status betokened by the ephemeral materiality of its periodical form. But a hefty anthology conveys authority and seals its judgments in the permanence of its stereotyped sentences and solid binding.

Even regarding the severity of his present judgments, Duyckinck admits that, "it would be trifling the reader to notice such absurdities did they appear in any other quarter than this national octavo." But the high ambitions of the anthology form all but demanded the sober scrutiny of critics, nor would critics lack for objects to ridicule since the task of anthologizing prose necessarily diminished its subject; since the ambitions of the anthology as a form faltered when confronting the limitations of the anthology-piece; since the volume's bearings gestured at representativeness while the act of excerption depended upon fragmentation, condensation, and a radically subjective process of selection.[54]

As Duyckinck would soon discover, however, criticizing anthologies proved much easier than compiling them. Yet Duyckinck's censure was not mere wheel spinning. Griswold's anthology had stirred something in him such that at times we can discern in the critical perorations of the review the plotting of his own editorial mind as early blueprints for a national anthology of his own began to take shape. In finding fault with Griswold's anthology, while many of his criticisms dwelt on relatively minor matters, others approached the subject of anthology construction from a more catholic perspective that understood the formal components of compilations as material expressions of abstract philosophies of literary history. For Duyckinck, who was himself primarily an editor, these theoretical concerns never strayed too far from nuts-and-bolts considerations, a practicality clearly displayed in his suggestion that in assembling literary histories, compilers had two options: either "industrious compends, confined to well-ascertained matters of fact, and well-settled judgments, with careful specimens of authors," or, alternatively, works "of the higher rank of original critical histories." The first mode was historical and objective, while the second was critical and therefore necessarily interpretive.

In drawing this binary, however, Duyckinck repressed the reality that both historically based compendiums and critical histories entail the subjective judgment of the compiler. Rather, we find a more nuanced distinction in David Perkins's suggestion that the two major forms that most literary histories take are either "narrative" or "encyclopedic." While traditional narrative literary history integrates material into a coherent, engaging, though necessarily constructed narrative, the encyclopedic form allows for greater heterogeneity and a more plausible representation of reality but sacrifices narrative coherence and, with it, popular appeal.[55] Duyckinck's problem with *The Prose Writers*, accordingly, is that it belongs "to neither one nor the other," to neither pure history nor pure criticism, to neither the encyclopedic nor the narrative form. Instead, "it is an unpleasant cross between the two. The reader is at one moment starved by a dry catalogue; at another, inflated by a windy disquisition, with little profit any way." In short, "Mr. Griswold seems to lack the simple habits of mind of the patient chronicler . . . while he is evidently unequal to the higher demands of criticism. His compilations of the Poets and Prose Writers are hence dry and chaffy, meagre, and unprofitable."[56]

While the editor of the *Literary World* opened the topic to debate, two weeks later in a set of reviews for the *United States Magazine and Democratic Review*, fellow Young American William A. Jones enlarged upon Duyckinck's preliminary considerations by interrogating the theoretical implications of the anthology as an expression of literary history. Jones began by agreeing with Duyckinck that the anthology form was better suited to poetry than prose since poetry, even poetry of the longer variety, was ready made for excerption. This was hardly the case for prose, however, for as Jones observes, "to give a few pages, here and there, of a novel, a treatise, a sermon, or an elaborate essay, in order to convey an idea of the author's qualities to a reader ignorant of them, is to repeat the old jest of Hierocles' silly fellow, who brought a brick as a sample of the house he lived in."

Like Poe and Schlegel before him, Jones insisted upon the Romantic principle of unity within artistic design, a requirement that prose anthologies violated in dramatic fashion. Judging a novel based on an excerpt was like judging the *Mona Lisa* based on a glimpse of eyebrow or *The Birth of Venus* by a bit of clamshell. Nor was the case any different for an accomplished prose stylist: "the more perfect his mastery of his art," Jones suggests, "the less likely we should be to know him fully by means of selections and extracts, or his effects would result, not so much from the finish imparted to single sentences, as from the unity and grandeur wrought into the whole piece." As a result, "Beauties of Burke" or "Elegant extracts" are "very apt to be stupid affairs, doing great injustice to the author whom they pretend to illustrate, and misleading the readers who are shallow enough to trust to such sources for their supplies."[57]

An explicitly national collection like *The Prose Writers* posed an even greater risk since it submitted for foreign review a jumble of fragments presented as a fair representation of America's intellectual achievements, a course that could cause nothing but injury to America's literary reputation. In lieu of a competent survey, Jones laments, "some sixty or seventy authors are thrown together in a heap . . . from each of whom, a page or less of extracts is taken, and the whole is set forth as a concise embodiment of what America has done in prose literature!" But one single, entire work by Cooper or Irving, Jones maintains, would have done more to establish America's literary distinction than all of Griswold's fragments taken together. "The editor, in his endeavor to do too much, has done nothing, or worse than nothing," Jones bemoans. "He has minced our literature until no substance remains—he has shorn it of its fair proportions—he has cut down our Brobdingnags into Lilliputians—made Tom Thumbs of our giants, and reduced American literature to its smallest dimensions, by causing it to be looked at through the smaller end of his telescope."[58]

Though Jones's dissatisfaction with *The Prose Writers* began with the practical problem of excerption, his larger critique stemmed more broadly from Griswold's approach to literary history. Specifically, with the nation nearing the century's halfway point, Jones had grown impatient with the inherited form of eighteenth-century literary historiography expressed by Griswold's volume, a tradition based upon a dryly erudite scholasticism that relied heavily upon bibliographic catalogues, biographical criticism, and a simplistic governing narrative of linear literary progress that inevitably reduced to rise or decline, or to patterns of cyclicality as derived from Vico. While such methods embraced a historical approach to literature, it was for Jones a naïve historicism operating in a one-way direction and guided by a simplistic nationalist impetus. According to these antiquated historiographic conventions, a nation's literature developed over time and was given its distinctive character by geographic forces (landscape, climate), reflected native political, social, and religious institutions and ideologies (democracy, Calvinism, self-reliance), and kept pace with the growth of the nation. These factors in turn shaped the national character, finding consummate expression in its writers, who both exhibited national traits as individuals and disseminated them to the public through their writings. In this fashion, a nation's literature developed along with the nation itself, expressing its native characteristics and fundamental ideals as well as its crises and conflicts.[59]

This historical theory of literary history was typical of the eighteenth century and of Romantic literary historians such as Warton and Campbell, while Griswold gestures at other sources when he footnotes Sismondi's *Literature of the South of Europe* in his introductory essay. As a way of understanding literature, however, this sort of non-self-interrogating historicism had run its course for Jones: "We know of few works in our language," Jones observes, "which come up to our ideal of literary history." Pointing to the prominent example of Henry Hallam's *Introduction to the Literature of Europe,* Jones notes that while the work is "masterly" and "inestimable" in many respects, still Hallam "is one of those authors who have a keen eye for the minute, and the utmost patience and impartiality in the investigation and decision of particular facts, but no capacity for great and comprehensive generalizations." For these grander conceptions, Jones suggests, "we must look to the continental writers—to the French and Germans—who write history, not as one makes an inventory of his shop, but in the spirit and according to the methods of a profound philosophy," to

Villemain, Guizot, and any number of German works that cannot help but suggest their "immense superiority to the dull and lifeless productions which crowd the shelves of English and American libraries."[60]

Jones wants a more nuanced and searching theory of the relationship between literature and history, one that is more than a dry catalogue of names and facts, and in this respect, he anticipates one of the fundamental critiques of historicism in general: that it is essentially reductive, flattening literature into its most conspicuous historical contexts.[61] Modern readers demand something more of literary history: "What the student of literature wants to know," Jones proclaims, is "not the when or where such and such writers were born, nor how many books they may have published, nor whether their style is 'terse' or 'eloquent,' or 'forcible,' &c., to use the slang adjectives of commonplace critics: but their respective influences upon the national life, and reciprocally the influences of the national life upon them, the degree in which they reflect the spirit of the age and country, and the degree in which they have carried that spirit on to its ultimate historical development, in laws, institutions, and manners." The loaded word here is *reciprocally* since one failure of the older model of historicism was that it betrayed a fundamental paradox in its patterns of influence: the nation influences literature, and literature influences the nation, yet these dual strains are presupposed and their tautological self-defining relationship seldom, if ever, explored.

These complex, uneasily parsed, reciprocal causalities are precisely what interest Jones, however, for as he insists, "Literature, when it is worth anything at all, is not a chance product: but like everything else, both in the moral and natural worlds, is the result of an infinite variety of co-operating agencies,—itself operating back again infinitely in various directions. Thus, it may be considered cause and effect at once; and great writers, who impress themselves upon the men of their day, are, in a certain sense, both the creatures and creators of the epoch in which they live."[62] Like Poe in "The Philosophy of Composition," Jones rejects the myth of Romantic inspiration while proceeding even further in his undercutting of the fanciful image of the isolated genius, a myth that Poe indulges. Rather, literature is a product of its place, its time, its moment, not in any simplistic sense but as a crystallization of innumerable social and historical forces that manifest themselves in works that immediately become part of the cultural milieu, thereby completing the feedback loop in their subsequent influence on the creation of new works. The linearity of the old model of influence is gone, and instead we begin to see the more complex models of history as explored by Hegel, Herder, and the Schlegels.

This is not to say that Jones was uninterested in material concerns, but these material considerations maintained a more theoretical cast in contrast to Duyckinck, whose observations tended toward practical applications. Jones's interest, on the other hand, was in exposing correlations between formal editorial choices and the theoretical and ideological assumptions that such choices silently carried with them. In Griswold's volumes, for instance, an organization structured around individual authors gave physical expression to the biographical method at the heart of neoclassical criticism. Griswold admits as much in his preface when he asserts that, "it seems necessary to a due understanding of an author's mind, that some of the circumstances of his education and general experience should be known to us," adding that, "To be able to think with him and feel with him, we must live with him."[63]

Jones's own theory of literary history, in contrast, founded itself on the structural unit of the epoch. Within the chaotic pattern of endlessly reciprocal influences, Jones suggests that one can demarcate periods with distinctive, defining characteristics that provide a semblance of order and coherence within the otherwise cacophonous play of history. Great writers "seldom come singly," Jones observes, but rather the "plans of Providence, in this respect, as in many others, are socialistic: for we find particular eras in the histories of nations, illustrated like the different spaces of the heavens by galaxies of stars or constellations more than by individual planets. Great men are grouped together, sometimes in a kind of equilibrium in regard to each other, but more often around some central figure, who is the pivot of his era." As evidence, Jones cites the Periclean Age, the Augustan Age, the Elizabethan Age, and the Age of Louis XIV. "These epochs are the salient points of history, and relieve its steady progress from the dead level of barren and monotonous uniformity."

This dynamic view of literary relations required a more flexible form than authors arranged chronologically by birth. A better alternative in

Jones's view would have been to expand upon the model adopted by Chambers' *Cyclopaedia of English Literature* "in which a chronological order is preserved, while a sufficient number of extracts, to illustrate the styles of different writers, as far as they can be thus illustrated, are interspersed." By extending this strategy of interspersion, Griswold "would have had an opportunity to do, what is not done in the Encyclopedia, viz., to present literature in its regular historical development; to connect it with the various external causes, political and religious, conspiring to modify its character, and to assign to each writer his relative place in the literary republic."[64]

In short, Jones locates in the textual interlacing of social and historical narratives with passages from related literature a formal correlative to his reciprocal theory of literary history. This integrated organization has the benefit of weaving literature and its historical contexts together into a single narrative arranged by chronology instead of segregating the two, counteracting the romanticized conception of literature as primarily the product of genius, of single actors disconnected from both history and one another, that was the silent implication of the biographically-based critical method employed by Griswold in *The Prose Writers*. Such a historically integrated formal arrangement was much better equipped to represent Jones's "socialistic" view of literary production with its emphasis on creative epochs, while more generally his critique of *The Prose Writers* expressed an organicist desire that the structures of anthologies correlate roughly to their underlying conceptions of literary history.

Jones was not in the anthology business, however. He was a critic and preferred to remain so. Evert Duyckinck, on the other hand, had always been actively invested in the material promotion of the national letters, most notably through his editorial tenure at influential journals such as the *Democratic Review* and the *Literary World* and through his editorial supervision of Wiley and Putnam's Library of American Books. And though his editorial plate was full in 1847, the desire to produce a national compilation persisted for nearly a decade until the mid-1850s when he and his brother finally began collecting material for an anthology of their own.

Confronting "the Material Limit":
The Duyckincks' *Cyclopaedia of American Literature*

When *The Cyclopaedia of American Literature* appeared in 1856, Evert and George Duyckinck were careful to pay due deference in their opening acknowledgments to their anthologizing predecessors. Even with such niceties, however, it was abundantly clear to readers and reviewers alike that the imposing compilation was meant to supplant Griswold's three major anthologies with a single work. In constructing their survey of American literature, the editors abandoned Griswold's biographically based model for that of Chambers' *Cyclopaedia*, discarding narrative literary history for the encyclopedic form and presenting chronologically arranged entries that interlaced biography, history, and restrained commentary with pertinent or representative extracts. And though the editors disclaimed any intention of comprehensiveness, the completed work belied such modesty, surveying American literary history in two weighty royal octavo volumes totaling over one thousand four hundred pages that exhaustively documented the progress of American letters from the early settlement of Virginia to the mid-nineteenth century.

In doing so, they returned to a conception of literary value as rooted in historical interest rather than aesthetic or critical judgments, asserting with echoes of Kettell that, "The history of the literature of the country involved in the pages of this work is not so much an exhibition of art and invention, of literature in its immediate and philosophical sense, as a record of mental progress and cultivation, of facts and opinions, which derives its main interest from its historical, rather than its critical value." For, as they add, "It is important to know what books have been produced, and by whom; whatever the books may have been, or whoever the men." In short, the Duyckincks fashioned themselves as impartial historians rather than biased critics. Indeed, as the editors demur, "the study and practice of criticism may be pursued elsewhere: here, as a matter of history, we seek to know in general under what forms and to what extent literature has been developed. It is not the purpose to sit in judgment, and admit or exclude writers according to individual taste, but to welcome all guests who come reasonably well introduced, and, for our own part, perform the character of a host as quietly and efficiently as practicable."[65]

If the metaphor for the volume was that of a party, the guest list was admittedly large, with the editors devoting lengthy entries not only to authors but to private and public institutions such as Harvard and Yale, the American Academy of Arts and Letters, and the New York Society Library, to publishers like Isaiah Thomas and Mathew Carey, and even to notable anthology editors such as Elihu Smith, Kettell, and Griswold himself. So too, they admit foreign-born authors, give more space to writers from the South and West, and dedicate the first six hundred pages to literature of the Colonial Period. Such marked departures from Griswold's editorial rubric betrayed the fact that, though the Duyckincks praised his anthologies as "the first comprehensive illustrations of the literature of the country," admitting their influence at home and abroad, nonetheless, much in the conception of their volumes came as a direct corrective to perceived inadequacies in his own compilations, a competitiveness that was equal parts ideological, Oedipal, and commercial.[66]

From the perspective of the material text, meanwhile, it was clear that the Duyckincks simply wanted to outdo Griswold. *The Cyclopaedia of American Literature* was bigger, longer, and much heavier, with scores more writers and a greater breadth of topics. Held in the hand, Griswold's *Prose Writers* presented itself by contrast as a tidy, elegant assertion of American cultivation in the field of letters: to peruse it might evoke pride and amusement, while to own it suggested refinement and a commitment to the national literature. The Duyckincks' book, on the other hand, was imposing and unwieldy, demanding to be spread out upon a table, and its length, density, and refusal to engage in entertaining critical polemics suggested serious study rather than casual perusal. Years earlier, a reviewer of Griswold's *Prose Writers* commended the volume by noting that "in this necessarily labor-saving age, in letters as in all beside, we do not know how a young American, especially one intending to travel, can spend the leisure hours of a month better than in making himself thoroughly acquainted with *The Prose Writers* and *The Poets of America*."[67] It would be difficult to say the same of the Duyckincks' volumes, however, since the physical aspects of the *Cyclopaedia* unsuited it both for leisure reading and travel.

Even among the editors themselves, there was a slight uncertainty as to how the books were to be received. At times they described the work as a handy reference book, naturally suited to "the public and private library [since] it is desirable to have at hand the means of information on a number of topics which associate themselves with the lives of persons connected with literature." At other moments, they present the volumes as intended to enrich and entertain, to "aid in the formation of taste and the discipline of character, as well as in the gratification of curiosity and the amusement of the hour." To this latter end, they embellished the volumes with numerous engravings, daguerreotypes by Southworth and Hawes, sketches of the houses of prominent authors, and authorial autographs, elements designed to pique the popular interest and to add commercial appeal to a work that might otherwise be mistaken as antiquarian in conception.[68]

This challenge of producing a work that was both historically comprehensive and commercially viable confronted the Duyckincks even more directly through the publisher's specifications regarding the work's material dimensions. For as the editors recount, "on consultation with the publishers, it was found that two royal octavos of the present liberal size could be afforded at a moderate price, which would place the work within the reach of the entire class of purchasers; that any extension beyond this would involve an increase in cost unfavorable to its circulation. This was the material limit."[69] Putting the volumes at a price point within reach of a large audience meant keeping the size of the book within reasonable page and size limits, a demand that reflected the further historical irony that as the push for comprehensive coverage grew, the size of anthologies shrank. In the eighteenth century, literary surveys were less restricted by space, spreading out either into numerous volumes devoted to individual authors or at the very least to multivolume compilations, as for instance with John Bell's cheap reprint series *The Poets of Great Britain Complete from Chaucer to Churchill,* appearing between 1777 and 1783 in 109 duodecimo volumes (which Griswold owned in its entirety) or with the projected series of books for which Samuel Johnson's *Lives of the Poets* were to serve as biographical prefaces.[70]

This condensing process, Julia Wright suggests, stemmed in part from a shift in emphasis as the impetus for comprehensive coverage became secondary to the propagation of the national narrative that connected the various authors. As the nationalist prerogative became more important, an anthology's success came to be measured less by the extent of its coverage and more by the extent of its distribution. Literary compilations in the eighteenth century were still largely the province of the wealthy, but by the early nineteenth century the democratization of literature enabled by innovations in print technology made affordability for the middle class both a practical and patriotic asset while the heightened importance attached to culture made such anthologies more widely sought after by the mass of general readers.[71]

When we add to these trends the further development that by the early nineteenth century, the unwieldy folio format had been all but abandoned in favor of the user-friendly octavo volume, we once again see the daunting challenges faced by editors of antebellum anthologies.[72] As a result, though the Duyckincks envisioned an exhaustive survey, practical commercial requirements provided a check on their ambitions for the book as comprehensive literary history. To afford as wide an audience as possible, some writers needed to be left out, otherwise "its extent would soon place it beyond the reach of ordinary purchasers." Still, if Chambers could squeeze a millennium of English literary history into his volumes, the Duyckincks surely could find room for a mere 250 years in theirs, or so they reasoned.

These space constraints in turn helped decide other editorial matters: for instance, that "under any principle of selection, the story should be as briefly told as possible; being confined to the facts of the case, with no more comment than was required to put the reader in ready communication with the author, while matters of digression and essay-writing should be carefully avoided." While it had been their design with the excerpts "to preserve the utmost possible completeness: to present a subject as nearly as practicable in its entire form," nonetheless, the space constraints of the volume naturally favored short forms—"the brief essay, the pertinent oration, the short poem"—forms that saved the editors from having to "mutilate the entire line of an argument of philosophy" or "violate the sanctity of a treatise of divinity, by parading its themes, plucked from the sacred inclosure of the volume." In this way the Duyckincks hoped to display with as much depth and as little critical bias as possible the achievements of two and half centuries of American literature, embracing the material constraints as factors that encouraged concision and promoted a streamlined editorial objective. And for a brief time, it seemed that they had succeeded.[73]

Early reviews of the Duyckincks' imposing volumes were enthusiastic, praising them as the new definitive work on the subject, then and for years to come. Yet Griswold had not forgotten Evert Duyckinck's slashing review of his *Prose Writers* from eight years earlier, nor was he about to sit passively by while the Duyckincks' *Cyclopaedia* eclipsed his life's work. When he sat down to review the hefty compilation in 1856, his health was precarious, the tuberculosis that had plagued him for years having relapsed, exacerbated by a drawn out legal battle with his second wife. As the prospect of death grew more probable, Griswold began to contemplate his legacy. While he had earned recent critical praise for his cultural history *The Republican Court* (1856), a study of American society during George Washington's presidency, he nonetheless knew that it was by his national anthologies that he was to be remembered, if at all. The Duyckincks' *Cyclopaedia* was a direct threat to that legacy; both the proportions and the pretensions of the new compendium were an insult to Griswold's pride, reducing his preceding efforts to a polite footnote and vaunting itself as authoritative and, at least in some sense, comprehensive.

In the lengthy review that appeared on February 13, 1856, in the pages of the New York *Herald,* Griswold set out to show that the Duyckincks' volumes were neither of these things. The result was spectacular. As Perry Miller notes, Griswold "slaughtered the *Cyclopaedia,*" unleashing what Miller characterizes as "the most destructive review in all American history."[74] Soon after the review's appearance, Griswold's friend and publisher Herman Hooker wrote to him, excitedly proclaiming that, "I never saw a more complete end made of anything. The fires of the last day could not have made a cleaner work of destruction . . . If I was the author of the book I should want to get into so little a place that no one could find me, or put my eyes out, so that I could see no one."[75] Other friends were so impressed by the performance that they encouraged Griswold to print it separately as a pamphlet, a suggestion that he promptly obliged.

Any way you looked at it, the review was brutal. What paradoxically made it so, moreover, was its stripped-down method of argu-

ment, embracing empirical evidence rather than critical grandstanding while avoiding arguments that could in any way be construed as
subjective. "The time has passed," Griswold observes, "when a reviewer's epithets, commending or condemning a book, were conclusive as
to its qualities"; rather, "criticism at present . . . is authoritative only as
it is demonstrative." And Griswold was nothing if not demonstrative
as, over the course of thirty-one pages, he systematically dismantled
the presumption that the Duyckincks' volumes were anything even
remotely approaching authoritative or comprehensive by exposing a
seemingly endless parade of errors and omissions.

In approaching this task, Griswold wastes no time, jumping into his
assault with a six-page catalogue of historical errors, faulty biographical information, textual misattributions, and incorrect chronological
dating. He follows this with six more pages of grammatical mistakes,
enumerating 155 separate examples of incorrect grammar, awkward
style, or inelegant expression, faults inflamed by the fact that, as
Griswold notes, "a history of literature, it will of course be admitted,
should itself be literature." Having proven that the work was neither
historically accurate, factually reliable, nor worthy of its literary subject, Griswold then demonstrated just how far the work was from being
comprehensive, as over the course of six pages he catalogued 191 distinguished American writers (arranged according to state) whom the
editors omit. He followed this up with forty-one more writers of foreign birth also deserving of inclusion, a tongue-in-cheek jab at the volumes' editorial principles since the Duyckincks insisted on including a
host of foreign writers in their supposedly *American* anthology.

Griswold was equally dismissive of the Duyckincks' saintly critical posturing, in particular the preposterous notion that they had
somehow abstained from critical judgment. "Let not the absurdity
be repeated, that their work is historical, and not critical," Griswold
insists, for beyond the obvious fact that selection is itself an act of criticism, "these volumes are full of what is meant for criticism, according to the common application of the word; and this criticism, when
not second hand, is often as feeble and preposterous in substance,
as puerile and vicious in expression."[76] These sorts of naive editorial
assertions combined with the seemingly endless stream of historical,
biographical, and grammatical blunders are for Griswold nothing less

than "conclusive as to the ignorance and incapacity of the authors of this pretentious performance." For as Griswold concludes, "We look in vain through every part of the work for such fruits of a loving familiarity with the intellect of the country, and its development, as should have been an assurance to the authors of their vocation. Many of the subjects demanded patient and sagacious research, and were susceptible of such handling as would have made them highly interesting. But every thing appears to have been done carelessly and feebly, which the compilers did not find already done by other hands."[77]

The review was critical karma, or at the very least, critical comeuppance, as years earlier Evert Duyckinck had made the exact same accusation of Griswold in insisting that his scholarly abilities were not up to the task of literary history. Now Griswold had a chance to return the favor. A key difference between the two reviews, however, was that while Duyckinck's criticisms had been largely unsubstantiated, in attacking the *Cyclopaedia*, Griswold amassed a surfeit of irrefutable evidence to back up his claims. Beneath the charges of incompetence, however, Griswold's review of the Duyckincks' *Cyclopaedia* offered a sharply deromanticized vision of the work of constructing literary history, as amidst the tempered vitriol of the article, he revealed his fundamental sense that writing literary history was above all hard work, a labor of love demanding "patient and sagacious research." Griswold had always been a pragmatist, had always approached the literary vocation from a practical, material perspective just as he had the promotion of the national letters. While Jones theorized the act of anthology construction without ever engaging in its labors, for twenty years Griswold had toiled in libraries pouring over dusty tomes and at his desk penning a never-ending stream of correspondence, had devoted the better part of his adult life to collecting and arranging materials, dealing with poets and publishers, bearing the rebuke of the slighted and the censure of the scorned, and all to have the next in line come along and appropriate the fruits of his toil with no more thanks than a hasty acknowledgment or a cursory footnote.

Years earlier, Evert Duyckinck had criticized Griswold's compilations for lacking a governing principle of selection, but eight years later, Griswold could not say the same of Duyckinck's. For as Griswold insisted, the *Cyclopaedia* was clearly governed by the principle of convenience, by easy access to materials, and by theft from the works of others, all to produce an inferior volume as shoddy and unreliable as it was large and pompous. Recalling an etymological point made by Henry Rogers for the *Edinburgh Review*, Griswold reflects at the close of his article that even though "compilation" is etymologically related to the Latin root "pilatio," meaning "pillage," still "it does not follow necessarily that compilation is to be literally pillage." The only sound parts of the Duyckincks' volumes, however, were those plagiarized from other sources; nor was Griswold the least bit shy in suggesting which works the two brothers pillaged most thoroughly: "In their first volume, they 'compiled' mainly from Mather, Elliot, Allen, and Kettell," while "for much of the rest, so far as it has any value, *The Poets and Poetry of America*, *The Prose Writers of America*, and other books and periodicals by the same author, have been liberally pillaged."[78]

Like Poe in his "Little Longfellow War," Griswold entered into tricky territory with the charge of plagiarism since the line separating theft, influence, and research was frequently thin. It is the nature of literary history that new works appropriate and build upon preceding ones; indeed, this was the very essence of Griswold's conception of the practical function served by anthologies — to present cultural digests of past literary achievements for current generations to assess, incorporate, and transcend. Just as Griswold pillaged Kettell's volume without due acknowledgment, so the Duyckincks pillaged his, and in the years to come, Edmund Clarence Stedman would do the same before the rise of the academic English department ushered in a century of collaborative pillaging in such works as *The Cambridge History of American Literature*, *The Columbia Literary History of the United States*, and most recently in Harvard University Press's *New Literary History of America*. Each generation's labor makes the path for future generations that much easier. Each new work draws upon its predecessors, and not the least irony of the literary historian's art is that though the work of literary history inevitably builds upon those that came before, in doing so, the historian becomes an actor within that history rather than the author of it.

Griswold's review of the Duyckincks' *Cyclopaedia* proved a bittersweet coda to a distinguished career, as in his last-ditch attempt to forestall the Duyckincks' volumes from supplanting his own, he displayed his prodigious mastery of American literary history one final time. In

the year that remained of his life, an exhausting legal battle with his ex-
wife drained his energy before the tuberculosis that had plagued him
for years finally finished the job, when on August 27, 1857, after months
of severe illness, Griswold died. In the decades to come, literary history would continue to prove unkind to Griswold as the penumbra
of Poe's lengthening shadow came to eclipse Griswold's own extensive achievements. Ironically, though Poe had made Griswold his literary executor in order to assure his own posthumous literary legacy, in
doing so he permanently tarnished Griswold's, not intentionally perhaps, but in a curious accident of literary history as Griswold came to
be the villain of Poe's biography rather than the protagonist of his own.
    So too, in the Duyckincks' *Cyclopaedia*, Griswold became a minor
character in the nation's literary history, despite having done as much
as anyone in the first half of the nineteenth century to write that history. Though Griswold devoted his life to literary history, though he
produced the first successful anthologies of America literature, giving
material shape to a national literary canon in the process, by the year of
his death, the Duyckincks' *Cyclopaedia* had realized Griswold's worst
fears: spreading out over a column and a half from the bottom of page
611 to the top of 612, tucked neatly between Jedidiah V. Huntington
and Benjamin Davis Winslow, was a sketched image of Griswold followed by a half-page account of his life's achievements.

CHAPTER 3

REVIEWERS REVIEWED

Poe, Monthly Magazines,
and the Critical Vocation

Perhaps the surest sign that Rufus Griswold had accomplished something impressive was that Edgar Allan Poe, that most uncompromising of critics, deigned to praise Griswold's *Poets and Poetry of America*. Though there was much in the volume with which Poe disagreed, nevertheless, as he conceded, "we know no one in America who could, or *who would*, have performed the task here undertaken, at once so well in accordance with the judgment of the critical, and so much to the satisfaction of the public. The labors, the embarrassments, the great difficulties of the achievement are not easily estimated by those before the scenes." As Poe concludes, "the book should be regarded as *the most important addition which our national literature has for many years received*. It fills a void which should have been long ago supplied," and in so doing, "Mr. Griswold in the 'Poets and Poetry of America,' has entitled himself to the thanks of his countrymen, while showing himself a man of taste, talent *and tact*."[1]

Griswold, for his part, had less patience for Poe's own destructive brand of criticism. In introducing Poe for *The Prose Writers of America* (1847), Griswold hastily dismissed Poe's extensive critical corpus with the brusque characterization that, "As a critic, he rarely ascended from the particular to the general, from subjects to principles; he was familiar with the microscope but never looked through the telescope."[2] While the specific charge is hardly an apt description of the man who would write "The Poetic Principle," to say nothing of *Eureka*, Griswold's analogy is nevertheless instructive: for though nicknamed the "Tomahawk," Poe preferred the comparison of the scalpel. While his ambitions for criticism were grand in theory, his practice of it was more frequently of the anatomizing variety, as he pinpointed errors in versification or grammar, exposed stylistic blunders, or quarreled with underdetermined plot construction. And while in the final years of his life Poe envisioned producing a full-length critical history entitled "Literary America," the project never got beyond the planning stages such that what we are now left with when surveying his critical oeuvre is more often than not the precise carvings of the scalpel rather than the larger historical patchwork to which he aspired.

   If observers disagreed on the merits of Poe's critical approach, however, no one was more conflicted about the proper role of criticism than Poe himself. Specifically, Poe worried that, within the expanding literary culture of antebellum America, critical practice was increasingly at odds with the true aims of literature. Nowhere was this concern more evident than when in the fall of 1849, while on a Southern speaking tour intended to raise money and attract subscribers for his long-standing project of a magazine of his own, Poe sat down in his Norfolk hotel room to answer a letter from an admirer. Susan Ingram had attended an intimate speaking engagement of his at the Hygeia Hotel the night before, and while admiring the beauty of the new poem he had recited, a mystical piece entitled "Ulalume," she nonetheless failed to grasp its broader meaning. Conscientious as always, Poe responded with a transcription of the poem and the following note:

> I have transcribed "Ulalume" with much pleasure, dear
> Miss Ingram,—as I am sure I would do any thing else,
> at your bidding—but I fear that you will find the verses
> scarcely more intelligible to day in my manuscript than
> last night in my recitation. I would endeavor to explain to
> you what I really meant—or what I really fancied I meant
> by the poem, if it were not that I remember Dr Johnson's
> bitter and rather just remarks about the folly of explaining
> what, if worth explanation, should explain itself. He has a

happy witticism, too, about some book which he calls "as obscure as an explanatory note." Leaving "Ulalume" to its fate, therefore, & in good hands, I am

Yours truly
Edgar A Poe[3]

Twenty-seven days later, Poe was dead. In the interim, he wrote only one final extant letter, a few paragraphs to his mother-in-law, Mrs. Clemm, informing her of his arrival in Richmond and his travel plans for the days to come. As such, his note to Miss Ingram, with its polite refusal to explain away the mystery of one of his more cryptic poems, exists as a curious final word of sorts, as well as a polite nod to the eighteenth century's most famous critic by one of the nineteenth century's most famous.[4]

As far as final words go, however, these were strange ones. Poe was never tight-lipped with his opinions, after all, either of his own work or that of others. Indeed, he spent the better part of his adult life "endeavor[ing] to explain" the inner workings of literature, boasting to his name just under a thousand critical pieces produced in his fourteen years as a practicing magazinist. His 1846 essay "The Philosophy of Composition" is one of literature's most famous poetic glosses, moreover, an exhaustive reconstruction of both the composition and intended effect of his most popular poem, "The Raven"—or at least, so the majority of Poe scholars have maintained.

This tension between the critical explication that by 1849 had been putting bread on Poe's table for well over a decade and his lingering sense of "the folly of explaining what, if worth explanation, should explain itself" was a nagging concern for Poe throughout his career as well as something that appeared to be on his mind during his final days. Just three months prior to his letter to Miss Ingram, a similar confusion appeared in the July installment of his *Marginalia*, a series of brief observations and critical miscellanies that Poe ran in various periodicals throughout the latter years of his life. In the first of these marginalia, appearing in the *Southern Literary Messenger*, where years before Poe had gotten his start as critic, he reflects that, "To see distinctly the machinery—the wheels and pinions—of any work of art is, unquestionably, of itself, a pleasure, but one which we are able to enjoy only just in proportion as we do *not* enjoy the legitimate effect designed by the artist:—and, in fact, it too often happens that to reflect analytically upon Art, is to reflect after the fashion of mirrors in the temple of Smirna, which represent the fairest image as deformed."[5]

In this observation, gleaned, we are told, from the margins of the books in his own personal library, Poe expresses his clear concern over the potentially deforming and inevitably disenchanting impact of literary criticism upon the intended effect of any given work of art. Yet in so doing, he explicitly calls into question his stated purpose in "The Philosophy of Composition," an essay in which he quite literally promises to give us "a peep behind the scenes, at the elaborate and vacillating crudities of thought . . . at the cautious selections and rejections—at the painful erasures and interpolations—" and, yes, "in a word, at the wheels and pinions" that ultimately resulted in "The Raven," language which his above marginal comment echoes verbatim.[6] While critical essays claiming insight into the mechanisms of poetry are, Poe admits, amusing, their interpolations are at odds with the true effect of literature, which, for poetry, is the rhythmical creation of beauty leading to an elevation of the soul and, for fiction, is the unified production of a psychological effect. Accordingly, the "legitimate effect" of a work of art is entirely beyond, even inversely related to, the analytic reflections of criticism. Something is lost in the process, moreover, and what we are left with is a deformed image reflected back to us as in a funhouse mirror.

That Poe violates this warning in not only "The Philosophy of Composition" but in scores of other reviews is enough to raise suspicion even before a page and a half later within the very same *Marginalia* installment he insists with equal confidence that, "It is folly to assert, as some at present are fond of asserting, that the Literature of any nation or age was ever injured by plain speaking on the part of the Critics. As for American Letters, plain-speaking about *them* is, simply, the one thing needed. They are in a condition of absolute quagmire."[7] The apparent contradiction is striking: while the first comment expresses concern as to the deforming effect of literary criticism upon art, the second observation insists upon the urgent *need* for criticism, arriving at the sober conclusion that the "plain-speaking" of critics is a commodity upon which nothing less than the fate of American literature depends.

The dialectical tension between these two strains of thought is the subject of this chapter. They represent two antithetical impulses that, I argue, were not only indicative of Poe's conflicted sense of the function of criticism, but of cultural ambivalences felt toward and within the institution of American criticism during its first great era of expansion. Though Poe conceived of literary criticism as essential to the development of a mature American literature, assigning the critic a pivotal, active agency in the creation of distinguished literary works, this is not to say that Poe was uncritical of criticism itself. Quite to the contrary, the heavy emphasis Poe placed on criticism's rarefying effect upon literature rendered him *more* rather than less exacting in the high standards he set for the critical institution in America. This tendency manifested itself not only in Poe's habit of attacking other critics in his reviews and essays, and of deconstructing both their theoretical assumptions and practical applications, but also, in its most extreme form, in Poe's own critical self-scrutiny. To put it bluntly, Poe on occasion turned his famed tomahawk on himself.

There is a pervasive tendency in Poe scholarship to view the author as somehow oblivious to the contradictoriness so prevalent in his life and art, or at best as a man whose convictions frequently bowed to the necessities of the moment. This view extends especially to treatments of his critical corpus, so seemingly rife with paradox, if not hypocrisy, a fact made all the more galling by the arrogant braggadocio of Poe's critical voice. Yet Poe was nothing if not self-aware, and in this chapter, I examine several of the occasions on which Poe directed his dissecting blade at his own critical methods. Poe was highly attuned to the contradictions within his critical practice, in other words, and in his reconciling of these apparent opposites, we see born in Poe the new embodiment of the American critic, struggling to assert his professional legitimacy while lacking the old marks of authority, and all the while facing the constant threat of corruption from the near proximity of the newly commercialized print industry.

Among Poe's other legacies as an innovative force for the short story, detective tales, or science fiction, one additional achievement is his contribution toward the codification of criticism as an independent vocation, operating in a public realm that combined the engagement of journalism with the rigor of scholarship and that rejected the appropriation of criticism as an advertising arm of the print industry while also eschewing the elitism of the quarterlies as they headed in the direction of what would become academic criticism. In a century marked by increasing professionalization across diverse vocations and disciplines, in advocating for rigorous standards for the American critic, Poe proved an influential force in the professionalization of criticism in America. As I'll argue, however, Poe was also a savvy self-promoter, cultivated critical feuds, and carefully crafted his persona as a severe, ruthless critic. All the while, he contributed frequently to popular monthly magazines the lighter brand of criticism that at other times he so vociferously decried.

Nowhere are the paradoxes of both Poe's own critical method and of the broader culture of American criticism more apparent than in "The Philosophy of Composition." Indeed, these paradoxes can help us begin to account for the long-standing controversy over "The Philosophy of Composition" and its proper reception, as for over a century critics ranging from T. S. Eliot and Remy de Gourmont to Daniel Hoffman and Kent Ljungquist have argued over whether the essay is poetics or hoax, a sincere expression of Poe's literary method akin to "The Poetic Principle" or a lark more properly suggestive of "The Balloon Hoax" or "Von Kempelen and His Discovery."[8] Moving past the hoax/poetics impasse, I instead read "The Philosophy of Composition" as a sensitive reflection on the culture of criticism in antebellum America, a barometer of the hyper-critical zeitgeist, and a meditation on both the promises and pitfalls of literary criticism by one of the era's most prominent critics. Residing at the core of the essay is Poe's deeply felt ambivalence toward the vocation of criticism as both necessary to the refinement of American letters and superfluous to the experience of literature itself. And while the essay brilliantly captures Poe's specific anxiety regarding his own practice as critic, it also reflects a much wider uncertainty held not only by other critics like Edwin Percy Whipple or Ralph Waldo Emerson, but by the historically self-aware antebellum culture more generally—anxiety over the province of criticism at a transitional moment when its function as entertainment or science, philosophy or advertisement, was still far from settled.

Much of this uncertainty was rooted, I suggest, in the unprecedented growth of antebellum America's most influential critical medium:

wide-circulation monthly magazines. It is no coincidence that "The Philosophy of Composition" appeared in *Graham's Magazine*, the very magazine that had first *rejected* "The Raven" months earlier, and a peri- odical Poe abandoned as editor because it was becoming too "namby-pamby," as Poe termed it, in its constant printing of sentimental fluff as well as its inveterate catering to the current vogues of the day, watered-down popular literary criticism among them.[9] The essay appeared a month before Poe began his popular "Literati of New York City" series in a second successful monthly magazine: *Godey's Lady's Book*. If Emerson relied on quarterly reviews for his career as lecturer, and Griswold focused his critical energy on anthologies, Poe was most deeply invested in the print genre of general monthly magazines, periodicals like *Graham's* and *Godey's* that were transforming the literary profession in America.

While by the 1840s critics had access to an increasing range of periodical venues, from scholarly quarterlies to penny newspapers, as Thomas Bender observes, Poe always understood his vocation as that of a "magazinist," eschewing the mantle of journalist while ridiculing the elitism of the quarterlies.[10] Over the course of his life, Poe contributed to no fewer than thirty magazines and was connected in an editorial capacity with five, from the *Southern Literary Messenger* and his own *Broadway Journal* to the influential *Graham's*, whose circulation he quadrupled during his fifteen-month editorial tenure from 1841–1842. In his commitment to eclectic, elegantly produced magazines, as Kevin Hayes argues, Poe saw an attractive, enduring alternative to the cheap pamphlet novels and foreign reprint periodicals that to Poe's mind were degrading literary taste and undercutting American authors.[11] Yet it was also Poe's dissatisfaction with existing magazines like *Graham's* that fueled his lifelong desire to start a magazine of his own, one which would set a new standard for periodical literature and criticism alike. It was magazines, finally, that grounded Poe's sense of both the capabilities and failures of American criticism, in particular the critical genres of lively book reviews, entertaining critical essays, personality criticism, and literary gossip that had become the monthly magazine's stock and trade.

The success of popular monthly magazines like *Graham's* and *Godey's* in the 1840s was, as Frank Luther Mott observes, one of the most significant developments of nineteenth-century US literary history. Between 1825 and 1850, the number of magazines increased dramatically, from less than one hundred to roughly six hundred, totaling between four or five thousand periodicals in the twenty-five-year period, though many had short lifespans. The types of these periodicals ranged from quarterlies, literary weeklies, and mammoth reprint papers, to women's magazines, religious quarterlies, antislavery papers, and specialized medical, scientific, and trade journals. Yet it was the general monthly magazines and the new model of operation they introduced that revolutionized the American literary marketplace. Specifically, editors like George Graham and Louis Godey began offering better pay for contributions, an innovation that resulted in higher quality contents, a more distinguished list of contributors, and increasing subscription numbers. In the process, the monthlies created a class of magazinists who could make a tolerable living by their pens while supporting the growth of American literature—and not merely through lofty rhetorical pronouncements but by paying American authors well for their writings.[12]

Beginning in the early 1840s, Graham began increasing payments for contributions. While a quarterly like the *North American Review* paid a dollar per page, and the *Democratic Review* paid on average two dollars per page, Graham started paying contributors from four to twelve dollars a page for prose and ten to fifty dollars for a poem, while famous authors received even more. The result was dramatic. In 1843, Poe earned around three hundred dollars for contributions to magazines, and by the end of his life he could receive fifty dollars for a single poem, while popular writers like Nathaniel Parker Willis, James Fenimore Cooper, and Henry Wadsworth Longfellow made significantly more. Other journals like *Godey's* and *Peterson's* quickly adopted *Graham's* model, creating a demand for magazine content that supported a growing roster of writers that included Poe, Willis, John Neal, Charles Fenno Hoffman, Charles Briggs, T. S. Arthur, as well as female authors like Lydia Sigourney, Ann Stephens, and E. F. Ellet. With more magazines came more editorial positions too, which provided an even more stable source of income.[13]

These magazines and their roster of contributors began producing a characteristic sort of content: light and lively, distinguished by variety, charm, wit, and worldly sophistication; printed on high quality paper and with expensive "embellishments" of copper and steel engravings by John Sartain, F. O. C. Darley and others. With the success of magazines catering to a female readership like *Godey's* and Snowden's *Ladies' Companion*, general monthlies began including fashion plates and sentimental tales and poems as well, marketing themselves as sophisticated parlor reading. These investments paid off: while the *Dial* had a subscription list of a few hundred, and the *North American Review* two or three thousand, in 1849 *Godey's* claimed forty thousand subscribers. *Godey's* standard rate for a year subscription averaged three dollars a year, meanwhile, the price charged by *Graham's*, though some monthlies like the *Knickerbocker*, the *Southern Literary Messenger*, and the *United States Magazine and Democratic Review* could cost as much as five dollars, and a surprising number of magazines attempted to lure readers with a low price of one dollar per year. While the content of these magazines was frequently derided as fashionable fluff, mostly good to kill an hour or two, these diatribes did little to stop the growing popularity of the monthly magazines or their impact on American literary tastes.[14]

The critical content of the monthlies was different, too, from the sober excurses of the quarterlies or the puffs and cursory notices that filled the newspapers. Rather, popular monthlies like *Graham's* created a demand for lively, jocular reviews and critical essays, written in stylish prose, that made for entertaining reading in its own right, and contributed by a growing list of distinguished contributors whose reputations were beginning to equal those of the authors they were reviewing. In monthly magazines like the *Knickerbocker*, the *Democratic Review*, *Sartain's Union Magazine*, *Holden's Dollar Magazine*, and *Arcturus*, readers followed the comings and goings of this cast of literary notables and were entertained by colorful feuds, witty critical evaluations, and biting takedowns. All the while, the more talented, enterprising, and sensational critics began to become more individuated from the mass of anonymous reviewers, cultivating reputations, and collecting their critical writings in separate volumes.

Accordingly, while the practice of anonymity was still common in quarterly reviews in the 1840s, book reviews in magazines like *Graham's* increasingly included the initials or full name of the reviewer if he or she was well known.[15] And with popular series like *Graham's* "Our Contributors," the *Knickerbocker's* "Editor's Table," and Poe's "Literati of New York City" in *Godey's*, increasingly, America's critics *were* known. For critics like Poe, that is, monthly magazines offered a new sort of livelihood. Yet this new professional identity came at a cost, as magazines expected a certain style of content, which Poe increasingly found beneath him. Contradictions such as these increasingly found articulation in Poe's growing corpus of metacritical pieces, moreover, critiques of critique and reviews of reviewers that sought to police critical practice, charting its abuses and defining its goals, even while committing many of the crimes with which he charged others.

"A Condition to Be Criticized": Poe and the Antinomies of Critical Practice

In the last three decades, new generations of Poe scholars have countered the romantic self-fashioning of his biography—of Poe as the poet Israfel at odds with the material world—as well as the ahistorical slant of his protoformalist aesthetics, instead presenting Poe as a savvy negotiator of the nineteenth-century literary marketplace. In the first decades of the twenty-first century, Poe has emerged as the representative man of antebellum print culture.[16] As J. Gerald Kennedy and Jerome McGann argue, "[Poe's] involvement in the magazine world and print culture, in the politics of reputation, in the problem of copyright, in the dilemma of sectionalism, in the cultural rivalries among eastern cities, and in his ceaseless promotion of 'Independence, Truth, [and] Originality' in American literature make him singularly representative of the practical realities of antebellum literary production."[17] As one of the era's most prolific (and polemical) critics, Poe offers us a unique window into the period's critical culture as well, which he both contributed to and commented upon extensively throughout his life.

It was into this fledgling vocation as professional critic that Poe found himself initiated when in 1835, he accepted the position of assistant editor at the *Southern Literary Messenger*. From this date until his death in 1849, Poe characterized himself as a poet, but made a name for himself first and foremost as a notorious critic. Criticism was more than a paycheck for Poe; it was a lifelong intellectual preoccupation, a subject that awakened in him both indignation and idealism. During his impressionable early years in Richmond, Poe was an avid reader of the British quarterlies and, as Michael Allen suggests, the deep impression of *Blackwood's* winning formula in the 1820s was formative of Poe's own artistic and critical development.[18] As a boy, Poe would page through the imported journals in his room above John Allan's mercantile house, and the education provided by models such as John Wilson and Francis Jeffrey was long when compared to the single year he spent at Jefferson's newly founded University of Virginia. Indeed, what Poe knew of purer philosophy and literary criticism—of Kant, Coleridge, and the Schlegel brothers—reached him largely by way of the quarterly reviews. Though many have tried to trace Poe's critical influences, as Arthur Hobson Quinn concedes, "it would be a brave critic . . . who would attempt to give the exact source of any particular passage in Poe's critical writing" since so much arrived secondhand through British periodicals.[19]

Within Poe's prolific critical corpus, this intellectual preoccupation with criticism manifested itself among other ways through a pronounced subset of reviews specifically concerned with the province of criticism itself, pieces that anticipate modern critical theory in their attempts to expose, define, and regulate critical practice. These metacritical pieces are numerous within Poe's critical oeuvre, ranging from passing commentary to sustained digressions to full-length articles devoted to the subject; they include his various magazine prospectuses, his reviews of other critics like Hazlitt and Macaulay, his engagement in topical reviews such as Lowell's *Fable for Critics*, and, most blatantly, in direct discussions of the subject in articles such as "Some Secrets of the Magazine Prison House" or his posthumous "About Critics and Criticism." So too must this subgenre be seen as distinct from Poe's various treatises on poetics—works such as "The Poetic Principle" or his reviews of Hawthorne—concerning itself not with the production of literature, not with unity, effect, and the heresy of the didactic, but rather with the critical evaluation of it.

Within this reflexive critical vein, the first important, sustained pronouncement came in an 1836 review of two American poets, Joseph

Rodman Drake and Fitz-Greene Halleck, which Poe feels compelled
to preface with "a few words regarding the present state of American
criticism" (*E&R* 505).[20] In surveying the native critical field, Poe asserts
that, "it must be visible to all who meddle with literary matters, that
of late years a thorough revolution has been effected in the censorship
of the press" (*E&R* 505). For the first three decades of the nineteenth
century, Poe observes, the major problem afflicting American criticism had been a wholesale subservience to European opinion and with
it a begrudging acceptance of the inferiority of American letters; but
of late, Poe laments, American critics have moved too far in the other
direction. "We are becoming boisterous and arrogant in the pride of
a too speedily assumed literary freedom," Poe warns. "We throw off,
with the most presumptuous and unmeaning hauteur, *all* deference
whatever to the foreign opinion—we forget, in the puerile inflation
of vanity, that *the world* is the true theatre of the biblical histrio—we
get up a hue and cry about the necessity of encouraging native writers
of merit—we blindly fancy that we can accomplish this by indiscriminate puffing of good, bad, and indifferent, without taking the trouble
to consider that what we choose to denominate encouragement is thus,
by its general application, rendered precisely the reverse" (*E&R* 506).

In short, Poe points out the unfortunate fact that we "often find ourselves in the gross paradox of liking a stupid book the better, because,
sure enough, its stupidity is American" (*E&R* 506). This is no trifling
matter for Poe. The indiscriminate praise of mediocre American productions is crippling the future of American letters, and it is against this
scourge of ubiquitous panegyric that Poe directs his own frequently
scathing brand of criticism. With this deleterious tendency of American critics to puff bad writing in mind, Poe explains that as editor of
the *Southern Literary Messenger*, it has been "our constant endeavor . . .
to stem, with what little abilities we possess, a current so disastrously
undermining the health and prosperity of our literature" (*E&R* 506).

A central tenet of Poe's critical doctrine was that a vital national criticism is an indispensable precondition for a thriving national literature,
a view that influenced Lowell's famous articulation of the same principle in his sketch of Poe for *Graham's*.[21] The latter cannot exist without the former, and in the Drake-Halleck review, Poe wagers that if
American literature is mediocre (and it is, he insists), a good part of

the blame must fall on the pandering, jingoistic swarms of lapdog critics who praise anything American regardless of intrinsic merit. Calling manure roses doesn't make it so. As for Drake and Halleck, the two overrated poets in question: "That we have among us poets of the loftiest order we believe—but we do *not* believe that these poets are Drake and Halleck" (*E&R* 539).

Though comments such as this rightfully earned Poe his reputation as a cruel reviewer, there was method to his meanness.[22] A mature American literature could for Poe come about only after the development of a mature and impartial critical establishment. In 1842, a year in which Poe produced some of his finest critical work, he stated this point bluntly in the pages of *Graham's Magazine* in a review of yet another undeservingly acclaimed American poet, John G. C. Brainard: "Among all the *pioneers* of American literature," Poe writes, "whether prose or poetical, there is *not one* whose productions have not been much over-rated by his countrymen" (*E&R* 404). This nationalistic literary self-aggrandizement was all the more frustrating for Poe because it made it difficult for Americans to recognize native works of true merit, which by the early 1840s, even by Poe's concession, were beginning to appear in greater number. "There is no longer either reason or wit in the query,—'Who reads an American book?'" Poe observed, echoing Sydney Smith's infamous jibe.

> In fact we are now strong in our own resources. We have, at length, arrived at the epoch when our literature may and must stand on its own merits, or fall through its own defects. We have snapped asunder the leading-strings of our British Grandmamma, and, better still, we have survived the first hours of our novel freedom,—the first licentious hours of hobbledehoy braggadocio and swagger. *At last*, then, we are in a condition to be criticized—even more, to be neglected; and the journalist is no longer in danger of being impeached for *lese-majesté* of the Democratic Spirit, who shall assert, with sufficient humility, that we have committed an error in mistaking 'Kettell's Specimens' for the Pentateuch, or Joseph Rodman Drake for Apollo. (*E&R* 405)

American literature could proceed no further without a critical apparatus free of bias; the two existed in a state of symbiosis with critics clearing away the dross so that works of true genius could find the audiences they deserved. What America needed, Poe consistently reiterated, was a fearless, independent criticism; what it currently *had* was a system hobbled by every sort of prejudice—national, commercial, personal, and political—which in turn held back the emergence of a distinguished American literature.

As a result, while Poe's more famous forays into poetics—works such as "Letter to B—," "The Poetic Principle," or his review of Thomas Hood—were generally constructive, his assessments of the current climate of American criticism tended to highlight systemic dysfunctions. While his theory of poetry sought to free readers from the crude materiality of the world, carrying them into a transcendent realm of ideality, Poe's critical theory was doggedly social; and while Poe was always attuned to the split roots of poetic composition in both ideal *poiesis* and practical *techne*, Aristotle never had to worry about New York publishers. Theorizing was all well and good, but there was also the business of letters with which to contend. These practical matters were no less important than poetics, moreover, for as Poe once quipped: "To be appreciated you must be *read*."[23]

What was holding back American literature, Poe insisted, was not lack of talent but rather a corrupt literary-critical establishment that failed to recognize and encourage writers of talent. It was this corruption in its various perfidious forms that Poe sought to expose through his own critical pieces when in review after review, he lambasted the literary establishment. He attacked its cliquishness; he attacked the Northern regional bias; he attacked its jingoistic nationalism. So too did he take repeated aim at the underlying financial concerns that favored known mediocrity over unknown genius. Like most of his fellow authors, he criticized the lack of an international copyright—for what publisher would take a chance on an unknown American author when cheap, reprinted copies of Dickens and Bulwer bore high returns on a small investment?

Despite Poe's deep concern over the manifold corruptions of the American literary scene, however, he nonetheless managed to retain a steadfast faith in the role criticism must inevitably play in the formation of a national literature. Indeed, his frustration over America's prodigal critical establishment emanated directly from his abiding sense of the vital function criticism must have if American literature was to become anything at all. With this in mind, Poe implores critics to scrutinize their own practices, for American literature can be only as good as American criticism demands it be. "When we attend less to 'authority' and more to principles," Poe writes in 1845, "when we look *less* at merit and *more* at demerit, (instead of the converse, as some persons suggest,) we shall then be better critics than we are." As Poe insists, "We must neglect our models and study our capabilities. The mad eulogies on what occasionally has, in letters, been well done, spring from our imperfect comprehension of what it is possible for us to do better. 'A man who has never seen the sun,' says Calderon, 'cannot be blamed for thinking that no glory can exceed that of the moon; a man who has seen neither moon nor sun, cannot be blamed for expatiating on the incomparable effulgence of the morning star.' Now, it is the business of the critic so to soar that he shall *see the sun,* even although its orb be far below the ordinary horizon" (*E&R* 1376–77). The fate of American literature, the heights it can reach, Poe maintains, rest on American criticism; without serious, exacting, uncompromising critics, America can never have a serious literature. Poe dedicated his life to this principle; ultimately, by his own admission, he sacrificed his reputation to it.

What Poe's detractors characterized as unnecessarily severe, mean-spirited criticism, Poe himself saw as a brave, honest corrective to the universal system of puffery that was the critical mode of the day. While the critical opinions of most periodicals were corrupted by incestuous relationships between magazines and publishers, or by an infection of back-scratching by cliques, coteries, and mutual admiration societies, Poe's life ambition was to start a literary journal of his own, free of these corrosive influences. This one ambition followed Poe through the various stages of his career, so much so, in fact, that we frequently get the sense that fiction and poetry took a back seat to Poe's desire for a magazine of his own, a way to make a little money while he tried to drum up support for first the *Penn Magazine,* then the *Stylus,* and finally the short-lived *Broadway Journal,* the closest Poe ever came to success when after two months under his full ownership, it folded from financial insolvency. It was in pursuit of this dream of a magazine of his own that Poe set off in 1849 on a Southern tour intended to raise money and subscription lists, a voyage that would prove to be his last.

Despite the different names, the vision for each magazine was exactly the same—to be a repository for "an honest and fearless opinion"—and each journal swears to a critical Hippocratic oath of sorts, pledging to uphold "an absolutely independent criticism—a criticism self-sustained; guiding itself only by the purest rules of Art; analyzing and

urging these rules as it applies them; holding itself aloof from all personal bias; acknowledging no fear save that of outraging the right;
yielding no point either to the vanity of the author, or to the assumptions of antique prejudice, or the involute and anonymous cant of the
Quarterlies, or to the arrogance of those organized *cliques* which, hang-
ing like nightmares upon American literature, manufacture, at the nod
of our principal booksellers, a pseudo-public-opinion by wholesale"
(*E&R* 1025). Though Poe could be inconsistent on some matters, this
was not one of them. The prospectus for each magazine, as well as the
letters which surround each campaign, reinforce this call for a fearless,
independent, and at times brutally honest criticism. Appended to this
central determination was a commitment to the world republic of letters rather than to any particular clique, publisher, region, and even
nationality. For as Poe repeatedly asserted, it was the world, rather
than the narrow bounds of the nation, that was the true stage for any
author worth the name.

Poe's lifelong commitment to the vocation of criticism renders it
all the more jarring that throughout his corpus we also find a subtle,
though no less persistent strain of uncertainty regarding the practical
impact of criticism upon the work of art. It is telling that Poe's first short
stories were neither Gothic horror nor tales of ratiocination but rather
satires upon the current literary scene, and in particular, contemporary
criticism. Long before *Tales of the Grotesque and Arabesque* (1840) or *The
Prose Romances of Edgar Allan Poe* (1845), Poe spent years trying in vain
to find a publisher for an abortive volume tentatively entitled "Tales
of the Folio Club." In the tradition of *The Decameron* or *The Canterbury
Tales*, the premise of the volume was that members of an elite literary
society meet every Tuesday to recite original tales to one another; and
while the author of the story judged to be the best ascended to the hon-
orary position of president, the author of the worst had to provide dinner at the following meeting. As Poe explained to publisher Harrison
Hall, not only was each individual tale meant as a satire upon some
popular story mode of the day, but in addition, "as soon as each tale is
read,—the other 16 members criticise it in turn—and these criticisms
are intended as a burlesque upon criticism generally." While by 1836
many of the individual stories had found homes in various periodicals, "the critical remarks, *which have never been published*," Poe informs

Hall, "will make about ¼ of the whole—the whole will form a volume of about 300 close pages."[24]

Though neither the volume nor the critical interpolations ever materialized, we get a good indication of their intended tone from his unpublished introduction to the proposed volume, which first resurfaced over a half-century later in James Harrison's 1902 edition of Poe's complete works. As Poe writes, the "Club is, I am sorry to say, a mere Junto of *Dunderheadism*. I think too the members are quite as ill-looking as they are stupid. I also believe it their settled intention to abolish Literature, subvert the Press, and overturn the Government of Nouns and Pronouns." Among this cast of club members intent on destroying literature are Mr. Horrible Dictû, the author of the Germanic "Metzengerstein," Mr. Blackwood Blackwood, responsible for the unbridled sensationalism of "Loss of Breath," Mr. Snap, "formerly in the service of the Down-East Review" and author of the pompously pedantic "Lionizing," as well as a host of others, each representative of some popular story genre with names such as Chronologos Chronology, Mr. Convolvulus Gondola, Mr. Solomon Seadrift, and De Rerum Naturâ, Esqr.[25]

The Folio Club was evidently born of the frustration Poe experienced while trying to break into the literary scene in the early 1830s; his proposed burlesque of criticism even preceded by several years his induction into the critical vocation in 1835. Since Poe goes out of his way to specify that the club meets on Tuesday, it seems likely that he modeled his Folio fraternity on a combination of the Tuesday Club, an eighteenth-century literary society based in Annapolis, and the Delphian Club, a group active in the 1820s to which two of Poe's acquaintances, John Neal and William Gwynn, both belonged—and whose members, we might add, employed eccentric pseudonyms.[26]

While Poe's Folio Club had identifiable social bearings, its professed intention to serve as a burlesque upon criticism also marks it as part of an established literary tradition. As far back as literature has existed, critics have existed right alongside it; and as long as there have been critics, there have been those who mocked the pretension of the endeavor as well as the arrogance of those who would profess to tell us what a particular play or poem means, something which by all accounts should be just as evident to us as to them. In short, critical satire—and by this, I mean satire of criticism or what Poe calls critical "burlesque" — is as old as criticism itself, a long-standing satiric sub-genre that traces itself back at least as far as Aristophanes's *The Frogs*.

As the institution of criticism expanded with the rise of print, critical satires also increased in number, registering on a basic level not merely authorial resentment of abuse by specific critics but a general anxiety over the transformations affecting the republic of letters in the eighteenth and nineteenth centuries. Perhaps the most famous practitioner of the genre was Alexander Pope, who wrote not only *An Essay on Criticism*, published in 1711, the same year Addison and Steele launched *The Spectator*, but also *Peri Bathous* (1728), a parody of the ars poetica mode as inaugurated by Horace, though here specifically Pope pokes fun at Longinus's classical treatise on the sublime, *Peri Hypsous*. While *An Essay on Criticism* mocks the social institution of criticism, as I'll suggest, *Peri Bathous* is a direct precursor to "The Philosophy of Composition" in its parodying deconstruction of manuals like those of Longinus that prescriptively delineate a practical guide to the creation of literary profundity. Though Poe never mentions these two verse satires by name, he does refer to Pope frequently, and it seems a safe assumption that Poe had some sort of exposure to them.

We know more definitively that Poe had read a nineteenth-century example of critical satire in Lord Byron's *British Bards and Scotch Reviewers* (1809), which Poe mentions by name in a review of James Russell Lowell's *Fable for Critics* (1848). The Lowell review suggests that we need not look to ancient Greece or even to England for examples of the genre, for Poe dealt with it first hand in reviewing Lowell's *Fable*. Not surprisingly, Poe was highly critical of Lowell's verse satire of the antebellum literary scene, in no little part because in it Lowell mocks Poe with the quip: "There comes Poe with his raven, like Barnaby Rudge / Three-fifths of him genius and two-fifths sheer fudge."[27] Personal animosity aside, however, *A Fable for Critics* is also for Poe indicative of America's more general deficiency within the satiric genre. "What have we Americans accomplished in the way of Satire?" Poe asks in the review's opening lines. His answer is *not much*. As Poe argues, "It seems to us that, in America, we have refused to encourage satire—not because what we have had touches us too nearly—but because it has been too pointless to touch us at all" (*E&R* 815). As Poe proceeds, he derides Lowell's satire for lacking "polish," lacking subtlety, lacking the proper tenor of sarcasm, and lacking "that skill in details" which was so central to Poe's literary philosophy. At times Lowell's poem devolves into "namby-pambyism," at other times into laughable acrimony, such that "we laugh not so much at his victims as at himself for letting them put him in such a passion" (*E&R* 817).

The lamentable irony for Poe is that the current literary scene is such a fertile field for satire; it offers ample fodder for ridicule, yet Americans seem unable to answer the charge. Lowell's execution is messy and "unpolished," meanwhile—it is "essentially 'loose'—ill-conceived and feebly executed, as well in detail as in general . . . it is so weak—so flimsy—so ill put together—as to be not worth the trouble of understanding" (*E&R* 816–18). The review is telling, less for what it says about Lowell than for what it reveals about Poe's own conception of satire. For Poe, satire must be subtle, clever, avoiding outright ire as well as sycophancy; so too must it be carefully controlled and constructed in both its overall conception and its details. Lastly, Poe tells us, if American satire has failed, "in part, also, we may attribute our failure to the colonial sin of imitation. We content ourselves—at this point not less supinely than at all others—with doing what not only has been done before, but what, however well done, has yet been done *ad nauseam*" (*E&R* 815–16). What American satire needs more than anything is originality, to break from the old, worn out molds of *Hudibras* or *The Dunciad* as emulated by American imitators in *M'Fingal* and *A Fable for Critics*; Americans need to look for new ways to mock the pretensions of the day, to fresh modes of satire suited to the tenor of the times.

During the 1840s alone, Poe not only reviewed Lowell's *Fable* but also encountered a second attempt at the genre in Lambert Wilmer's *Quacks of Helicon* (1841). While Poe dismissed Lowell's satire as poorly conceived and even more shoddily executed, his earlier review of Wilmer's poem, a short critical satire of Baltimore literati, managed the daunting task of earning Poe's respect, prompting as part of the review one of Poe's most important pronouncements on the state of American criticism. Poe liked Wilmer's satire so much that in a letter to his friend Joseph Evans Snodgrass, he insisted, "You must get this satire & read it—it is really good—good in the old-fashioned Dryden style. It blazes away, too, to the right & left—sparing not." The satire sparked Poe's enthusiasm to such an extent that, as he tells Snodgrass, "I have made

it the text from which to preach a fire-&-fury sermon upon critical independence, and the general literary humbuggery of the day."[28]

The "fire-&-fury sermon" in question does not disappoint. "As a literary people," Poe asserts, "we are one vast perambulating humbug";
and amid this general melee, "surely there can be few things more
ridiculous than the general character and assumptions of the ordinary
critical notices of new books" (E&R 1006–8). As Lara Langer Cohen has
argued, such charges of literary humbuggery were not issued by Poe
alone but rather were typical of a wide-ranging antebellum concern
over what Cohen terms "literary fraudulence," inflated estimates of
American literature akin to currency speculation and land bubbles that
collectively constituted a powerful counter-narrative to that of literary
nationalism, both in the antebellum period's penchant for nationalist
puffery and in twentieth-century scholarship's exceptionalist accounts
of early American literary history.[29]

American criticism, Poe tells us, is corrupt, clique-ridden, hamstrung
by puffery; it praises everything it sets its eyes upon and revels in mean-
ingless generalities. As for the quarterlies, their insipidity masks itself
beneath an "air of sufficient profundity"; what the reviewer lacks in
original ideas, he makes up for in "verbiage" — "'Words, words, words'
are the secret of his strength," Poe rails (E&R 1009). What American
criticism needs is honesty, severity, critical independence, nor are these
insignificant matters. The fate of American literature depends upon a
rigorous, disciplined critical institution, and with puffery rampant, Poe
admonishes, American literature cannot progress: "Trivial as it essentially is, it has yet been made the instrument of the grossest abuse in the
elevation of imbecility, to the manifest injury, to the utter ruin, of true
merit" (E&R 1010). Ultimately, however, it is the *truth* of Wilmer's satire rather than its execution that Poe admires; it is refreshingly candid
on a subject close to Poe's heart, and this fact goes a long way in making up for its servile imitation of Pope and Dryden as well as for its
technical deficiencies as verse.

As with his review of Lowell, we get the sense that while Poe saw
an ardent need for satire of the literary and critical status quo, he felt
that the form of these satires was stale and antiquated. Poe was not
interested in heroic couplets or mock epic; these modes had run their
course. The question was not whether American criticism needed to

be mocked, moreover, but rather what new form this mockery should take. Poe had already tried his hand at explicit parodying grotesques in tales such as "How to Write a Blackwood Article" or "Lionizing." And though the satirizing critical interpolations of "The Folio Club" never materialized, as I want to suggest, the spirit that conceived of them—the desire to produce a burlesque of criticism—found its belated expression in "The Philosophy of Composition." Poe was always one for variety as well as for originality, and in his peculiar reconstruction of "The Raven," he gave new shape to an old theme.

"The Philosophy of Composition" as Critical Burlesque

Published in the April 1846 issue of *Graham's Magazine,* where years before Poe had served as literary editor, "The Philosophy of Composition" capitalized upon the tremendous popularity of "The Raven" by following it up with a behind-the-scenes look at his compositional process for the poem. As Poe observes, "I have often thought how interesting a magazine paper might be written by any author who would—that is to say, who could—detail, step by step, the processes by which any one of his compositions attained its ultimate point of completion." Why no such paper exists baffles Poe, though he surmises the real reason is authorial vanity, or specifically the fact that, "Most writers—poets in especial—prefer having it understood that they compose by a species of fine frenzy—an ecstatic intuition—and would positively shudder at letting the public take a peep behind the scenes, at the vacillating crudities of thought—at the true purposes seized only at the last moment . . . at the cautious selections and rejections—at the painful erasures and interpolations . . . which, in ninety-nine cases out of the hundred, constitute the properties of the literary *histrio*" (*E&R* 14). If this passage is quoted frequently, it is for good reason: for it is here that Poe famously rejects the romantic myth of the "spontaneous overflow of powerful feelings" made famous by Wordsworth and Coleridge in the preface to *Lyrical Ballads* (1798), the fanciful notion that poetry is composed in a state of "fine frenzy," as Poe calls it, emerging fully-formed from the lips of inspired poets. Against this romantic fantasy, Poe explains that in the reconstruction of "The Raven" to follow, "it is my design to render it manifest that no one point in its composition is referrible [*sic*] either to accident or intuition—that the work proceeded step by step, to its completion with the precision and rigid consequence of a mathematical problem" (*E&R* 14–15).

In the pages that follow, Poe provides not only a detailed iteration of his poetic process in constructing "The Raven," but a convenient checklist of his main aesthetic principles. Though none of the principles is new exactly, this is one of the first times that Poe gathers them all together under one roof and with a view to practical application rather than abstract theorization. It is perhaps this comprehensiveness combined with the pragmatic quality of the piece that could have prompted Poe to refer to the essay as his "best specimen of analysis," though, as I want to suggest, there may be other reasons as well.[30] As the essay proceeds, we get a catalogue of Poe's core critical doctrines: "beauty [as] the sole legitimate province of the poem," insistence on unity of effect leading toward an "intense and pure elevation of the soul," the parameters of a single sitting and conversely the impossibility of a long poem (*E&R* 15–16). So too do we get matters of a more technical nature: Poe's theory of the refrain by which monotonous repetition produces connotative variation, the need for originality in versification, the careful calibration of metrical deviations. In all of this, the uniting theme is backwards composition following Poe's opening assertion that, "nothing is more clear than that every plot, worth the name, must be elaborated to its *dénouement* before any thing be attempted with the pen." For as Poe explains, "it is only with the *dénouement* constantly in view that we can give a plot its indispensable air of consequence, or causation, by making the incidents, and especially the tone at all points, tend to the development of the intention" (*E&R* 13). Only when you know where you are heading can you actually begin; in this way, everything tends towards that final outcome, nothing is wasted.

While all of this is good in theory and *as* theory, however, Poe's implementation of his various tenets in his step-by-step reconstruction of "The Raven" repeatedly tests the reader's credulity, as what seems plausible enough in the abstract is rendered absurd in the application. Poe famously claims, for instance, that the duration of a poem must be limited to one sitting, but in his elaboration of this principle, he pushes the suggestion to its breaking point. As Poe calculates, "Within this limit, the extent of a poem may be made to bear mathematical relation to its merit—in other words, to the excitement or elevation—again in other words, to the degree of the true poetical effect which it is capable of inducing . . . Holding in view these considerations, as well as that degree of excitement which I deemed not above the popular, while not below the critical, taste, I reached at once what I conceived the proper *length* for my intended poem—a length of about one hundred lines. ['The Raven'] is, in fact, a hundred and eight" (*E&R* 15–16). Moments earlier Poe insisted that in contradistinction to the romantic myth of fine frenzy, poetic composition must proceed "with the precision and rigid consequence of a mathematical problem," yet now that we see this statement practically carried out, the specificity of the calculations comes across as impossibly precise and over-determined. We have a vision of Poe secluded in a stormy turret, abacus in hand. Or perhaps less fancifully, we see poetic creation reduced to algebra, to plugging variables into equations—in a sense, the nineteenth-century version of computer-generated art. If the romantic myth of "ecstatic intuition" is as Poe suggests unrealistic, his depiction of the poet as actuary is no better.

The entire essay flounders in precisely this manner. Backwards composition is fine in theory, nor do we question the validity of Poe's concern that a poem or short story must be sketched out in advance and constructed with careful deliberation and design; yet the actual essay serves not so much as a proof of these points than as a *reductio ad absurdum* deflation of them. To give a second example, Poe reasons that since the sole province of poetry is beauty, and since melancholy is "the most legitimate of poetical tones," he was therefore then able to use "ordinary induction" to determine "a key-note in the construction of the poem—some pivot upon which the whole structure might turn." Knowing too that he wanted a single word as the refrain, "these considerations inevitably led me to the long *o* as the most sonorous vowel, in connection with the *r* as the most producible consonant" (*E&R* 17). In other words, Poe claims that "The Raven" began with a single phoneme: specifically, "-ore." Assertions such as these put our willing suspension of disbelief, as Coleridge termed it, to the test—more so, indeed, than many of Poe's most fantastic Gothic plots, more than criminal orangutans, imploding houses, and dead wives taking over the bodies of present wives.

Nor are we dealing with a couple of isolated moments in the essay. Rather, "The Philosophy of Composition" is a catalogue of improbabilities, if not deliberate provocations, the most notorious of which is Poe's perverse, much cited pronouncement regarding the choice of a theme, asserted with an air of infallibility, that "the death . . . of a beautiful woman is, unquestionably, the most poetical topic in the world" (E&R 19). Or there is Poe's offhand opening quip, in which he nonchalantly instructs us to "dismiss, as irrelevant to the poem *per se*, the circumstance—or say the necessity—which, in the first place, gave rise to the intention of composing a poem that should suit at once the popular and the critical taste" (E&R 15), a suggestion that is all but impossible to reconcile with Poe's lived experience, his struggle for survival and recognition as a writer, and the market pressures he was constantly forced to negotiate. In stark contrast to Poe's flippant dismissal, Terence Whalen and Jonathan Elmer have both argued persuasively that Poe's negotiation of the conflict between popular taste and his own high standards was in fact one of the formative struggles of his career.[31] So much of our sense of Poe—so much of his own sense of himself—is of an artist whose ideals are tested and frequently compromised by the demands of editors and publishers, by necessity and hunger, and by the vagaries of popular taste. Even in the passage quoted above regarding the determination of a suitable length, Poe himself, in a telling lapse, admits that in deciding such a matter, he needed to pay heed to the "degree of excitement which I deemed not above the popular, while not below the critical, taste," or exactly what he just said was *not* a factor.

These moments of hyperbole in the practical applications of his theoretical principles combined with suspicious understatement regarding the pressing social and personal exigencies of authorship are compounded by two final pressure points at the close of the essay. The first is a peculiar argument that creeps up in Poe's explanation of why the narrator persists in tormenting himself by continually asking the raven, which he knows to be a mere animal, questions about his lost Lenore. In the middle of the essay, Poe gives a reading of his own poem when he explains that the narrator, though beginning rationally, eventually turns to superstition. Influenced by this mystical susceptibility and exacerbated by his psychological vulnerability, he "wildly propounds queries of a far different character—queries whose solution he has passionately at heart—propounds them half in superstition and half in that species of despair which delights in self-torture," ultimately deriving a "phrenzied pleasure" from the sorrow produced by the raven's inevitable answer of "nevermore" (*E&R* 19). What Poe is suggesting is a sort of emotional masochism on the narrator's part; he delights in sorrow just as the Gothic reader takes a certain pleasure in melancholy themes, the death of a beautiful woman included.

Just as the narrator experiences a delight of self-torture in conjuring up painful memories of Lenore, so too in "The Philosophy of Composition," Poe performs a species of *critical* self-torture, of analytic masochism in which he dissects the living body of his poem for his own delight and that of the public—and in the very magazine that rejected "The Raven" no less. This ambivalence regarding the critical act takes its most explicit form in the very next line in which Poe pauses to suggest the limits of the type of analysis he has up to this point been enacting: "But in subjects so handled, however skillfully, or with however vivid an array of incident," Poe reminds us, "there is always a certain hardness or nakedness, which repels the artistical eye" (*E&R* 24). While Poe has been working to lay bare the mechanisms of his poem, to provide a candid exposé of the laborious poetic process, now he arrives at the last stage. Like a painter globbing on a final coat of varnish, Poe suggests that the final step of the poetic process is to add "some amount of complexity, or more properly, adaptation; and secondly, some amount of suggestiveness—some under current, however indefinite of meaning," for "it is this latter, in especial, which imparts to a work of art so much of that *richness* . . . which we are too fond of confounding with the *ideal*" (*E&R* 24). So, just like that, Poe tacks on an "under current of meaning" by adding the final two stanzas, stanzas which "dispose the mind to seek a moral" and encourage the reader "to regard the Raven as emblematical." And what is that moral, we might ask? As Poe pithily informs us, it is nothing other than *"Mournful and Never-ending Remembrance"* (*E&R* 25).

Just moments earlier, Poe warned us that there is a "hardness or nakedness" to criticism which "repels the artistical eye." Yet surely there is little that could be more unceremoniously demystifying than glossing your own poem's underlying meaning in four words. Early in the essay, Poe mocked the notion of romantic inspiration by which a poem spills fully formed onto the page; but so too throughout the essay and with vitriol at the close does Poe excoriate the equally ridiculous idea that a poet's process can be reduced to a step-by-step manual, to a machine-like assembly line, while simultaneously burlesquing the arrogance of critics—himself included—who think that the way to approach, understand, and appreciate a poem is through the cold analytic explication that had come to characterize the dissecting *zeitgeist* of antebellum criticism. To be sure, Poe is guilty of this himself. This awareness is, I would suggest, the driving force of the essay, a self-scrutiny akin to the bereaved lover's "thirst for self-torture." Thus, while Poe calls for a scientific criticism, for rules in both the construction and analysis of literature, he also knows full well the limits of critical inquiry.

If this critical masochism is subtle here, it is all but explicit in an unpublished piece entitled "A Reviewer Reviewed" in which Poe ruthlessly reviews himself under the pseudonym Walter G. Bowen. The self-review was prompted specifically by a versified attack appearing several months after "The Philosophy of Composition" in the December 1846 issue of *Graham's Magazine*, where an antagonist who went only by "W." blasted Poe's arrogance in presuming to criticize his own poem. The barb, entitled, "On P—, the Versifier, reviewing his own Verses," quipped: "When critics scourged him, there was scope / For self-amendment and for hope; / Reviewing his own verses, he / Has done the deed—*felo de se*" (*E&R* 1046). Though Mabbott assumes that Poe wrote his rejoinder years later, the suggestion seems unlikely; rather, Poe probably began drafting the article soon after the attack appeared in late 1846. For his own part, Mabbott doesn't know quite what to do with the article, calling it a "*jeu d'esprit*," and reading it as of a piece with other literary satires like "How to Write a Blackwood Article" or "The Literary Life of Thingum Bob, Esq.," though this too seems unlikely.[32] There are deeper motives at play than either simple retaliation or lighthearted literary satire; and though Poe had written puffing self-reviews before, one as recently as the previous year, this one was of a markedly different tone and intensity.

"A Reviewer Reviewed" is no puff, nor is it a self-defense. It is a mer-
ciless self-excoriation, a piece of fearless, honest criticism, but this time
directed by Poe squarely at himself. As Poe argues, since "Mr. Poe . . .
has done little else than 'ride rough shod' over what he is in the facetious habit of denominating the 'poor devil authors' of the land . . . I pre-
sume that neither you nor any body else will think it unreasonable that,
sooner or later, he should have the bitter chalice of criticism returned
to his own lip" (*E&R* 1046–47). Though the review begins with harm-
less self-praise regarding his fiction and poetry, it quickly turns sour on
the matter of criticism. "Of his criticisms I have not so much to observe
in the way of commendation," Poe writes, for while his reviews show
"scholarship, and the peculiar analytic talent which is the ruling feature in everything he writes," nonetheless, in almost all other respects
they are contemptible. "They show no respect for persons . . . they seem
to me bitter in the extreme, captious, faultfinding, and unnecessarily
severe . . . As for the beauties of a work, he appears to have made up
his mind to neglect them altogether . . . Real, honest, heartfelt praise is a
thing not to be looked for in criticism by Mr. Poe" (*E&R* 1047–48).

Admittedly, few of these criticisms were altogether novel since Poe
on numerous occasions defended his method of severe criticism against
attacks of a precisely similar sort; yet even so, Poe's review of himself
is as unflinchingly severe as he is in his most scathing reviews of others. "Even when it is his evident intention to be partial," Poe writes
of himself, "to compliment in an extravagant manner some of his *lady*
friends (for he never compliments a gentleman) there always seems to
be something constrained, and shall I say malicious, at the bottom of
the honey cup." "These blemishes," Poe concludes, "render his critical
judgments of little value. They may be read for their pungency, but all
the honesty they ever contain may be placed upon the point of a cam-
bric needle" (*E&R* 1048). It is no exaggeration to say that this review,
coming from Poe's own pen, is the harshest he ever received.

So too does Poe show a clear sense of his own critical hypocrisy, his
tendency to perpetrate literary crimes of which he himself incessantly
accuses others. Poe asserts, for example, that "as he has a most unman-
nerly habit of picking flaws in the grammar of other people, I feel justified in showing him that he is far from being immaculate himself,"
proceeding to catalogue a number of his own grammatical mistakes,

but not before beginning with his favorite charge of plagiarism. On this count, Poe is, we are told, as guilty as Longfellow or any of the others upon whom he has laid the accusation (*E&R* 1050). Finally, as for "The Philosophy of Composition," that "laudatory criticism on ['The Raven'] which he lately published in 'Graham,'" it is a "criticism which displayed, perhaps, more analysis than modesty." This last claim is telling, among other reasons, because it calls into question Mabbott's supposition that "A Reviewer Reviewed" was written in Poe's final months, suggesting instead through internal evidence that its composition date fell closer in proximity to the publication of "The Philosophy of Composition."

Even more interesting for our purposes is Poe's sense of his essay as both self-indulgent and, more significantly, as a display of "analysis" rather than a credible view into his actual methods. Here we come full circle to the epistolary exchange that opened this chapter and concluded Poe's life: for as Poe tells Miss Ingram, some things are beyond the province of the critic or even the artist to explain. There is something deforming in the act of critical analysis, moreover, something anathema to the true impact of poetry upon the soul. Those, like Yvor Winters, who chastise Poe for his supposed affirmation of the intentional fallacy, might do well to read his letter to Miss Ingram or the final paragraphs of "The Philosophy of Composition" more closely.[33] For in those final lines we find one of Poe's greatest and most enduring fictions in his assertion that a poet controls all elements of his poem, including something as abstract and intangible as "suggestiveness," of "under current[s], however indefinite of meaning." Rather, Poe's elaborate display of critical hubris and God-like authorial intention is both farce and self-torture, a perhaps too subtle joke (for indeed so few have gotten it) and an equally subtle display of critical masochism.

The tension of the essay is that while Poe's essay contains many key tenets central to his compositional philosophy and consistent with both his wider critical oeuvre and his literary practice, the essay *expresses* these principles in exacting, overblown language accompanied by displays of practical application that hinge on the improbable if not, at times, the absurd. In other words, the theories are sound, but their critical articulation is suspect. For past critics, the paradoxes of the essay have divided readings toward either our sense of Poe as prankster or our sense of him as romantic visionary; yet Poe was not exclusively one or the other, but both, and playing many other roles in addition to these two, including that of critic. Indeed, many of the essay's problems derive from the simple circumstance that Poe is playing two roles at the same time, roles generally kept distinct. Specifically, in writing a critical analysis of his own poem, and moreover, in claiming to lay bare his methods of composition, Poe is acting as both critic *and* poet.

While Poe famously claimed in his early "Letter to B—" that one must, in a sense, be a poet to be a critic, paradoxically, if "The Philosophy of Composition" tells us anything, it is that criticism and composition are emphatically different arts, and that skill in one does not necessarily translate to heightened perception in the other. It is this distinction that Poe admits early in the essay when he acknowledges that he has taken on the task at hand in part "since the interest of an analysis, or reconstruction . . . is quite independent of any real or fancied interest in the thing analyzed," and therefore, "it will not be regarded as a breach of decorum on my part to show the *modus operandi* by which some one of my works was put together" (*E&R* 14). This concession proves to be the seed of his failure, however, hinting at the impossibility of his task. It is in carrying out multiple literary offices at once—of critic and poet—that Poe reveals the limits of criticism in unveiling the mechanisms of art and the limits of constructivism in creating art. Poetic meaning is subjective and ineffable, while poetic construction is often haphazard, idiosyncratic, and its motives and methods frequently either mundane or inscrutable. Poetic construction occurs no more "with the precision and rigid consequence of a mathematical problem" than it does in a "fine frenzy," and it is in the clashing of Poe's dual vocations as critic and poet that we see a debunking of the mythic aggrandizement of each, of the idealization of the poet as God-like craftsman and of the critic as possessing access to secret realms of knowledge that ordinary readers lack.

It is my sense that the contradictions of "The Philosophy of Composition" are carefully within Poe's control and are meant to satirize the arrogance of criticism, an arrogance of which Poe was himself knowingly guilty. Though to call the essay a hoax is to miss its serious engagement with the problem of criticism on both a philosophical and a social level. Rather, the essay is more properly a burlesque of criticism, a concept which had been floating around in Poe's mind for well over a decade since the days of his earliest short stories. Situating the essay within the rapidly expanding culture of antebellum criticism, as well as in line with Poe's lifelong preoccupation with the analytic art, we can see the essay not simply as mischievous prank or straightforward poetics, but as a not altogether subtle commentary on the increasingly popular genre of literary criticism and the critical essay, a genre which in the 1830s and '40s was proving more and more difficult to ignore.

This isn't to say that Poe was above catering to popular tastes with his criticism, however. Indeed, one final irony of Poe's career as critic is that, while he insisted upon the importance of criticism to the fate of the national literature and observed with concern the potentially deforming impact of criticism on the experience of literature itself, Poe was also directly implicated in the growth of criticism as a popular, sensational form of entertainment in its own right. If Poe's critical burlesques—works like the abortive "Tales of the Folio Club" or the self-critical "A Reviewer Reviewed"—offer one window into the mischievous intent of "The Philosophy of Composition," his popular "Literati of New York City" series, commencing the same month that his deconstruction of "The Raven" appeared in *Graham's*, reveals just how strategic Poe was in crafting his critical persona, both in "The Philosophy of Composition" and throughout his critical career. If Poe's notoriety rested on his image as the Tomahawk, this was hardly by accident. Rather, for Poe, a critic's success increasingly depended on his or her ability to craft an effective critical persona. It is this process of critical self-fashioning that I turn to in the final section of this chapter.

Critical Personae: Sensation, Embodiment, and the Art of Critical Scandal

In April of 1846, the same month that "The Philosophy of Composition" was entertaining readers of *Graham's*, the first installment of Poe's "Literati of New York City" created a sensation when it debuted in the popular *Godey's Lady's Book*, a "namby-pamby" magazine if ever there was one. On the most practical level, the series was trying to reproduce both the form and the success of Lewis Gaylord Clark's "Editor's

Table," a segment which appeared with each installment of his New York *Knickerbocker* and traded in literary gossip as well as colorful portraits of New York literati. As Perry Miller notes, "the primary appeal of the *Knickerbocker*—especially outside the city—was that it dazzled a glamour-starved people by the sheen of a circle reputed to be, or that could present itself as, the ultimate in metropolitan sophistication."[34] Capitalizing upon Clark's strategy and pandering to the fad for literary gossip, Poe, in introducing the series, observes that, "with one or two exceptions I am well acquainted with every author to be introduced, and I shall avail myself of the acquaintance to convey, generally, some idea of the personal appearance of all who, in this regard, would be likely to interest the readers of the magazine" (*E&R* 1120–21).

Apparently the formula worked. Within a week and a half, the magazine's publisher, Hiram Fuller, noted that "the article on the 'New York Literati' in the April number of Godey's Lady's Book has compelled the publisher to print a second edition," adding piquantly that, "There is nothing in this country that sells so well as literary scandal."[35] By mid-May, demand for the first installment of the series and anticipation of the second was so high that proprietor Louis A. Godey offered to buy back copies of the previous issue for twenty-five cents each, only then to republish the first literati installment alongside the second in the June issue. Finally, in December of 1846, after a number of installments, Poe wrote to George Eveleth that with the November issue he had finally decided to conclude the series: "I was forced to do so," Poe wrote, "because I found that people insisted on considering them elaborate criticisms when I had no other design than critical *gossip*."[36] Poe admits as much in the series itself when he qualifies the ensuing portraits with the disclaimer that they are little more than "simple *opinion*, with little of either argument or detail" (*E&R* 1120). The success of the format was nevertheless a powerful argument in its favor, and though Poe dismissed the series as trifling, its popularity reinvigorated his determination to produce a critical history of American letters.

The sketches themselves are uncharacteristically amiable. Though Poe had become notorious for his critical severity, there is something decidedly genial about the "Literati" series. Of the thirty-eight sketches, there are far fewer cringe-inducing condemnations or far-fetched plagiarism accusations than we come to expect from Poe. He is liberal with both faint and fervent praise, meanwhile, and reins in his assessments of less gifted poets. As Poe writes, "in the series of papers which I now propose, my design is, in giving my own unbiased opinion of the *literati* (male and female) of New York, to give at the same time, very closely if not with absolute accuracy, that of conversational society in literary circles," and in this capacity, "it must be expected, of course, that, in innumerable particulars, I shall differ from the voice, that is to say, from what appears to be the voice of the public" (*E&R* 1120).

Throughout the series, Poe's founding premise is that there is a glaring discrepancy between written, public opinion regarding American authors and private, spoken opinion. In other words, we tend to flatter in print and tell the truth in person. Or as Poe puts it: "We place on paper without hesitation a tissue of flatteries, to which in society we could not give utterance without either blushing or laughing outright" (*E&R* 1119). This works both in terms of overestimation and underestimation, and Poe displays the principle by reference to Nathaniel Hawthorne, who while "scarcely recognized by the press or the public" is generally hailed as one of the best American authors in drawing rooms and salons. Conversely, Longfellow, though lauded ubiquitously by the press, is generally held by most literary men to be a decent, though overestimated poet.

A second and equally important distinction that Poe articulates in his introduction to the series is between authors whose esteem is based upon literary merit and authors who have merely gained the advantage of being in the public light. As he observes, "the most 'popular,' the most 'successful' writers among us, (for a brief period, at least,) are, ninety-nine times out of a hundred, persons of mere address, perseverance, effrontery—in a word, busy-bodies, toadies, quacks . . . In this way ephemeral 'reputations' are manufactured which, for the most part, serve all the purposes designed—that is to say, the putting money into the purse of the quack and the quack's publisher" (*E&R* 1118). Authors of true genius, on the other hand, invariably scorn "chicanery," as Poe calls it, and therefore seldom receive the public notice they deserve. In this way, so-called pioneers like Halleck, Willis, and Lydia Maria Child, though not without merit, are nonetheless overestimated simply because they were some of the earliest Americans to make a name for themselves and thus have been on the public stage the longest.

If being in the public eye is, as Poe observes, a key component to success, certainly he himself is aiming for the same attention in the *Godey's* series. With hits like "The Raven" and "The Gold Bug" behind him, Poe seems to have learned that the quality of one's work matters little unless one is actually known. In the transformed American literary marketplace of the 1840s, even literary genius needs a good publicist. If Hawthorne lacked this, Poe now understood that the savvy author needed to get himself noticed by whatever means necessary. And with the platform of the popular *Godey's*, Poe found that he did not always have to resort to his sensation-making, mean-spirited criticism. Publicity produced by the series was indeed two-fold: it brought attention to Poe and to those about whom he wrote. Everyone benefited.

It was one of the professed intentions of the series not only to evaluate the productions of the various literati but to conclude with "occasional words of personality," with "personality" meaning descriptions of the author's physical appearance, temperament, social standing, and even phrenological attributes. Over the course of the series, perhaps the harshest accusation Poe makes is when, in referring to Lewis Gaylord Clark, he notes that "as a literary man, [Clark] has about him no determinateness, no distinctiveness, no saliency of point . . . he is noticeable for nothing in the world except for the markedness by which he is noticeable for nothing" (*E&R* 1206). Though the estimation is clearly influenced by Poe's personal ire—for as Poe jests, "Mr. Clark once did me the honor to review my poems, and—I forgive him"—it also speaks to Poe's sense of the importance of personality, individuation, and embodiment on the part of the critic (*E&R* 1205).

If in the early days of the republic, anonymous disinterestedness was the mark of a good critic, the realities of the new literary marketplace rendered this antiquated notion obsolete. While criticism in the early republic generally went unsigned, marking it as part of the disinterested public sphere that Michael Warner, drawing on Habermas, has argued comprised the spiritual core of the early American republic of letters, it was one of Poe's central tenets that a just and honest criticism could *not* be anonymous.[37] Not only did anonymity degrade intellectual exertion into hackwork, it gave carte blanche to the

culture of puffery that already had a stranglehold on the critical vocation in the United States. As Poe observed, "The name of a writer being
known only to a few, it became to him an object not so much to write
well, as to write fluently, at so many guineas per sheet" (*E&R* 1028). For
criticism to maintain integrity and resist degradation, the author must
be held accountable for both the claims and quality of his work. Consequently, in articulating his guiding criteria for his projected magazine,
the *Stylus*, Poe assures us that, "it will eschew the stilted dullness of
our own Quarterlies, and while it *may*, if necessary, be no less learned,
will deem it wiser to be less anonymous" (*E&R* 1035).

In *Representations of the Intellectual*, Edward Said suggests that effective intellectuals are always publicly visible, representing their ideas as
much through their own embodied persona as through their writings
or speech. As Said argues, "in the outpouring of studies about intellectuals there has been far too much defining of the intellectual, and not
enough stock taken of the image, the signature, the actual intervention
and performance, all of which taken together constitute the very life-
blood of every real intellectual."[38] In the antebellum period, this principle is most readily evident in a figure like Frederick Douglass, whose
physical presence as a lecturer and public figure was one of his strongest arguments against claims of black intellectual inferiority and of
the institution of slavery more generally. Alternatively, N. Bryllion
Fagin has argued that it was from the theater that Poe, the child of two
actors, derived his keen sense of the performative quality of character,
or what in "The Philosophy of Composition" he refers to as the "the
literary *histrio*."[39] Either way, Poe's notorious life, his frequent literary
battles, his hoaxes and lecture antics, his semi-obsession with his own
daguerreotype image, as well as literary side projects like his "auto-
graph" series, his marginalia, and his "Literati" sketches all worked to
give physical shape to himself and others, to embody the disembodied
figure of authorship *literally* through Said's enumerated categories of
"the image, the signature, the actual intervention and performance."

Anticipating poststructuralism's emphasis on the cultural construction of identity, Poe seemed well aware, even in the 1840s, of the degree
to which the figure of the author is a deliberate construct. Indeed, on
the most general level, the "Literati" series speaks to the growing cen-

trality of personality criticism in antebellum magazines, those aspects of authorship that bordered on celebrity, that took an interest in biography, in the comings-and-goings of literati, of criticism as gossip, and the author as socialite. From the 1820s on through the 1850s, commentators debated the propriety of personality criticism and of the ad hominem attacks that such criticism frequently entailed, as for instance when, in a series of articles in the *Literary World*, the editor Charles Fenno Hoffman and a correspondent Charles Bristed debated the legitimacy of personal criticism in light of a reader's recent request for a "Spicy Cut-Up of an Author."[40]

Whether approved or disapproved of, however, the growing vogue for personality criticism framed Poe's legacy as well as his sense of the critical vocation. It is in this regard that Poe commends Nathaniel Parker Willis as remarkable even when his writings are decidedly unremarkable. For Poe observes that, "At a very young age Mr. Willis seems to have arrived at an understanding that, in a republic such as ours, the *mere* man of letters must ever be a cipher, and endeavoured [*sic*], accordingly, to unite the *éclat* of the *littérateur* with that of the man of fashion or of society. He 'pushed himself,' went much into the world, made friends with the gentler sex, 'delivered' poetical addresses, wrote 'scriptural' poems, traveled, sought the intimacy of noted women, and got into quarrels with notorious men. All these things served his purpose—if, indeed, I am right in supposing that he had any purpose at all" (*E&R* 1124). As Poe concludes, "it is quite probable that, as before hinted, he acted only in accordance with his physical temperament; but be this as it may, his personal greatly advanced, if it did not altogether establish his literary fame" (*E&R* 1124). While Willis has some estimable qualities, the final source of his fame must, for Poe, be attributed "to those *adventures* which grew immediately out of his animal constitution" (*E&R* 1124).

Not surprisingly, in his own career, Poe's methods for attaining notoriety looked suspiciously similar to those he describes for Willis. This insistence on the authorial body, on the "animal constitution" of the literary figure, is a far cry from the cold, analytic critical persona of "The Philosophy of Composition," moreover. In his deconstruction and aggressively anti-romantic reconstruction of "The Raven," the persona of the piece insists that the poem was assembled with the "precision and rigid consequence of a mathematical problem," phrasing which connotes more of a domino-like process of causality than a human artistic endeavor. While the essay brushes aside the worldly considerations of the poet, presenting the author as a poetry assembly line, a cold, calculating beauty machine, the "Literati" series boldly, and in an emphatically literal sense, *embodies* both the critic and the author. This sharp contrast between the two works is rendered even more striking on account of the fact that "The Philosophy of Composition" and the first of the "Literati" series appeared in the same month. The icy, almost disconcertingly intellectual, disembodied analysis of the former was the very same mind that for six months devoted itself to the literal embodiment—to the detailed physical, phrenological, and temperamental delineation—of New York's literary notables.

One way to understand this contrast is to view the essay alongside "The Murders in the Rue Morgue," in which a disembodied Dupin—pure intellect without any more physical description than that he is youthful—is startlingly juxtaposed to the brutal carnality of the orangutan, perhaps the most literal instance of "animal constitution" we are likely to find in Poe's oeuvre. Yet as Poe reminds us in a letter to Philip Pendleton Cooke, Dupin is smoke and mirrors, a fantastical creation who dazzles us with his "method, or *air* of method" while we as readers marvel at his "ratiocination." It was not Dupin alone that made "Rue Morgue" one of Poe's three most popular stories: surely the sensation of a murderous ape who stuffs a young woman up a chimney while all but decapitating her mother must account for at least part of the tale's success. In another sense, however, the story is remarkable for marrying the ethereal analytic ability of Dupin with the brutish corporeality of the ape, for successfully merging ratiocination with sensation, the pleasure of the higher faculties with a simultaneous indulging of the baser.

"Rue Morgue," and the mechanism of the Dupin tales more generally, bears close affinity to the so-called modus operandi of "The Philosophy of Composition." For as Poe candidly admits to Cooke, "You are right about the hair-splitting of my French friend:—that is all done for effect." As Poe explains, "These tales of ratiocination owe most of their popularity to being something in a new key. I do not mean to say that they are not ingenious—but people think them more ingenious than they are—on account of their method and *air* of method. In the 'Murders in the Rue Morgue', for instance, where is the ingenuity of unravelling a web which you yourself (the author) have woven for the express purpose of unravelling? The reader is made to confound the ingenuity of the suppositious Dupin with that of the writer of the story."[41]

It is in this very same letter that Poe refers to "The Philosophy of Composition" as his "best specimen of analysis," which is not mere coincidence. Just as Dupin impresses readers with his seemingly unassailable "*air* of method," the narrator of "The Philosophy of Composition" engages in a similarly ostentatious display of cold, critical logic. In both cases, the underlying trick is the same: namely, backwards composition. As Poe cagily asks, where's the difficulty in "unravelling a web which you yourself . . . have woven for the express purpose of unravelling?" In reviewing the British critic Thomas Macaulay, Poe points tellingly to "a tendency in the public mind towards logic for logic's sake—a liability to confound the vehicle with the conveyed—an aptitude to be so dazzled by the luminousness with which an idea is set forth, as to mistake it for the luminousness of the idea itself." Macaulay's logical style obscures the fact that his criticism lacks substance, or as Poe suggests, "it is indeed questionable whether they do not appertain rather to the trickery of thought's vehicle, than to thought itself—rather to reason's shadow than to reason" (*E&R* 321–22).

It is this very same symbiosis—between intellect and sensation, between critical analysis and critical posturing—that Poe came to accept and master regarding the figure of the antebellum critic. A successful critic weds analysis with an embodied persona. As he suggests with Hawthorne, genius is only part of the equation, for if no one is reading you, all the genius in the world will do you little good. Poe was sincere when he insisted that what America needed and what he would give it was a "fearless, honest criticism," but by 1845, after a series of dashed hopes in the quest for his own journal, after years of oblivion while lesser poets like Longfellow reveled in the spotlight, after years of lessons learned through pain and hunger, Poe knew that fearless honesty was nothing if no one was paying attention.

So Poe adapted. He gave popular magazines literary gossip while quietly working on his own book on the higher life of American letters. He employed an exaggerated "air of method" not only in his tales of ratiocination but in critical pieces like "The Philosophy of Composition," a mode of rhetoric that dazzled even while its substance might contain little truth. He learned to stir things up, to ruffle feathers, to cultivate hoaxes and feuds, scenes and scandals, all the while insisting upon a rigorous scientific discipline for critics. He flamboyantly wielded the tomahawk, not only against small-fry literati but against luminaries like Dickens and Bryant. And amidst the slashing, he injected his original critical theory and his exacting standards for literature, aspects through which he genuinely sought to elevate American letters.

Long before the advent of publicists and tabloids, Poe seemed precociously aware of the modern dictum "no press is bad press." This is explicitly evident in a letter he wrote to his friend and fellow Philadelphia journalist George Lippard regarding some abuse his friend had recently suffered at the hands of critics: "As for these personal enemies," Poe advised, "I cannot see that you need put yourself to any especial trouble about THEM . . . Let a fool alone . . . Besides—as to the real philosophy of the thing—you should regard small animosities—the animosities of small men—of the literary animalculae (who have their uses, beyond doubt)—as so many tokens of your ascent—or, rather, as so many stepping stones to your ambition." For as Poe reflects, "I have never yet been able to make up my mind whether I regard as the higher compliment, the approbation of a man of honor and talent, or the abuse of an ass or a blackguard. Both are excellent in their way—for a man who looks steadily up."[42]

This was a lesson Poe had learned years earlier, when, in 1835 in a letter to Thomas White justifying the gruesome, sensational quality of "Berenice"—a story which ends with an obsessed lover pulling out the teeth of his not-quite-so-dead beloved—he argues for the general utility of *Blackwood's* style sensation. While admitting that "the subject is by far too horrible," nonetheless, Poe insists that, "the history of all Magazines shows plainly that those which have attained celebrity were indebted for it to articles *similar in nature — to Berenice —* although, I grant you, far superior in style and execution." And "in what does this nature consist," Poe asks?

> In the ludicrous heightened into the grotesque: the fearful coloured into the horrible: the witty exaggerated into the burlesque: the singular wrought out into the strange and mystical. You may say all this is bad taste. I have my doubts about it . . . But whether the articles of which I speak are, or are not in bad taste is little to the purpose. To be appreciated you must be *read*, and these things are invariably sought with avidity. They are, if you will take notice, the articles which find their way into other periodicals, and into the papers, and in this manner, taking hold upon the public mind they augment the reputation of the source where they originated.[43]

Gore, violence, and scandal were neither incidental nor needlessly histrionic; rather, they were part of a deliberate strategy for drawing attention to oneself, for gaining notoriety through the cultivation of sensation.

It was a strategy Poe employed not only in his fiction but in his criticism as well. In a letter to his friend George Eveleth in 1848 regarding his feud with Thomas Dunn English, we see the degree to which Poe's scandals were deliberately cultivated, if not contrived outright. Calming the concerns of his friend, Poe assures him: "Believe me there exists no such dilemma as that in which a gentleman [is] placed when he is forced to reply to a blackguard. If he have any genius then is the time for its display. I confess to you that I rather *like* that reply of mine in a literary sense — and so do a great many of my friends. It fully answered its purpose beyond a doubt — would to Heaven every work of art did as much!" For as Poe candidly admits, "You err in supposing me to have been 'peevish' when I wrote the reply: — the peevishness was all 'put on' as a part of my argument — of my plan: — so was the 'indignation' with which I wound up. *How* could I be either [peev-]ish or indignant about a matter so well adapted to further my purposes? Were I able to afford so expensive a luxury as personal and especially as *refutable* abuse, I would [w]illingly pay any man $2000 per annum, to hammer away at me all the year round."[44]

Among Poe's many skills, not the least of his accomplishments resided here in the art of scandal. In his private comments regarding his battle with English, we see that Poe's critical reputation as the

Tomahawk was at least in part a deliberately constructed persona, a pose that was "put on" as a way to attract free publicity. So too, Poe suggests that his feuds have a certain artful quality to them, exhibiting a distinctive "literary sense" in playing up postures of peevishness and irritation, which proved both pleasing and amusing to himself and his friends. It is not the least of Poe's many contradictions that while he reiterated his call for a serious, near-scientific criticism, he also simultaneously perfected the art of self-publicity via literary scandal. If Poe frequently made headlines, it was not by accident.

In admitting that his critical postures were frequently put on, Poe draws a line of continuity between his criticism and his fiction. The notion of a first-person speaking voice distinct from that of the author is, in a literary sense, simply that of the persona, a narrative device with which Poe was extremely familiar. His stories are full of them, scores of nameless madmen narrators whose ability to produce rational discourse is but a thin veil to their insanity; or sometimes the unreliability of these narrators is more perfidious, cloaking itself in an air of carefully wrought authoritativeness, artfully calibrated to lend force to the deception. In *The Narrative of Arthur Gordon Pym*, for instance, Poe claims to be not the author but the editor of the ensuing manuscript, a supposedly true life account of a voyage to the South Pole. Poe's art, the verisimilitude of his tales, rested on these authoritative poses, and this narration is a key aspect of the romantic irony that defined so much of Poe's artistic achievement.[45] While Poe excelled at conjuring madmen, one of his other accomplished personae was what we might call the man of science—more properly, the jargon-wielding confidence man—a figure which bore much resemblance to his persona as critic and who relied on what Neil Harris has termed the "operational aesthetic," an increasingly popular mode of discourse that sought to explain and demystify the ongoing parade of technological marvels that by the 1840s had become a permanent aspect of antebellum cultural life.[46]

Poe was not alone in employing personae in his critical writings. Rather, the concept of the persona was crucial to the development of the essay as a genre. Though the twentieth-century essay largely established itself as a nonfictional form, distinct and apart from fictional literature, in its formative stages, particularly in the eighteenth and early nineteenth centuries, the line between fancy and fact was much thinner. In England, the essay and the novel developed alongside one another, each blending together elements of fiction and nonfiction and filtering social reality through the lenses of carefully constructed literary personae. Instead of Joseph Addison, Richard Steele, or Samuel Johnson, we see English society described through the eyes of the "Spectator," the "Tatler," or the "Rambler."

This convention persisted long into the nineteenth century as Thomas De Quincy's confessing opium-eater showed readers the seamy side of London life or Charles Lamb's cosmopolitan Elia toured the sunnier sides of the metropolis. "As developed from the popular broadsides of Joseph Addison and Richard Steele," Denise Gigante explains, "the periodical essay tradition afforded a peculiar opportunity for an author to create a character—more nearly, a pose or persona—who participated directly in the public sphere, thereby becoming something more than a fictional character." One benefit of the literary dimension of these essays, Gigante suggests, is that it forced readers to take a more active role and to be more critical of what they read. The critical persona of the essayist served as a constant reminder of the inevitable personal bias that lay behind all writing, whether novel or newspaper, forcing the public to approach their reading with a healthy air of critical detachment.[47]

Throughout his career, Poe constructed not one, but many personae. As a result, different readers are likely to encounter different Poes depending on what they are reading and which of Poe's personae they are confronting. In accounting for the proliferation of biographies, myths, and portrayals of Poe, meanwhile, each contending for a different vision of the author's life, we must look not only to the poststructuralist sense of the malleability of literary history, but less anachronistically to Poe's own highly conscious attention to and refinement of his authorial persona—or rather *personae*—as well as to his active efforts to give physical form to the disembodied figure of the critic more generally. It was in pursuit of this objective that the "Literati" series sought to embody the prominent figures of the New York literary scene.

The fact that the "Literati" series commenced the same month "The Philosophy of Composition" appeared suggests, moreover, that for Poe, criticism covered not one, but a range of functions from literary

gossip to analytic science. Nor does the fact that Poe accepted the taw-
drier sides of criticism preclude his more elevated conceptions of the
critical vocation as both science and as spur to the national literature.
That Poe was savvy about the cultivation of critical personae, the pro-
motional value of critical controversy, or the popular appeal of critical
analysis for its own sake is not to say that Poe doubted criticism's pivotal role within antebellum literary culture. The question, rather, was
what precisely that role should be. It was a question that Poe wrestled
with throughout his life as he produced not just reviews but a series of
works that reflected, often in experimental fashion, upon the place of
criticism in American culture, from "Tales of the Folio Club" and "The
Philosophy of Composition" to "The Literati of New York City."

Within the arc of Poe's critical career, while his first phantom collection, "Tales of the Folio Club," provided a first word regarding its
author's creative engagement with the vocation of literary criticism, a
second phantom volume at the end of his life adds a concluding unity
to that lifelong preoccupation. Just as Poe spent the early 1830s assembling a "burlesque upon criticism" for which he never found a publisher, so too did he spend the final years of his life in the late 1840s
intermittently working on a full-length critical study tentatively entitled "Literary America." As early as 1844, Poe mentioned in an offhand comment to James Russell Lowell that of late he was "very
industrious—collecting and arranging materials for a Critical History of Am. Literature."[48] When in 1846, the "Literati" series proved
immensely successful, Poe revived the idea with a new intensity, for as
he wrote to George Eveleth, "the unexpected circulation of the series,
also, suggested to me that I might make a hit and some profit, as well
as proper fame, by extending . . . the plan into that of *a book* on American Letters generally, and keeping the publication in my own hands."
Poe admits that in the "Literati" sketches "I thought too little of the
series myself to guard sufficiently against haste, inaccuracy, or prejudice," but he insists that in the projected critical volume, "I intend to be
thorough—as far as I can—to examine analytically, without reference

to previous opinions by anybody—all the salient points of Literature
in general—e.g. Poetry, The Drama, Criticism, Historical Writing—
Versification etc. etc."[49] While Poe brushed aside the "Literati" series
as literary gossip, something produced to be popular rather than pro-

found, "the book" as he called it, "will be *true*—according to the best of my abilities." As for writing it: "I am now *at* this—body & soul."[50]

Like "Tales of the Folio Club," "Literary America" never materialized, though references to it dot Poe's letters from 1846 to the end of his life. Today all that exists of the projected book is a manuscript held by the Huntington Library in San Marino, California, consisting of a handwritten title page and three articles along the "Literati" series line: specifically, sketches of Richard Adams Locke, "Thomas Dunn Brown" [i.e. English], and Christopher Pearse Cranch. As Arthur Hobson Quinn demurs, "if the three articles which comprise the manuscript represent Poe's conception of literary history, it is just as well that he did not publish it."[51] Yet we could also argue that Locke, editor of the sensational literary weekly the New York *Sun* and famous for the notorious "Moon Hoax," as well as English, with whom Poe had one of his most publicized and protracted critical feuds, might indeed represent a more honest, if cynical, vision of American critical culture as Poe saw it. Based on Poe's earlier remarks in letters, however, it seems safe to say that the existing manuscript does not reflect a full conception of the project. For in Poe's earlier expressed vision, we see the blueprints for a wide-ranging survey of American letters, one which is "true" to the best of his abilities, its spirit best conveyed, according to Poe, in pieces like his review of Hawthorne with its theory of the short story or "The Rationale of Verse."

Unfortunately, Poe died before "Literary America" ever came to fruition. In Poe's final years, after the death of Virginia in early 1847, he was increasingly distracted and unstable, putting his energy toward hasty courtships or further attempts to realize his dream of a magazine. Yet these two book projects—one abandoned, the other unfinished— are, I suggest, biographical bookends that provide remarkably consistent insight into Poe's lifelong intellectual investment in the theory and practice of criticism. Taken together, the two projects reveal both an ambivalence and a certain flexibility in Poe's conception of what criticism was and should be, a range of possibility visible not just in Poe's critical corpus but in antebellum critical culture more generally.

It is a testament to the precarious, multifaceted, and unsettled place of the critic in antebellum society that while Poe set out to redefine American criticism according to rigid artistic criteria, he also enjoyed the notoriety produced by the lower brand of tabloid criticism. Though modern critics like to imagine a tortured Poe resisting the adulterating demands of the literate mobs as best he could, in practice Poe was able to reconcile a lofty criticism with low literary gossip, though not always without a certain discomfort or hesitation, as "The Philosophy of Composition" suggests. He saw himself as a force for the elevation of American letters while cultivating petty feuds and scandals with other authors. He gave popular magazines literary gossip while quietly working on his own book on the higher life of American letters. And ultimately, he made a name for himself as a fearless critic while quietly maintaining that the true purpose of poetry and fiction was at best beyond and at worst distorted by the act of criticism.

Perversely, it is "The Philosophy of Composition," that classic deconstruction of the poetic process, which manages to unite the antithetical cultures of criticism that Poe struggled to negotiate throughout his career. For while others have debated its status as either sincere poetics or unabashed hoax, it is paradoxically both of these, a simultaneous exemplification and burlesque of Poe's own mode of coldly analytic criticism. It is in the same letter to Philip Pendleton Cooke expounding on Dupin that Poe refers to "The Philosophy of Composition" as his "best specimen of analysis," and in a sense it is, but not for the reasons it is most commonly anthologized as a straightforward presentation of his fundamental artistic philosophy. Rather, it is his "best specimen of analysis" because of the way it registers with a perceptive subtlety unrivaled by few of his best fictional and poetic works both the strengths and weaknesses of his own critical method. It is a fearless, honest criticism of *himself* as critic, and of his own brand of blade-wielding criticism at a moment when he and other critics were slowly but surely assuming a greater prominence on the American cultural stage.

CHAPTER 4

BLACK, WHITE, AND READ ALL OVER

Margaret Fuller and the Newspaper Book Review

FOUR MONTHS INTO his "Literati of New York City" series, when Edgar Allan Poe began drafting his sketch of fellow New York critic Margaret Fuller, he promptly encountered a difficulty. Though the conceit for the series had been that authors are frequently different in person from how they appear in print—a gap his series addressed—when it came to Fuller, Poe observed, "her personal character and her printed book are merely one and the same thing. We get access to her soul *as* directly from the one as from the other—no *more* readily from this than from that—easily from either." As Poe adds, "her acts are bookish and her books are less thoughts than acts," such that, "her literary and her conversational manner are identical." By August 1846, when Poe's sketch of Fuller appeared in *Godey's*, however, Fuller's reputation was linked less to "bookish" acts than to a different print media altogether. As Poe noted early in his sketch, though a former editor of the *Dial*, and author of *Summer on the Lakes* and *Woman in the Nineteenth Century*, "at present, she is assistant editor of 'The New York Tribune,' or rather a salaried contributor to that journal, for which she has furnished a great variety of matter, chiefly critical notices of new books, etc. etc., her articles being designated by an asterisk." He admired her criticism, moreover, remarking that her account of American publishing in her review of Harro Harring "did her infinite credit," "frank, candid, independent," while her review of Longfellow's poems is "one of the very few . . . ever published in

America, of which the critics have not had abundant reason to be ashamed."[1]

As two of antebellum America's most prominent critics, Poe and Fuller offer a study in contrasts. As critics, their orbits circled one another, with each reviewing the other on multiple occasions. Each writer had also made recent career moves to New York—Poe from Philadelphia, Fuller from Boston—a city that by 1840 had emerged as the center of the US publishing industry. For all their similarities, however, they managed their critical reputations differently. While Poe relished critical theatrics, savoring acts of critical destruction and cultivating feuds as a means of self-promotion, Fuller took pains to avoid drama. Though she was no less exacting in her reviews of mediocre authors or her assessment of the current state of American letters than Poe, she took no pleasure in cutting an author down, seeing such severity as a necessary means of improving that writer.

In this regard, Poe frustrated her. Of the class of "professed critics" in the country, Poe is "of all the band the most unsparing to others," Fuller lamented. Though honesty from critics was preferable to unmerited praise, still, "let their sternness be in the spirit of Love. Let them seek to understand the purpose and scope of an author, his capacity as well as his fulfilments, and how his faults are made to grow by the same sunshine that acts upon his virtues." Though the garden of American literature required careful tending, one must be careful "lest the flowers and grain be pulled up along with the weeds." Poe's flailing attacks, cataloguing of grammatical mistakes, and repeated accusations of plagiarism (typically from his own works) revealed no such discernment. Indeed, Fuller went so far as to suggest that Poe should give up criticism altogether and stick to writing tales, which she found excellent, even encouraging him to undertake a longer "metaphysical romance."[2]

In contrast to Poe's destructive critical approach, Fuller's critical theory was sympathetic and reproductive, maintaining that the critic's task was to judge a work according to the aims of the writer rather than by fixed standards, to clarify those aims to readers, and to help them understand the work by placing it within a series of elucidating contexts, whether biographical, historical, or philosophical. If Poe was tirelessly self-promoting, meanwhile, Fuller's critical persona was simultaneously effaced and asserted by the characteristic asterisk with which she signed each of her columns. Though at least one aggrieved author saw this signatory choice as a way to mask her gender, it was also an assertion of intellectual ownership over her *Tribune* pieces, a refusal to hide behind critical anonymity by leaving periodical pieces unsigned, as was common with newspapers, and a way for her to take credit for her work by distinguishing her own columns from those by Horace Greeley.[3]

Of all their differences, however, none was more pronounced than their respective investments in different periodical forms. While Poe always understood his literary vocation as that of a magazinist, Fuller's career had recently undergone a substantial shift from elite intellectual quarterly to popular daily newspaper, as she gave up her post as editor of the avant-garde Transcendentalist quarterly the *Dial* to become literary editor of Greeley's *Tribune*. She was still a critic and an editor, but like others immersed in the world of newspapers, Walt Whitman among them, she now assumed the mantle of journalist as well, a title Poe eschewed.[4]

These shifts in critical venue mattered. They mattered to Fuller's sense of her vocation, to the development of her critical theory, to the construction of her critical legacy, and ultimately to the ways we understand both antebellum critical culture and critical authority itself. While early twentieth-century accounts of Fuller as critic focus on her romantic critical theory, her role as an American interpolator of German literature and philosophy, Goethe in particular, and of French writers like George Sand and Madame de Staël, her tenure as a critic for one of the nation's leading newspapers at a moment when newspapers were establishing their dominance on the American cultural scene proved equally formative to her sense of the critical vocation.[5]

Only in the past thirty years, as more of Fuller's *Tribune* writings have been made available in modern editions, have scholars begun to assess her career as literary journalist, as well as the reasons for its long neglect.[6] While her career as newspaper critic transformed her sense of criticism's cultural role, as Fuller's anxiousness regarding her one published critical volume, *Papers on Literature and Art* (1846), suggests, it also explains at least partially her marginalization within histories of American criticism. For as Susan Belasco Smith notes, while the widespread male chauvinism of American literary scholarship in the first half of the twentieth century plays a role in this neglect, as does the tendency of her dramatic biography to eclipse her impressive critical oeuvre, equally significant is the fact that Fuller published the majority of her reviews in a medium whose power resided in its contemporaneity and cheapness, a form that is difficult to preserve and access from an archival perspective, and that resists both Foucault's author-function and literary canonization in ways that books and magazines do not. As such, Fuller's career as newspaper critic offers a compelling case study for how critical forms shape critical history in acknowledged and unacknowledged ways.[7]

Since the expansion of cheap newspapers in the 1830s, newspaper criticism has posed a challenge to literary history and to culturally embedded notions of critical authority, with literary journalism segregated, if not passed over completely, in surveys of antebellum criticism. For commentators both in the antebellum period and today, newspaper criticism falls short of widely accepted standards of critical value, prompting a series of recurring critiques that justify its neglect: newspaper criticism is written hastily by journalists unqualified for the critical task by their lack of expertise; it caters to the degraded tastes of the masses, on the one hand, and the interests of publishers, on the other; it speaks to the faddish concerns of the moment with little value beyond the present day; it is bad writing and offers subjective judgments rather than carefully formulated arguments; it trades in vulgar purchasing advice rather than eternal truths, serving the market rather than the mind, sales rather than souls. These sorts of critiques, still common in the twenty-first century, began to be voiced in the 1830s alongside the rise of the penny press, revealing the deep-seated biases of the critical institution as it developed in the nineteenth and twentieth centuries, a period when competing visions of professionalization—academic versus journalistic, specialist versus generalist, expert versus public intellectual—began to contend with one another.[8]

Alongside these prejudices against journalism, a complementary set of affirmative critical values became codified as well: the privileging of professional expertise and specialization; the construction of a critical hierarchy with academics at the top and journalists at the bottom; the valuing of long gestation periods and original argumentation for critical writing; the rejection of direct financial compensation as writing

motive; the identification of good critical writing with dense, technical language rather than a polished style or accessible prose; and mea-
suring critical success by professional metrics rather than by extent of
readership. As numerous scholars have observed, these distinctions
grew more robust in the late Victorian period in the careers of author-
critics like Matthew Arnold, William Dean Howells, and Henry James
before being institutionalized in the early twentieth century with New
Criticism and the emergence of academic English departments. They
are visible in nascent form in the debates over newspaper criticism in
the middle decades of the nineteenth century, however, debates largely
ignored within accounts of antebellum criticism.[9]

The scholarly neglect and devaluation of literary criticism published
in newspapers is particularly evident in estimations of Margaret Fuller's place within critical history. Beginning in the summer of 1835,
with critical submissions to her friend James Freeman Clarke's *Western
Messenger* then to Park Benjamin's *American Monthly Magazine*, Fuller
went on to earn her critical stripes as editor of the Transcendentalist
Dial, as for two years of fatiguing editorial labor without pay she cor-
ralled a frequently fractious group of writers, each with different agendas, levels of commitment, and literary ability. By the time the exasper-
ated and exhausted Fuller handed the editorial reins over to Emerson
in 1842, she had nonetheless managed to make a name for herself, both
through her series of so-called Conversations among Boston society
women and as one of the nation's most adept critics at the country's
most controversial, if not quite as widely read, intellectual quarterly.
During this period, she established her expertise in European literature, in burgeoning criticism of art and music, and, with the publication of "The Great Lawsuit: Man vs. Men, Woman vs. Women" in July
1843, as one of the strongest voices in the growing movement for wom-
en's rights.

The industrious New York editor Horace Greeley was one of many
readers who noted Fuller's career with interest, praising the *Dial* as
"the most interesting and valuable as well as the most original work
ever published in America," and reprinting excerpted material first
in his literary weekly the *New-Yorker* (1834–1841) and then in the
newly launched *New-York Tribune* (1841–1966), noting in the preface to a lengthy excerpt from "The Great Lawsuit" that "there is but

one woman in America who could have written it."[10] The following year, with the departure of Henry Raymond, who covered book
reviews and culture for the *Tribune*, Greeley at the suggestion of his
wife Mary, who had attended several of Fuller's Boston Conversations, asked Fuller to take over as literary editor at the paper. While
the *Dial* at its height had a circulation of three hundred, when Fuller
finally accepted the position at the *Tribune* and began work in December 1844, it claimed thirty thousand daily subscribers—fifty thousand
for the weekly edition—and twice as many actual readers stretching
from New England to Ohio.[11]

During the year and half that Fuller worked as literary editor of the
Tribune, she wrote two to three feature-length pieces a week at mini-
mum (though Greeley wished she would write faster), producing two
hundred and fifty articles signed with her characteristic "star" on subjects ranging from Emerson's *Essays: Second Series* in her first review to
Beethoven's symphonies; summer pleasure reading and the plight of
Irish immigrants; from verse collections by working-class poets to editorials on the treatment of female prisoners at Sing-Sing. In her capacity as literary editor, moreover, as Catherine Mitchell notes, Fuller contributed a range of other content beyond reviews and editorials, much
of which went unsigned, from translations and brief notices to introductions for the literary excerpts that she selected for the paper's pages.
On days when her longer pieces appeared, Mitchell adds, it was not
uncommon for Fuller to provide over a quarter of the paper's editorial
copy, calling into question Greeley's frequently cited complaint that
Fuller wasn't pulling her weight as editor.[12]

In her work as a literary critic, meanwhile, Fuller reviewed with discernment and restraint many of the most popular authors of the day,
including several who would become central to the US literary canon—
Emerson, Hawthorne, Melville, Poe, Douglass—balancing a temperate nationalism with a commitment to introducing foreign writers and
strains of thought to American audiences. Rather than merely passing
judgment on works that came across her desk, Fuller endeavored to
instruct readers more broadly on how to engage with literature, articulating and enacting a romantic critical theory grounded in the social
and political realities of urban-industrial America, and transforming
the abstracted Transcendental notion of self-culture into a socially-

engaged, reform-minded theory of reading geared not just to personal growth but to social and political change.

In carrying out her critical charge at the *Tribune*, finally, Fuller elevated the institution of criticism in America by refusing to engage in puffs or diatribes, book promotion or partisanship, reviewing works with a clarity, equanimity, and honesty that amounted to a new standard of critical professionalism—and without lowering herself to the kind of cruelty and pettiness indulged by critics like Poe. As Thomas Wentworth Higginson reflected years later, "[Fuller] entered on her work at a time when the whole standard of literary criticism, not only in America but in England needed mending," with insipid notices commonplace and the "tomahawk theory" of revenging slights still prevalent. "To the bad tendencies of the time her work furnished an excellent antidote," Higginson concludes. "In that epoch of strife which I so well remember, that storm-and-stress period, that *Sturm-und-Drangzeit*, she held the critical sway of the most powerful American journal with unimpaired dignity and courage. By comparing a single page of her collected works with any page, taken almost at random, of Edgar Poe's, we see the difference more clearly than it can be expressed in words."[13] If twentieth-century scholars were slow to come to the same appreciation of Fuller as her own contemporaries, today, in the second decade of the twenty-first century, Fuller has finally achieved her due recognition, assuming her place in the national canon she helped define.[14]

Though Fuller held sway at the "most powerful American journal" of its time, however, the irony of her tenure at the *Tribune* was that her critical output was simultaneously empowered and undercut by its publication within a daily newspaper. Her writing reached a large audience that was more diverse along socio-economic lines than any competing print media of its day but taken less seriously by the intellectual community. While the newspaper medium allowed her writing to have a broad cultural impact in the 1840s, the ephemerality of the material form limited her legacy as a critic. And while the journalistic vocation put her in closer contact with the social and political concerns of her moment, it gave her less time to reflect on the books under review and to refine her critical views. In many ways her post at the *Tribune* was the antithesis of what Emerson advocated for in his vision of the scholar—swayed by currents of the day rather than insulated from them—but it also lent her criticism greater urgency and impact.

To treat Fuller in the *Tribune*, accordingly, is to confront questions about how critical values, theories, and legacies are bound up with the print media that disseminate them. Ironically, as Fuller's corpus demonstrates, the critical works with the broadest cultural reach are often afforded the least authority within critical history. Prejudices that Fuller faced in the 1840s, prejudices linked to the newspaper medium itself, were reinforced by those who subsequently wrote literary history, as Fuller was allotted a second-tier status beneath that of Emerson, Poe, and Lowell, when mentioned at all. This neglect, as Bell Gale Chevigny notes, is due in part to idiosyncrasies of Fuller's life, cut short as she reached her intellectual prime and clouded by scandal regarding her marriage to Giovanni Ossoli, the uncertain circumstances of the birth of her child, and the young family's tragic demise in a shipwreck within sight of Fire Island. It was exacerbated too by the unreliable record of her life produced by those who commemorated it in the posthumous *Memoirs of Margaret Fuller Ossoli* (1852), as her life and achievements were distorted, bowdlerized, censored, and sanitized by friends and acquaintances who found her unconventional model of femininity off-putting, if not outright threatening, and gallantly endeavored to make it conform to more conventional social narratives.[15]

Yet Fuller's marginalization within critical history is also due to biases against the intellectual purity of literary journalism in contrast to academic scholarship and to literary criticism in higher prestige periodical forms—quarterlies like the *North American Review*, the *Dial*, and the *Christian Examiner* or wide circulation monthly magazines like *Graham's* or the *Atlantic*—as well as to material challenges inherent in the newspaper form itself. Her articles flew on the "paper wings of every day," as Fuller put it, but had brief flights.[16] The precarious material existence of newspapers made them ubiquitous when first published but difficult to access after their initial appearance. Their cheapness was both asset and liability, giving them a wide audience geographically but a limited one temporally and making them difficult to preserve. Even while working at the *Tribune*, as Fuller assessed her future prospects while surveying her past achievements, the ephemerality of her critical medium worried her, and it proved debilitating to her critical legacy after her death.

Though Fuller's concern over her critical legacy was understandable, the power of newspapers has also never resided in their longevity and permanence. Rather, as a print form, newspapers embody contemporaneity, reach, and diversity of contents. Their power, as Benedict Anderson has argued, is to create a sense of temporal simultaneity and geographical continuity among disparate readers, organizing diverse contents under a single banner and date. And though numerous scholars have endeavored to puncture the print-capitalist fantasy of Anderson's "imagined communities," his view of newspapers as fostering a sense of simultaneity and connection, projecting visions of coherence, national identity, as well as systems of values to a vast constituency of readers, Anderson's theoretical framework remains intact.[17] Fuller stated the appeal of newspapers herself more bluntly, observing in a letter that, "I value my present position very much, as enabling me to speak effectually some right words to a large circle; and while I can do so, am content."[18]

Such debates over the comparative power and limitations of newspapers, their demographic reach and temporal constraints, their unquestionable influence weighed against their dubious intellectual authority, are hardly confined to twentieth and twenty-first century scholarship. Rather, throughout the antebellum period, contemporary observers responding to the rapid growth of the newspaper industry amid the rise of the penny press debated the potential value of newspapers as well as the threats it posed. In these debates over the legitimacy of newspaper criticism, we see early articulations of still lingering biases against literary journalism, as well as the emergence of a long overlooked antebellum critical genre: the newspaper book review.

Debating Newspaper Criticism:
Literary Criticism and the Rise of the Penny Press

As countless commentators from Alexis de Tocqueville to Paul Starr have noted, the growth of newspapers in antebellum America was dramatic, with far-reaching implications for all aspects of American social and political life. "After 1833, the newspaper became the key element in a web of mass production, mass consumption, and mass communication that has come to characterize life in America," Christopher Daly observes. "If we live in a media age, it is because of decisions made, struggles fought, and power wielded in the crucial period before the Civil War."[19] In 1790, Americans published ninety-nine newspapers, only eight of which were dailies. These papers were produced on wooden handpresses, a technology that, as Andie Tucher notes, remained fundamentally unchanged since Gutenberg, sold by subscriptions payable in advance, with a year's subscription to a daily newspaper costing up to ten dollars and a weekly just under five dollars. The high price and advance subscription model limited readership primarily to wealthy citizens engaged in the worlds of commerce and politics, a model that persisted through the 1820s as newspapers continued to be primarily either mercantile or explicitly partisan in orientation, giving precedence to reports of ship arrivals and commodity prices or political news directed toward the parties that bankrolled them.[20]

This all changed in the 1830s with the advent of the penny press. When Benjamin Day's New York *Sun* issued its first number on September 3, 1833, it marked a new stage of development for the news, lowering the price of papers from the six cents charged by the commercial and party papers to one cent. Day expanded beyond an exclusive subscription model as well, enlisting newsboys to hawk papers on the streets and at railroad depots and introducing a new business model for newspapers that relied on low price, high circulation, and advertising revenue instead of subscription payment or party subsidies. Following a consumer-based market logic, as Michael Schudson describes, editors like Day and James Gordon Bennett created a product that they sold at a reduced price to an enlarged readership and then sold that readership to advertisers. That product was the "news," a formula they refined as editors and publishers worked to make newspapers more appealing to general readers.[21]

Freed from a reliance on political patronage and from the business concerns of the mercantile class, the penny papers became less restricted to political and commercial dealings and more committed to attracting and sustaining a wider demographic of readers through diverse and engaging content. In Day's *Sun,* staples of modern news culture became permanent features of the papers. Rather than printing speeches or transcripts of Congressional proceedings, editors enlisted paid reporters and domestic and foreign correspondents to gather political news and present it in a lively manner. Editors entertained readers with human interest stories, sensational police and court reporting, sports news, and colorful accounts of social life drawn from high society and the seedier world of the bars and tenements. Features like the notorious "Moon Hoax," which caused a stir when the *Sun* reported that a high-powered telescope had discovered winged bat-men on the moon, were only extreme examples of Day's push to make the news engaging to a wider range of readers. And though political affiliations didn't disappear altogether, coverage of events began to trump the promotion of partisan causes. A moralizing tone began to disappear as well, as editors accepted any advertisement that could pay the paper's rates, from beer gardens and vaudeville performances to gonorrhea pills. While editors presented such inclusivity as a principled stance, in their coverage of news, as Schudson notes, they touted the virtues of accuracy, comprehensiveness, and timely reporting.[22]

Despite frequent charges of sensationalism and immorality, particularly from the six-cent papers, the penny weeklies thrived, expanding the focus of the newspapers from the affairs of the wealthy, from business and politics, to the social world of its diverse urban readership, which now extended to the increasingly literate middle and working classes. In the process, the newspaper began to serve as a way for readers to make sense of a social world that was rapidly transforming under the forces of industrialization and urbanization. Careful to resist the temptations of technological determinism so prevalent in histories of the penny press, Schudson reminds us that it was the innovative content of the newspapers as much as the reduced price that drove their increasing circulation. For readers, the newspaper presented itself as essential reading for any enterprising American who hoped to rise in the world, quickly establishing itself as indispensable a guide to urban-industrial America as the Farmer's Almanac had been for colonial and republican readers.[23]

The growth that resulted from the reduced cost and livelier contents was dramatic. While in 1830 the United States counted sixty-five daily newspapers with a combined circulation of 78,000, by 1840 that number more than doubled to 138 dailies with a total circulation of 300,000.[24] By 1830, New York emerged as the nation's publishing center, outpacing Boston and Philadelphia, the former centers of colonial publishing, while the introduction of the telegraph quickened editors' abilities to report national political news from Washington. Of the 1,631 periodicals recorded in the 1840 census—a number that increased to 2,526 by 1850 and 4,051 by 1860—New York State led the pack with 302 papers, followed by Pennsylvania (229), Ohio (143), Massachusetts (105), and Indiana (76), reflecting both the lingering strength of colonial publishing centers and the westward push of the nation.[25]

The New York City directory for 1845 listed seventy newspapers in the city alone. While Day's *Sun* introduced the penny daily to New York, within years it faced fierce competition from Bennett's *Herald* and Greeley's *Tribune*, as well as from more expensive papers like the six-cent *Courier and Enquirer* and William Cullen Bryant's *Evening Post*.[26] As large circulation papers aimed at a mass audience, each of the three major penny papers rode the wave of the cheap press, though they worked to differentiate themselves as well, quickly coming to occupy different urban niches as by the mid-1830s a growing number of papers began catering to specific demographics, not just at the top of the social ladder but up and down it, as well as by race, religion, and ethnicity. The innovation of Day's *Sun* was to cater to a large working-class audience through sensational material, shifting the motive from politics to sales. When Bennett started his *Herald* in 1835, he imitated Day's model, though he geared his paper toward more affluent middle-class readers. Greeley in turn launched his more reform-minded, Whig-leaning *Tribune* in 1841, pushing the *Herald* to become more firmly Democratic in its own politics.

Though politics continued to play a role, orienting each paper toward its readership and differentiating the papers from one another, however, it was less decisive than in the days of the early partisan press of the republican and national periods. As John Nerone observes, the entire stance of editors toward the place of politics within the news shifted as editors like Day, Bennett, Greeley, and Bryant endeavored to strike a sustainable balance between broad commercial appeal and competitive differentiation along political lines, distinguishing and increasingly segregating ideological editorials from the factual reporting of political events, as well as from commercial and general interest subjects. If Greeley's innovation was to take the format of the penny press, which leaned Democratic in Bennett's *Herald*, and to apply it to a more progressive Whig sensibility, he did so without sacrificing a large readership.[27]

While scholarly accounts of the development of antebellum newspapers are numerous, as are studies of American literary criticism, however, scholars have paid little attention to the place of literary criticism in antebellum newspapers. Rather, within both nineteenth-century assessments and twentieth-century periodical studies, newspapers have frequently been dismissed as a print media incapable of producing critical judgments of enduring value, with literary journalism, even by major names like Whitman and Lydia Maria Child, underrepresented in critical histories and anthologies. Most accounts of nineteenth-century literary journalism within twentieth-century literary studies instead focus on the formative impact of journalistic careers on canonical authors' developing literary style and subject matter—the "apprenticeship" model of journalistic influence as Mark Canada terms it—whether of Walt Whitman's populist poetics or the emergence of realism in the works of one-time journalists like Stephen Crane, William Dean Howells, Mark Twain, or Frank Norris.[28]

In this teleological model, newspaper writing is a means rather than an end, an early career stage to be transcended as an author's artistic ambitions find expression through more respectable, enduring forms and genres. And while periodical studies as a subfield situated at the intersection of book history, New Historicism, and reception studies has flourished in the past twenty years, with dedicated journals, edited collections, and standing conference panels, when it comes to histories of American criticism, there has been little accounting of the ways in which cultural hierarchies and material affordances within and among competing antebellum periodical forms shaped literary criticism as a practice in the nineteenth-century and continue to do so today.[29] This gap is all the more notable given that for antebellum critics, as I've argued, periodical forms signified more powerfully than either political affiliation (Whig versus Democrat; Knickerbockers versus Young Americans) or critical school (neoclassical versus romantic; moralistic versus aesthetic) as a way to understand comparatively and taxonomically their own critical practice in relation to others.

The marginalization of newspapers specifically has a long history

that began with the growth of the cheap press in the 1830s and in the
frequent debates over "newspaper criticism," as observers termed it—
that is, of reviews published in newspapers—in which the impact of
the newspaper medium on critical content became a subject of contention among antebellum commentators. While debates over criticism in
the 1820s centered on the quarterly reviews and the "paper wars" of
Anglo-American cultural feuding, in the 1830s the growth of the penny
press sparked a new discussion over the value of criticism in different types of periodicals. In addition to continued concern over literary nationalism playing out in the quarterlies, critics began to weigh in
on the comparative merits of criticism in quarterly reviews, monthly
magazines, and the newest contender on the antebellum print culture
stage: cheap daily newspapers. These concerns were less bound up
with nationalist anxieties than with explicit and implicit class anxieties
and with the steadily growing influence that newspapers were coming
to play on the social and political scene, not just among wealthy readers but among the middle and working classes who could increasingly
afford the cheap price of newspapers, and whose contents grew in sensational allure as they decreased in price.

Beginning in the 1830s, a recurring strain of criticism emerged that
dismissed newspaper criticism as trash, little more than puffs and
advertisements masquerading as critical judgment. As a commentator for the New York *Mirror* wrote in August 1833, "the criticism to
be found in newspapers, both British and American, is worse than
worthless. Weak tea and bread and butter—milk and water—we cannot think of any thing stale, diluted, insipid enough for comparison."
The insipidness of newspaper criticism, which provided no moral or
aesthetic value, traversed national boundaries, as the commentator
substitutes different periodical forms, hierarchically arranged, for the
standard differentiation along national lines. Nor is there any question as to what one might expect from newspaper criticism: "With
very rare exceptions, but one character pervades all the dailies, weeklies and monthlies wherever the English language is written—puff—
puff—puff; morning, noon and night—summer and winter—octavos,
quartos, folios—blue covers, yellow covers, white, green and brown.
Nothing but puff."

Newspapers have stripped criticism of all credibility, moreover,

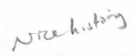

with Shakespeare, Addison, and Pope placed on the same level as the day's most recent versifier, puffed vociferously by booksellers. "Works described as of the most intense and fearful interest, and extraordinary merit, have turned out to be no better than catch-penny concerns—old uninteresting materials wrought up anew, and garnished with all kinds of ridiculous and improbable events. We read tales of the 'most exquisite wit,' with imperturbable gravity. We yawn over the 'incidents of an awful description' . . . Occasionally, it is true, we accidentally alight upon a book worth reading, but it is quite likely that it is one which has been woefully overlooked by the sleepy Aristarchuses of the press, because the author was too proud to send it round on a begging expedition."[30]

Such views of newspaper criticism were ubiquitous, singling out newspapers as the worst offender in the plague of puffery afflicting criticism. The commentator for the *Mirror* doesn't bother to distinguish among newspapers—daily, weekly, or monthly—but rather dismisses all newspaper editors as publishers' lackeys, alternately too corrupt and too distracted to offer legitimate criticisms of works forwarded to them by publishing houses. It seems no coincidence, moreover, that the *Mirror*, which billed itself as a literary weekly "Devoted to Literature and the Fine Arts" but formatted like a newspaper to benefit from postage rates, and which had made a cottage industry of similar attacks on critical malfeasance of all sorts, wanted to separate itself from the pack, elevating itself by putting down its competition. Whatever else they might be good for, the *Mirror* suggests, newspapers were not a reliable source of guidance on literary matters. Such critiques could do little to stem the tide of cheap newspapers, however. Indeed, just one month after the *Mirror*'s wholesale attack on newspaper criticism, on September 3, 1833, Day issued the first number of his *Sun*, setting in motion the transformation of the newspaper business and the birth of the mass media in America.

While penny papers took antebellum America by storm, transforming the nature of the news and expanding its readership, however, daily papers remained largely unconcerned with literary matters. The critique of newspaper criticism by the *Mirror* in this sense overestimates the degree of literary coverage in the daily papers. With one or two exceptions, as of 1833 when the *Mirror* issued its attack, daily

papers barely treated literature at all, with coverage limited to an occasional bookseller's advertisement or a few lines announcing a new
work. Its coverage of culture more broadly, meanwhile, generally consisted of announcements for musical or theatrical performances, muse-
ums, or sideshows, with a few lines of perfunctory praise. And while
more substantial treatment could be found in a select few papers like
Charles Greene's Boston *Post* or in literary weeklies like the *Mirror* or
Greeley's own *New-Yorker*, these were the exceptions rather than the
rule. Rather, as Joan Shelley Rubin notes, most criticism that did appear
in antebellum newspapers was of the literary "news" variety—brief,
unsigned notices announcing new works with a line or two of perfunctory comment—rather than full-blown reviews.[31]

What little criticism *did* appear in newspapers, however, began to be
of greater concern to commentators as the status, readership, and influence of newspapers continued to grow. For William A. Jones, in his
two-part survey of contemporary criticism in the *Democratic Review*,
reviews in newspapers barely qualify as criticism at all: "Newspaper
criticism, in this country at least . . . discovers the very lowest phase of
the art of criticism," Jones insists. "It is indeed a perversion of the term
to apply it to the paragraphs of alternate praise and blame, alike indis-
criminating and exaggerated, which pass under that name." As for
newspaper critics themselves: "They are the least of the small critics;
the most microscopic of the minute philosophers; their judgments are
purely fragmentary and as detached, if not as deep, as the maxims of
the old Gnomic philosophers, or the more modern Orphic (transcendental) sayings." And though some might deem it a waste of energy
even to critique these "ephemeral scribblers," as Jones asserts, "any
one who knows the vast influence the daily press exerts upon public
opinion, will not think a little earnest remonstrance against the vices
of this kind of writing (which may be brought to a high pitch of per-
fection, and for that reason deserves the more reprehension because
so egregiously abused) and the evils it occasions, thrown away or ill
judged."[32]

Only in the second installment of his survey does Jones qualify his
censure somewhat, acknowledging the practical challenges that newspaper editors face. For starters, they have too much on their plates:
"Too often, politics, news, city gossip, theatrical criticism, notices of

new books, come from the same hand which indites paragraphs on pictures, the streets, and the health of the city." Editors face social pressures as well, as in their capacity as reviewers every author expects praise while political parties expect loyalty to their espoused causes and members. The more serious problem, however, is that editors lack the necessary training as critics. "With such slight preparations, how is a writer to be able, almost extemporaneously, to form opinions on questions of political economy or national law—to judge accurately and describe vividly the characters of leading public men or popular writers—to discriminate merit in a new author?" Jones asks. "How can a puritanical New Englander manage to convey his impression of a theatrical performance, distinguish the meshes of a plot, or analyze the incidents of a ballet? With what an untutored eye he will regard paintings! and a thousand things quite new to him, but which he should know everything about, if he ever expects to become a clear critic."

Rejecting the belletristic critical model of the national period described by William Charvat, with doctors, lawyers, and ministers moonlighting as critics, Jones insists that criticism is a profession in its own right, requiring specialized training, tempered judgment, broad erudition, and wide reading. Not just any old newspaper editor can do it, however clever and well-meaning he might be. Nor is this a trifling matter: performed properly, a "pure literary criticism" could be invaluable in contributing to "the work of popular reformation." It is precisely for this reason, Jones concludes, that "we look for a better, a purer, a more enlightened and liberal school of criticism than has yet subsisted here."[33]

To be sure, Jones, who was part of a growing class of professional critics who managed to eke out a living writing for magazines like the *Democratic Review* and *Graham's,* imagined himself as representative of this "enlightened . . . liberal school of criticism." He had a decided interest in asserting his own critical authority as superior to that of newspaper editors whom he characterized as shrewd and well-meaning but lacking the sort of literary expertise that devoted critics like himself undoubtedly possessed. In his assertion of the authority of the professional critic, it isn't only newspaper editors at whom he takes aim. Rather, for those interested in obtaining a "literary caste," the two professional options available are college professor and journal editor, and

of these the journalist is far superior, "uniting the opposite characters
of scholars and men of the world: both readers and writers; authors
and critics; at the same time, men of action and speculative observers
of the great Drama of Life going on before them." In short, college professors are out of touch with the real world while literary critics at the
journals are forced to confront it on a daily basis—a fact that lends their
judgments a grounded, practical quality.[34]

The more newspapers came to dominate American print culture, the more vocal the attacks on newspaper criticism became. The
fact that newspapers were rapidly eclipsing other forms of periodical reading gave urgency to the critiques of newspaper criticism. If in
1844 Jones derided newspaper editors as "the least of the small critics," unequipped to the particular demands of reviewing, by January
1856 a commentator for the *American Publishers' Circular* writing under
the initials T. W. M. worried still further that "the PRESS has gradually
sapped the influence—literary, political, and secular—of the priest."
"There are now but few intelligent citizens in the land," the commentator notes, "who do not peruse the morning newspapers before they
take coffee." Nor is it only political news they glean from it; increasingly, discussions of moral and religious questions as well as art and
literature all find their way to the public through the daily newspapers.
"To the mechanic, the farmer, the clerk, and the merchant, this consti-
tutes the principal medium of information as well as of education; and,
if properly conducted, it would constitute, after the Bible, one of the finest 'Institutions' of which a free country might justly boast." Though,
of course, it has not been conducted properly, and its power for harm is
equal to, if not greater than, its potential for good.[35]

In wielding this powerful engine of influence, it is in their capacities as critics specifically that newspaper editors have proven themselves most deficient, the commentator insists, carrying out the critical
office in a careless, perfunctory manner and thereby neglecting their
duty as arbiters of literary taste, defenders or morality, and proponents
of national education. In the remainder of the article, accordingly, the
commentator enumerates the necessary qualifications for a critic: he
must be a man of "accomplished and cultivated genius"; he should be
conversant in classical literature, the literature of Germany and France,
and the English classics; he should know the world of painting and

sculpture; be well versed in scientific discovery, philology, theology, history and the philosophy of history. In reviewing works, he should be impartial and magnanimous, avoiding meritless praise as well as intemperate censure, admitting freely those assumptions on which he differs from the author under review.

This critical ideal is far from the current practice of newspaper criticism, however, in which, "Week after week, the same stereotyped nonsense and exaggerations—about 'pathos,' 'intense interest,' 'general usefulness,' 'tenderness,' 'fine type,' beautiful paper,' and 'rich binding,'—by which the last as well as the present generations were so often swindled out of their money, and seduced into the perusal of bad books—are printed in the columns of influential newspapers." As the commentator concludes, "It is the unblushing scandal of which the American people have so completely sickened; and not of literature. Give them honest, candid, fearless, able and elegant criticism; and it will be found more acceptable to the public, and more generally welcomed in the family circle, than the longest reports of murders, seductions, and the general catalogue of crimes, which are the result and disgrace, alike, of the baser passions." In short, "Every literary review could be made useful, instructive and interesting."[36]

For those actually engaged in the labor of producing a daily newspaper, however, such a daunting list of qualifications was laughable. Four days after the *Publishers' Circular* article appeared, an editor from the *New York Times*, which by 1856 had joined the ranks of the *Tribune* and *Herald* as one of the city's most influential papers, responded by pointing out the impossibility of such a critical polymath as the *Publishers' Circular* envisioned:

The literary critic of a daily paper, according to the requirements of the *Circular*, should be a gentleman of great natural endowments, and of a liberal education, of unimpeachable morals and infallible taste; he should have the health of a HERCULES to enable him to bear up under the labor of reading everything; he should be as industrious as MACAULAY, and as learned as MAGLIABECHI; . . . and in addition to all his other qualifications, natural and acquired, he should possess the faculty of always pronouncing a right judgment, and of being better informed on any subject he reviews than the author whose work furnishes him the occasion for an article . . . In short, the literary critic of a newspaper should not only be an impossible person, but he should perform impossible feats. We will wish the *Publishers' Circular* nothing worse than that it may continue to prosper until it shall meet with its idea of what a literary critic should be; and if, in the meanwhile, it should happen to find a person having only a moiety of the qualifications desired, we shall be most happy to secure the services of such a Phenix [sic].[37]

In other words, the *New York Times* points out how much easier it is to wax philosophical about what criticism should be than to meet the practical task of criticism in a daily paper. No one person can be an expert in all things, nor does the editor tasked with the critical office have limitless time. He can't read all books or know the subjects of the works reviewed better than the authors themselves. The commentator for the *Publishers' Circular* demands too much, envisioning an impossible ideal.

The *Times*'s response in turn prompted a rejoinder from the *Publishers' Circular*. It is the steadily increasing power of the press, T. W. M. retorts, that raises the bar of responsibility for critics who, for good or ill, have become gatekeepers of national culture. "When it is remembered that the weekly circulation of that journal [the *New York Times*] surpasses the actual number of 'Uncle Tom's Cabin' sold in the American market, it cannot be doubted that its means of cultivating public taste is almost boundless." "There is no other power in the United States . . . which has within its immediate reach the means of doing so much public good as the Press," the commentator insists: "Compared with it, the schoolhouse, the bar, the pulpit, sink into insignificance." The newspaper positions itself as judge and arbiter of matters of greatest import, claims a wide and growing influence, and therefore must hold itself to a higher standard. Even admitting the practical challenges that newspaper editors face, T. W. M. insists, it is incumbent upon them to rise to the challenge. It is a shame, too, that particularly in matters of literature and culture, newspapers have proven so woefully deficient, failing in the critical office that falls to them by inadequately guiding readers who turn to the papers for advice in navigating the tide of books that flow daily from the press.[38]

As early as 1840, there was wide agreement among commentators as to the enormous power of the press, its ability to reach huge swaths of the population, to shape public opinion and serve as a tool of education. "Give me the making of the newspapers of a nation, and I will make its minds," a commentator for the *Democratic Review* proclaimed in 1842: "The newspaper is everywhere, in the counting-house and in the parlor, in the bar-room and in the bed-room, on board of the steamboat and in the student's chamber. All subjects are discussed in it; all classes of men read it; and all men, to an extent, are affected by what it contains." Unlike the preacher, teacher, or orator, however, the editor's power is not limited to Sunday church services, the class-room, or to public occasions but rather exerts itself constantly. Yet for this observer, the growing demand for newspapers is cause for cele-bration rather than concern: "One of the best signs of the times is the growing demand for newspapers, cheap books, and literary and sci-entific lectures," the writer notes. "It is a sign that the love of knowl-edge is spreading through all classes; that the treasures of philosophy and poetry are no longer to be shut up in rare caskets, to be the posses-sions of the few; that the general mind, too long satisfied with low and sensual delights, is seeking for higher aliment. The mass of men are availing themselves of the means of improvement which a condition of freedom furnishes, and call for an increased number of instructors and guides."

The more perplexing question, rather, was why, given the indisput-able influence of the press, more writers of talent hadn't joined its ranks. "Why is it that a vehicle so intimately connected with human happiness as the press, so powerful over social issues and human destinies, has so seldom been desired by men of the loftiest endowments?"[39] The cul-tural importance of the medium demanded editors of talent who rec-ognized "the momentous responsibilities that hang upon their power," who perceived "the elevation and might of their position," and who rose to the dignity of the office. By January 1842 when the *Democratic Review*'s article on journalism appeared, few had answered that call, however. And though the commentator could name Orestes Brownson and William Cullen Bryant as editors who brought passion and ability to their office, they were the exceptions rather than the rule.[40]

Just the previous year, however, another figure of note entered the ranks of newspaper editors when Horace Greeley ceased publication of his struggling literary weekly the *New-Yorker* to launch a daily news-paper. In starting the *New-York Tribune*, Greeley envisioned a paper

that would complement news coverage with a serious literary and critical department, giving to culture the same sort of rigorous treatment
that he devoted to political and social concerns. Yet he also knew that
such a task was beyond his own purview. To aid him in this endeavor,
accordingly, he conscripted a critic who had attracted his attention as
editor of an intellectual Boston quarterly, a critic who would go further
than anyone yet had to answer the call put forth by the commentator in
the *Democratic Review*.

Building the "Literary Department"

Though Fuller's editorship of the *Dial* was a distinguished though not
necessarily formative chapter in the progress of American quarterly
reviews, a short-lived, small-circulation venture that folded after a
few years, her tenure at the *Tribune* marked the emergence of serious
book reviewing in American newspapers, a legacy we see today in the
power and prominence of the *New York Times Book Review*. If today, in
the first decades of the twenty-first century, book review sections are in
decline, with traditional print media destabilized by the expansion of
digital media and online publications, Fuller's tenure as literary editor
of the *Tribune* marked the origins of the newspaper book review section in America.[41]

In Frank Luther Mott's expansive treatment of American journalism, the sole reference he makes to book reviews in newspapers is in
his discussion of Greeley's *Tribune*: "In its literary phase, the *Tribune*
developed unusual excellence," Mott notes. "Short book notices had
been common on the editorial pages of many newspapers, but the *Tribune* appears to have been, in 1856, the first daily to establish a regular
department for such reviews." Though a "regular department" would
come into being more completely under Fuller's successor, George
Ripley, who took over the literary department in 1849 and ran it for
thirty-one years, the determination to make criticism a central feature
of the paper was evident in Greeley's decision to hire Fuller a decade
earlier. Similarly, while brief, unsigned announcements of new books
rather than full reviews was the critical norm for antebellum newspaper criticism, as Rubin notes, "the only notable exception to the general
absence of genuine critics was Margaret Fuller, who contributed essays

on books and other subjects to Horace Greeley's *Tribune* two or three times a week between 1844 and 1846."[42]

In doing so, the *Tribune* set a new standard for newspaper criticism. Greeley's paper along with Greene's Boston *Post* "were both leaders in expanding the scope and reach of the daily newspaper to give new prominence to discussions of books and ideas," Robert Scholnick observes, pioneering a new form of literary journalism devoted "at once to social critique and extended discussions of books and ideas and aimed at the widest possible readership." Before these two papers, Scholnick notes, "few if any daily papers in antebellum America devoted the space and editorial resources for the kind of substantive discussions of literature and the arts." Charles Capper goes one step further: "In an era of longwinded gentlemanly quarterlies that hemmed and hawed and newspaper puffs and hatchet jobs, often stolen from other papers and sometimes libelous (especially when paid for by an author's or artist's rival), 'the Star' signaled the first serious book review section in the country." In hiring Fuller, Capper notes, Greeley transformed a "largely partisan newspaper into America's first mass-circulation periodical of ideas." And while there is a problematic scholarly tendency to elevate Fuller at the expense of her surrounding critical culture, treating Fuller and Poe as exceptional rather than typical of the sophistication of antebellum criticism, even indulging some of the same exaggerated critiques of critical culture as contemporary commentators, there is nonetheless agreement that in the domain of newspaper literary criticism, the *Tribune* under Fuller was distinctive.[43]

In bringing Fuller to the *Tribune*, Greeley signaled his desire to give serious, sustained treatment to literary culture in his paper, and he backed up this commitment by directing both resources and space to the coverage of literature. It was Fuller who made this vision of bringing literary culture to the masses a reality, however. Nor is the invocation of the "masses" mere rhetorical flourish: riding the wave of the penny-press revolution, Greeley's paper expanded the readership of literary criticism more dramatically than any previous development in American critical history. Greeley and Fuller made criticism not only affordable and accessible but culturally central, their placement of literary reviews alongside political news, economic reports, and urban reporting signaling materially that literature was, and should be, indispensable to the everyday world of its readers. To the degree that newspapers created a cultural field of vision, a metonymic composite of the social world, oriented toward practical use, literary culture was now included in that vision. And it was Margaret Fuller who presided over this newly democratized conception of literary criticism.

On September 25, 1844, Fuller announced in a letter to her friend Maria Rotch that she'd accepted Greeley's offer to be the new literary editor of the *Tribune*. She planned to spend the autumn up the Hudson at Fishkill Landing, expanding her *Dial* essay "The Great Lawsuit" into what would become *Woman in the Nineteenth Century* before heading in December to New York "to try that city for the winter with a view to living there, if my position suits me." For as she informs her friend, "I am to *edit* the literary department of the N.Y. Tribune. If you remember Mr Greeley, one of the editors, such an arrangement may not seem to you seducing, but as a's [sic] not gold that glitters, so some things that do not glitter may turn gold. It is a position that offers many advantages and may be turned to much good. I cannot expect, however, to remain free from the usual foibles of Editors and I warn you that, if you write me anything good, it is likely to figure as 'interesting communications from a foreign correspondent' in the columns of *my department*."[44]

Fuller arrived in New York in early December 1844, and soon after Greeley announced Fuller's hiring as literary editor in the paper, praising her as "already eminent in the higher walks of Literature" while promising that her addition to the editorial staff "would render this paper inferior to no other in the extent and character of its literary matter."[45] On December 7, 1844, Fuller's first review appeared, reprinted in the weekly edition on December 14 in what would become standard operating procedure. Her choice to review Emerson's *Essays: Second Series* in her first column was fitting, marking her transition from the Boston Transcendental circles that she'd formerly travelled in and grown weary of and her new, more cosmopolitan New York environment, a "centrifugal evolution" that, as Chevigny observes, signaled her intellectual break with her New England associates.[46]

If in the past three decades, the surge of interest in Fuller has shown her to be a woman very much of our time, a natural fit for the evolving critical concerns of the twenty-first century, she was also very much a product of her own time as well.[47] When she accepted Greeley's offer to serve as contributing literary editor of the *Tribune*, she was riding the wave of her own moment's media revolution, a move that provoked its fair share of skepticism from Fuller's circle. In a letter to Samuel Ward regarding Ellery Channing's recent contributions to the *Tribune*, Emerson remarked that he thought these writings "unworthy of him." "The Tribune office may be good treatment for some of his local distempers," Emerson averred, "but it seems a very poor use to put a wise man & a genius, to. Is it any better with Margaret?" he adds. "The Muses have feet, to be sure, but it is an odd arrangement that selects them for the treadmill. Our grand machine of society must be sadly disjointed & ricketty [*sic*], if this is its best result."[48]

Fuller was only too aware of this contempt for what Emerson elsewhere derided as the "foaming foolishness of newspapers" and to his opinion that she was wasting her talents at the *Tribune*.[49] As Fuller admitted candidly to James Freeman Clarke a year into her tenure at the paper, "I was pleased with your sympathy about the Tribune; I do not find much among my own friends. They think I ought to produce something excellent, while I am well content for the present to aid in the great work of mutual education in this way." The *Tribune* office, the pace of the journalist's life, its close integration into the life of the city, was invigorating to Fuller and quickly shifted her critical philosophy away from the more rarefied romantic theory espoused in the *Dial* to the social concerns of her *Tribune* columns. As she continued to Clarke, "I never regarded literature merely as a collection of exquisite products, but as a means of mutual interpretation. Feeling that many are reached and in some degree aided the thoughts of every day seem worth writing down, though in a form that does not inspire me. Then I like to feel so fairly afloat in mid-stream, as I do here. All the signs of life appear to me at least superficially, and, as I have had a good deal of *the depths*, an abode of some length in *the shallows* may do me no harm. The sun comes full upon me."[50]

To be sure, Fuller internalized some of the prejudice against newspapers held by her New England friends and the culture more broadly, but she also quickly came to feel the power of her new position, her capacity to turn criticism into a tool for social good in ways that would have been inconceivable at the *Dial*. As she noted in March 1845 to her brother Eugene, "As to the public part; that is entirely satisfactory. I do just as I please, and as much or little as I please, and the Editors express themselves perfectly satisfied, and others say that my pieces *tell* to a degree, I could not expect. I think, too, I shall do better and better. I am truly interested in this great field which opens before me and it is pleasant to be sure of a chance at half a hundred thousand readers." From her new station in New York, away from the influence of Emerson and the Harvard Unitarian set, it was easy to see how hampered intellectually she had been in New England, how much she had "given almost all my young energies to personal relations," as she laments to her brother. "I no longer feel inclined to this, and wish to share and impel the great stream of thought[.] I really have nothing, at present, to communicate to any one, except what you may see indications of in print. I am observing my new field this occupies me." It was now her public career that concerned her and to which she desired to direct her energies; she no longer wanted to be pinned down by the personal obligations that had formerly held her back— taking care of her family, her brothers in particular, after the death of her father; corralling the fractious contributors to the *Dial* for no pay. And it was newspapers, that medium which so many derided, that offered her the prospect of a "noble career."[51]

While Fuller initially struggled to adapt to the intensive demands of newspaper writing, by the time she was set to embark for Europe to serve as foreign correspondent, she saw clearly that it was newspapers that offered her the clearest path for growth as well as a way to leave her mark. While her mind was already largely formed such that she no longer viewed the European trip as the potentially formative experience she once had, "still, even in this sense, I wish much to go. It is important to me, almost needful in the career I am now engaged in I feel that, if I persevere, there is nothing to hinder my having an important career even now. But it must be in the capacity of a journalist, and for that I need this new field of observation"[52]

One of the most surprising developments of Fuller's career is indeed that she became one of the nation's most ardent newspaper advocates. One wouldn't have predicted such a shift during her *Dial* days. Four years earlier, when Fuller published her "Short Essay on Critics" in the first issue of the *Dial*, her mind was far from the world of newspaper reviewing. In dismissing the alternately authoritarian and somnolent criticism of the quarterlies, she noted that, "scholars sneer and would fain dispense with them altogether; and the public, grown lazy and helpless by this constant use of props and stays, can now scarce brace itself even to get through a magazine article, but reads in the daily paper laid beside the breakfast plate a short notice of the last number of the long established and popular review, and thereupon passes its judgment and its content." The daily paper, with its superficial gloss of the contents of other periodicals, is all that the public has patience for anymore, Fuller chides, such that they can't even muster the strength to read a magazine article. The newspaper signals the easiest form of reading: cursory, disposable, something to consume with tea and toast at breakfast and then toss aside. In distinguishing among subjective, apprehensive, and comprehensive critics, newspaper reviews don't seem to register as belonging to any of the three.[53]

In launching the *Dial*, by contrast, Emerson and Fuller aspired to elevate criticism to new heights. "All criticism should be poetic; unpredictable; superseding, as every new thought does, all foregone thoughts, and making a new light on the whole world," Emerson proclaims in the opening "Editors to the Reader": "It has all things to say, and no less than all the world for its final audience." As Fuller continues in "A Short Essay on Critics," "The critic is not a base caviller, but the younger brother of genius. Next to invention is the power of interpreting invention; next to beauty the power of appreciating beauty. . . . The critic, then, should be not merely a poet, not merely a philosopher, not merely an observer, but tempered of all three." In describing the task of the apprehensive critic to enter into the spirit of the creator, and of the comprehensive critic, to put the work's achievement in relation to both history and set standards of nature, Fuller singles out for condemnation the subjective critic, with his degraded, impressionistic judgments, and the sober quarterly critic with his stale, pompous pronouncements. She notes too in opening that much of what goes by the name of criticism today is either "epistles addressed to the public through which the mind of the recluse relieves itself of impressions" or, alternately, "regular articles, got up to order by the literary hack writer, for the literary mart" whose "only law is to make them plausible."[54]

While the *Dial* had noble aspirations, however, it could have used a stronger basis in the market. For her two years of editorial labor, Fuller was paid nothing. By the time she sent her letter of resignation to Emerson, her health was failing, and she was broke. It was all too easy to dismiss criticism written for money, but after her experience at the *Dial*, Fuller was determined to get paid for her work. While her tenure as editor of the *Dial* had exhausted her and depleted her health without financial compensation, her first months at the *Tribune* were no less demanding, though more rewarding both financially and experientially. The learning curve as newspaper writer was steep but invigorating. At the end of her first month at the *Tribune*, Fuller reported back to Samuel Ward that, "My life here is a queer one and presents a good many daily obstacles of a petty sort, but I find the way to get along. I like the position; it is so central, and affords a far more various view of life than any I ever before was in. My associates think my pen does not make too fine a mark to be felt, and may be a vigorous and purifying element. I cannot judge so well of this, but I begin to find the level here." As she adds, "I shall be much employed for some time in visiting public institutions and writing short pieces on such subjects as are thus suggested to me. This will suit me well."[55]

It was the pace of production that initially posed the greatest challenge, and Greeley made it known to Fuller that he wished she would write more articles and faster. Yet she also liked Greeley and felt supported by him in a way that contrasted with Emerson's emotional coldness and distance. As she remarked in 1845, "Mr. Greeley is in many ways interesting for me to know. He teaches me things, which my own influence on those, who have hitherto approached me, has prevented me from learning. In our business and friendly relations, we are on terms of solid good-will and mutual respect. With the exceptions of my own mother, I think him the most disinterestedly generous person I have ever known." She put the case even more bluntly to her brother Eugene: "Mr. Greeley I like, nay more, love. He is, in his habits, a slattern and plebeian, and in his heart, a nobleman. His abilities, in his own way, are great. He believes in mine to a surprising extent. We are true friends."[56]

Within months, under Greeley's guidance and encouragement, Fuller adapted to the life of literary editor of a newspaper, and by early 1845 she was producing two to three long articles per week as well as a constant stream of shorter content. More than the pace of

journalism, however, it was her life in the city, the new experiences it
opened up to her as critic, combined with the power of the newspaper to reach large and diverse audiences, that altered Fuller's understanding and practice as critic most dramatically. What was conveyed
visually and materially through juxtaposed columns of the paper
found reinforcement in Fuller's reviews themselves and in her evolving critical theory at the *Tribune*: namely, that literature, mediated by
the sympathetic, discerning judgment of the critic, could help readers navigate and improve the social world. As Jeffrey Steele argues,
Fuller's *Tribune* writings comprised a "new kind of journalism—
one that brought the discernment of the literary critic to the social
problems of the city," collapsing the gulf between literature and
life, and offering readers interpretive frameworks for making sense
of the increasingly overwhelming urban world around them. "Pioneering a new model of urban critique," Steele writes, "Fuller interpreted the city the way she read the books she reviewed—as a multi-
layered text that intersected with her unfolding consciousness. What
resulted from this process was a complex literary awareness that connected the city's disparate spaces to passages from a wide variety of
published sources. In her New York essays, streets and texts, urban
institutions and books, illuminate each other, as different facets of the
same cultural geography that—like all geographies—is situated in
the writer's and reader's minds."[57]
   This critical vision, fusing the literary and social, books and streets,
took material shape in the formal layout of the newspaper page itself.
Even more directly than with other print forms, in reading newspapers, as Kevin Barnhurst and John Nerone argue, readers enter into
a textual "environment": the form of the news "invites readers into a
world molded and variegated to fit not only the conscious design of
journalists and the habits of readers, but also the reigning values in
political and economic life. . . . Form structures and expresses that environment, a space that comfortably pretends to represent something
larger: the world-at-large, its economics, politics, sociality, and emo-
tion." "At each phase of US history," Barnhurst and Nerone conclude,
"newspapers have matched that history not with a picture of the world
or a particularly reliable witness of events but with an environment: a
paper armchair, a newsprint backdrop, a surround that itself proposes

a way to see." Amid this textual environment, "readers don't read the news; they swim in it."[58]

In the *Tribune* particularly, literary coverage was part of Greeley's social vision of the cultural work of criticism, given material shape in the pages of the newspaper. The placement, thematic content, and style of Fuller's reviews in the paper revealed an expanded sense of literary criticism's role within US culture broadly as well as the host of particular functions it served more locally. Yet to see these functions clearly necessitates a direct confrontation with Fuller's reviews in the context of the *Tribune*'s pages. To be sure, this is easier said than done; nor has the digitization of newspapers solved the problem of mediation in replicating the originating scene of dissemination. Rather, to begin to understand Fuller's criticism in the *Tribune*, a development which marks the origins of the newspaper book review section in America, requires a return to the material site of the *New-York Tribune* itself, as well as reflection on the experience of reading Fuller in that context.

Reading Fuller in the *Tribune*

At just under two feet tall by one and a half feet wide with six closely printed columns across, the *Tribune* presented an imposing appearance. On September 13, 1845, Greeley and McElrath listed the cost for a one-year subscription to the wider circulation *Weekly Tribune* as two dollars paid in advance. The daily edition, published every day except Sunday at a cost of five dollars per year or sold for two cents on the street, was four pages, while the weekly edition, published each Saturday, numbered eight pages with fewer advertisements comparatively than the daily and much of its content reprinted from the previous week. In the standard practice of antebellum newspapers, the most recent political news, as well as Greeley's editorials, appeared not on the front page but on the second page, where the ink of freshly printed political news risked less chance of running.[59]

The first few columns of the first page were generally reserved for Fuller's reviews and for other literary matter like poems or excerpts from prose works. Like Hawthorne's tales, Fuller's reviews were "twice-told," printed first in the daily edition of the *Tribune* and then reprinted in the weekly edition. While a daily issue might have one or two pieces by Fuller, the *Weekly* edition often carried four or five articles, if not more, reprinted from the previous week's issues. These pieces varied greatly in length, from a brief notice of a few hundred words to feature-length reviews of three to four thousand words. In the weekly edition of Saturday, December 27, 1845, for instance, a year into her tenure at the *Tribune*, the paper carried two short paragraphs on Hannah Gould's *Gathered Leaves* followed by an excerpted poem; reviews of Charles Fenno Hoffman's *Vigil of Faith and Other Poems* and J. T. Headley's *Alps and the Rhine*; and a lengthy review of Thomas Carlyle's *Letters and Speeches of Oliver Cromwell*. Viewed in the context of the full newspaper, the length of Fuller's columns stands out. While Greeley's column on "The Oregon Question" on page five of the paper fills most of a single column, for instance, Fuller's review of Carlyle on the following page extends through three and a half columns, or almost half the full page.

Indeed, one thing that is immediately apparent when looking at the original *Tribune* pages is that Fuller's reviews were often the longest, most intellectually developed articles it contained since most of the paper was filled with short reports or notices from two or three lines to a few paragraphs in length. Fuller's reviews, by contrast, took up two to three columns generally, though much of this was frequently excerpts. Her review of "Browning's Poems" on the front page of the April 1, 1846, issue, to take a second example, took up five columns of the *Daily Tribune*—almost the entire first page—interspersing critical commentary with extensive excerpts from poems (figure 9). As Fuller concludes at the close of the piece: "These poems will afford some idea of Browning's compass. Of his delicate sheaths of meaning within meaning which must be opened slowly, petal by petal, as we seek the heart of a flower." Such a sense "can only be gained by reading him a great deal," however, and Fuller concludes the review by adding her wish "that the 'Bells and Pomegranate,' at least, may be brought within reach of those American readers who have time and soul to wait and listen for such."[60]

Fuller's criticism not only helped readers open up the poems' "delicate sheaths of meaning within meaning," it helped bring the poems themselves "within the reach of American readers." The manner in which Fuller interspersed critical commentary with sample poems and

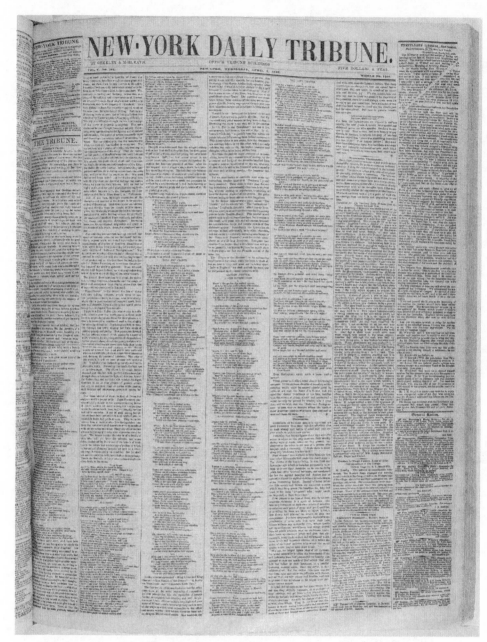

FIGURE 9. Margaret Fuller, "Browning's Poems," *New-York Daily Tribune* (April 1, 1846), 1. Courtesy of the American Antiquarian Society, Worcester, Massachusetts.

prose excerpts was itself emblematic of her critical practice at the *Tribune*, revealing the newspaper's desire to provide not just purchasing advice but wholesome entertainment for its readers in contrast to the sensational content of the *Sun* and the *Herald*. Her task wasn't simply evaluation or to use reviews as occasions for topical essays—two common expressions of antebellum critical practice—but rather to present new work to readers alongside a contextualizing and educational apparatus. In this sense, the choice by editors to exclude extracts from many twentieth-century collections of Fuller's writings, while understandable given the practical and financial exigencies of scholarly publishing, also distorts the experience of reading Fuller's columns in the *Tribune*.[61]

Yet if modern editors privilege critical commentary over literary extracts in their selections, the excerpted passages were as central as the critical judgments, providing the *Tribune*'s readers with liberal samplings of literary content under the guise of critical evaluation, allowing them to compete with both the mammoth reprint papers *Brother Jonathan* and the *New World* and literary weeklies like the *Mirror*. In this sense, Fuller's heavy sampling of the literature under review alongside its critical estimation points to a crucial, if often overlooked, function of criticism: to expose readers to literature directly through the frame of the review, a feature that has largely disappeared from twentieth-century book reviewing. Fuller oversaw not just the critical department but the "literary department"; reviews served not just as critical judgment but as literary entertainment, using the occasion of the review to reprint sizable portions of the work in question, situating reviews firmly within the culture of reprinting described at length by Meredith McGill.[62] Yet reviews also coupled literary entertainment with critical guidance, as Fuller educated readers on how to best understand the work they were reading, enacting both the apprehensive and comprehensive critical vocations laid out in "A Short Essay on Critics," while also showing readers how to profit personally from literature and making explicit the social reform messages frequently implicit in it.

The content of these excerpts was not mere filler. Rather, in Fuller's reviews, some of the most politically charged arguments came not from Fuller's commentary but from the excerpted passages themselves. In this regard, Fuller should not be thought of as the sole author of these reviews, in which she frequently gave space to lengthy excerpts where voices other than her own, including those of the marginalized or powerless, were placed center stage, their voices and concerns amplified through the powerful platform of a wide-circulation newspaper. Many of her reviews, indeed, make little impression stripped of their excerpts, in which the heart of an argument lay in the excerpted passage itself, as when she devotes half of her review of Frederick Douglass's *Narrative* to quoting Douglass himself, pointing to the brilliance of his writing as itself a refutation of spurious charges regarding the intellectual inferiority of the black race.

If Steven Mailloux has focused on Fuller's sparring with Garrisonian abolitionists and religious apologists in the main body of the review as the discursive context for the rhetorical occasion of the piece, in its original context, Fuller's own commentary, for all its interest, is not the main event—Douglass's is. "If any one wishes to be impressed with the soul-killing effects of Slavery," Douglass proclaims, "let him go to Col. Lloyd's Plantation, and, on allowance-day, place himself in the deep pine woods, and there let him, in silence analyze the sounds that shall pass through the chambers of his soul,—and if he is not thus impressed, it will only be because 'there is no flesh in his obdurate heart.'"[63] With pathos, eloquence, and a restrained fidelity to life as he experienced it, Douglass dismantles the common apologist argument that slaves sing because they are content, revealing instead the unfathomable sorrow, pain, and fortitude that slave spirituals express, a pain that Douglass himself had to learn to apprehend, just as the *Tribune*'s readers must now as well. As such, there is a doubling effect to the review as both Fuller in her commentary and Douglass in his excerpted passage instruct readers on how to extract true meaning from texts: Douglass from the slave songs and Fuller from Douglass's *Narrative*. For each writer, moreover, the purpose of accurate interpretation is social change; criticism is not about evaluation, purchasing advice, or critical grandstanding but about honing the interpretive faculties, separating truth from falsehood, and seeing through the illusions of the world, before enlisting that clarity in the cause of social reform. Fuller's review of Douglass doesn't just perform the critical office, it models the stakes of interpretation itself through the very text it reviews.

The high value Fuller placed on reprinted content is even more plainly evident in her regular practice of translating pieces from foreign and immigrant newspapers. These translated pieces, as Christina Zwarg suggests, contained some of the most radical, provocative, and overtly political views Fuller expressed in *Tribune,* as when she translates Gottfried Kinkel's essay on the revolutionary potential of popular literature, "Popular Literature in Germany," or translates from the *Deutsche Schnellpost* one of the first notices of Marx and Engels published in the United States. Rather, as Zwarg argues, the equal intellectual weight carried by translations or quoted materials printed by Fuller in the *Tribune* testifies to her career-long investment in unconventional, "anticanonical" literary forms (translations, dialogues, criticism, journalism, and histories) and to providing space for voices other than her own. Yet in studies of Fuller's canon and collections of her writings, translations are regularly ignored and excluded, dismissed by scholars "trapped within the somewhat useless idea of originality," as Zwarg puts it. In the pages of the *Tribune,* by contrast, translations, excerpted passages, and Fuller's own critical commentary all received central billing, greeting readers in the first column of the first page as visually indistinguishable from one another, with the subject matter of the column taking precedence over its authorship.[64]

Just as Fuller's voice mingled with those of the authors she reviewed, her columns formed a complex web of relation with the adjacent news stories, sharing the page with arrivals of steamships from Europe, reports on Congressional sessions, murder trials, and news of the war with Mexico. Occasionally a breaking news story would cause her review to be bumped from its usual spot on the front page, as when in the issue for June 10, 1846, a feature on the fortified army camp at Point Isabel, Texas, illustrated with a large sketch of the compound, caused her review "Critics and Essayists" to be printed not on the front page but in a supplement, emphasizing just how different her own critical milieu was from those of the critics under review. As she notes at the close of the piece, which surveyed volumes of critical essays by primarily three critics—Richard Henry Horne, George Gilfillan, and Henry T. Tuckerman—she wished to say more about Tuckerman's views of British poets, "but newspaper limits forbid, and indeed we have made the present writing so long, that it is doubtful whether the war with Mexico lets it see the light."[65] The occasion reminds us of a fact that was omnipresent for *Tribune* readers: that in the pages of the newspaper, literature and news shared space, with Fuller's reviews expanding or contracting when major stories broke, existing alongside a host of paratextual contexts that enacted materially the constitutive relationship between criticism and politics.

As with the content of excerpts, these paratextual relationships complicated and complemented the content of Fuller's reviews, opening up new avenues for reading intertextually across the page of the newspaper. In the *Daily Tribune* for June 28, 1845, for example, two pieces by Fuller appeared one page apart: her review of the most recent volume of Commander Charles Wilkes's *Narrative of the United States Exploring Expedition* on page one and an editorial on "Irish Character" on page two, following closely on the heels of Greeley's editorial "Immigrants Abused." In the two pieces, the first addressing Christian hypocrisy and imperialist violence overseas, the second an editorial addressing anti-Irish sentiment at home, two policies underwritten by racism and jingoism are linked to one another through the physically bound pages of the June 28 *Tribune*, their thematic connection rendered material rather than speculative.

The epistemological orientation suggested by the material presentation is significant too: for while twentieth-century edited collections of Fuller's writings present these two essays sequentially one after the other, in the pages of the *Tribune*, Fuller's two pieces with their respective treatments on imperialism and nativism occur synchronically rather than diachronically, their material positioning suggesting simultaneity rather than chronology while connecting domestic and international concerns through a single field of vision and under the banner of a single date, or what Anderson terms the "meanwhile" effect.[66] In each column, moreover, Fuller encourages sensitivity to other cultures, promotes sympathy between fellow men, and sardonically attacks both capitalist rapacity and Christian hypocrisy in which the white man "extends the Bible or crucifix with one hand and the rum-bottle with the other."[67]

While Fuller makes some of these connections explicit, she also encourages her newspaper audience to be active rather than passive readers, forging these critical links themselves. If she once derided newspapers as promoting the laziest sort of reading, she was now doing her part to change that. When Fuller said that she was engaged in the work of "mutual interpretation" with her readers, what she meant was that she didn't just want to pass judgment on books *for* readers, she wanted to teach them how to interpret for themselves, for critic and reader to interpret the work *together*, mutually. As she wrote in "Critics and Essayists," which reviewed several volumes of collected critical essays, "such books are interesting companions, and at intervals, guides—not that the critic should ever be allowed to guide our judgment, but he may show us *where* to look, and warn us not to *over*look in learning to judge for ourselves."[68]

Fuller was as concerned with teaching readers how to read critically as she was with telling them what to read. As Robert Hudspeth notes, unlike earlier critics who addressed criticism toward authors, guiding them on how to improve their craft in the service of encouraging the growth of a national literature, Fuller redirected her focus from the author to the reader, serving as a "mediator and advocate," turning all readers into critics, asking the reader rather than the writer to raise his or her standards, and "schooling her readers in ways of better reading."[69] Her concern was not how authors might be improved but how literature might improve the lives of its readers. As she notes in her review of Emerson's *Essays: Second Series*, "the only true criticism of these, or any good books, may be gained by making them the companions of our lives. Does every accession of knowledge or a juster sense of beauty make us prize them more? Then they are good, indeed, and more immortal than mortal."[70]

In carrying out this mission, her practice of the critical vocation was intertwined and dependent upon the vocation of the daily newspaper, empowered by having a huge readership that crossed geographical and class boundaries. If in the first decades of the nineteenth century, as William Gilmore argues, reading became a necessity of everyday life, as the growing book and periodical trade made print a mainstay of US culture, this did not necessarily mean that readers knew *how* to read, how best to turn the riches of contemporary print culture to their profit. Much as James Machor has argued that books and authors instructed readers on habits of reception, a "historical hermeneutics" whereby works set their own horizons of expectations, establishing conventions of reception and guiding reading practices, in her *Tribune* columns Fuller instructed readers on how to be astute critics more directly, showing them not just how to read but how to read for personal growth, not merely passing judgment but encouraging readers to judge for themselves.[71]

The kind of socially oriented, active reading made possible by newspapers was not just material but theoretical, as increasingly for Fuller criticism and politics pursued aligned vocational concerns. Specifically, for Fuller, as numerous scholars have observed, criticism became a platform for social reform while books became an effective tool for the promotion of sympathy among Americans of all classes, races, and creeds.[72] As Fuller asserts in one of her last pieces for the *Tribune*, a review of Anna Jameson's *Memoirs and Essays Illustrative of Art, Literature, and Social Morals*, published in the *Daily Tribune* for July 24, 1846, and again in the *Weekly Tribune* on August 1, 1846, the day Fuller set sail for Europe, "literature has become not merely an archive for the preservation of great thoughts, but a means of general communication between all classes of minds, and all grades of culture." "If charity begin at home," she writes in her Thanksgiving Day reflections a year and half earlier, "it must not end there"; rather, "no home can be healthful in which are not cherished seeds of good for the world at large." And increasingly, the value of literature resided in its capacity to generate in readers empathy for the less fortunate. As she writes in her review of the British working-class poet William Thom, "literature may be regarded as the great mutual system of interpretation between all kinds and classes of men. It is an epistolary correspondence between brethren of one family, subject to many and wide separations, and anxious to remain in spiritual presence of one another."[73]

Just as literature cultivates empathy by providing windows into the experiences of others, her columns helped readers to see those whom their eyes had become accustomed to gloss over, those at the social margins: servants, prisoners, immigrants, prostitutes, the sick and disabled. This sympathy must be converted from the realm of fiction to the real world, however, from sentiment to action, if it is to be of any use. As she writes in her account of the Asylum for Discharged Convicts, "Have you entertained your leisure hours with the Mysteries of Paris or the pathetic story of Violet Woodville? . . . Do you want to link these fictions, which have made you weep, with facts around you where your pity might be of use? Go to the Penitentiary at Blackwell's Island . . . Think what 'sweet seventeen' was to you, and what it is to them, and see if you do not wish to aid in any enterprise that gives them a chance of better days . . . Is not the hope to save, here and there *one*, worthy of great and persistent exertion and sacrifice?"[74] Don't just read about urban desperation, Fuller implores, do something about it.

Just as the pages of the *Tribune* juxtaposed literature and sociopolitical concerns, Fuller sought to make the link between the two explicit, instructing *Tribune* patrons in a radical theory of reading for social change, as Zwarg describes it, "one meant to develop a form of political agency that would include a more diverse group of people than those who traditionally hold power."[75] And though Fuller's genteel understanding of charity, which frequently entailed voyeuristic pathos or lecturing prostitutes on morality, is not without its own problems, she nonetheless insisted that the sympathy gleaned from reading needed to be translated to the actual world, redirecting the aims of reading from the personal growth of Transcendental self-culture to improving the lives of those less fortunate. Or as she asserts pithily, quoting from the preface of Thom's *Poems*, "'MAN, KNOW THYSELF,' should be written on the right hand; on the left, '*Men, know* EACH OTHER.'"[76]

In keeping with her desire to put literature in the service of social reform, Fuller's contributions to the *Tribune* quickly came to extend well beyond literary matters. In her capacity as literary editor, she began reviewing works that fail to qualify under even the most expansive definitions of the "literary." In the first few months of 1846, for instance, Fuller recorded the speech of Kentucky abolitionist Cassius Clay, reflected on John Wesley and Methodism, addressed the treatment of the insane, reports on prisons and the treatment of criminals, criticized capital punishment in a piece titled "Darkness Visible," and reviewed the "Twenty-Seventh Annual Report and Documents of the New York Institution of the Deaf and Dumb."[77] As she becomes equally a social critic as a literary critic, that is, her columns begin to depart further and further from the essays of quarterlies or the reviews of monthly magazines and to adopt the concerns of newspapers themselves, anticipating her subsequent position as foreign correspondent, in which Fuller reported on the battles of the Italian Risorgimento from the streets of Rome.

Fuller contributed occasional pieces as well, using Thanksgiving, the Fourth of July, and the New Year as opportunities to reflect broadly on American values and the direction of the country, confirming her evolution from a book critic to a cultural critic. Indeed, while Lawrence Buell has argued that Emerson's career signaled the emergence of the public intellectual in America, as John Evelev counters, Margaret Fuller fit the description much better.[78] In her New Year's column for January 1, 1846, for instance, Fuller stands back and assesses the current state of America and of the world, charts the failures and hypocrisies of American democracy, observes the juxtaposition of rich and poor, prosperity and suffering that fill the streets of New York.[79]

The pages of the paper bear witness to her account, imbuing it with the force of truth. In the weekly edition, her account of the Irish potato famine finds an echo two pages later in a letter from a Dublin correspondent, "Synopsis of Irish News—Awful Prospects of Famine—Criminal Apathy of Government." A column on page four addresses the "Support of the Destitute." On page six, Fuller retains her more traditional role as critic in reviewing an American edition of *The Poetical Works of Percy Bysshe Shelley*, but she is no longer restricted to this role. In the *Weekly Tribune* for April 11, 1845, to take one final example, Fuller contributes a front-page account of Caroline, a young girl afflicted by a spinal disease and of the way her town banded together to take care of her. Over and over again, Fuller's columns turned to the vulnerable in the community and to social issues in and out of New York, enacting an expanded sense of critical vocation that contrasted sharply the subjects that filled her essays in the *Western Messenger* and the *Dial*.

Reading Fuller's reviews in their original material context in the pages of the *Tribune*, we also get a strong sense of the writing pressures that she was working under. While the system of quarterly publication allowed time for significant reading and reflection, for crafting an argument and refining one's style, the demands of daily and weekly publication necessitated a different mode of writing: faster, more observational, less argument driven, frequently announcing new works or performances and offering a few thoughts rather than developed arguments. Though both Greeley and Clarke remarked to Fuller that her time at the *Tribune* had improved her writing style, imparting to it a "directness, terseness, and practicality" lacking in her earlier critical writings, as Greeley put it, such fast turnaround also had its drawbacks, occasionally resulting in hastily formed judgments.[80]

In Fuller's review of Schoolcraft Jones's *Ellen: Or Forgive and Forget*, for instance, published in the January 10, 1846, issue of the *Daily Tribune*, we see Fuller's maturation as a newspaper critic as she admits that, "in this connection we must try to make amends for the stupidity of an earlier notice of the novel called 'Margaret, or the Real and Ideal,' &c. At the time of that notice we had only looked into it here and there, and did no justice to a work full of genius, profound in its meaning and of admirable fidelity to Nature in its details. Since, we have really read it, and appreciated the sight and representation of 'soul-realities,' we have lamented the long delay of so true a pleasure."[81] In this candid remark, we get a brief glimpse of the haste with which Fuller was compelled to review books. In this case, she repents of a harsh review she gave of an earlier novel by Jones, having read it too cursorily to appreciate its merits. One refrain in critiques of newspaper reviewers was that they read books too quickly to do them justice, and here Fuller concedes the point, repenting of her former oversight.

One of Greeley's main complaints when Fuller began at the *Tribune* was, indeed, that she took too long to mull over the books under review. In those first few months, "she could write only when in the vein," Greeley recalled, "and this needed often to be waited for through several days, while the occasion sometimes required an immediate utterance." For if she waited too long, other papers would beat the *Tribune* to the punch, at which point, "even the ablest critique would command no general attention." And while waiting for the "flow of inspiration" might not seem unreasonable to outside observers or for other genres of writing, "to the inveterate hack-horse of the daily press, accustomed to write at any time, on any subject, and with a rapidity limited only by the physical ability to form the requisite pen-strokes, the notion of waiting for a brighter day, or a happier frame of mind, appears fantastic or absurd." As a result, Greeley failed to appreciate adequately her earliest reviews for the *Tribune* since in his mind, "they often seemed to make their appearance 'a day after the fair.'" Both Fuller and Greeley adapted, however: Fuller got faster at reviewing and Greeley grew to appreciate the "intellectual wealth and force" of her pieces.[82]

If Fuller was initially hesitant about working for the *Tribune,* by the
time she left New York on August 1, 1846, she had been fully converted
to the power of the newspaper medium. In the last months before her
departure, as Fuller made final preparations for a foreign tour she'd
looked forward to for much of her life, she produced what would
become one of her most anthologized essays, a survey of America's
literary prospects written specifically for *Papers on Literature and Art,*
a volume of critical writings she was assembling. As the sole original
contribution to Fuller's only critical volume, "American Literature; Its
Position in the Present Time, and Prospects for the Future," claims the
distinction of being Fuller's last published piece of literary criticism,
Wilma Ebbitt notes, a final word of sorts before she exchanged the title
of literary editor for that of foreign correspondent.[83] Written at the end
of her time in New York, the essay offers a condensed summary of
many of the views she had expressed in her *Tribune* reviews over the
past year and a half. In particular, it articulates Fuller's restrained literary nationalism; her realistic, if grim appraisal of America's modest literary accomplishments to date and her hopes for its future; as well as
her longstanding belief that the most effective inspiration for native talent might come not from America but from abroad, from invigorating
strains of foreign thought coming out of Germany, France, and Italy,
and from the great works of previous eras.

Amid her doleful assessment of the state of American literature,
what is perhaps most surprising about "American Literature," however, is that Fuller reserves her highest praise not for any particular author, not for American accomplishments in the fields of fiction,
poetry, or drama, but for America's thriving periodical culture. "The
most important part of our literature, while the work of diffusion is
still going on," Fuller declares toward the close of the essay, "lies in the
journals, which monthly, weekly, daily, send their messages to every
corner of this great land, and form, at present, the only efficient instrument for the general education of the people." While she ranks magazines lowest in the periodical hierarchy, their object "principally to
cater for the amusement of vacant hours," and finds quarterly reviews
more creditable, if injured by a "partisan spirit, and the fear of censure
from their own public," it is ultimately newspapers that offer the greatest promise for the nation in its current stage of development. "The life

of intellect is becoming more and more determined to the weekly and daily papers," Fuller observes, "whose light leaves fly so rapidly and profusely over the land." "This mode of communication is susceptible of great excellence in the way of condensed essay, narrative, criticism, and is the natural receptacle for the lyrics of the day," Fuller continues. "The means which this organ affords of diffusing knowledge and sowing seeds of thought where they may hardly fail of an infinite harvest, cannot be too highly prized by the discerning and benevolent."[84]

Despite the power of newspapers to educate the populace and nourish the growth of American literature, however, even after a year and a half at the *Tribune* Fuller knew that there was still a strong prejudice against journalism, expressed not least by Fuller's own Boston friends toward her current occupation. As Fuller observes,

> Minds of the first class are generally indisposed to this kind of writing; what must be done on the spur of the occasion and cast into the world so incomplete, as the hurried offspring of a day or hour's labour must generally be, cannot satisfy their judgment, or do justice to their powers. But he who looks to the benefit of others, and sees with what rapidity and ease instruction and thought are assimilated by men, when they come thus, as it were, on the wings of the wind, may be content, as an unhonoured servant to the grand purposes of Destiny, to work in such a way at the Pantheon which the Ages shall complete, on which his name may not be inscribed, but which will breathe the life of his soul.

This is not to say that newspaper writing was without dangers: "The confidence in uprightness of intent, and the safety of truth, is still more needed here than in the more elaborate kinds of writing, as meanings cannot be fully explained nor expressions revised." Indeed, "newspaper writing is next door to conversation, and should be conducted on the same principles. It has this advantage: we address, not our neighbour, who forces us to remember his limitations and prejudices, but the ideal presence of human nature as we feel it ought to be and trust it will be. We address America rather than Americans." While newspaper writing had the speed and immediacy of conversation, a field in which Fuller established her renown in Boston, it was also able to speak beyond local prejudices and constraints, addressing in the abstracted nation of readers "the ideal presence of human nature," "America rather than Americans."[85]

There is something counterintuitive though essential for Fuller here in the idea that newspapers, that most practical and utilitarian of instruments, grounded in the daily needs of localized readerships, written under temporal constraints and obsolete with the next morning's edition, is the medium that can best address "the ideal presence of human nature." The breadth of its audience, ever increasing with the capacities of rotary presses, postage acts, and new railroad lines, addressed an abstracted audience too large to be particularized or fully comprehended. In contrast to the familiar roster of names on the subscription list of the *Dial*, in which she was writing for friends and associates, we get a sense that Fuller felt the abstracted power of her position at the *Tribune*, speaking to innumerable, unknown readers, far-flung subscribers, and anonymous men and women who purchased the paper from newsboys and magazine depots.

The geographical extent of its distribution cancelled out the petty squabbles of the local, and it seems not coincidental that while Poe in the *Broadway Journal* carried out countless personal feuds, even taking aim at Fuller on one occasion, Fuller engaged in no such wrangling with local personalities or feuds over her critical judgments. Her letters were devoid of the sorts of petty animosities that consumed Poe. With her high perch at the *Tribune*, Fuller was above the fray, as she imagined it. Perhaps this came from the confidence Greeley put in her, perhaps from her own self-assurance, but in her position at the *Tribune*, Fuller came to feel that she was speaking true, high, sincere if particularized ideals to "America rather than Americans," and developed a faith in newspapers as the medium best positioned to propel the nation forward.

Fuller's "American Literature" is a complicated document, and her own prefatory assessment that it is "a very imperfect sketch," written hastily, is borne out by its disorderly and unsystematic treatment of her broad topic, as well as its improvised ending in which she attaches reviews of Hawthorne, Charles Brockden Brown, and Longfellow. Yet if imperfect, "it is, however, written with sincere and earnest feelings, and from a mind that cares for nothing but what is permanent and essential. It should, then, have some merit, if only in the power of suggestion."[86] The irony is that Fuller reserves her greatest praise, rests the greatest hopes for the nation's literary future, on perhaps the least "permanent and essential" form of writing, not poetry, drama, or the novel, but newspaper journalism, a genre borne on the "wings of the wind." The great hero of her survey of the current state of American letters, the figure upon whom the literary prospects of the nation rest, is not the poet, the sage, the scholar, or the man of letters in Goethe and Carlyle's abstracted sense, but the journalist.

In her "Farewell" column for the *Tribune,* published on August 1, 1846, the day she sailed for Europe, Fuller reiterated this faith in the journalistic vocation one last time. "Farewell to New-York City," Fuller declares, "where twenty months have presented me with a richer and more varied exercise for thought than twenty years could in any other part of these United States." If her time in New York confirmed some of her views of the great metropolis and of the picture of human nature contained there, new opinions, new "leadings" have been opened up to her as well, in particular, "the superlative importance of promoting National Education by hightening [*sic*] and deepening the cultivation of individual minds, and the part which is assigned to Woman in the next stage of human progress in this country." While her own career provided evidence of the latter, as literary critic for the *Tribune* she had spent the last eighteen months engaged in the former, using her post as critic at one of the nation's leading newspapers to devote herself to the task of not just critical judgment but popular education.

She felt confident, moreover, in having found a receptive audience. "The degree of sympathetic response to the thoughts and suggestions I have offered through the columns of this paper has indeed surprised me . . . It has greatly encouraged me, for none can sympathize with thoughts like mine who are permanently ensnared in the meshes of sect or party; none who prefer the formation and advancement of mere opinions to the pursuit of Truth." In her columns, she had contributed to the work of national education, had attempted to guide readers as they navigated the waters of literature and culture, guided them in the act of "mutual interpretation," pursuing not party views or hasty opinion but truth—and all through the pages of a daily paper. Though she was now departing the new world to survey the Old World of Europe, she did so with a sense of hope in what her own country seemed poised to produce, of the harvests yet to come, cultivated by the medium of the newspaper itself. And though she did as much as anyone in antebellum America to sow the seeds of that harvest, it was one she would not live to see herself.[87]

"Paper Missives": Newspapers and Critical Legacy

If Fuller came to develop a sincere faith in the cultural power of journalism, the precarious materiality of newspapers has paradoxically posed enduring difficulties for Fuller's critical legacy. This question of critical reputation was on Fuller's mind during her final months in New York. Just as Poe spent his final years envisioning a full-length critical volume, in the summer of 1846, as Fuller prepared to embark for Europe where she would serve as foreign correspondent for the *Tribune*, she hurried to make final arrangements for a volume of her critical writings. When several months earlier Fuller proposed the idea to Evert Duyckinck, editor of Wiley and Putnam's Library of American Books, Duyckinck readily agreed. As the literary critic at one of the nation's leading newspapers, the volume would add new dimensions to the series while supporting Fuller and Duyckinck's shared commitment to the growth of a national literature. Yet Fuller was excited at the prospect of the volume for more practical reasons as well.

While her travel book *Summer on the Lakes* (1844) had sold well, and her feminist tract *Woman in the Nineteenth Century* (1845) made her famous (and in some circles infamous), her critical writings were scattered through a handful of magazines and scores of newspaper columns. Though Fuller had spent the better part of her adult life working as a critic, the fruits of that labor were buried amid the dusty pages of periodicals. Bringing them together in a collection "would be very agreeable to me," Fuller observed to Duyckinck, "as copies of them are continually borrowed and I think, if more accessible, they would command a good deal of sympathy." Fuller had recently reviewed critical volumes by James Russell Lowell and Henry Theodore Tuckerman, moreover, and she began to worry that her own critical reputation depended on just such a collection. She knew that the financial prospects for the book were not great. "As it takes two thousand copies to pay expenses, I may make nothing or very slowly," she reported to her brother Richard. "Still I shall be content as it is an object to me to get the pieces in an accessible form."[88]

The volume that resulted, *Papers on Literature and Art,* published in the fall of 1846, assembled reviews and essays from an eleven-year period, from Fuller's earliest articles in the *Western Messenger* and the *American Monthly Magazine,* through her editorship of the *Dial,* to her recent tenure at the *Tribune.* While her early letters to Duyckinck record her initial excitement at the prospect of the collection, however, that enthusiasm quickly turned to frustration as Wiley and Putnam produced a book that was too thin and too conservative to Fuller's mind. "The translation . . . of the matter from a more crowded page to its present form has made such a difference," Fuller complained. Of the twenty-seven essays that Fuller proposed in her original plan, the final volume included only seventeen, while her original vision of four thematic sections was reduced to just two.

She had planned to include essays on a wider variety of topics, several of a more radical stamp, and to include extracts, as they would provide "far more harmony and interest for the general reader." But she was forced to abandon her original plan, cut the extracts, and drop a number of the pieces, including those of a "controversial character or likely to offend the religious public." Had she been aware of the restrictive limits that Wiley and Putnam would put on the volume, Fuller noted in the book's preface, "I should have made a different selection, and one which would do more justice to the range and variety of subjects which have been before my mind during the ten years that . . . I have written for the public." Indeed, as she admits to Duyckinck, she might have made different publishing plans altogether.[89]

Fuller's frustration with *Papers on Literature and Art* was more than mere griping. Rather, it reflected her concern over the continued accessibility of her critical corpus and the prospects for her critical legacy, concerns that the newspaper medium exacerbated. "The last twenty months is the first period of my life when it has been permitted me to make my pen my chief means of expressing my thoughts," Fuller observed in the volume's preface, "yet I have written enough, if what is afloat, and what lies hid in manuscript, were put together, to make a little library, quite large enough to exhaust the patience of the collector, if not of the reader. Should I do no more, I have at least sent my share of paper missives through the world."[90] But what would happen to the intellectual fruits of the past decade, Fuller worried, to say nothing of the past eighteen months? Unless preserved in a more permanent and accessible form, her sizable journalistic output, enough for a "little library," would be lost to history. For a time, Fuller thought *Papers on Literature and Art* might solve this problem. It didn't, however. If anything, it only highlighted her predicament, presenting a brief collection of critical pieces that failed to align with her own sense of her critical accomplishments.

Fuller's concerns proved warranted. In closing her preface to *Papers on Literature and Art*, Fuller noted that should the volume receive a warm reception, she would follow it up with more in the same vein. As fate would have it, however, the lone volume proved to be the last before her death. For though she would go on to become America's first female foreign correspondent, giving Americans a front row view of the European uprisings of 1848 through the pages of the *Tribune*; and though she sailed back to America with a manuscript about the Italian revolution in tow; neither she nor her manuscript ever reached the shore. As a result, the slim collection, which Fuller found so meager and unsatisfactory, became the last published volume of her life, a very partial record of her career as mid-nineteenth-century America's most widely read critic.

Not until the twenty-first century would the broad range of Fuller's critical output be readily available to readers. Until then, readers had to make do with the few selections that filled *Papers on Literature and Art*; the select additions included by her brother Arthur Buckminster Fuller in two posthumous volumes; and in the occasional pieces published in twentieth-century critical editions. Indeed, before Judith Mattson Bean and Joel Myerson released *Margaret Fuller, Critic* in 2000, only thirty-eight of Fuller's two hundred and fifty signed critical pieces from her *Tribune* years in New York (roughly 15 percent) had appeared in twentieth-century editions. Bean and Myerson's volume addressed this neglect by reprinting eighty-eight pieces in the book and including all two hundred and fifty on an accompanying CD-ROM.[91] Though Fuller had indeed sent her fair share of "paper missives through the world," until recently the vast majority of them were inaccessible to readers. Rather, it was not through bound volumes but through the pages of the *Tribune* that Americans got to know Margaret Fuller and her critical vision for American literature.

Today, in the twenty first century, we finally have access to Fuller's *Tribune* writings both in edited volumes and through periodical databases like American Periodical Series and Chronicling America. From a material perspective, however, newspaper criticism continues to pose problems for scholars of critical history. At research library archives, newspapers are preserved in fewer numbers than monthly magazines and quarterlies. They were built for cheapness, for short-term use, and thus have not endured as well or in complete runs, requiring serious commitments of space and resources to maintain. Reading them is challenging too: small print strains the eyes; fragile texts crumble in your hands; while daily publication has generated massive print archives that lack paratextual aids like tables of contents, indexes, and even clear headings to help guide scholars. Nor have microfilm and digitization resolved these problems of access. Unlike magazines, the large format of newspapers doesn't lend itself well to digital reading, forcing panning, clicking, and zooming that strains the eyes even more than hard copies. The poor print quality of the newspapers poses challenges for OCR technologies, meanwhile, rendering keyword searches unreliable, while a single downloaded file can be five or six megabytes, making the process of moving between pages tedious.

The act of remediation, whether in scholarly print editions or digital surrogates, effaces the experience of the material text, sacrificing the physical encounter with periodical criticism even as it increases our access. Periodicals that are strikingly different in physical size, production quality, or presentation appear to readers through a uniform digital interface, with three-dimensional objects flattened into two-dimensional images, sprawling pages shrunk down to the size of a laptop screen, and elaborate full-color fashion plates rendered dull and grey. We read differently, too: tactile engagement becomes visual; trackpad and mouse replace hands; the experience of flipping through a magazine, scanning the classifieds, or cutting out an article becomes the more detached experience of looking at a screen. And while technologies of digital remediation are improving, the fact of remediation remains the same.

With digitized newspapers, the loss of the material experience of reading is especially pronounced. The newspapers of the 1840s were designed to dazzle with their size. At the Huntington Library, as I surveyed mid-nineteenth-century newspapers, readers paused with curiosity to glance at the *Tribune* and the *New-York Evening Post* spread out in front of me across an entire table, with news of the annexation of Texas mingled alongside classifieds for lost dogs, Congressional reports juxtaposed to advertisements for pianos and notices of arriving ships. The overwhelming size, the clutter of information, the visual noise, the variety of contents were designed to astonish. Its imposing physical form and cosmopolitan clutter were visual arguments for American progress and the advanced state of civilization in New York. And while the pages of the *Tribune* presented the dizzying stir of modern culture, increasingly for critics like Fuller, literature and literary criticism became a way to make sense of it.

If Fuller's critical output has been slow to achieve the recognition it deserves within American critical history, finally, it is in part because much of it appeared in newspapers, a context that still in the twenty-first century falls lower in hierarchies of critical authority than quarterlies, monthly magazines, and bound books. Part of this low esteem is material, part of it is cultural. From Margaret Fuller to Michiko Kakutani, newspaper criticism has been, and still is, viewed as a lower form of the critical art—hasty, brief, unserious, speaking to the fleeting tastes of the moment, and compromised by close proximity to the publishing industry—and despite the fact that newspapers speak to a much larger audience than organs of greater prestige. Such biases aren't new, though they persist. As low as newspaper criticism falls in hierarchies of critical value, however, another critical form falls still lower: reviews *reprinted* from other sources. For if newspaper reviews are hasty and amateurish, they're at least original. Reprinting criticism from other periodicals opens up a whole new set of concerns, challenging both assumptions about critical authority and the very definition of criticism itself. It is to this problem of reprinted criticism that we turn in the final chapter.

CHAPTER 5

SLAVERY REVIEWED

Uncle Tom's Cabin, Frederick Douglass,
and the Politics of Critical Reprinting

I N THE CLOSING episode of Maria McIntosh's 1863 proslavery novel
*Two Pictures; or What We Think of Ourselves, and What the World
Thinks of Us*, the story's heroine, Augusta Moray, chances upon a
review of *Uncle Tom's Cabin* while perusing a periodical one day. Wit-
nessing the distress in her face, her husband, Hugh, immediately surmises the cause: "You are reading that review of 'Uncle Tom,' with
its unflattering portraiture of Southern planters," he wagers with a
smile. For Augusta, however, the review is nothing to smirk at: "'That
they should think thus of you!'" she proclaims indignantly, her face
reddening as she "contrasted the picture of the vulgar and beastly
tyrant just presented to her, with the image enshrined so reverently in
her heart." "'You know, love, there are two sides to every picture,'"
her husband demurs. "'True; and I thank God there are,'" Augusta
replies sharply, "'that we are not obliged to see ourselves or each
other as the false world see us.'"[1]

In this final scene of McIntosh's novel, which closes the story and
lends it its title, the referential ambiguity of the pronoun "its" in Hugh's
observation "You are reading that review of 'Uncle Tom' with its
unflattering portraiture of Southern planters," renders it unclear as to
just who is providing the disparaging portrait of southerners: Stowe or
the reviewer. Yet either way, it's the review, not the novel, that disturbs
Augusta. Nor were such episodes merely the stuff of fiction. Rather, in

the months and years following the publication of *Uncle Tom's Cabin*, both proslavery and antislavery critics picked up where Stowe left off, extending or revising her portraits of southern life through lengthy critiques of the novel, much as McIntosh did herself in *Two Pictures*. As Augusta's emotional confrontation with the review suggests, literary criticism could inflame passions just as easily as Stowe's novel, and as such, the episode highlights the central role that not just *Uncle Tom's Cabin* but reviews of it played in fomenting the slavery crisis in the decade that elapsed between the novel's serialization in the *National Era* beginning in June 1851 and the outbreak of war in April 1861.[2]

Amid the clamorous hyperbole of press accounts of the novel, it's easy to forget that the publishing phenomenon eventually tapered off, with sales of *Uncle Tom's Cabin* dropping off abruptly in the spring of 1853. As Claire Parfait notes, Stowe's novel saw no reprinting between the spring of 1853 and the fall of 1862, precisely the years we might expect the political ramifications of the novel to be greatest and those implicated in Abraham Lincoln's apocryphal (and in modern scholarly accounts, compulsory) proclamation, "So you're the little woman who wrote the book that made this great war!"[3] Rather, while Stowe's novel captured the imagination of the country, roused its sympathies and passions, it was reviews of the novel that kept Stowe's story a current topic of controversy long after everyone had finished reading it. It was criticism that distilled Stowe's sentimental portrait into the political arguments that sped the nation toward war, prolonging the cultural impact of the novel while translating its message into political terms that evolved alongside the escalating sectional crisis.

When in 1866 the American historian and linguist John Russell Bartlett published his bibliography *The Literature of the Rebellion*, he described its contents in his subtitle as "A Catalogue of Books and Pamphlets relating to the Civil War in the United States, and on Subjects growing out of the Event, together with Works on American Slavery, and Essays from Reviews and Magazines on the Same Subjects." At 477 pages, the volume testified not only to how extensively the topic had been discussed in the years and decades preceding the war but also to the formal and generic diversity that the debates over slavery took, including not just books but also reviews, essays, and pamphlets. In reviewing Bartlett's volume, a critic for the *North American Review* commended the author's labor, noting that the catalogue "contains six thousand and seventy-three entries, many of them titles of ephemeral publications which have already become of extreme rarity; and it is not unlikely that of some of them the only trace hereafter to be found will be that which will exist in this list." Besides illustrating the conditions that brought about the war, as the reviewer observed, "Its pages present a brief abstract of the various forms in which public opinion found expression, and of the modes in which it was addressed." As such, "They contain the condensed record of the thoughts of the nation; and in the short titles may be read the story of the war, and the nature of the principles from which sprang the conflict of arms."[4]

While literary history tends to privilege books, bound codex volumes whose form suggests lasting value, as Bartlett's catalogue suggests, in practice the arguments that fomented the Civil War played themselves out largely through more ephemeral print mediums. Reviews, essays, and pamphlets were often better suited to the fast-paced exchange of arguments amid the rapidly evolving slavery debate, as critics for and against the peculiar institution responded to current events as they transpired. While books might convey authority, they were too slow to keep up with the front page of the newspaper. Conversely, an article in a periodical or a well-attended lecture had a built-in limit on its audience while articles frequently had length restrictions as well. As a result, amid the high stakes of the slavery debate, advocates on either side of the issue became adept at exploiting the specific capacities of various print forms in order to best promote their position. It is here that liminal material forms such as pamphlets and reviews became crucial to the debates over slavery.

In the following chapter, I conclude the present study by arguing that the critical response to *Uncle Tom's Cabin* reveals in dramatic fashion the role that print forms play in the mobilization of literary criticism as an agent of political change. While most scholars have emphasized those critical statements that are most readable by modern standards of critical value—reviews or essays by named authors, known critics, or appearing in prestigious journals—in the following pages, I instead focus on less stable critical iterations: hybrid texts, often with unattributed or mixed authorship, and circulating in ephemeral forms that carry low or uncertain cultural authority. By focusing on the material periphery of critical discourse, we gain not only a more accurate picture of antebellum critical practices but of how these practices turned criticism from second order discourse into the main event, primary texts designed to have a broad social and political impact. In this sense, the chapter is both an attempt to historicize critical practice and to reveal literary criticism's cultural power.

In performing this task, I focus on three sites of critical response to *Uncle Tom's Cabin*: lengthy pamphlet reviews by southerners; Stowe's book-length critical rebuttal in *A Key to Uncle Tom's Cabin*; and reprinted critical responses in the black press. These three areas of reception, each with its own distinctive, material form, conclude the broader study by offering a picture of how nineteenth-century critics strategically used the material forms of critical discourse to forward their respective agendas, agendas that extended far beyond the realm of entertainment. If Poe worried that the critical institution had become commercialized and corrupt, with the success of *Uncle Tom's Cabin*, critics instead began to worry that both literature and criticism had become too political, a concern that gestured at the shifting cultural work of criticism in the second half of the nineteenth century.

Approaching the critical response to *Uncle Tom's Cabin* from a print culture perspective generates a series of insights about mid-nineteenth-century critical culture, while reinforcing several scholarly trends in treatments of Stowe and the literature of slavery. The first is that *Uncle Tom's Cabin* precipitated a full-scale reassessment of the current state of American literary and critical values. In particular, the critical response to Stowe's novel blurred the lines between fact and fiction, pushing literary and critical standards toward realism.[5] Stowe's novel also accelerated the reorientation of critical tensions from a transnational to a sectional axis, or more precisely, it entangled transatlantic literary competition with sectional concerns.[6] Second, reviews of *Uncle Tom's Cabin* unhinged the physical form of criticism, fostering hybrid and genre crossing critical practices that blurred distinctions among criticism, advertising, sociology, and political activism. The reception of *Uncle Tom's Cabin* also prompted innovative critical practices such as the publication of critical companion volumes like *A Key to Uncle Tom's Cabin* and the reprinting of lengthy reviews as pamphlets. This includes the phenomenon of anti-Tom novels like McIntosh's *Two Pictures* as well, in which southern authors employed the novel form to rebut

Stowe's portrait of slavery, responding critically through fiction rather than reviews or political tracts.[7]

Third, Stowe's novel provided a platform for the development of African American literary criticism by legitimizing the novel form within the black press. Yet this development paradoxically relied upon the widespread practice of reprinting reviews and on appropriating a range of non-literary discursive forms for the critical office. Finally, the critical uproar over Stowe's novel legitimated the vocation of criticism as a social practice, pushing it further from the eighteenth-century realm of belles lettres toward the emergence of academic criticism in the closing decades of the nineteenth century. Indeed, we might even argue that, while *Uncle Tom's Cabin* is a book that anticipates criticism within its original narrative, it also contributed to the emergence of what we might think of as new historical critical practice, with critics emphasizing the reciprocal relationship of literature and history as well as the sociopolitical discursive underpinnings of fiction.

"But We Are Fast Nearing the Utmost Limits of Our Article": *Uncle Tom's Cabin* and the Constraints of Criticism

From its earliest serialized appearance in the *National Era* in June of 1851, the success of *Uncle Tom's Cabin* was bound up with its materiality.[8] When Boston publisher John P. Jewett issued the novel in two volumes on March 20, 1852, it was in three formats: a cheap version in paper covers for $1.00, a cloth edition for $1.50, and an ornate gilt version for $2.00. Jewett's appeal to a variety of consumer sensibilities intensified what was already a strong pre-sale demand. Within a month, the first run of five thousand copies had been exhausted, while by March 22, Jewett reported that fifty thousand copies had been printed.[9] Throughout March and April, it was difficult to distinguish advertisements from reviews or to separate critical remarks from book promotion as the magazines reported the details of what was quickly proving to be a publishing phenomenon. Advertisements clipped critical praise from early notices and printed them as blurbs alongside sales numbers. Conversely, the earliest reviews took spiraling print runs and commercial excitement as jumping off points for their own critical responses. It was nothing short of media frenzy.

Almost immediately, critics fanned out to cover what had rapidly turned into a cultural event. They reported on the novel's unprecedented sales and on Jewett's attempts to keep up with them. They reported on spin-offs, reception abroad in England and elsewhere, and published remarks by prominent figures. Above all, criticism reprinted and responded to other criticism as the cycle of reviewing became a self-generating engine distinct from the novel itself. The orderliness with which Stephen Railton's invaluable digital database *Uncle Tom's Cabin and American Culture* indexes and organizes critical responses to the novel in a sense obscures the cacophony and unreadability of the novel's reception and of the workings of antebellum critical culture more generally.

Instead of signed reviews by known critics, magazines relied heavily on reprinting notices from other papers. And while occasionally the author of a review was known, more frequently he or she was not. Instead authorship was more closely identified with the political and religious stance of the journal or the geographical location of the periodical from which the review was clipped. Nor were responses limited to the review section. News of the novel was frequently a front-page story, focusing on the numerous controversies that arose from the novel's publication, printing letters by correspondents or accounts of Stowe's travels. Indeed, the clearest way to understand the critical reception of the novel is by the modern analogy of the twenty-first century media landscape in which internet articles are shared, "liked," tweeted, and commented upon through the frequently inscrutable, systemic logic of social media.[10]

It's difficult to fathom the scale of the critical response to *Uncle Tom's Cabin*. It is the tendency of literary scholarship to clean up and categorize, to find through-lines and common themes: the southern response, the British response, the African American response. But the critical reaction to *Uncle Tom's Cabin* was sprawling and disorganized, repetitive and redundant both in argument and article, with stories re-inscribed and reprinted in structures more evocative of Deleuze's branching rhizomes than in organized camps of uniform response. The flood of responses forced criticism into instant self-reflexivity. Within weeks, commentators couldn't begin an article without reference to the redundancy of their task. Southerners couldn't attack the novel without first noting that all refutations had already been made. As such, *Uncle Tom's Cabin* tested the habits of the critical vocation, forcing critics to regroup and take different approaches, particularly critics from the South.

As George Frederick Holmes observed halfway through his lengthy review in the December 1852 *Southern Literary Messenger*, "the misstatements of Uncle Tom's Cabin, have already, as we have said, been frequently exposed, but the refutation has been entirely disregarded in those quarters where alone the disproof of its mis-representations could be required. But, if for these and other reasons, we will not so far degrade ourselves as to retrace the beaten track, what remains for a Southern writer to do?"[11] Criticism for Holmes was both futile, an attempt to convince those who refused to be convinced, and more crucial than ever before. It forced a self-examination of how criticism was to proceed, as well as of the place of letters within the political life of a nation more generally. Indeed, for Holmes, the South was in large part to blame for the enormous and devastating popularity of *Uncle Tom's Cabin* since as a region it had long neglected the proper development of a native literary culture.

As Holmes laments, the lack of a southern literature had left the region defenseless. Accordingly, in a call that would be taken up by the rising generation of regional writers who would dominate the American literary scene of the postbellum period, Holmes insisted that, "The only true defence of the South against this attack, and the swarms of similar insults and indignities which its success and the prevalent fanaticism will generate, is to create and cherish a true Southern literature, whose spontaneous action will repel and refute such accusations, and command a respectful consideration wherever intellect is honored, or truth even dimly sought. Let the South honestly and cordially sustain her own periodicals, and her own writers, and such productions will cease to alarm or annoy her, or if they should attempt to fret her, they will be brushed aside without effort, and without producing even momentary injury. Let her fail to do this, and no one can complain if she is slandered, without contradiction and maligned without defence."[12] Decades later, Thomas Nelson Page would continue to echo Holmes's insistence that *Uncle Tom's Cabin* exposed the folly of the South in neglecting the literary vocation, revealing the urgent necessity of a strongly fortified literary' establishment for the promotion of a region's political interests. In doing so, the novel paved the way for writers like Page who abandoned the legal vocation for that of the man of letters, vocations in which the same sociopolitical battles were adjudicated via different means.[13]

While for Holmes, Stowe's novel exposed the vulnerability and underdevelopment of a southern literary establishment, countless other critics took the occasion of the review to celebrate the novel's American-ness and to refute English charges that American literature was merely derivative. As one reviewer for the *Christian Examiner* writes, "This is an American book. Our English critics will have no occasion to propose, as they so frequently do in treating our productions, some book of their own of which they can say that it is an imitation."[14] In a January 1853 article entitled "Uncle Tomitudes," an anonymous reviewer for *Putnam's Monthly* went even further. In surveying the preceding year, the critic describes the unprecedented publishing success of *Uncle Tom's Cabin* as nothing less than the commencement of a new epoch in the long history of print. As the critic proclaims,

> Here is a miracle! or something at least, that has not happened before, and consequently, for which the world was not prepared . . . Never since books were first printed has the success of *Uncle Tom* been equaled; the history of literature contains nothing parallel to it, nor approaching it; it is, in fact, the first real success in book-making, for all other successes in literature were failures when compared with the success of *Uncle Tom*. And it is worth remembering that this first success in a field which all the mighty men of the earth have labored in, was accomplished by an American woman. Who reads an American book, did you inquire, Mr. Smith? Why, your comfortable presence should have been preserved in the world a year or two longer, that you might have asked, as you would have done, "who does not?"[15]

This strain of transatlantic literary nationalism, as noted in previous chapters, had been a vocal refrain of critical debates from 1820 on. Yet more loudly than ever before, reviews of *Uncle Tom's Cabin* declared the decades long cultural feud over, with Sydney Smith's infamous charge now irrefutably put to bed.

The reviewer goes on to chart the book's unprecedented success: it exceeded one million copies in its first nine months; four presses running day and night couldn't keep up with demand; translations had appeared in France, Italy, and Germany while in England the lack of international copyright had produced even more sales and editions than in America. All of this "announces the commencement of a miraculous Era in the literary world," one born of "our steam-presses, steam-ships, steam-carriages, iron roads, electric telegraphs, and universal peace among the reading nations of the earth." Above all, it relies upon an expanded market of readers. The phenomenon spreads like an epidemic. It has given birth to an entire literature of anti-Tom novels devoted to refuting the portrait given by Stowe, "something entirely new in literature." And beyond America and England, the remaining nations of the world wait to be "Uncle Tomitized."[16]

If in reviews of *Uncle Tom's Cabin* critical positions on regional strife, transatlantic literary relations, and the developing publishing industry became entangled, no critical bias was more exposed by the success of Stowe's novel than the treatment of gender within contemporary reviewing. Critics raised the issue of Stowe's sex incessantly. For those who praised the novel, Stowe's femininity was a source of its emotional power since female writers had a natural aptitude for affairs of the heart—or so the argument went. For hostile critics, both in the South and elsewhere, meanwhile, Stowe's gender was an affront, compounding the insult of the novel's antislavery rabble-rousing with the author's transgression of gender boundaries through her decision to enter into the sphere of politics in the first place. The fact that the author of so infamous a novel was a woman proved a test for male southern critics, raised amid culturally embedded notions of honor, who frequently assumed the mantle of chivalry in their critical writings.

As an early review in the *Southern Literary Messenger*, unsigned but most likely by John R. Thompson, avers, to review Stowe's novel at all raises "the question whether lady authors should or should not be dealt with according to strict critical justice." In proceeding, therefore, "we beg to make a distinction between *lady* writers and *female* writers." A well-meaning "lady" of course deserves gentle treatment by critics. "But where a writer of the softer sex manifest, in her productions, a shameless disregard to truth and of those amenities which so peculiarly belong to her sphere of life, we hold that she has forfeited the claim to be considered a lady, and with that claim all exemption from the utmost stringency of critical punishment." Stowe had chosen to abuse her talents by sowing the seeds of strife, the critic insists, and in so doing, she has trespassed beyond her proper sphere in the home, meddling in politics where she doesn't belong, and violating the biblical injunction to subject herself to the authority of her husband. "We know that among other novel doctrines in vogue in the land of Mrs. Stowe's nativity—the pleasant land of New England—which we are old-fashioned enough to condemn, is one which would place woman on a footing of political equality with man, and causing her to look beyond the office for which she was created—the high and holy office of maternity—would engage her in the administration of public affairs; thus handing over the State to the perilous protection of diaper diplomatists and wet-nurse politicians."[17]

Or as George Frederick Holmes so graciously put it in the December 1852 issue of the *Southern Literary Messenger*, though the critic typically treats with care those writers of the softer sex, nonetheless, "if she deliberately steps beyond the hallowed precincts—the enchanted circle—which encompasses her as with the halo of divinity, she has wantonly forfeited her privilege and immunity as she has irretrievably lost our regard, and the harshness which she may provoke is invited by her own folly and impropriety." In short, "we cannot accord to the termagant virago or the foul-mouthed hag the same deference that is rightfully due to the maiden purity of untainted innocence." But our benevolent reviewer is too much of a gentleman, naturally, to deride the fairer sex, even the most reprehensible specimen of it. And so, "with this, we dismiss Mrs. Stowe: and we claim credit for our forbearance in thus resisting the temptation to castigate the improprieties of a woman, who has abandoned the elevated sphere appropriate to her sex and descended into the arena of civil dissension and political warfare—to say no more—where the gladiators contend naked and *a l'outrance*."[18]

Yet while for southern critics gender was a liability for Stowe as the author of the offending work, it was paradoxically an asset for critics attacking the novel when that critic happened to be a woman. Accordingly, while most reviews of *Uncle Tom's Cabin* were left unsigned, Louisa McCord's expansive, forty-page response for the *Southern Quarterly Review* appeared under the signature of McCord's well-known initials "LSM."[19] To have Stowe's novel refuted by a woman bestowed authority upon the critique. And though Holmes, Thompson, and other southern critics launched repeated ad hominem attacks upon Stowe's femininity, ironically, one of McCord's refrains in her own review was that Stowe did not understand the ingrained gentility of southerners. "Need we say to any reader who has ever associated with decent society anywhere, that Mrs. Stowe evidently does not know what 'a gentleman' is," McCord chides. Southern honor is taken as unfailing and constant, the guiding principle which Stowe's caricatures fail to comprehend or represent. For no decent southern gentleman would act as Shelby does, McCord insists, or be as blind to his own self-interest; no decent lady would behave as cruelly as Marie St. Clare had; no slaveholder would be as impotent to reconcile his principles with his actions as Augustine St. Clare. Only Mrs. Shelby's shrewish tirades, meanwhile, might drive a husband to such rash behavior as Shelby's selling of Tom.

Rather, as McCord sardonically affirms, "Ay, Mrs. Stowe, there are pious slaveholders; there are Christian slaveholders; there are gentlemanly slaveholders; there are slaveholders whose philosophic research has looked into nature and read God in his works, as well as in his Bible, and who own slaves because they think it, not expedient only, but right, holy, and just so to do, for the good of the slave—for the good of the master—for the good of the world." Slavery requires no apology but rather for McCord is a positive blessing, preserving an inferior race from extinction though the benevolence of the southern master class, "a Godlike dispensation, a providential caring for the weak, and a refuge for the portionless." Slavery is God's plan, such that, "the civilized world must totter to its foundations, when, if ever, African slavery in America ceases to exist."[20]

In setting forth her argument, McCord's overriding objection is that Stowe has taken theoretical possibilities regarding slavery, or at best exceptional cases, and presented them as typical and representative. Yet "evils, to be felt, must be tangible and not theoretic evils," McCord insists. "It is not enough that a master *might* do this, and might do that." Rather, "theory has done, and is doing, wild work in our world, of late years," and we must discard theoretical possibilities for the real state of things.[21] For McCord, however, Stowe is completely ignorant of the actual state of the South and has clearly traveled no farther than the border states where slavery has been perverted by its proximity to the fanaticism of abolition. She forms her picture based only on hearsay, tall tales from friends, and her brother's warped anecdotes.

In asserting these arguments, McCord's review, like many other southern reviews, offered a condensed litany of apologist arguments distilled through criticism of Stowe's text, proslavery manifestoes that proliferated through every periodical, month after month, for the better part of a decade. It was not simply that Stowe's novel stoked abolitionist sympathies in the general populace of the North; it solidified passionate resentment in the South as well while persuading the nation of the intractability of the sectional disagreement. As reviews of Stowe's novel revealed, the question of slavery was nothing short of a clash of civilizations.

For McCord, the task of criticism was an unpleasant burden, moreover: to even comment upon the book was painful while to disprove the truth of her portraits was futile since the case was prejudged. Refuting Stowe's slanders is the "labour of Sysiphus," McCord observes, fruitless in that the northern mind is already made up. "But what argument avails against broad, flat, impudent assertion? The greatest villain may swear down an honest man: and the greatest falsehoods are oftenest those which it is impossible to disprove." Indeed, it taxes the very conventions of criticism. As McCord notes toward the end of the forty-page review, "But our argument is becoming so prolix, that we must cut it short. We could run on for fifty pages, showing our author's blunders and inconsequences." A few pages later, she notes that, "These quotations are so delightfully racy, that we find it difficult to abridge them. But we are fast nearing the utmost limits of our article, and must stop."[22] McCord was hardly alone in feeling constrained by the formal parameters of the critical review. Rather, for southerners, Stowe's novel tested the limits of the review as a genre. It confronted them with what McCord and others felt to be a Sisyphean critical task.

In book reviews traditionally defined, the novel pushed the material limits of the form, as reviews sprawled into lengthy treatises spread out over multiple issues, as when a review by a southern critic writing under the name "Walpole" spanned four issues of the *New York Daily Times*.[23] For some critics, even these expanded parameters proved too limiting, if not in terms of length than in terms of audience. The result was that southerners took to new forms that offered more space for argument and more freedom to circulate widely, including that most adaptable of forms, the pamphlet. In the widespread practice of reprinting reviews as pamphlets, we see not only the search for a more flexible critical form but the shifting vocation of literary criticism as well, as reviewers came to embrace criticism's capacity to effect political change.

"Impassioned Pamphleteers":
Pamphlet Reviews and the Politics of Criticism

As both northern and southern reactions to *Uncle Tom's Cabin* suggest, the critical controversy over the novel centered around the fundamental question of what literature was for. In review after review, critics began with definitions of terms as they laid out the multiple provinces of literature and clarified those aspects with which he or she was primarily concerned. One writer for the *Mercersburg Review,* for instance, began by noting that, "the writer of fiction may have two objects in view: first, to produce a story which shall carry with it attraction and power as a work of art; second, to inculcate certain principles or doctrines."[24] While most reviews couldn't dispute the power of Stowe's novel as a work of art, as a "literary work merely," as one review put it, in regards to design, conception, and execution, many took issue with putting fiction to work for political ends.[25]

Accordingly, while the *Putnam's* reviewer locates the success of the novel in Stowe's consummate artistry, he nonetheless sees its antislavery sentiments as not a strength but a defect, "the great blemish of the book" without which "*Uncle Tom's Cabin* would be a nearly perfect work of art." While southern critics objected to the divisive effect that the novel must inevitably have, the *Putnam's* reviewer by contrast was skeptical that the book had produced any effect at all. The weakest moments, he notes, are those that betray the author's antislavery sympathies too nakedly, while the book as a whole presents a far more agreeable picture of slavery in the South than many other works treating the region. In sharp contrast to many reviewers who marveled at the political revolution the book must invariably effect in transforming sentiment around slavery, the *Putnam's* reviewer instead closes with the sobering observation that, "our last presidential election certainly did not afford any reason to believe that the minds of our countrymen had been at all influenced by Mrs. Stowe's enchantments."[26]

A reviewer for the *Southern Press Review,* in addressing the book's political efficacy, stated the case even more bluntly: "Now, what is the value of a work of fiction in this controversy? What would be its value even if [every] incident it contains were founded on fact, as the writer intimates? Why, just nothing at all." Comparing Stowe's novel to a recent proslavery pamphlet by Elwood Fisher, the reviewer notes that while "the system of the South relies on fact—the sentiment of the North flies to fiction. This is significant."[27] Indeed, this distinction between fiction and fact, between romance and politics, continued to be significant in the long critical controversy over *Uncle Tom's Cabin,* as the question for critics grappling with Stowe's novel became, if a novel embraced a political motive, did it continue to be good art?

For critics, whether proslavery, antislavery, or somewhere in between, *Uncle Tom's Cabin* was evidence of the shifting vocation of the novel as fiction embraced the social gospel of reform. Writing for the *Southern Literary Messenger,* an anonymous reviewer, likely George Frederick Holmes, began his lengthy review by observing that, "This is fiction—professedly a fiction; but, unlike other works of the same type, its purpose is not amusement, but proselytism." Yet this new mantle violated the pure aims of the older sort of romance. As Holmes opined, "The romance was formerly employed to divert the leisure, recreate the fancy, and quicken the sympathies of successive generations, changing its complexion and enlarging the compass of its aims with the expanding tastes of different periods; but never forgetting that its main object was to kindle and purify the imagination, while fanning into a livelier flame the slumbering charities of the human heart." This was no longer the case, however: "In these late and evil days, the novel, notwithstanding those earlier associations, has descended from its graceful and airy home, and assumed to itself a more vulgar mission, incompatible with its essence and alien to its original design. Engaging in the coarse conflicts of life, and mingling in the fumes and gross odours of political and polemical dissension, it has stained and tainted the robe of ideal purity with which it was of old adorned." The modern reader must accordingly be on his or her guard when picking up a novel lest she admit a wolf in sheep's clothing. Rather, the purpose of literature for Holmes should be to console, to ease our afflictions and expand our sympathies, not to be "the heralds of disorder and dissension."[28]

While the critic for the *Southern Press Review* drew a distinction between the northern propensity for fiction and the southern reliance on fact by juxtaposing Stowe's novel to Fisher's apologist pamphlet, the critical response to *Uncle Tom's Cabin* did far more to confuse and conflate the two genres than to demarcate them. Nowhere is the conflict between the politics of the novel and its ambitions as an art form more clearly stated than when in 1949, just short of a century after the first appearance of the novel, James Baldwin, in his essay "Everybody's Protest Novel," observed retrospectively that, "[Mrs. Stowe] was not so much a novelist as an impassioned pamphleteer; her book was not intended to do anything more than prove that slavery was wrong; was, in fact, perfectly horrible. This makes material for a pamphlet but it is hardly enough for a novel; and the only question left to ask is why we are bound still within the same constriction."[29] If Baldwin's critique of Stowe as not a novelist but an "impassioned pamphleteer" is often quoted, as we've seen, its argument was hardly new. Yet few scholars have taken this comparison seriously for the insight it offers regarding the material dimensions of antislavery critique.

Though Baldwin intends the comparison as a slight, a critique of Stowe's dehumanizing representation of her black characters, he also isn't wrong: Stowe's novel both drew upon and contributed to a vibrant culture of pamphleteering that informs not only the way we understand the text but the way the text circulated within antebellum literary culture. Within a year of its publication, the book appeared in not one but two cheap editions: a $1.00 edition in paper wrappers and, soon after, a 37 1/2 cent "Edition for the Millions." In each case, inexpensive reprinting in paper covers gave material shape to the novel's abolitionist ambition to spread antislavery sentiment far and wide. In doing so, it drew upon the pamphlet's generic properties as a printed form, its capacity to serve as "anti-slavery missiles," as Armistead Wilson termed it in his announcement of a campaign to deluge the nation with half a million abolitionist pamphlets.[30] In this sense, Stowe's novel was its own century's *Common Sense*. Yet by 1852 the novel had also joined the polemical pamphlet as an effective medium for political agitation and one particularly well-suited to widespread dissemination.

Beyond the novel's own political aims, signified through its republication in cheap, paperbound editions, *Uncle Tom's Cabin* also sparked a critical pamphlet war. On November 5, 1852, in an article entitled "Pro-Slavery Literature," William Lloyd Garrison's *Liberator* reviewed a series of apologist works written in response to Stowe's novel, including responses to two "handsome pamphlets" in addition to accounts of anti-Tom novels by W. L. G. Smith, Mary Eastman, and J. Thornton Randolph. The shorter of the two pamphlets, *Uncle Tom in England*, first appeared as a review in the *London Times* on September 3, 1852, before the *New York Times* reprinted it on September 18 under the title "American Slavery. English Opinion of 'Uncle Tom's Cabin.'" The New York publishers Bunce and Brother, known for printing cheap editions of popular novels, soon extracted the review and printed it as an eight-page standalone pamphlet under the revised American title (figure 10).

Though the publishers gloss the contents on the title page with the headings "Evils of Slavery" and "Method of Its Removal," the author's position is best summarized by the third gloss: "Danger of Agitation." For as the critic informs us, despite being a "decided hit," the book cannot disguise its true nature: that is, "Mrs. Harriet Beecher Stowe is an abolitionist, and her book is a vehement and unrestrained argument in favor of her creed." And though the critic cannot help but praise her artistry, he worries about the book's effect. "That she will secure proselytes we take for granted, but that she will help, in the slightest degree towards the removal of the gigantic evil that afflicts her soul, is a point upon which we may express the greatest doubt." Instead, Stowe's novel will only "rivet the fetters of slavery" by exciting the indignation of slaveowners.

In the remaining pages of the review, the critic proceeds to attack Stowe's abolitionist fanaticism as dangerous, urges gradualism, and commends southern slavery as softening yearly. He points out that slaves are better off than English peasants and insists that if any solution is to occur, it cannot be forced upon slaveowners but must be "voluntarily undertaken, accepted and carried out by the whole community."[31] The pamphlet offers a concise, calmly argued litany of familiar apologist arguments, in other words, and yet it comes from England, from an anonymous reviewer for the *London Times*, and thereby avoids the easy charge of regional bias. As such, there were surely many pro-

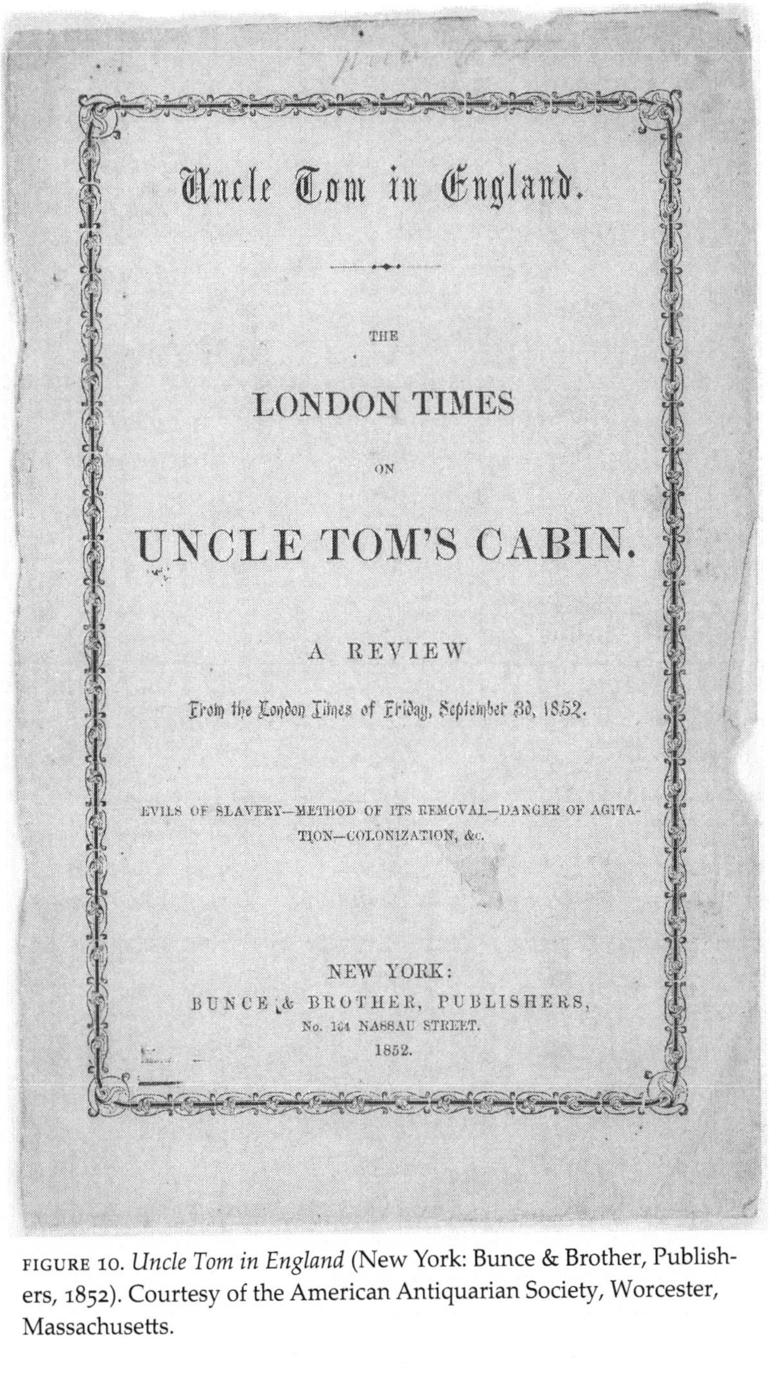

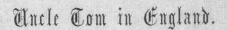

Uncle Tom in England.

THE

LONDON TIMES

ON

UNCLE TOM'S CABIN.

A REVIEW

From the London Times of Friday, September 30, 1852.

EVILS OF SLAVERY—METHOD OF ITS REMOVAL—DANGER OF AGITA-
TION—COLONIZATION, &c.

NEW YORK:
BUNCE & BROTHER, PUBLISHERS,
No. 144 NASSAU STREET.
1852.

FIGURE 10. *Uncle Tom in England* (New York: Bunce & Brother, Publishers, 1852). Courtesy of the American Antiquarian Society, Worcester, Massachusetts.

slavery advocates who wished to ensure that the review had a wide circulation.

The second pamphlet reviewed by the *Liberator* followed a different path, though many of its arguments were similar. Attributed to a "Carolinian" later identified as Edward J. Pringle, the essay originally appeared under the title *Slavery in the Southern States*. Just as the authority of *Uncle Tom in England* rested on the reviewer's supposed objectivity as an Englishman, Pringle's pseudonym in turn emphasized his authority as a southerner. As he accuses Stowe in the opening lines, "to preach distant reform is very cheap philanthropy,—the cheaper in proportion to the distance." Yet though Stowe professed to offer a true picture of the South, as the reviewer balks, "We know more of slavery than she does, though she has undertaken to tell all the world about it."[32] For Pringle's arguments to have any effect, however, ironically, "distant reform" was the precise thing required. This is where pamphlets came in. While in *Uncle Tom in England,* a book review was reprinted as a pamphlet, with *Slavery in the Southern States,* Pringle's pamphlet was reprinted in periodicals as a review.

A native Carolinian attending school at Harvard, Pringle composed his essay on Stowe's novel as a response to a British friend's query, "What do you think of 'Uncle Tom's Cabin' at the South?" He then published the response as a pamphlet in Cambridge, Massachusetts, which soon crossed the Atlantic and was reprinted as an article in *Fraser's Magazine* before the reprint journal *Littell's Living Age* spotted the piece there, clipped it, and reprinted it back in Boston complete with *Fraser's* preface. When a critic identifying himself as a "North Carolinian" responded to the article in a lengthy piece spreading across three issues of the *National Era*, he accordingly drew from *Littell's Living Age,* which he learned only belatedly had abridged Pringle's original. That is to say, while the authority of the argument rested on the critic's status as a "Carolinian," for the essay to achieve its purpose, it needed to travel beyond its author's geographical point of origin in the South—or rather the South by way of Massachusetts. Pamphlets helped achieve this goal, as the essay quickly moved from Boston to London back to Boston and then finally back to North Carolina where a fellow Carolinian responded to the piece in the Washington DC-based *National Era,* the very journal where Stowe's novel had its start. There's a pleasing, if dizzying, circularity to it all. In the meantime, the original pamphlet was reissued in two more editions, disclosing Pringle's name in the third, a substitution that paradoxically carried less weight than his anonymous signature as a "Carolinian."

As these two examples suggest, much of the power of pamphlets as a material form lay not only in their versatility, speed of production, and low cost, but also, as Laurel Brake suggests, in their fluid relationship to adjacent print forms.[33] In this case, the pamphlet and periodical book review complemented one another, shifting back and forth through networks of reprinting and remediation. In the case of *Slavery in the Southern States,* by circulating in two forms—as a magazine article and a pamphlet—Pringle and other interested parties increased the likelihood that readers, whether hostile or sympathetic, could get it, read it, and respond to it. And while the pamphlet's preface announced the work as literary criticism, thereby capitalizing upon the popularity of *Uncle Tom's Cabin,* in practice the arguments that unfolded were more properly within the province of political economy, seldom referring to the novel itself. Instead Pringle set forth a thoroughgoing paternalist argument, insisting that what Stowe doesn't see is the deep sense of duty and responsibility slaveholders feel toward the wellbeing and moral cultivation of their slaves. The notoriety of his pamphlet today, meanwhile, rests on his second argument: a scathing critique of the conditions of labor in the North. To the degree that Pringle shows up in the footnotes of histories by Eugene Genovese, Bertram Wyatt-Brown, and others, it is because he so clearly articulates the notorious wedding of a proto-Marxist critique of capitalism with a reactionary defense of plantation slavery, an effect that produces a vertigo of sorts, with radical socialism, drawing upon the revolutionary spirit of 1848, enlisted to prop up the blight of chattel slavery.[34]

In closing his review of *Uncle Tom's* reviewers, the critic for the *Liberator* brushes aside the argument of *Uncle Tom in England,* which, in typical apologist fashion, derides Stowe's portrait of slavery as an "altogether exaggerated and overdrawn account . . . too shocking for belief." Yet before concluding, the reviewer pauses to mention that, "this long article was briefly, but very effectively, replied to in the *Times* a few days after, by one who said that, though not familiar with *American* slavery, he was well acquainted with *slavery* . . . and gave his judgment that in that work the evils of slavery were too feebly rather than too strongly stated," before then proceeding to offer ample evidence by way of rebuttal. Yet despite the effectiveness of the rejoinder, as the critic observes, "no notice was taken of this reply in the pamphlet referred to." This offhand remark cuts to the heart of pamphlet reprinting as a political strategy. For while reprinting a book review as a pamphlet worked to extend the argument's reach, it also worked to control the terms of the debate as it played out within the more unruly periodical press. In this instance, the reprinted pamphlet included the proslavery argument that appeared in the *Times* while excluding the effective rebuttal that followed.[35]

As these two pamphlets also suggest, part of what's significant about *Uncle Tom's Cabin* to the development of American literary criticism was the way that critical responses to the novel blurred disciplinary boundaries and genre demarcations. A hundred and thirty years before Stephen Greenblatt and Walter Benn Michaels, Stowe had southern and northern critics acting as proto-historicists, tethering their literary exegesis to the adjacent disciplines of history, economics, politics, law, and anthropology, just as Stowe soon would in *A Key to Uncle Tom's Cabin*. This disciplinary blurring was signified through the material form of the pamphlet, a form more closely associated with political disputes, radicalism, and doctrinal religious debates than with belles lettres.

Pringle's *Slavery in the Southern States* was just one of many pamphlets that eroded and expanded the boundaries of literary criticism. Sir Arthur Helps's *Letter on Uncle Tom's Cabin* (1852), for instance, an eloquent epistolary response to Stowe's novel by a British dignitary, circulated in multiple pamphlet editions, which were in turn reprinted widely in the periodical press. Conversely, Nassau William Senior's pamphlet *American Slavery* (1856) served as an improvised anthology of sorts, republishing an article on Stowe's novel from the *Edinburgh Review* together with a speech by Charles Sumner. *The Discussion Between Rev. Joel Parker, and Rev. A. Rood* (1852), meanwhile, capitalized upon the reverend Joel Parker's threatened libel suit of Stowe by reprinting as a single pamphlet the entire sixteen-installment debate that took place six years earlier in the Philadelphia *Christian Observer* and which served as background to the controversy. And then there were the numerous anti-Tom novels, which, though possessing the contentious soul of a pamphlet, responded to Stowe's fiction with fiction.[36]

Though the precise motivations for pamphlet reviews differed from case to case, whenever an interested party reprinted a book review as a pamphlet, it nonetheless signaled a repurposing of literary criticism for some greater cause beyond the realm of literary entertainment, a protean gesture that simultaneously revealed the communicative constraints of antebellum print media while working to overcome those constraints. While reviews published in periodicals, whether magazine or newspaper, had a limited audience and a brief temporal lifespan, pamphlets endeavored to overcome these limitations by broadening the readership and prolonging the circulation of the article. The pamphlet was also a way to overcome the ephemerality of periodicals while still capitalizing upon their timely engagement with current events. And though the nature of remediation could differ dramatically from pamphlet to pamphlet, it was seldom if ever neutral, while the very fact of republication signaled some instrumental purpose in and of itself. An author, publisher, or interested third party reissued a review as a pamphlet when he or she wanted it to reach new or different or larger audiences than it had previously. Finally, pamphlet reviews of *Uncle Tom's Cabin*, in particular, signaled the conflation of literary criticism with other discursive genres as well as the elevation of the figure of the critic within antebellum culture as literary criticism became closely intertwined with the political affairs of the nation.[37]

From a book history perspective, however—a title that still betrays, whether intentionally or not, the privileging of the codex over more ephemeral print forms—pamphlets retain a liminal status, residing in the limbo between the historical weight of the bound codex and the temporal urgency of the periodical. The former records the grand narratives while the latter glimpses the progress of history as it happens. One grasps at the transhistorical, the diachronic, while the other revels in the contemporaneity and temporal cacophony of the synchronic. Pamphlets offered a middle ground, however, between the authoritativeness of the book and the quick turnaround of the periodical. They were cheap to print and easy to distribute. Indeed, as David Paul Nord suggests, perhaps their most crucial characteristic was

that their low production cost allowed them to be published and purchased in bulk and given away for free.[38] For African American authors
in particular, as Richard Newman, Patrick Rael, and Phillip Lapsansky suggest, pamphlets offered not only generic versatility and dis-
tributive power but greater expressive control, free from the meddling
constraints of white editors and publishers.[39] Unlike reviews in periodicals, they had no length restrictions, meanwhile, and could be anywhere from a few pages to over a hundred while still responding to a
recent event or publication. So too, they could reach audiences beyond
those who might subscribe to a particular magazine, or who may have
missed a particular newspaper article.

Still, for some critics even the enlarged format of pamphlets proved
too constricting, prompting the development of a new phenomenon in
American critical history: the production of book-length reviews, point
by point critical rebuttals of Stowe's novel stretching to hundreds of
pages and issued as standalone volumes, often with elaborate production value in their own right. In 1853, for instance, A. Woodward published his 216-page *Review of Uncle Tom's Cabin; Or, an Essay on Slavery*, which F. C. Adams followed soon after with his 142-page *Uncle
Tom at Home. A Review of the Reviewers and Repudiators of Uncle Tom's
Cabin* (1853) (figure 11). The critical uproar eventually prompted Stowe
to issue her own rejoinder in *A Key to Uncle Tom's Cabin* (1853), a companion volume responding to those critics who, for the past year, had
systematically attacked the truth of her portrait. Stowe's volume in turn
prompted Reverend E. J. Stearns to issue *Notes on Uncle Tom's Cabin:
Being a Logical Answer to Its Allegations and Inferences Against Slavery
as an Institution. With a Supplementary Note on The Key, and an Appendix of Authorities* (1853), a work which, at 314 pages, won the prize for
both overall length and length of title.[40] Finally, with a clear eye for the
absurdity of these nettling, bloated critical volumes, one author writing under the pseudonym Nicholas Brimblecomb, Esq. issued toward
the end of 1853 the attention-grabbing *Uncle Tom in Ruins! Triumphant
Defence of Slavery!*, a work which, for those who actually took the time
to read it, proved to be a full-length satire of book-length apologist
attacks of Stowe's novel, itself running to 162 pages.

Despite the clear satirical intent of the volume, however, by
this point nobody could tell what was what, as evidenced by the

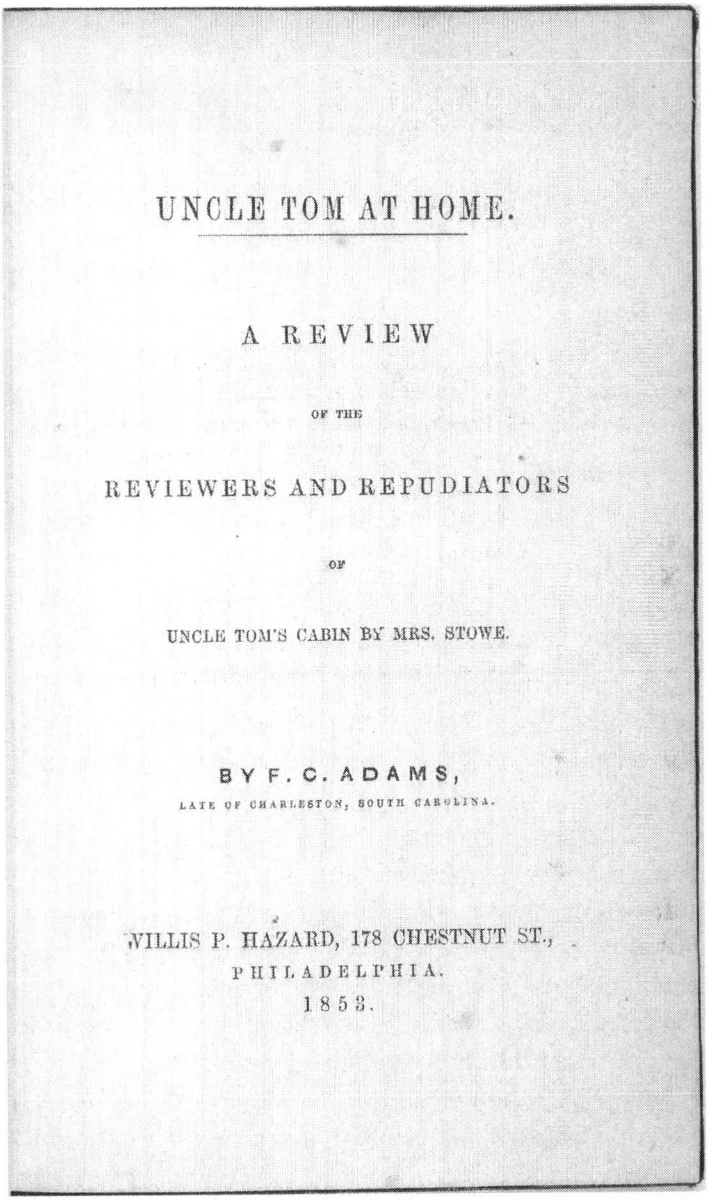

UNCLE TOM AT HOME.

A REVIEW

OF THE

REVIEWERS AND REPUDIATORS

OF

UNCLE TOM'S CABIN BY MRS. STOWE.

BY F. C. ADAMS,

LATE OF CHARLESTON, SOUTH CAROLINA.

WILLIS P. HAZARD, 178 CHESTNUT ST.,

PHILADELPHIA.

1853.

FIGURE 11. F. C. Adams, *Uncle Tom at Home* (Philadelphia: Willis P. Hazard, 1853). Courtesy of the American Antiquarian Society, Worcester, Massachusetts.

response of *Frederick Douglass' Paper*, which missed the joke completely, perfunctorily noting the existence of Brimblecomb's volume before excerpting a passage as evidence of the weakness of the ostensibly proslavery arguments. In the melee of critical responses, the editor, most likely Julia Griffiths, could hardly be blamed for not reading yet another apologist defense or for mistaking as sincere the laughably weak proslavery arguments since earnest apologist logic was often no better.[41] Indeed, as both the pamphlets and book-length reviews suggest, we might even say that *Uncle Tom's Cabin* taxed antebellum criticism to its breaking point—at the very least, it changed its course. And nowhere is this new path more evident than in the new material forms that criticism took, including Stowe's own book-length defense.

"Truth Stranger than Fiction": Stowe's *Key* and the Critical Companion Volume

It was amid the deluge of critical attacks that Stowe finally found it necessary to defend herself, issuing early in 1853 *A Key to Uncle Tom's Cabin*, 262 closely printed, double-columned pages of counterattack, which, much like *Uncle Tom's Cabin* itself, Jewett published in multiple editions, including a cheap version in paper wrappers. If readers were expecting more of what they found in *Uncle Tom's Cabin*, they must have been sorely disappointed. What the volume lacked in emotional absorption, however, it made up for in argumentative acumen, as over the course of the volume's four subdivided sections, Stowe amassed an arsenal of evidence to prove once and for all the accuracy of her portrait of slavery while rebutting the attacks of her critics. In entering into the critical fray, much of Stowe's argumentative power in *A Key* emerged from her deeply intuitive understanding of the workings of antebellum print culture. As Cindy Weinstein notes, Stowe's ingenuity resided in her ability to turn southerners' own statements against themselves, assembling in her *Key* a collage of accounts, a slavery commonplace book, designed to prove beyond question the horrible truth of chattel slavery to those who had never confronted it directly.[42] In doing so, however, Stowe's *Key* also revealed the degree to which the original novel was itself a print culture patchwork.

As with Louisa McCord's review of the novel, Stowe begins *A Key* by acknowledging that, "this work which the writer here presents to the public is one which has been written with no pleasure, and with much pain."[43] Rather, the motivation for the volume resided in the full title itself: *A Key to Uncle Tom's Cabin; Presenting the Original Facts and Documents Upon Which The Story Is Founded. Together With Corroborative Statements Verifying The Truth Of The Work.* The title page, like the volume to follow, leaves little to misconstrue, its typography emphasizing that the purpose of the volume was to prove the truth of the facts upon which her narrative was based. For as Stowe explains, "At different times, doubt has been expressed whether the representations of *Uncle Tom's Cabin* are a fair representation of slavery as it at present exists. This work, more, perhaps, than any other work of fiction that ever was written, has been a collection and arrangement of real incidents,—of actions really performed, of words and expressions really uttered,—grouped together with reference to a general result, in the same manner that the mosaic artist groups his fragments of various stones into one general picture. His is a mosaic of gems,—this is a mosaic of facts."[44]

Like Poe in "The Philosophy of Composition," skeptical of the demystifying effect that authorial exposés must invariably have on the work under dissection, so too Stowe admits that from an artistic perspective such a volume is folly. "Artistically considered, it might not be best to point out in which quarry and from which region each fragment of the mosaic picture had its origin," she concedes, "and it is equally unartistic to disentangle the glittering web of fiction, and show out of what real warp and woof it is woven, and with what real coloring dyed. But the book had a purpose entirely transcending the artistic one, and accordingly encounters, at the hands of the public, demands not usually made on fictitious works." In short, "it is *treated* as a reality,—sifted, tried and tested, as a reality; and therefore as a reality it may be proper that it should be defended." Yet though her current companion volume threatened to destroy the artistic effect of her novel, her course of action was paradoxically justified since, as Stowe admits, as a work of fiction her novel could never do justice to the true horrors of slavery. "It is so, necessarily, for this reason,—that slavery, in some of its workings, is too dreadful for the purposes of art. A work which should represent it strictly as it is would be a work which could not be read. And

all works which ever mean to give pleasure, must draw a veil somewhere, or they cannot succeed."[45] For Stowe, that is, to represent slavery throws into question the very distinction between fiction and reality, dissolving the gap between the two.

This documentary emphasis on the textual sources for her narrative further eroded the romantic critical emphasis on originality, much
as slave narratives had done in the preceding decades. In a section of
A Key "authenticating" the chapter from Uncle Tom's Cabin entitled
"Select Incidents of the Lawful Trade," for instance, and in particular
the account of the separation of an aged slave woman from her young
son, Stowe observes with wry irony that, "The writer is sorry to say that
not the slightest credit for invention is due to her in this incident. She
found it, almost exactly as it stands, in the published journal of a young
Southerner, related as a scene to which he was eye-witness."[46] Rather,
throughout A Key Stowe recorded the degree to which literary composition was a process of assembling from pre-existing materials instead
of an act of outright invention. This practice was reinforced by the critical response to her novel itself, which demanded that incidents related
to slavery be based upon reality rather than invention. By carefully documenting the sources for her fiction and the materials she drew upon
in crafting her work of imagination, however, Stowe gave historical
grounding to Poe's aesthetic principle that true originality exists in artful combination rather than in creating an artistic vision ex nihilo.

To the degree that A Key proved an effective counterattack, it was
paradoxically Stowe's southern critics—reviewers like George Frederick Holmes and Louisa McCord—who precipitated this course of
action in their insistence that her account couldn't be trusted because it
was mere fiction. In constantly reminding readers of the line between
fact and fiction, moreover—a line whose blurring is the very history
and origin of the novel itself—southern critics compelled Stowe to
puncture the fanciful notion that artistic composition is anything other
than weaving together existing threads, or assembling a "mosaic of
facts," as she put it. Moving from the vision of romantic genius to that
of the realist painter of modern life, Uncle Tom's Cabin recast artistic
accomplishment as the skillful handling of materials and as the craft of
representing life in a manner that is either true or that achieves worth-
while social effects.

In drawing back the fictional veil in her *Key*, meanwhile, Stowe answered southern attacks upon the veracity of her portrait with a cavalcade of testimonies, source materials, and authentications of the facts upon which her novel was founded. In assembling these materials, however, the paradox that became clear amid the spiraling, self-enveloping reception to *Uncle Tom's Cabin* was that the material contexts in which literary criticism circulated both mattered tremendously to the authority of the views expressed and were constantly blurred, recast, effaced, and tampered with for deliberate effect by a culture that was particular savvy as to the argumentative weight that different print forms and contexts carried with them. In short, publication contexts mattered, as Stowe relied as much on the source of a statement for its authority—or, alternately, its ironic effect—as she did on the content of the statement itself.

In a section entitled "The Spirit of St. Clare," for instance, Stowe collects positive reviews of her novel appearing in southern newspapers or letters from southerners attesting to the novel's veracity published in northern papers. She published advertisements for runaway slaves and announcements of slave auctions, frequently retaining the precise visual and typographical effects of the original. Part of the volume's power, indeed, lay in the variety of its contents, as over the course of the four sections Stowe brought every sort of evidence to bear, from personal conversations and observations by Stowe herself, first-hand testimony extracted from slave narratives by Frederick Douglass, Lewis Clarke, and Josiah Henson, to the frequently damning accounts contained within published defenses by slavery apologists. Nor was Stowe the first to apply a curatorial strategy to the antislavery cause. Much of the material Stowe clipped was already second hand when she got to it, as when she quotes newspaper articles that published letters from contributors or culls excerpts from Theodore Dwight Weld's *American Slavery As It Is: The Testimony of a Thousand Witnesses* (1839), itself a compilation of first-hand testimony from an eclectic array of sources. In doing so, Stowe, like Weld before her, both removed texts from their original contexts while relying on the signifying power of those very contexts.

Turning critical attacks on her novel on their heads, Stowe's patchwork process placed fact and fiction into generative and dynamic relation. For while she did her best to hide the stitching in the original novel, in *A Key* Stowe shined a light on the seams, sacrificing the enchantments of artifice for the argumentative authority of her sources. If *A Key* exposed the *un*originality of *Uncle Tom's Cabin*, that is, its diligent account of the story's source materials proved a powerful rejoinder to southern critics. Her authorial strategy, meanwhile, beyond the work of gleaning and gathering the print record of slavery, lay in the arrangement, juxtaposition, and treatment of these source materials. In this vein, as Weinstein notes, throughout *A Key* Stowe repeatedly wielded the rhetorical weapons of irony, documentation, and direct citation, providing a preponderance of evidence that allowed the absurdity of apologist accounts to speak for itself. This strategy avoided the charge of polemic, moreover, by putting the task of judgment in the reader's hands, airing apologist accounts alongside antislavery descriptions. In deploying this rhetorical weaponry in *A Key*, Weinstein argues, Stowe produced a "devastating counterattack" against southern critics, "an irate and ironic critique of critiques of *Uncle Tom's Cabin* which aims to prove the mutual exclusivity of being both pro-slavery and sympathetic."[47]

For while Stowe drew authority from a text's original source of publication, her most ingenious tactic in the *Key* was to render apologist defenses of slavery ridiculous by juxtaposing them to a parade of conflicting accounts by fellow southerners. After providing pages of testimony regarding the impoverished living conditions of slaves from a panoply of sources, for instance, many of them southern in origin, Stowe follows up with an account by a cheery-eyed apologist, J. H. Ingraham, who reports on a slaveowner who purportedly indulges the whims of his slaves, providing four-post beds, mosquito nets, tobacco, Christmas gifts, and porches on their cabins for shade. "How far these may be regarded as exceptional cases, or as pictures of the general mode of providing for slaves," Stowe observes sardonically, "may safely be left to the good sense of the reader." For as Stowe sarcastically adds, after excerpting a lengthy passage from Ingraham's work, "The writer [Stowe] would not think to controvert the truth of these anecdotes. Any probable amount of high-post bedsteads and mosquito 'bars,' of tobacco distributed as gratuity, and verandas constructed by leisurely carpenters for the sunning of fastidious negroes, may be con-

ceded, and they do in no whit impair the truth of the other facts. When
the reader remembers that the 'gang' of some opulent owners amounts
to from five to seven hundred working hands, besides children, he can
judge how extensively these accommodations are likely to be provided.
Let them be safely thrown into the account, for what they are worth."[48]

In Part Two of *A Key*, meanwhile, Stowe reverses tactics in her interrogation of the line between fiction and fact, exposing, not the factual sources for her fiction, but rather the imaginative feats required
of southern legal statutes, case law, and judicial decisions regarding
slavery. If her fiction relied on fact, as her *Key* took pains to prove, conversely, southern slave law was a tissue of fictions. Observing a particularly heinous bit of statute, for instance, Stowe notes that, "This
passage of the Revised Statutes of North Carolina is more terribly suggestive to the imagination than any particulars into which the author
of Uncle Tom's Cabin has thought fit to enter." In recounting a second
case in which a master emancipates and marries a slave while residing in Ohio, and has a son with her, only to have both mother and son
claimed as property by distant relatives in Mississippi after the husband dies, Stowe observes bitterly that, "Had this case been chosen
for the theme of a novel, or a tragedy, the world would have cried out
upon it as a plot of monstrous improbability. As it stands in the law-
book, it is only a specimen of that awful kind of truth, stranger than
fiction, which is all the time evolving in one form or another, from the
workings of this anomalous system."[49] In subjecting case law to literary
exegesis while documenting the factuality of her novel, Stowe reverses
the authority of legal discourse and fiction. It is the cruel, dispassionate
logic of law that sanctions the gross injustices committed daily within
the institutions of slavery, while, by contrast, it is literature, with its
imaginative scenes and fabricated characters, that promotes visions of
humanity, sympathy, love, and even basic decency.

In exposing the grotesque romance of slave law, Stowe's argument once again relies on the authority of the printed text. In prefac-
ing one chapter that treats southern slave law, Stowe pauses to note
that, "the author must state, with regard to some passages which she
must quote, that the language of certain enactments was so incredible
that she would not take it on the authority of any compilation whatever, but copied it with her own hand from the latest edition of the

statute-book where it stood and still stands."[50] By juxtaposing her critique of slave law as fundamentally fictional with the defense of her
novel as founded on fact, Stowe effectively inverted the positions of
romance and legal discourse while recasting the act of criticism as that
of legal advocate. She did so, moreover, by drawing on a range of documentary evidence whose authority rested on its original publication
context, while its argumentative force depended on its redeployment
and arrangement in new contexts. The result of this blurring of material contexts, these patterns of re-inscription, recycling, and repackag-
ing, was a redefinition of the meaning of both literature and criticism,
as the nineteenth-century critical vocabulary began to shift. Verisimilitude replaced imagination; real replaced ideal; and craft replaced originality as the mark of artistic genius.

So too, the standards of critical judgment began to shift as well, as for
editors like Frederick Douglass, as for Stowe in her *Key*, critical authority began to depend as much upon *where* a piece of criticism originated
as it did upon the reputation of the individual critic him or herself. For
as both Stowe and Douglass perceived, paradoxically, the editorial act
of reprinting a piece of criticism from another paper often carried more
argumentative weight than publishing an original review. If this was
Stowe's strategy in *A Key*, Douglass made it a guiding editorial principle within his own periodical *Frederick Douglass' Paper*, particularly
when it came to the matter of literary criticism. To confront the full
range of the critical response to *Uncle Tom's Cabin* in *Douglass' Paper*,
however, challenges the very definition of criticism itself as well as the
relation of critical print forms to critical authority.

Beyond the "Proper Notice":
Critical Reprinting in *Frederick Douglass' Paper*

In July of 1852, Douglass included within the pages of his paper an
account of a recent three-day trip to Ithaca, New York. In recounting
the details of his tour, Douglass paused to express his astonishment
at the "pleasing change in the public opinion of the place" in its stance
toward slavery since his last visit ten years earlier. He observed that
while the Fugitive Slave Act and the cumulative effect of antislavery
lecturers and papers must be held partly responsible for this shift, "It

must be conceded that the most efficient agent in changing the sentiment of Ithaca, as well as elsewhere, must be set down to the circulation of 'UNCLE TOM'S CABIN.' That book is but at the beginning of its
career, and it goes like fire through a 'dry stubble,' sweeping all before
it." While acknowledging the important work Stowe's novel had
accomplished, however, just one day earlier, Douglass also recorded
his surprise and discomfort when, arriving at a scheduled address to
the black congregation of Zion Church, he discovered that the audience was, "contrary to my expectation, and partly to my wishes,
largely composed of white persons," adding his concern that, "there
are some things which ought to be said to colored people in the peculiar circumstances in which they are placed, that can be said more effectively among themselves, without the presence of white persons." For
as Douglass notes, "We are the oppressed, the whites are the oppres-
sors, and the language I would address to the one is not always suited
to the other." In the remarks that followed, Douglass recalls, "I aimed
to impress upon my friends, in my speech, the importance of helping
themselves," a lesson that took on a decidedly ironic coloring given the
largely white audience.[51]

Though the dissonance between his message and the context is glaring, Douglass made no attempt to mask or apologize for the contradiction. Instead, he rendered it legible to his readership by narrat-
ing it through the form of an editor's letter, comprised of three-days'
worth of journal entries recording his travels and experiences in Ithaca,
a form that provided a wide berth for such contradictions to express
themselves. For while, on the one hand, Douglass couldn't help but
marvel at the positive impact that Stowe's novel was having on the
white population, on the other, he insisted that northern blacks needed
to take their future into their own hands and expressed concern that
to speak without restraint required a venue "without the presence of
white persons."

It was this question of who should plead the cause of African Americans that formed the crux of Douglass's debate with Martin R. Delany
over *Uncle Tom's Cabin*. On this point, Delany does not mince words:
"We have always fallen into great errors in efforts of this kind going to
others than the *intelligent* and *experienced* among *ourselves*; and in all
due respect and deference to Mrs. Stowe, I beg leave to say, that she

knows nothing about us, 'the Free Colored people of the United States,' neither does any other white person—and, consequently, can contrive no successful scheme for our elevation; it must be done by ourselves." Yet by 1852, Douglass was too pragmatic to make such categorical claims or to deny aid from white allies. As he responded to Delany, "that colored men would agree among themselves to do something for the efficient and permanent aid of themselves and their race 'is a consummation devoutly to be wished;' but until they do, it is neither wise nor graceful for them, or for any one of them to throw cold water upon plans and efforts made for that purpose by others. To scornfully reject all aid from our white friends and to denounce them as unworthy of our confidence, looks high and mighty enough on paper; but unless the back ground is filled up with facts demonstrating our independence and self-sustaining power, of what use is such display of self-consequence?"[52]

This clash between pragmatism and principle, results and rhetoric, was visible throughout the literary criticism appearing in *Douglass' Paper*. For Douglass, as Robert Levine notes, the moral and aesthetic value of *Uncle Tom's Cabin* resided in its capacity to effect social change, its "cultural work" in Jane Tompkins's formulation.[53] Douglass's approach to both literature and criticism was practical and instrumental, rooted in the ability of each to combat slavery and promote the elevation of the race. It was this pragmatic attention to outcomes that prompted him to chastise Delany for assertions that might appear "high and mighty enough on paper," but which produced no quantifiable results. Or as Douglass put it in remarks upon Stowe's much publicized tour of England, "Heaven, according to Swedenborg, consists of '*uses*;' whether this be so or not, down here among men, things are valued according as they are useful, or discarded and thrown away as they are useless. The colored people in this country, will in the end, stand or fall by this test."[54]

While Douglass's remark referred specifically to the necessity of industrial schools for black freedmen, and to the prospect of financial assistance from Stowe, it applied equally to Douglass's sense of the critical vocation. For Douglass, that is, both literature and criticism were valuable to the degree that they were "useful" and dispensable when they weren't. In practice, however, this meant that much of the literary criticism that Douglass included in his paper privileged political utility over aesthetic evaluation, while discarding longstanding markers of critical authority such as originality, length, known authorship, or even generic signposting as a review. Rather, more frequently critical content was reprinted from other periodicals, left unsigned, contributed by correspondents, or embedded in forms that didn't clearly register as literary criticism. Indeed, while Douglass included a Literary Notices section in most issues, the literary discussions of greatest urgency and broadest cultural stakes—those tied to slavery, social uplift, and the political prospects of African Americans—seldom were restricted to the review section and instead were spread throughout the paper's featured contents.

If Douglass's expansive definition of criticism comprised a deliberate editorial strategy, however, it could also make it difficult for readers to discern Douglass's own critical opinions, as amid reprinted articles and unconventional critical forms his direct authorial voice could at times seem notably absent. In the same July 30, 1852, issue describing his Ithaca trip, for instance, a correspondent from nearby Herkimer, New York, O. A. Bowe, wrote in to remark that, "Among the most encouraging signs of the times, I think we may reckon the publication and wide diffusion of Mrs. Beecher Stowe's graphic and powerful work, 'Uncle Tom's Cabin.'" Of Stowe's novel, however, "I do not recollect to have seen any proper notice, either editorial or communicated, in your columns." This editorial silence struck Bowe as a missed opportunity, for "it is, indeed, a mighty book—a perfect moral thunderbolt—and is making dreadful havoc among the 'refuges of lies' in which the political, clerical, and cotton apologists for slavery are accustomed to hide themselves."[55]

Yet despite Bowe's objection, by July of 1852, Douglass had already included not one but several critical responses to Stowe's novel, including letters from Ethiop [William J. Wilson] and William G. Allen, as well as the unsigned literary notice by either himself or his literary editor, Julia Griffiths. For Bowe, however, none of these pieces quite registered as a "proper notice," at least none that could be confidently taken as Douglass's response to Stowe's novel. As if to prove Bowe's point, it was in this same issue that Douglass published the account of his travels in Ithaca, New York, with his conflicted sense of the impact of

Stowe's novel on the American public. In doing so, Douglass revealed a critical dissonance between the familiar sort of review that Bowe was calling for (and failing to find) and the brand of hybrid, eclectic, reprinted critical forms that Douglass favored.

To consider literary criticism in *Frederick Douglass' Paper* is to reflect upon the very nature of criticism itself, of what counts as criticism, and what generic assumptions we bring to the table when we study America's critical past. The editorial privileging of unsigned, unoriginal, genre-blurring literary criticism was hardly limited to *Douglass' Paper*. Rather, it was a staple of antebellum critical practice in antislavery papers like the *Liberator* or the *National Era*, early African American periodicals like *Rights of All* or the *Colored American*, and in the antebellum periodical press more broadly. As Meredith McGill has shown, reprinting was ubiquitous within antebellum literary culture, destabilizing literary history's emphasis on originality. For Ryan Cordell, the prevalence of reprinting within antebellum newspapers specifically reorients conceptions of authority away from individual authorship and toward repetition, circulation, and the "network author," "a model of authorship that is communal rather than individual, distributed rather than centralized."[56]

In contrast to quarterlies and monthly magazines, which often prided themselves on original content, given the demands of frequent publication, as Ellen Gruber Garvey suggests, newspapers relied heavily upon reprinting for both copy and for coverage outside their local purview, content that expanded the geographical scope of a paper by introducing far-flung domestic and international fare. Far from haphazard, this practice of clipping and reprinting was orchestrated by a developed system of periodical "exchanges" that, as Frances Smith Foster observes, was commonplace in the early black press as well, with newspaper exchanges recorded in Douglass's regular distribution lists.[57] His reliance on clipping and reprinting from a vast print culture, meanwhile, as Garvey suggests, was a powerful rhetorical strategy employed by other antislavery advocates like Theodore Dwight Weld, Sarah and Angelina Grimké, and Stowe herself in both *Uncle Tom's Cabin* and its *Key*.[58]

Yet while reprinting features prominently in current scholarly conversations, and while studies of American criticism are as old as the institutional study of American literature itself, little attention has been paid to the widespread practice of critical reprinting or to the ways reprinted reviews reconfigure entrenched assumptions about critical authority. Despite the vitality of print culture studies as a methodology for revising and complicating longstanding narratives of literary history, scholarly treatments of American criticism remain surprisingly conservative in their criteria of critical value, continuing to rely on a selective roster of sources and a narrow definition of criticism that paradoxically replicates Bowe's limited sense of the "proper notice," with its focus on originality, attribution, and generic self-identification, as the standard-bearer of critical authority.

In the remainder of this chapter, accordingly, drawing on Douglass's approach to criticism in *Frederick Douglass' Paper*, I offer two interrelated claims. First, I argue that antebellum critical culture relied upon a diverse range of critical forms beyond reviews and literary notices, many of which were diffuse, anonymous, unoriginal, tangential, and generically hybrid, and that taken together unsettle naturalized notions of critical authority. The unprecedented scale of *Uncle Tom's Cabin's* success, as argued in this chapter's previous sections, cast this critical diversity into relief, propelling critical practice into reflexive self-examination while taxing its generic bounds still further. In doing so, it highlighted the political potential inherent in literary criticism broadly and individual critical forms specifically, including forms typically dismissed by modern scholarship as marginal, if criticism at all.

Second, I argue that in his capacity as editor Douglass wielded the power of reprinted, generically hybrid criticism to create a polyvocal critical forum that privileged the values of community debate over the authority of a single critical perspective, his own included. In choosing the two canonical, if not hyper-canonical texts of *Uncle Tom's Cabin* and *Frederick Douglass' Paper*, my intention is not to suggest that either is fully representative or exceptional in its respective evocation and display of antebellum critical practice. While there were certainly other novels that generated a political response in their reviews, and while literary criticism has never in its long history *not* been political, even (if not especially) amid assertions of disinterestedness or objectivity, the cultural ubiquity of *Uncle Tom's Cabin* made this political agency impossible for observers to ignore, accelerated its embrace by segments of the literary population heretofore reticent to take fiction seriously, and gave these political valences material shape through the forms that various critical constituencies seized upon to promote their respective agendas. The sheer extent of *Uncle Tom's Cabin's* critical reception within antebellum culture laid bare the variety of critical forms in operation by 1850 as well as the political utility that even the most unassuming of those forms could carry. The critical response to *Uncle Tom's Cabin* in *Frederick Douglass' Paper* thus offers a prime occasion for rethinking the material bearings of literary criticism itself, of what counts as criticism, and the various ways it functions within our culture.

To be sure, neither Stowe nor Douglass is at any risk of scholarly neglect. Since the 1980s *Uncle Tom's Cabin* has become a representative text of New Historicism, a case study in feminist, cultural, and reception-based scholarship, while Douglass, as John Ernest and Eric Gardner have separately cautioned, has long served as a lodestone in studies of antebellum black writing in a fashion that risks obscuring rather than revealing the vitality and diversity of early African American print culture.[59] Yet this attention is hardly new: Douglass and Stowe's contemporaneous fame prompted near constant cultural commentary. Douglass's embrace of reprinted, generically eclectic criticism by a chorus of voices under the banner of his own name, meanwhile, a simultaneous assertion and subversion of Michel Foucault's author-function, complicates charges by Ernest and others that continued scholarly attention to Douglass comes at the expense of other antebellum black voices. To the contrary, Douglass exploited the notoriety of his name to create a platform for other members of the black community, both known and obscure, to debate issues central to the wellbeing of the race while solidifying a black critical counter-public. No one was more aware of the problematics of "the politics of representative identity," as Levine terms it, of the risk of being a stand-in for his race, than Douglass himself, and he used the venue of his paper to counteract this tokenizing tendency.[60] For though the journal blazoned his name across its front page, Douglass's editorial policy favored debate and community dialogue rather than autocratic insistence on ideological conformity.

Douglass's use of reprinted reviews, moreover, came to embody materially the cross-racial antislavery strategy that he articulated in his debate with Delany, with reviews simultaneously asserting and effacing the identity of their writers while providing a flexible space for the airing of controversial views. Finally, the fact that scholars have previously discussed the reception of *Uncle Tom's Cabin* in the black press at some length, turning it into a model of critical reception studies, offers an opportunity to examine the ways scholarly technologies shape critical history. That no small amount of ink has been spilled on this topic, in other words, enables a clearer view of the complex, reciprocal relationship between generic definitions of literary criticism in the critical present and constructed narratives of critical history, as well as between the digital technologies of twenty-first century scholarship and our understanding of the print-based critical practices of the past.

In returning to the critical reception of *Uncle Tom's Cabin* in *Douglass' Paper* then, I redirect our gaze from the center to the fluid edges of critical practice, as I focus not on original, signed reviews by familiar figures but on less stable critical iterations: hybrid texts, often with unattributed or mixed authorship, and circulating in forms that carry low or uncertain cultural authority. If scholars have privileged prestigious or high circulation journals in their critical histories, in practice it was commonplace for editors to reprint critical reviews from obscure, short-lived journals or from newspapers with a small, primarily local readership, cutting and pasting at their discretion, while citing only the source journal rather than any named critic in attributing the reprinted piece. This general disregard for reprinted criticism despite its cultural prevalence is less a fault of scholars than a sign of the changing scholarly times, of new technologies and shifting methodologies, the emergence of searchable digital periodical databases in tandem with a renewed interest in the material experience of literary consumption that is an ongoing legacy of book history. This combination of new digital technologies and an ideological return to the archive have enabled new generations of scholars to reclaim the critical margins, organizing countless two-line fragments, advertisements, and critical responses printed outside the domain of a journal's review section into a coherent narrative, using powerful search engines to identify where a piece was reprinted from, what editorial changes it underwent, and even who wrote it. If scholarship has tended to focus on more predictable, authoritative critical forms—lengthy, attributable reviews in established journals—as often as not antebellum readers confronted the sorts of brief, unsigned, reprinted notices that filled *Frederick Douglass' Paper*, a daily confrontation with peripheral modes of criticism that shaped the day-to-day, page-by-page haptic experience of perusing an antebellum periodical.

If Douglass's reliance on reprinted criticism makes it difficult to get a clear view of Douglass as critic, the question of literary criticism in *Douglass' Paper* is complicated further by the fact that, unlike prominent critics like Poe or Margaret Fuller, Douglass issued no explicit remarks on the practice of literary criticism generally or an African American critical enterprise specifically. Yet as Elizabeth McHenry has argued, Douglass's editorial commitment to literature and criticism is evident within the pages of his various journals through both the manner and the extent of his treatment of literary subjects. For McHenry, in reconstructing Douglass's critical voice, three principles become evident: first, that Douglass sought to provide a forum for the promotion of black authors, whose work he both excerpted and reviewed; second, that he measured literature by European American and black American writers dually according to both political *and* imaginative standards, asserting creative license for black writers and freeing them from what McHenry calls the "verbal bondage" of a compelled verisimilitude; and, lastly, that by placing work by European, European American, and black writers side by side within the pages of his papers, he advanced the radical idea of "creative parity" between black and white writers. Though critical principles began to coalesce especially around Douglass's reviewing of a series of slave narratives, as McHenry notes, it was Stowe's *Uncle Tom's Cabin* that provided a "concrete center" and "a point of departure" for Douglass's consideration of the role of literature and criticism within efforts for black liberation, elevation, and equality.[61]

For Barbara Hochman, meanwhile, *Uncle Tom's Cabin* was more than a focal point for discussions; it was a cultural watershed that for Douglass and the antebellum reading public more generally legitimated fiction as a literary genre, disarming a still lingering resistance to the novel as a discursive form.[62] The success of *Uncle Tom's Cabin* was also the largest single factor in overcoming the widespread resistance to fiction in the early black press, visible not only in pioneering newspapers like *Freedom's Journal* and the *Colored American*, but in Douglass's first journalistic enterprise, the *North Star*, which, compared to his later periodical ventures, treated fiction less frequently and with greater ambivalence. While in the *North Star* (1847–1851) Douglass encouraged literary pursuits primarily for the purposes of self-culture, community building, and to refute charges of black intellectual inferiority, when the journal merged with the Liberty Party's newspaper in June of 1851 to form *Frederick Douglass' Paper* (1851–1863), the same month that serialization of Stowe's novel began in the *National Era*, Douglass's inclusion of both literature and literary criticism became more extensive and less confined to moral and intellectual improvement.

Literary treatments became increasingly prevalent not only in the Literary Notices or Miscellanies sections but as front-page news. Among literary treatments included, Douglass and his literary editor Julia Griffiths prioritized reviews of works by black authors like the poetry of Phillis Wheatley and Frank J. Webb's *Garies and Their Friends* (1857). The editors also routinely reviewed antislavery novels such as Richard Hildreth's *White Slave* (1836) and Mary Langdon's *Ida May* (1854), reformist works like Thurlow Weed Brown's temperance novel *Minnie Hermon* (1854), as well as including critical reviews of proslavery anti-Tom novels like Mary Eastman's *Aunt Phillis' Cabin* (1852) and W. L. G. Smith's *Life at the South; or, Uncle Tom's Cabin As It Is* (1852).[63]

The literary coverage extended to canonical writers as well, with Griffiths including pieces by Longfellow, Cooper, Whittier, Lydia Maria Child, and even an excerpt from Melville's *Typee*. In looking across the Atlantic, meanwhile, she included works by Sir Walter Scott, Samuel Taylor Coleridge, and Felicia Hemans, while for eighteen months Douglass dedicated the final page of his paper to a lengthy serialization of Dickens's *Bleak House*.[64] He included less well known fiction as well, often of a political nature, ranging from William J. Wilson's original story "Terance Ludlam" (1854) and Laura J. Curtis's radical woman's rights novel *Christine, or, Woman's Trials and Triumphs* (1856) to Elizabeth Livermore's *Zoë, or The Quadroon's Triumph* (1855). Nor was Griffiths above including lighter fare, excerpting from Fanny Fern's *Fern Leaves* (1853), reviewing Ellen Louise Chandler's *This, That, and the Other* (1854), and including a range of short sketches by Stowe and Dickens. In the Miscellanies section, finally, discussions ranged from "The Author of 'Jane Eyre,'" "Anecdotes of Milton," and a sketch of *Blackwood's* critic Christopher North [John Wilson], to Henry Ward Beecher on "The Duty of Owning Books."[65] And then, of course, there was the fanfare that accompanied the release of Douglass's expanded autobiography, *My Bondage and My Freedom* (1855).

It was *Uncle Tom's Cabin,* however, that above all dominated literary discussions in *Frederick Douglass' Paper.* Typically, scholarly accounts of the critical reception of Stowe's novel in *Douglass' Paper* focus on responses with a specific critical profile: contributions by prominent black spokesmen (Douglass, William G. Allen, William J. Wilson), long enough to be generically recognizable as a review, and written explicitly for Douglass's paper. They also tend to offer critical—or at least skeptical—readings of Stowe's novel, with commentators balancing an acknowledgement of its political efficacy with a critique of the novel's degrading representation of blacks, its commercialization, and its conservative espousal of colonization. In cases where authorship is ambiguous, as with unsigned reviews in the Literary Notices section, scholars like Stephen Railton or McHenry occasionally attribute the authorship to Douglass by default, even in some cases with reviews that bear Julia Griffiths' explicit signature "JG."[66]

Within this broader discussion, several individual critiques are almost invariably singled out for consideration, including the initial unsigned notice praising the effects of the novel written by either Douglass or Griffiths; William G. Allen's critique of Tom as too pious, along with his attack on Stowe's colonizationist stance and his insistence upon amalgamation as the only path forward for America; William J. Wilson's wry account of Uncle Tom mania in Brooklyn; and Douglass's report of a visit to Stowe's house in Andover, Massachusetts, in which he endeavored to convince Stowe of the pressing need for an industrial college for black freedmen.[67] The centerpiece of most accounts, meanwhile, is the heated epistolary exchange between black nationalist Martin Delany and the more restrained Douglass over the question of whether Stowe, a white woman, could or should speak for the black race.[68] Taken together, the collective portrait we receive in these accounts is of an engaged community of black intellectuals who cautiously responded to both the promise and potential perils of Stowe's novel within the pages of the era's foremost black periodical.[69]

While there is much truth to this account, the handful of reviews of

Uncle Tom's Cabin typically foregrounded by scholars makes up only a small fraction of the critical responses to the novel that appeared in *Douglass' Paper*. In the ten-month interval that elapsed between Wilson's report from Brooklyn in June of 1852 and the opening volley of the Douglass-Delany exchange in April 1853, Douglass published scores of other responses, the majority of them reprinted from other papers. He did so at the height of the novel's popularity, moreover, between Jewett's release of the two-volume book edition in March of 1852 and the tapering of sales in late 1853. In his account of the novel's reception in *Douglass' Paper*, Levine proves duly sensitive to both uncertain authorship and to the presence of reprinted material, devoting several pages to reprinted articles that appeared in the year between Ethiop's report from Brooklyn and Delany's first letter, articles in which, as Levine suggests, Douglass as editor offered testimonials regarding the influence and accuracy of Stowe's depictions, charted the reception in England, and responded critically to anti-Tom novels. Yet Levine's astute account doesn't fully convey either the extent or the formal and thematic diversity of the material that Douglass reprinted in response to Stowe's novel.[70]

This is less a comment on the thoroughness of Levine's study, which refocused scholarly debates over Stowe's novel with African American voices at the center, providing a new model of reception studies in the process, than evidence of the expanded access to periodical archives enabled by the rise of OCR capabilities, keyword-searchable periodical databases, and digital humanities projects like Railton's *Uncle Tom's Cabin and American Culture*, resources unavailable to Levine in 1992 when his influential study first appeared in the pages of *American Literature*. These technological developments make it possible for twenty-first century scholars, myself included, to identify, collate, and evaluate all mentions of Stowe's novel, however cursory or indirect, from two-line blurbs on sales numbers to critical discussions buried in seemingly tangential or unrelated articles. With this expanded periodical archive, building upon Levine's foundation, we see the degree to which discussions of *Uncle Tom's Cabin* permeated political debates over slavery both in *Douglass' Paper* and in antebellum culture at large.

Frederick Douglass, Critical Reprinter

In the single year that elapsed between April 8, 1852, when the first notice of *Uncle Tom's Cabin* appeared, and April 1, 1853, when Delany's first letter was printed, Douglass included no fewer than seventy-five pieces that responded to Stowe's novel in some form or other. Of these, over forty articles, well over half, were culled from other papers, a percentage that increases to two-thirds when we include reprinted addresses, minutes, and proceedings that addressed Stowe's novel. That is to say, the majority of Douglass's critical engagement with *Uncle Tom's Cabin* came not through editorial commentary or original reviews but second-hand through reprinted articles.

From the perspective of literary history, the challenge of reprinting in assessing the critical legacy of *Frederick Douglass' Paper* is that it threatens to undermine the critical authority of Douglass's voice as well as that of his paper. As a result, there is a scholarly tendency to apologize for reprinting and to assimilate diverse and eclectic voices, sources, and discursive genres into a unified editorial vision. Though Levine, following Benjamin Quarles, is right to suggest that Douglass's "selection process needs to be considered as a central part of his efforts to shape a particular way of reading the novel," and to remind us that the journal blazoned Douglass's name across its banner in every issue, still, the individual pieces were rarely signed.[71] This absence of attribution poses a problem for scholars, as even within editorial content like the Literary Notices section, it is frequently impossible to determine whether Douglass or Julia Griffiths was the author. This constant ambiguity is compounded by the fact that Douglass did occasionally sign pieces "Ed." or Griffiths mark her notices "JG.," highlighting in the process just how many of their contributions *weren't* signed.

If twenty-first century critics are anxious to attribute authorship to Douglass, paradoxically, Douglass often seemed unconcerned that pieces be credited to him. Despite the fact that the journal carried his name, he was remarkably willing—indeed, ideologically committed—to publish positions with which he strongly disagreed, as is evident in his heated exchange with Delany over *Uncle Tom's Cabin*. Or as he put it in introducing a letter by Delany in the *North Star*, "Identity of color, does not forbid a difference of opinion: and having a common object, does not prohibit a free expression of that difference."[72] Respectful, spirited disagreement was the hallmark of a free press for Douglass. In practice, meanwhile, Douglass's near constant lecture engagements and antislavery traveling drew him away from the editorial chair for long periods, as evidenced by the frequent printed apologies for his editorial silence. The result was that letters from correspondents and reprinted articles were as characteristic of *Douglass' Paper* as were editorials by Douglass himself. If most scholars point to the strong authorial stamp that the journal's title inevitably exerted over the paper's diverse contents, Douglass himself, in responding to William Lloyd Garrison's charge of egotism for the paper's new name, dismissed the title as little more than "simple, unpretending and truthful," certainly less grand or presumptuous than the *Liberator* or the *National Era,* and more functional, for "it is 'Frederick Douglass' Paper,' in name, and in fact." "The great advantage is distinctness," he adds, though as he sardonically quips by way of conclusion, "Do let a colored man in the United States have the pleasure of calling something after his own name, even though it should savor a little of 'egotism.'"[73]

To be sure, Levine is correct to point out that reprinting and editorial selection were part of Douglass's antislavery strategy. Instead of a unified perspective rendered legible under the author-function of Douglass's name, however, that strategy more closely resembled what Lara Langer Cohen describes as a "patchwork aesthetic," a practice of reprinting, assembly, and collage that was widely employed within the early black press. To understand African American print culture properly, Cohen and Jordan Stein suggest, requires new critical paradigms that dispense with the traditional emphasis on originality, print capitalism, and authorship as principles of value and coherence. "As literature written *by* (rather than *for* or *about*) African American persons is the almost universal criteria for defining African American literature," Cohen and Stein note, "theoretical arguments for displacing the author have usually been read as hostile to the intellectual and political project that has carved out space for that literature."[74] This revisionist paradigm, with its embrace of *un*original, *un*remunerated, and *un*signed writing helps make sense of Douglass's career as literary critic, a tenure in which he privileged other voices over his own and expressed critical opinions by reprinting a generically diverse array of criticism from other sources.

Nor can the response to Stowe's novel in *Frederick Douglass' Paper* either be subsumed under Douglass's individual interpretation or reduced to a unified "black response."[75] Rather, in curating the response to *Uncle Tom's Cabin* in his paper, Douglass included multiple, conflicting viewpoints, often in the same issue, even on occasion within the same article. To do so, he relied upon the generic power of a diverse array of critical forms: letters, addresses, minutes, testimonies, reviews, prefaces, sales notices, advertisements. And while Douglass frequently remediates these forms to suit his purposes, he also exploited the inherent capacities of specific generic forms. This savvy awareness of the signifying potential of diverse and overlapping generic forms and methods of circulation was, as Sarah Meer suggests, typical of Douglass's strategy as an editor.[76] Indeed, as a critic, Douglass displayed his understanding of the cultural work of both literature and literary criticism not through direct editorial statements but through the variety of material and generic forms that he included in his paper.

Ultimately, as Levine proposes, these forms collectively point to a "social-transformative reading" of *Uncle Tom's Cabin,* and of literature more generally, that estimated a literary work based on its cultural impact rather than its aesthetic value.[77] This instrumental sense of the utility of criticism is visible, I suggest, through the types of critical forms Douglass reprinted in his paper in which the value of criticism was linked to its practical power to effect social and political change. To see Douglass in his capacity as critic accordingly requires an openness to forms of criticism that for various reasons—brevity, anonymity, unoriginality, or a non-literary focus—have traditionally undercut their authority, and even legitimacy, as literary criticism. Such liminal forms often don't strike us as criticism at all, yet they paradoxically gesture at Douglass's nimble, wide-ranging, and activist conception of the critical vocation, as well as his privileging of community debate over the sovereignty of a single viewpoint.

In the May 27, 1852, issue, for instance, Douglass reprinted the minutes of a meeting of the American and Foreign Anti-Slavery Society in which *Uncle Tom's Cabin* featured as a main topic of discussion. The treatment of the novel began when James McCune Smith moved that the society officially record its gratitude toward Stowe for writing *Uncle Tom's Cabin.* "Its success—unexampled as it was—proved the depth and breadth of the anti-slavery feeling in this country," Smith asserts, and that "the writer had touched a vein richer than California gold, and would be followed by a host of Grub street imitators." For as Smith reflects, echoing Theodore Parker's famous pronouncement, "If there was romance in the country, it was in relations between masters and slaves, and in the mixed relations growing out of them."

As the meeting proceeds, the attendees eulogize Stowe's novel; they record its positive influence on the acceptance of romance in the country; Smith goes on to "criticise the critic of the Literary World"; Louis Tappan and others personally acquainted with Stowe and the *National Era*'s editor, Gamaliel Bailey, narrate personal anecdotes regarding the book's origins and serialization; members recount anecdotes about its reception, discuss strategies about its proposed reprinting in a cheap pamphlet edition, and debate the novel's colonizationist sympathies.[78] In short, we see the range of reactions prompted by Stowe's novel as well as the various ways in which its cultural impact was measured. We see the manner in which Stowe's contemporaries discussed the novel as well as how it came to exert a political impact, a process described not through abstract encomiums or the perfunctory recourse to Lincoln's apocryphal sound-bite about the "little lady" who started the war, but rather through the novel's treatment within the proceedings of an *actual* political gathering. Above all, the antislavery society minutes gave material shape to Douglass's sense of the cultural and political work of criticism.

This particular discussion of Stowe's novel is, I suggest, emblematic of the dialogic nature of literary criticism within *Frederick Douglass' Paper.* While these sorts of unwieldy critical responses—eclectic and meandering, contradictory and anecdotal—are seldom discussed in scholarly accounts of the novel, they possessed many advantages for an editor like Douglass. For one, they were free in terms of both cost and critical labor. They also allowed Douglass to present a clash of critical opinions instead of a single reader's response, amplifying the political resonance of criticism by collapsing the distance between literary-critical discussions and adjacent political debates. If Douglass's critical repurposing of criticism for political ends was implicit in much of his journal's critical contents, it was all but explicit when he reprinted remarks on *Uncle Tom's Cabin* couched within the minutes of anti-slavery society meetings, transcripts of congressional proceedings, or addresses from foreign fundraising celebrations in Stowe's honor. At other times, he authenticated the truth of Stowe's literary portraits through testimonials from southerners or with accounts of real life incidents that for observers seemed torn from the pages of Stowe's novel, evidence of that ubiquitous epithet, "truth stranger than fiction."[79] The longest response to the novel, meanwhile, came in Douglass's reprinting of Henry Ward Beecher's exhaustive reconstruction of the controversy surrounding Reverend Joel Parker's threatened libel suit of Stowe, a nine thousand word account of a single sentence that Stowe attributed to Parker in her novel through a footnote: specifically, Parker's notorious assertion that slavery has "no evils but such as are inseparable from any other relation in social and domestic life." In his exacting reconstruction of the events of the controversy, spanning the front page of the November 5 and 12, 1852, issues of *Douglass' Paper*, Beecher adjudicated the precise relationship between fiction and fact through a blend of letters, legal consultation, citations, and personal reminiscence.[80]

At the other end of the spectrum was the ticker tape stream of two-line blurbs culled from other papers in which Douglass reported on the ever-increasing sales of the novel, on translations in Germany and France, the warm reception in Hawaii, or the astonishing account on August 5, 1853 of a man who, difficult to fathom, had not yet read *Uncle Tom's Cabin*.[81] Douglass reprinted more recognizable critical forms as well. On December 17, 1853, he copied a lengthy biographical sketch of Stowe by an "Alabama Man" originally published in *Fraser's Magazine*. He printed accounts of dramatizations and dioramas of Stowe's novel as well as reviews, both original and reprinted, of anti-Tom novels. He paid close attention to the British reception of Stowe's book, reprinting the entirety of Sir Arthur Helps's lengthy response to the novel in *Fraser's*, the Earl of Carlisle's introduction to the British edition of the novel, and the *London Examiner's* frequently reprinted review, "Uncle Tom's Cabin in England," which, as noted earlier, circulated widely in pamphlet form.[82] He printed addresses delivered at celebrations held in Stowe's honor during her trip to Great Britain in Glasgow and Belfast. He reprinted reviews of reviews, critics responding to other critics, even an apologist attack or two, including lengthy passages from George Graham's virulently racist screed, "Black Letters, or Uncle Tom Foolery in Literature."[83]

The newspapers Douglass drew from, meanwhile, were as eclectic as the critical genres they inhabited. While he clipped most frequently from the New York *Independent* and the Washington DC-based *National Era*, and from papers issued in New York City, upstate New York, and London, he also drew from periodicals as geographically diverse as the Honolulu *Friend*, the Leeds *Mercury*, and the international *Revue des Deux Mondes*. All said, in a two-year period, Douglass reprinted articles from over twenty-five different papers, while many of the notices he selected were themselves reprints already. Only on one occasion did he apologize for the necessity of drawing from a specific periodical, namely, when he reprinted a letter by William Wells Brown from William Lloyd Garrison's *Liberator*, prompting Douglass's justification that, "We copy the above letter from the *Liberator*, because we are always glad to lay anything from Mr. Brown before our readers."[84]

In each case, reprinting served as both copy and antislavery strategy. As with Stowe's *Key* or Weld's *American Slavery As It Is*, notices from southern papers gave credibility to authenticating accounts, while articles from northern proslavery papers like the Boston *Post* increased the value of any positive notices they issued. Notices from British papers lent an air of neutrality, of opinion unbiased by vested regional interests, while papers from exotic locales revealed the impressive reach of the novel's influence, as did statistics of Jewett's ever-increasing print runs. Nor did reprinting imply lesser intellectual value, but rather many of the most searching examinations of Stowe's novel in *Douglass' Paper* came not from original contributors but from reprinted reviews, as with Helps's nuanced meditation on the challenge of political action in the face of seemingly insurmountable evil or the incisive essay "Negro Intellect.—Ellis and Douglass, and Uncle Tom," reprinted from the *National Era*, in which the unknown contributor "E" critiques the model of black victimhood represented by Uncle Tom, suggesting that both Douglass and the "learned black blacksmith" Harrison W. Ellis, viewed by some as the model for Stowe's Uncle Tom, were both preferable to Stowe's vision of pious submission. As the anonymous critic writes, "Such a demonstration for fitness for freedom, and all the offices of civil life and business, is worth much more for the cause of emancipation than all the sacrifices which submission can make to the spirit of masterdom. Let us have more blacksmiths, scholars, orators, philosophers, and natural noblemen of the race. We have victims enough already, and sympathy for suffering will be most profitably replaced by admiration for evincible magnanimity."[85]

In using the above review, Douglass exploited yet another benefit of reprinting: the ability to distance himself from opinions that might strike readers as radical or offensive. For while much of the success of Stowe's novel lay with its evangelical spirit as embodied by Tom's piety, for the above reviewer, Tom's religion encouraged only submission. "Piety, as in the case of Uncle Tom, and apparently in that of the Rev. Ellis," the reviewer asserts, "is capable of being prostituted in the service of slavery. Because it acts upon the life mainly as a sentiment, it can be perverted into a sort of spiritual and moral handcuff, and made to answer the master as a restraint upon natural liberty." In Stowe's famous letter to Douglass, written as she was still composing the serialized novel, the author cautioned Douglass against his distrust of organized religion evident in his 1845 *Narrative*.[86] By ventriloquizing such apostasy through the mouths of anonymous critics cited from other papers, however, Douglass could both expose the "spiritual and moral handcuff" of Christian piety while continuing to solicit Stowe for contributions to his project of a black industrial college. Through reprinting, that is, Douglass could voice controversial critiques without bearing personal responsibility for them.

This editorial buffer applied not only to reprinted material but also to the original contributions Douglass published in his magazine. As with the essay "Negro Intellect," Douglass occasionally gave space to views that were more radical or militant than those he explicitly espoused in his capacity as editor. On August 6, 1852, for instance, in one of the earliest responses to the novel, Douglass published a letter by a correspondent from Sodus Bay, New York, under the signature "Sans Nom" which argued that the clear moral of Stowe's novel, in keeping with the example of George Harris, is that the north needed to arm fugitive slaves. For the contributor, this is no idle opinion; rather the inevitable result of reading *Uncle Tom's Cabin* is "that it is proper and necessary to provide arms for fugitives at convenient places, and to encourage and instruct them in their use; and that for this purpose 'material aid' should be called for to constitute a fund to be called 'The Fugitives' Arms Fund' or any other appropriate name." The critic then proceeds to a practical consideration of which gun is best suited to the purpose.[87]

Such a suggestion, anticipating the militancy of John Brown, would have been disconcerting, to say the least, to those northerners who saw moral suasion or colonization as the answer the problem posed by slavery, who preferred Uncle Tom's piety to George Harris's forceful resistance, to say nothing of southerners who had an inveterate fear of black revolt. Yet like the reprinted review from the National Era, Douglass could not be held personally to account for such militant views, though he came close to endorsing violent revolt himself in "The Heroic Slave," with its ennobling account of Madison Washington and the Creole revolt. While in Sans Nom's piece, Douglass used the epistolary form to distance himself, however, in "The Heroic Slave," serialized in four installments in March 1853, as Robert Stepto has suggested, Douglass shielded himself through the fictional veneer of the short story.[88]

Those responses to Stowe's novel that were original to Douglass's paper, and those most frequently cited by scholars, meanwhile— critiques by Allen, Wilson, and Delany—didn't take the form of traditional reviews at all or appear in the Literary Notices section, but rather appeared as letters to the editor, a generic framing that, as Meer suggests, simultaneously gave shape to a community of readers, fostered a sense of intimacy, and encouraged debate within that community.[89] This reliance on epistolary criticism from correspondents turned Frederick Douglass' Paper less into a mouthpiece for Douglass himself than into a community forum harkening back to the late eighteenth-century public sphere, a discursive model that, as Robert Fanuzzi has argued, was central to the self-conception of the abolitionist press.[90] This isn't to say that contributors agreed in their responses to Stowe's novel, far from it. Rather, by channeling the critical reception of Stowe's novel through a range of correspondents, Douglass presided over a spirited debate while consolidating a network of black intellectuals, as he did even more directly in May 1853 in his call for a Colored National Convention. To approach Douglass in his capacity as editor, indeed, runs counter to the prevailing emphasis, both in his own day and ours, on his embodied form, on the circulation of his daguerreotype image and his body on the lecture circuit in the service of the antislavery cause, and in the visible refutation of charges of racial inferiority.[91] Yet, as editor, Douglass effaced his embodied persona just as frequently as he promoted it, privileging polyvocality and dialogism instead of making his paper into a platform for his own voice alone.

His editorial preference for published correspondence instead of conventional reviews, meanwhile, enabled Douglass to promote ties with white allies and to seek philanthropic assistance from Stowe for his proposed industrial college, even while pieces within his paper delivered pointed critiques of Stowe's novel. Allen, in one of the earliest epistolary notices, for instance, worries that Tom is too pious, noting that he himself prefers resistance to submission, before chastising Stowe for her espousal of colonizationism. For ultimately, he argues, it is only by racial amalgamation that the nation will advance, a view not particularly popular with whites of either the antebellum north or south. Or Wilson, writing under the familiar pseudonym Ethiop, mocks the debased *Uncle Tom* mania sweeping through Brooklyn, a frenzy that marks abolitionism as the reigning ism of the moment, with Stowe's novel displacing the old black stereotypes of Zip Coon and Jim Crow in shop windows with the new and improved stereotypes of Uncle Tom and Aunt Chloe. Wilson laments that whites are leading the abolitionist charge rather than blacks, inverting the natural order in a manner that bodes ill for both antislavery efforts and the future of the black race.

Such opinions contrast sharply with the unsigned literary notice of April 8, 1852, in which one of the editors, Griffiths or Douglass, announced that, "the friends of freedom owe the Authoress a large debt of gratitude for this essential service, rendered by her to the cause they love." The editor's sense that Stowe "invests her characters with a reality perfectly life-like" flies in the face of critiques by Allen and Delany, while the assertion that "we doubt if abler arguments have ever been presented, in favor of the 'Higher Law' theory," clashes with the numerous commentators who viewed Tom's Christian piety as an impediment to his freedom, if not an outright shackle. Then, of course, there are the debates between Delany and Douglass himself over whether any good can come from whites like Stowe pleading the antislavery cause on the behalf of their black allies.[92] And while Douglass sides with Stowe in this debate, as editor he includes numerous articles that take issue with both Stowe and her novel, Delany's letters among them. The result is that Douglass possesses two voices: his direct authorial voice, which tends to be more moderate, and the more unruly, cacophonous voice heard in his capacity as editor, in which he selects pieces of a more militant, critical nature.

In short, reprinting wasn't simply a matter of editorial convenience, nor was it used to replicate Douglass's individual editorial viewpoint. Rather, the eclectic range of discursive forms that Douglass gathered in response to Stowe's novel gave physical shape to his sense of the cultural and political work of criticism. Each instance of reprinting, each discursive genre he drew upon, represented a strategy through which Douglass sought to extract political gains from fiction, a realm that he treated much more frequently after the serialized publication of *Uncle Tom's Cabin* and the launch of *Frederick Douglass' Paper* in 1851. This practice of reprinting reviews was, of course, not limited to *Douglass' Paper* or to the antislavery press. In venues such as *Frederick Douglass' Paper*, however, reprinting dovetailed with concerns over the politics of critical identity, with who exactly should advocate on behalf of African Americans, and with anxieties over the unity of the black community that such papers existed to promote. At the heart of *Frederick Douglass' Paper* was a series of tensions between the antebellum public sphere and a black counter-public; between the imagined community that such papers worked to create and realities of fragmentation, dispersal, and dissensus that Benedict Anderson's print culture thesis frequently belies; and between black nationalist principles of racial autonomy and a political pragmatism that prioritized results over rhetoric.

By reading literary criticism in light of rather than apart from the material and generic forms that transmitted it to readers, we gain a greater appreciation of the complex and wide-ranging role that criticism played in nineteenth-century American culture during the first age of industrial print. Today, in the first decades of the twenty-first century, amid the transformations of the digital revolution, an attention to the material practices of critical culture continues to offer new ways of viewing our critical landscape. In a moment of self-proclaimed crisis within the humanities, amid diminishing enrollments of English majors, the constriction of academic publishing, and disappearing book review sections, a print culture methodology with an eye for proliferating forms of criticism helps us answer those Cassandras who loudly proclaim the death of a discipline, the end of theory, or the close of the Gutenberg Era. Instead, we might see the dispersed, communal vision of critical authority visible in *Douglass' Paper* as offering an alternative vision to the concentrated authority of scholarly monographs or critical reviews at major journals, anticipating the sorts of online critical communities represented by reader comments sections, *Amazon* reviews, or even the *Los Angeles Review of Books*.

Douglass's use of critical reprinting allows us to reconfigure critical value in ways less concerned with authorship, generic conventions, or originating context than in the uses that criticism accrues through circulation, remediation, and editorial appropriation, dimensions particularly salient to the reiterative, networked critical pathways of the twenty-first century digital media landscape. If Douglass's promiscuous clipping and reprinting of criticism obscured authorship as frequently as it preserved it, however, today an ethos of attribution prevails, with embedded links, Twitter handles, and Google searches providing a trail of digital breadcrumbs back to a remediated text's original source. Still, the continuities—and discontinuities—are productive.

Finally, if Douglass's use of reprinted reviews helps us see our critical present in new ways, perhaps the most dramatic act of remediation comes today in the digitization of periodical archives themselves. As Meredith McGill and Andrew Parker suggest, the digital media of the present enable us to view the print media of the past through new eyes.[93] Twenty-five years ago, scholars working with antebellum periodicals sat in archives, paged through journals by hand, scrolled microfiche, consulted bibliographies like *Poole's Periodical Index*, and combed the footnotes of scholarly biographies, methods that produced a more in-depth knowledge of fewer periodicals. Today digitized periodicals and new search tools allow us to do much of the same work from the comfort of our homes, as with a click of the mouse, we can instantly search hundreds of periodicals and thousands of articles, providing unprecedented access to not just to the center but the far edges of antebellum print culture.

As our access to expanding archives changes, our narratives change with it, reinforcing one final time the constitutive impact of critical form on critical history, in this case with the evolution of academic research practices. Such ease of access to a seemingly endless array of evidence, as Maurice Lee cautions, is not without risks, contributing to a culture of flimsy, unfalsifiable evidentiary practices and "intertextual promiscuity." And while digitization makes previously inaccessible, scattered, and physically vulnerable archives widely available, the process of digital remediation from page to screen, as James Mussell reminds us, once again sacrifices the original, material form for the digital surrogate.[94]

My own sense, and the approach that informed this study, is that we must carefully balance the expanded access provided by digital databases and keyword searches with continued direct engagement with the physical texts themselves, as each confrontation, whether digital or analog, yields different sorts of insight and understanding. In the archive reading rooms of the twenty-first century, computer and codex sit side by side, with scholars toggling back and forth from screen to material text, from the algorithms of the search engine to the powerful sweep of the eye over the spread newspaper page. And while our media may differ from those of the antebellum period, as we move from print to screen and back again, the methodological imperative remains the same. To grasp the complexities of critical culture, we need to remain attentive to the signifying power of critical form, the uses it reveals, and the cultural tensions it exposes. For hidden in the materiality of literary criticism is the story of its past, present, and future, its conflicts and capabilities, its communities and commitments, as well as a final affirmation that literary criticism, in whatever new and unforeseen forms it takes, will continue to remain central to the way American culture makes sense of itself.

FROM THE STEAM PRESS
TO AMAZON.COM

Critical Forms for the Twenty-First Century

NOT LONG AGO, while spending a summer in Seattle, I had a chance to visit Amazon.com's much publicized brick-and-mortar bookstore: Amazon Books. The store opened its doors several months earlier in November 2015 in the upscale University Village shopping center and has since expanded to nineteen stores in ten states. With bookstore chains like Borders closing due in no small part to online retailers like Amazon, the decision to open Amazon Books at the time seemed as much a vanity project or publicity stunt on Jeff Bezos's part as anything else. Yet the store also claims troves of online user data from its website as a competitive advantage over rivals like Barnes and Noble. When I asked the sales clerk if the store had been profitable since opening—if Bezos even expected that—the clerk was polite but evasive, replying with a shrug. For Bezos, meanwhile, as George Packer has reported, books served as an entry point into online sales of other products rather than the real motivation for starting Amazon. It wasn't Bezos's love of books that launched Amazon but the degree to which books lent themselves to efficient distribution and shipping.[1] All of this predisposed me to cynicism.

Yet though I wanted to dislike the store, I couldn't help but be struck by its novelty—or perhaps more accurately, by the degree to which it laid bare the mercenary marketing motives behind most large chain stores. Almost all of the selections lining the tables and shelves followed the dictates of consumer tastes and user-generated sales statistics. On the table when I walked in, for instance, were selections that a sign informed me had been "rated 4.8 or above by users," the cream of the crop, as it were. Other subject sections—Fiction, History, Society, Graphic Novels, Business—followed a similar logic, featuring books that topped Amazon's charts in terms of sales or rankings. All of the books on the shelves faced cover out instead of spine out, replicating the experience of internet browsing and prioritizing bestsellers over an extensive backlist of slower-selling, though consistently stocked classics. You might be able to find Nabokov's *Lolita*, though you'd be hard pressed to find *Ada* or *Speak, Memory*. It was a marketing strategy that centered on what was currently popular, rather, what would reliably sell, and on consumer rankings of the "Top 50 Novels of All-Time" variety.

Amid the Kindle displays, Amazon Echo demonstrations, and carefully staged aisles, perhaps the most striking feature, however, was that beneath each book a small card was fastened containing a blurb culled from user-generated Amazon reviews. Under Margaret Atwood's *Handmaid's Tale*, for instance, a response from a reviewer identified only as "A Customer" praised the novel as, "Chilling, moving, vivid, terrifying and sometimes even humorous, The Handmaid's Tale is a profoundly moral story. It is a true masterpiece of power and grace that will someday attain the status of a classic." Validating the authority of this anonymous reader still further, the card informs us that 217 people found this review helpful. It also lets us know that of 2,063 reviews and ratings, Atwood's novel earned an average star rating of 4.1 out of 5. If you wanted to read more reviews, meanwhile, you could go to the Amazon app on your smartphone and use your camera to scan a barcode, which takes you directly to the full panoply of reviews on the Amazon website.

If Atwood's novel presents a vision of a dystopian future in which women are reduced to breeding slaves, the presentation of her book in Amazon's store offers a parallel vision of our critical future, which depending on whom you ask, carries either a utopian or apocalyptic cast. As I walked the aisles of the store, gone were the critical gatekeepers of old: professional critics with their reviews; English professors with their syllabi; and even chain bookstore marketing execs or small indie bookstore cognoscenti who assemble eye-catching displays based on various logics, monetary or esoteric. Instead, at the Amazon store, the selections followed the preferences of readers, operating according to the leveling dictates of user sales, reviews, and rankings. With the cozy logic of the "If you like x, you might also like y" so familiar to internet shoppers, the works on display at Amazon Books were reader approved and reader reviewed. The future of bookselling had arrived. Or rather, the antiquated world of brick-and-mortar bookselling had finally caught up with the market-conquering logic of online book sales.

The display cards accompanying each book presented a vision of criticism on the brink of a new era. The judgments of Amazon product reviews, easy to mock and dismiss as the pablum of amateurs, impressions untempered by knowledge, tact, or writing ability, were validated and authorized by their physical presentation on each small card, much as back cover blurbs by notable authors had been for the past century. If blurbs typically feature snippets of praise from fellow authors or from critics at prestigious journals, however, now you, your neighbor, and each member of your book club had a shot at critical glory. Yet despite my unease with the entire endeavor, my sincere desire to dislike it, the Amazon store was hard to resist. It sparkled with newness; light streamed in from large windows; readers lounged on long, cushioned seating areas; outside a fountain trickled. Was this the future, I wondered? And was it really so bad?

For *New York Times* film critic A. O. Scott, it is precisely the sort of seductive vision of a democratized critical future embodied by Amazon reviews that prompted him to write *Better Living Through Criticism: How to Think About Art, Pleasure, Beauty, and Truth* (2016), a book-length meditation on the role of criticism in modern life. As Scott reflects in an interview with *Vulture*'s Christian Lorentzen, in critical developments such as Amazon reviews, "there's a certain kind of false populism . . . that I think is actually always in defense of corporate interests, spuriously in the name of democracy." On the one hand, readers confront a triumphalism that hails the dissolution of professional criticism amid the tide of digital reviewers as a democratic evolution for criticism; on the other, box office sales are extolled as a more reliable metric of quality than the idiosyncratic and prejudicial opinions of lone reviewers. And all the while, critical amalgamators like Metacritic or Rotten Tomatoes flatten critical discourse into a raw score. In short, consumers in the age of the internet seem to have lost sight of what exactly criticism is for, of what functions it serves, and how exactly a film review by Scott in the *Times* might differ qualitatively from a blog rant or a Metacritic rating.[2]

Though Scott approaches this question from a variety of vantage points and through a cavalcade of case studies, moving seamlessly from Kant's *Critique of Judgment* to Pixar's *Ratatouille*, Harold Bloom to Marina Abramović, Keats to Tweets, his ennobling vision of criticism ultimately situates the critical enterprise at the center of American cultural life. For Scott, criticism is above all a mode of disciplined thinking. It is a rejection of intellectual passivity and apathy, a mandate to subject creative work to thoughtful, critical scrutiny and to resist the seduction of anti-intellectualism that currently has such a firm grip on our national discourse. In today's cultural climate, Scott notes, "there is little room for doubt and little time for reflection as we find ourselves buffeted by a barrage of sensations and a flood of opinion. We can fantasize about slowing down or opting out, but ultimately we must learn to live in the world as we find it and to see it as clearly as we can. This is no simple task. It is easier to seek out the comforts of groupthink, prejudice, and ignorance. Resisting those temptations requires vigilance, discipline, and curiosity." It is just this sort of disciplined, vigilant, inquisitive thinking that the best criticism models and enacts. "That everyone is a critic," Scott notes, "means, or should mean, that we are each of us capable of thinking against our own prejudices, of balancing skepticism with open-mindedness, of sharpening our dulled and glutted senses and battling the intellectual inertia that surrounds us. We need to put our remarkable minds to use and to pay our own experience the honor of taking it seriously."[3]

In the chapters that follow, Scott does just that, modeling a vision of balanced, engaged, restrained critical inquiry as he goes on to treat other larger concerns: the role of criticism in relation to the reception and appreciation of art; an account of competing schools of criticism (formalist versus humanist, traditional versus avant-garde, backward-looking versus forward-looking); the social and cultural origins of aesthetic taste; the commodification and institutionalization of artistic value in late-capitalist culture; as well as other related topics. Through-out these discussions, the point Scott returns to most frequently is that the line between critic and artist is blurry at best; that every good critic is an artist and every artist is on some level a critic since art, whether Shakespeare's plays or avant-garde performance art, always emerges from a critical conversation with the cultural achievements of the past. In walking a tightrope between competing critical orientations, Scott refuses to be boxed into a narrow and overdetermined critical posi-tion, arguing instead that given the range of viable critical orientations, above all, "the job of critics is to be wrong."

Whatever position you take, Scott concludes, "you are guaranteed to be wrong—to insult good taste, to antagonize public opinion, the judg-ment of history, or your own uneasy conscience." "There is no beau-tiful synthesis," moreover, "no mode or method of criticism that can resolve these contradictions. They cannot be logically reconciled, any more than a safe, sensible middle path can be charted between them. Still less is it possible to declare a decisive allegiance, to cast one's lot with the party of form or the party of content, the armies of tradition or the rebel forces of modernity, the clique of skeptics or the church of enthusiasts." For, as Scott concludes, "it should go without saying that every good critic, every interesting critic, will commit some of the crimes enumerated above, whether brazenly or unwittingly. A great critic will be guilty of all of them."[4]

In treating these topics, Scott anticipates almost every criticism that could be leveled at him, including alongside his affable tours of aesthet-ics and hermeneutics, four dialogues on topics ranging from "What Is Criticism?" and "The End of Criticism" to a "Self-Criticism" in which a cynical interlocutor takes aim at Scott's own critical biases. Despite the humility, relativism, and self-interrogating propensities of Scott's critical philosophy, however—an orientation that more than one of the book's critics attacked as an evasion of critical responsibility or lack of intellectual conviction—the limitation of the book for other review-ers is that Scott never properly acknowledges the privilege of his own position at the New York Times and the way it influences his conception of the critical vocation. In a review for the New Republic, for instance, Calum Marsh reflects that the book is a call for thinking, a manifesto against intellectual laziness, but "it's also a book about what it means to be a critic—and, less obviously, a book about what it means to be A. O. Scott. Its 277 pages hardly mention his sixteen years on the job. But they're there. The book patently bears the weight of its author's tenure . . . The eminence of Scott's platform glistens in every word that he writes." Yet despite the power inherent in his post, Marsh avers, "Scott's book deals with this unusual position only glancingly."

Though Scott has written a book about contemporary criticism, Marsh complains, he doesn't put his cards on the table, he doesn't interrogate the limitations and entitlements of his own critical position as reviewer at one of the most respected, widely read papers in the world. "This matters," Marsh concludes, "because Scott writes with a certain presumption of universality. His survey, in the early chapters of the book, of the history and evolution of criticism as a philosophy trade are bolstered by what is plainly a staggering erudition. But as he approaches the practice in its modern condition he is confronted by the limitations of his privilege—the prestige and elevation that insulate him from the realities of writing for a living without the patronage of the *Times*. 'Criticism is not a matter of technique or form,' Scott writes, 'so much as it is a matter of personality, of who you imagine is doing the talking.' But equally important is on whose behalf the talking is being done. Blog or trade? Alt-weekly or the paper of record? It matters a great deal."[5]

Critical context matters a great deal for *Slate*'s Laura Miller as well. For while Miller agrees with much of Scott's vision of the critical office, particularly his notion that it's the critic's job to be wrong, she also doesn't feel that criticism needs defending, certainly not from the sorts of puerile complaints typical of the comments section beneath an online review. "Unlike Scott," Miller chides, "I can't receive any of these bogus provocations as sincere inquiries into the nature and purpose of criticism, for one simple reason: Such questions instantly evaporate the moment the reader agrees with the critic." As for the legitimacy of criticism as a profession, "It's a job because people (sometimes) pay you to do it, and many more people pay attention to it," Miller demurs. "Write whatever you want to me about the irrelevance and superfluity of critics when you're complaining that my top-10 list left off your favorite novel; you've just proved you care enough about critics to gripe to and about one."

For Miller, rather, petty complaints against critics need to be taken with a grain of salt. "When you are a critic," Miller quips in opening her review, "you often find yourself listening to other people's opinions on how, ideally, a critic ought to ply her trade. It's wisest to keep a straight face and avoid explaining that the answer to this is often relative depending on the platform." To assess a critic, Miller suggests, we need to take into account his or her particular critical medium since different forms carry different expectations. "At the *New Yorker*, for example, the critics are essayists first and foremost," Miller notes. "If they brandish fierce prejudices or, as in the case of Anthony Lane, are sometimes willing to sacrifice information on the altar of witticism, so much the better: That's what *New Yorker* critics do. Editorially, their performance takes precedence over the works they write about." Indeed, we see just this in Nathan Heller's witty, biting, if vapid review of Scott's book for the *New Yorker*, as we do in Leon Wieseltier's slashing, curmudgeonly review for the *Atlantic*. "A film critic at the *New York Times*, on the other hand," as Miller concludes, "is arguably the film critic of record for the nation and therefore has a lot less wiggle room. His reviews are expected to be a pleasure to read, accurate, fair, pertinent, informed, open-minded, authoritative, and addressed to the interests of a wide readership."[6]

Toward the close of *Better Living Through Criticism*, Scott arrives at a similar conclusion. "Criticism is complicated," Scott notes. "The sheer variety of schools, styles, temperaments, and theories—to say nothing of the endless proliferation of objects and activities that invite critical scrutiny—makes it almost impossible to define." Part of the problem, Scott continues, is the number of venues that contain criticism and the number of people who call themselves critics: scholars, newspaper reviewers, bloggers, tweeters, Yelpers, and the disembodied soundbites of *Zagat* guides or Rotten Tomatoes. "To sort out these claimants and adjudicate their claims would require a separate critical discipline," Scott concludes, and "as it happens, the landscape of contemporary criticism is packed with canyons of meta, recursive formations in which reviewers are perpetually reviewed and judgments extensively judged . . . Meanwhile, on the green and tranquil lawns of academe, there are subfields devoted to the taxonomy of critical methods and theories, drawing and policing the lines that separate specialists from generalists, formalists from historicists, humanists from deconstructors, belle-lettrists from cultural studies zeitgeist surfers."[7]

This description of academic critical taxonomists, of course, applies to myself in my current undertaking. Yet one way to make sense of the pervasive contradictoriness that besets the critical vocation, Scott's own account and its reviews included, is to view critical form—or what Marsh and Miller term the critical "platform"—as a lens through which to understand and distinguish the various functions criticism serves. Throughout this book's five chapters, I've argued that the forms criticism takes provide indexes of cultural usage, of the ways that criticism functions socially and politically within our culture. In defining criticism, there's a temptation to swing wildly to one pole or another: to define criticism narrowly from its etymological roots as judgment, the act of aesthetic evaluation based in fixed standards of taste, on the one hand, or as an expansive, amorphous intellectual activity, on the other, summed up by the inevitable question, "what isn't criticism?" It's the longstanding discomfort with this broad latter definition of criticism that I suspect provoked some of the anxiety and scorn of Scott's reviewers when he used his book to assert the more catholic perspective, eroding the line between art and reviews, creativity and criticism, critical judgment and thinking itself. Criticism, it would seem, must be either narrowly defined and stable or broadly defined and unstable; cut-and-dry evaluative judgment or a freewheeling, discipline-crossing form of cultural discourse at risk of meaning nothing at all.

Part of the impasse between these two conceptions, I'd suggest, is the perennial disregard for the forms that criticism takes. To the extent that form is admitted into considerations, it is generally done so dismissively: Scott is *just* a newspaper reviewer, Wieseltier demurs, his reviews are fluff, disposable "fun," as he terms it; she is *just* a blogger, hastily recording the whims of the moment and calling it criticism; he is an academic critic, writing jargon-filled esoterica in obscure journals locked behind institutional paywalls.[8] These associations are natural, perhaps unavoidable, and not altogether wrong. Yet critical forms do more than frame and explain away critical judgments; they point to the ways that criticism circulates within our culture, the ways readers consume it, and, ultimately, to the roles it serves within our society, roles that extend beyond the realm of judgment, aesthetics, scholarship, or even simple entertainment. Indeed, it is the conflation and occasional clash of interests between these various critical functions that produce some of the paradoxes that Scott charts in his survey of the contemporary critical scene.

An attention to form doesn't solve the problems associated with the critical enterprise, but it does help us clarify the terms of contest and to present a less anarchic view of the cultural field of criticism. While criticism approached abstractly is, as Scott suggests, all but impossible to define, to ask what challenges are posed by, say, the newspaper reviewer specifically is a more manageable task, as it would be of the Yelp reviewer or the scholar of critical history. Rather, the idea that criticism is expansively—sometimes exasperatingly—broad as a category is encouraging, a sign of criticism's cultural vitality and functional diversity. With the advent of cheap print, the mass media, and an expanding print industry in the early nineteenth century, criticism began to take more forms and to serve more roles in US culture. To be sure, these functions have frequently clashed with one another, and will no doubt continue to do so, fracturing a single coherent definition of criticism. Yet this proliferation is also a hopeful portent of criticism's future, particularly in answer to those doomsayers who routinely lament the death of criticism. To the contrary, criticism has never been practiced more widely or more energetically than today; and there have never been more critics than now in the digital era, even if this criticism takes new and unsettling forms.

We are all in turn influenced by the critical forms that we write from and within. They shape our horizon of expectations; they attach goals and restrictions to our judgments, position us in relation to audiences, from the popular to the scholarly, dinner conversation to a newspaper circulation of hundreds of thousands. These forms aren't simply constraints on our ability to think freely and clearly; they point to the register criticism speaks within, the purposes it orients itself toward, and the objectives it pursues, from entertainment to ideological conversion, purchasing advice to aiding self-actualization. Yet though attention to critical form reveals the centrality of criticism to the daily intellectual operations of our world, literary criticism is also one of the few remaining disciplines within literary studies in which arguments are routinely divorced from their material bearings. This book has worked, accordingly, to situate criticism within its print contexts. In this endeavor, I have not been exhaustive. The book is an opening rather than a final word, a first volley, and an invitation to think materially when it comes to literary criticism. It is also, I hope, a reminder that criticism is not in crisis, nor does it risk extinction. Rather, the more productive question is, what new forms is criticism taking? And how do these forms gesture at new roles criticism plays within our culture?

In an interview with Scott for *Slate*, Isaac Chotiner concludes by asking whether the internet has changed Scott as a critic. "It absolutely has, and I think mostly in positive ways," Scott replies. "It's a lot less lonely, because writing is very lonely. First of all, to have Twitter, which is my main Internet vice or addiction. To have the company of other writers. Then there's also just the feeling that people are reading you, that you're not just sort of tossing something out into the void and thinking 'well maybe.'"[9] This sense that criticism in the age of the internet is somehow a less solitary endeavor, that it offers a form of connection, gestures finally to a less glaring, if no less important role of criticism in the twenty-first century: namely, critics turn the private act of reading into a communal activity. They initiate a public conversation, a community forum to reflect on literature, to provoke, incite, or validate our own reactions. They do so more articulately than the rest of us, moreover, or so we would hope.

Criticism today is also a participatory activity, as in online comments sections and Twitter threads, on Goodreads.com and in Amazon reviews, in the Oprah Book Club or countless local reading groups, we turn the solitary act of reading into a social endeavor. We read a review for many reasons, but perhaps the most essential is that we want to feel connected to others in our experience of art. Reviews by Scott or Emily Nussbaum, Daniel Mendelsohn or Geoff Dyer are cultural gathering places; they offer articulate, informed, entertaining reflections on contemporary art—which is to say, on life—but they do so publicly with a sense of shared experience. In this way, reviews in the twenty-first century counter the isolation of late-capitalist culture and bring us together through and around the act of critical reflection. In doing so, criticism has never been more vital to our lives.

It is this sense of criticism as a stay against isolation, as well as the de facto diary of the twenty-first century, that Rick Moody captures in his novel *The Hotels of North America* (2015). If Amazon Books gives us a glimpse of our critical future, in Moody's *Hotels of North America*, we get a refracted vision of our critical present. Drawing on the spirit of the epistolary novel, *Hotels of North America* stitches together the story of aging motivational speaker Reginald Edward Morse—his dissolving marriage, his separation from his child, his floundering career—out of his reviews for the fictional website RateMyLodging.com, a Yelp-like enterprise devoted to the reviewing of hotels. Like Nabokov's *Pale Fire*, the main narrative of Morse's reviews is framed by a paratextual apparatus that includes an introduction by Greenway Davis, Director of the North American Society of Hoteliers and Innkeepers, the group responsible for collecting and publishing Morse's scattered writings as a "novel," and an afterword by Rick Moody that comments on Morse's writings and his subsequent disappearance.

The heart of the novel, however, is Morse's reviews, which use the form of the online customer review to offer an account of his life, with the loneliness and frustration of his failed relationships given physical shape through the series of lodgings that serve as staging grounds for his life's downward trajectory. The entries, arranged sequentially to tell a story rather than simply chronologically, range from the Plaza Hotel in New York (four stars) to a meth-addled Rest Inn in Tulsa, Oklahoma (one star), from the Davenport Hotel in Spokane (five stars) to the parking lot of the New Haven Ikea where Morse spends a night in his car (two stars). In rating the hotels, Morse is, in essence, reviewing significant episodes in his life, moments of budding love, marital strain, infidelity, alcohol-fueled binges, and career deterioration, ultimately revealing a pervasive loneliness through his embrace of the disreputable form of the online review.

It is here that the critical mode of the online review captures for Moody the zeitgeist of our current moment, a genre that aspires to community and connection but ultimately exposes the isolation of modern life, an isolation doubly revealed in the form of the review itself and the subject under review, the hotels of North America, sites of transience and anonymity, surrogates for home that never quite manage to reach their aspiration. As Moody writes in the afterword, reflecting on his abandoned plan to stay in many of the same motels that the aptly named R. E. Morse visited, "I could have gone on and stayed at a few of the choicer residences described in these pages, like the Emerald Campsites, or the Norse Motel, or the bed-and-breakfast that is last in this sequence, but I would have learned only what is obvious, that this is not a book about hotels but a collection of writings about what it means to be alone." As Moody continues,

> The context of the work is crucial too, by which I mean its online publication, the contemporary world of the fast, cheap, and out of control. Despite Morse's brief infamy in that world, he's not even at the top of the comments section anymore. He's down in the archive now, deep in the space of the digital, in that sequence of nothing and somethings, a ghost inside a ghost of a machine. We like him, ultimately, because he's like us, but also not like us. He's a shadow, an imago, an ephemeral avatar of a human being, a voice in the wilderness whose work will never be troubled by an actual author appearing on daytime television. Morse is fragmentary, in that the pieces he wrote are themselves fragmentary, episodic, nonlinear, ending with new love simply because that is where he stopped.[10]

Like Nabokov's *Pale Fire*, which uses the conceit of a long poem and a prolonged exegetical critical commentary to satirize academic intellectual life in the late 1950s, for Moody, the ephemeral stuff of online reviews reveals something of the ghostliness of modern life, a world in which our lives, our experiences, are increasingly mediated by screens, apps, and profile names until we can only be known by the scattered traces of our online avatars.

If Moody's afterword is doleful, however, Morse's own sense of his critical endeavor is slightly more hopeful. For Morse, his reviews are an attempt at human connection, at reaching out through the ether of modern life, and he accrues a loyal group of followers who read and comment upon his work. Much of this response is comical—the trolling harassment of commenters like WakeAndBake, who posts Morse's social security number, or of KoWojahk283 and TigerBooty!, who speculate wildly about Morse's identity and involvement in a variety of scandals and international incidents. Other online interactions give way to real life meetings, as with his romantic rendezvous in Detroit with a talkative Midwestern fan he met in a chat room. Yet ultimately it is the connecting thread of reviews themselves that give shape and coherence to Morse's life story, his narrative assembled out of his careful ordering of the significant hotel stays of his life. If, as Morse suggests toward the close of his narrative, hotels aspire to, but fail to meet, the condition of home, online reviews aspire to, but fail to meet, the desire for interpersonal connection.

Whatever we finally make of Reginald Morse's life as revealed to us through his online reviews, Moody's conceit of a novel made up of reviews offers us a fully imagined vision of the way one very particular type of criticism functions within our current society. This vision travels far beyond the online review's typical associations as petty, ill-formed judgment by questionably literate masses of entitled, anonymous consumers. Rather, as Morse anticipates toward the end of his narrative, "Many readers insist that online reviewing is shallow, that the reviewers are vindictive, that their prose is bad, that they want for human feeling, that their physical isolation from the person they are attacking suggests that the worst possible instincts are liable to come to the surface in this online-reviewing process. I want to prove otherwise."[11] In Morse's (and Moody's) hands, rather, online reviews become an emblem of our cultural moment. As Moody concludes in the closing lines of his afterword, ultimately Morse's reviews tell us more about the future of mankind than they do about hotels: "I don't know if Morse's work is true, or genuine, or even if it's good," Moody notes, "but I know that his work is a sign of the times, and that his laughter and his laments compose a novel in fragments in which the traces of human pulsation are still audible at this distance, despite his silence."[12] At times, too, the prose of Morse's reviews rises to the heights of poetry, revealing the critical review's aspiration to something lofty and enduring.

In Moody's reflections and in his protagonist's embrace of the critical review as a genre of boundless expressive possibility, we see a literary rendering of Scott's central argument: that the line between criticism and creativity, between reviewing and art, is thin at best. That critics like Wieseltier or Heller dismiss Scott's hopeful vision of criticism's artistic potential for lacking an easily glossed argument suggests nothing so much as a lack of imagination on their own parts, an inability to see the potential that lies within an expansive genre, and an unarticulated desire to corral criticism back within its traditional confines as judgment. This is not to say that criticism shouldn't offer evaluations or purchasing advice, or present scholarly arguments rooted in competing theoretical and methodological camps. Nor is this to say that criticism shouldn't be instructive or entertaining, a home for ideological conviction and playful contention. This is not to suggest, in other words, that criticism should or shouldn't perform any or all of the roles it has been fruitfully tasked with since antiquity. Rather, we should simply remain open to the multiplicity of criticism's uses.

So too, we should resist the tendency to flatten out and homogenize criticism, to ignore the subtle ways it speaks to us in our hasty quest for the argument. Finally, we should be open to the diverse roles that criticism plays within our culture and to the possibility that criticism has new, emerging, and as yet unimagined roles still to play. If criticism is at the heart of the experience of being human, of consuming and responding to art and literature as both individuals and a community, then to trace the developing forms that criticism takes, whether scholarly monograph, anthology, or Amazon review, is to observe the ways our culture interacts with the world of ideas and, ultimately, with each other.

NOTES

INTRODUCTION: THE CRITIC IN THE AGE OF INDUSTRIAL PRINT

1. [Edwin Percy Whipple], "Criticism: Coleridge," *American Review* 3, no. 6 (June 1846): 581.
2. There are of course many existing studies that treat nineteenth-century American criticism from a variety of vantage-points. For several early accounts of American criticism focused on catalogues of literary and critical principles or on a handful of well-known critics, see Norman Foerster, *American Criticism: A Study in Literary Criticism from Poe to the Present* (Boston: Houghton Mifflin Co., 1928); Floyd Stovall and Harry Hayden Clark, eds., *The Development of American Literary Criticism* (Chapel Hill: University of North Carolina Press, 1955); William Charvat, *The Origins of American Critical Thought, 1810–1835* (New York: A.S. Barnes and Co., 1961); John Paul Pritchard, *Criticism in America* (Norman: University of Oklahoma Press, 1956); and John W. Rathbun, *American Literary Criticism, 1800–1860* (Boston: Twayne Publishers, 1979). For two studies that emphasize the political feud between Whig Knickerbockers and Democratic Young America, see Perry Miller, *The Raven and the Whale: Poe, Melville, and the New York Literary Scene* (Baltimore: Johns Hopkins University Press, 1997) and John Stafford, *The Literary Criticism of 'Young America': A Study in the Relationship of Politics and Literature, 1837–1850* (Berkeley: University of California Press, 1952).

For two strong studies of antebellum critical culture focused on the developing genre of fiction, see Nina Baym, *Novels, Readers, and Reviewers: Responses to Fiction in Antebellum America* (Ithaca, NY: Cornell University Press, 1984) and James Machor, *Reading Fiction in Antebellum America: Informed Response and Reception History, 1820–1865* (Baltimore: Johns Hopkins University Press, 2011). One particularly valuable resource regarding the careers of less prominent critics is John Rathbun and Monica Grecu, eds., *American Literary Critics and Scholars, 1800–1850*, v. 59 of *The Dictionary of Literary Biography* (Detroit, MI: Gale Research, 1987). For studies that treat the professionalization and institutionalization of literary criticism specifically, see Terry Eagleton, *Literary Theory: An Introduction*, 2nd ed. (Minneapolis: University of Minnesota Press, 1996); Gerald Graff, *Professing Literature: An Institutional History* (Chicago: University of Chicago Press, 2007); and Kermit Vanderbilt, *American Literature and the Academy: The Roots, Growth, and Maturity of a Profession* (Philadelphia: University of Pennsylvania Press, 1986).

Many other studies trace criticism through individual critical careers (Poe, Henry James, etc.) or broader movements like Transcendentalism or literary realism; through genealogies of particular strains of influence from philology and liberal Christianity to Scottish Common Sense philosophy; or through studies of transatlantic romanticism. For a small selection of these genealogies, see Jerry Wayne Brown, *The Rise of Biblical Criticism in America, 1800–1870* (Middletown, CT: Wesleyan University Press, 1969); Lawrence Buell, *New England Literary Culture: From Revolution through Renaissance* (New York: Cambridge University Press, 1986); and Barbara Packer, *The Transcendentalists* (Athens: University of Georgia Press, 2007). For the influence of Scottish Common Sense philosophy, see Franklin E. Court, *The Scottish Connection: The Rise of English Literary Study in America* (Syracuse, NY: Syracuse University Press, 2001). A full bibliography of works that touch on literary criticism would, indeed, extend to countless areas of American literary studies and is too extensive to cite here.

3. The dominance of literary nationalism is pervasive both in studies that codify and those that oppose the framework. For several notable examples, see Benjamin T. Spencer, *The Quest for Nationality: An American Literary Campaign* (Syracuse, NY: Syracuse University Press, 1957); Robert Weisbuch, *Atlantic Double-Cross: American Literature and British Influence in the Age of Emerson* (Chicago: University of Chicago Press, 1986); Paul Giles, *Transatlantic Insurrections: British Culture and the Formation of American Literature, 1730–1860* (Philadelphia: University of Pennsylvania Press, 2001); and Joseph Eaton, *The Anglo-American Paper War: Debates about the New Republic, 1800–1825* (New York: Palgrave MacMillan, 2012). Literary nationalism is evident too in the countless studies that assert the emergence of a distinctive American literature, represented most famously by F. O. Matthiessen's *American Renaissance: Art and Expression in the Age of Emerson and Whitman* (New York: Oxford University Press, 1941).

So too do we see the continued centrality of literary nationalism as an organizing framework in recent studies that challenge the exceptionalist orientation of older narratives of American literary emergence. See, for instance, Leonard Tennenhouse, *The Importance of Feeling English: American Literature and the British Diaspora, 1750–1850* (Princeton, NJ: Princeton University Press, 2007) and Elisa Tamarkin, *Anglophilia: Deference, Devotion, and Antebellum America* (Chicago: University of Chicago Press, 2008). That is to say, even scholarship that challenges, complicates, or rejects the terms of literary nationalism as a historical paradigm end up reaffirming its hold on American literary history.

In recent years, a growing number of scholars have worked to move beyond the paradigm of literary nationalism altogether. In *Liberty of the Imagination: Aesthetic Theory, Literary Form, and Politics in the Early United States* (Philadelphia: University of Pennsylvania Press, 2012), for instance, Edward Cahill demonstrates "not only that early U.S. literary culture was a transatlantic phenomenon but also that U.S. nation formation was utterly dependent on British (and sometimes even French, German, and Italian intellectual materials." Yet at the same time, American writers "rarely understood their engagement with [aesthetics] in narrowly national terms" (9–10). So too, in *Republic of Intellect: The Friendly Club of New York City and the Making of American Literature* (Baltimore: The Johns Hopkins University Press, 2007), Bryan Waterman sidesteps the traditional scholarly focus on nationalism, challenging and complementing such approaches "by examining the ways in which the Friendly Club's literary offerings were perhaps less oriented toward a new nationalism than to authority-making rituals of civic fraternity that constituted a transnational intellectual culture" (9–10). Like these studies, while not denying nationalist concerns, I nonetheless seek to decenter them, thereby opening up new avenues of inquiry.

4. Noah Webster, *An American Dictionary of the English Language*, 2 vols. (New York: S. Converse, 1828), s.v. "criticism"; René Wellek, "Reflections on My History of Modern Criticism," in *The Attack on Literature and Other Essays* (Chapel Hill: University of North Carolina Press, 1982), 137.

5. Andrew Ford, *The Origins of Criticism: Literary Culture and Poetic Theory in Classical Greece* (Princeton, NJ: Princeton University Press, 2002), 3; Michael Gavin, *The Invention of English Criticism, 1650–1760* (Cambridge, UK: Cambridge University Press, 2015), 4.

6. René Wellek, "Literary Theory, Criticism, History," *Concepts of Criticism*, ed. Stephen G. Nichols Jr. (New Haven, CT: Yale University Press, 1963), 1.

7. Ibid., 3.

8. For a good introduction to twentieth-century mappings of critical practice, see David H. Richter, introduction to *The Critical Tradition: Classic Texts and Contemporary Trends*, ed. David H. Richter (New York: Bedford Books, 1989), 1–14. Studies interrogating the ideological bases of criticism, particularly from the vantage-point of poststructuralist and Marxist critique, became the default approach in the latter decades of the twentieth century. Two influential examples include Terry Eagleton, *The Function of Criticism: From the Spectator to Post-Structuralism* (London: Verso, 1996) and Jonathan Culler, *Framing the Sign: Criticism and Its Institutions* (Norman: University of Oklahoma Press, 1988). Ford, *The Origins of Criticism*, x; Gavin, *The Invention of English Criticism*, 9, 18–19.

9. Caroline Levine, *Forms: Whole, Rhythm, Hierarchy, Network* (Princeton, NJ: Princeton University Press, 2015), 1–11. As Levine notes, the category of *form*, which she defines broadly as "all shapes and configurations, all ordering principles, all patterns of repetition and difference," has over the centuries come to connote a dizzying range of conflicting, often contradictory meanings, from Plato's ideal forms to the material categories of Aristotle, superficial trappings to essential qualities, historically situated or transhistorical, structures that reify political ideologies or that insulate works from political considerations. Rather than resolving these paradoxical meanings or choosing one definition, Levine focuses on the clash of competing conceptions and, by association, the systems of social organization they enforce. For the concept of affordances, see Don Norman, *The Design of Everyday Things* (New York: Basic Books, 2013), 10–13.

10. As Leon Jackson cautions in *The Business of Letters: Authorial Economies in Antebellum America* (Stanford, CA: Stanford University Press, 2008), commonplace

narratives of the emerging "profession of authorship" promoted influentially by William Charvat and others simplify the financial relations of authors, obscuring the blurry line between amateurs and professionals, fetishizing financial compensation as the metric of professionalism while ignoring the multiple authorial economies that supported writing careers. The discourse of professionalization glosses the fact that professional authors, defined narrowly as those who make a living by their writing, were, and still are, a minority. Rather, as Jackson reminds us, "authors in early national and antebellum America lived sometimes solely from the products of their pens, at other times solely from other forms of income, but most typically from a continuous combination of both, practicing what economic anthropologist Rhoda Halperin calls 'multiple livelihood strategies'" (17).

11. As Paul Fussell in *Samuel Johnson and the Life of Writing* (New York: W. W. Norton and Company, 1971) notes, "The fact is that genuine creativity shows itself not in the invention of forms or modes but in the accuracy with which distinct public forms of all kinds are recognized and the appropriateness with which they are exploited." For Fussell, Johnson is the "prime example of 'the writer,'" for "his own life of writing took place in the midst of a heady profusion and variety of genres. Indeed, to think of what an open, 'free' literary world would be like, a world where the available forms are almost numberless and infinitely variegated, is to imagine oneself in something like Johnson's literary circumstances" (38).

12. Vincent Leitch, William E. Cain, Laurie A. Finke, Barbara E. Johnson, John McGowan, T. Denean Sharpley-Whiting, and Jeffrey J. Williams, eds., *The Norton Anthology of Theory and Criticism*, 2nd ed. (New York: W. W. Norton and Company, 2010). The *Norton* is of course invaluable in the service it provides for students and scholars alike, collecting an extensive range of literary criticism across centuries, excerpted at length, and with learned, accessible introductions. It is the nature of such an enterprise, however, to transform the physical form of the excerpted criticism, whatever its material origins, into the now ubiquitously familiar tissue-thin, small-type format of the *Norton Anthology* itself. And while head-notes may acknowledge the social contexts for a body of criticism, the larger effect of the anthology is to assimilate all forms of literary criticism into dematerialized, uniformly printed critical theory, while some forms of criticism such as the puff or the anthology itself don't make it into the *Norton* at all.

13. Of the ninety-eight critical pieces included in Richard Ruland's influential anthology *The Native Muse: Theories of American Literature from Bradford to Whitman* (New York: E. P. Dutton & Co., 1976), to take one example, a full quarter of Ruland's selections come from the *North American Review* alone. The vast majority of the remainder are also from quarterly reviews (the *Edinburgh Review*, the *Dial*, *Brownson's Quarterly Review*) with a smattering of excerpts from monthly or weekly magazines (the *Knickerbocker*, the *Literary World*, the *United States Magazine and Democratic Review*).

14. Meredith McGill's *American Literature and the Culture of Reprinting, 1834–1853* (Philadelphia: University of Pennsylvania Press, 2003) reexamines Poe, Hawthorne, and others within the context of international copyright

debates and what she terms a "culture of reprinting." Jackson in *The Business of Letters* replaces Charvat's streamlined notion of the "profession of authorship" with a less unified portrait of the business of letters, characterized by multiple economies, diverse exchange rituals, and complicated webs of remunerative literary affiliation. Lara Langer Cohen's *The Fabrication of American Literature: Fraudulence and Antebellum Print Culture* (Philadelphia: University of Pennsylvania Press, 2012) situates debates over critical puffery within broader concerns over literary nationalism, fraudulence, and the growth of print-capitalism, forces that together "fabricated" the idea of American literature in all senses of the term. If for Cohen print culture aided the fabrication of American literature, for Trish Loughran in *The Republic in Print: Print Culture in the Age of U.S. Nation Building, 1770–1870* (New York: Columbia University Press, 2007), the "virtual nation" produced by both print culture and print culture theorists like Benedict Anderson obscures the degree to which print culture was a force not for national consolidation but fragmentation and disintegration, masking the fracture lines of deep-seated local and regional division beneath the rhetoric of print nationalism.

15. Michael Gavin, "Writing Print Cultures Past: Literary Criticism and Book History," *Book History* 15 (2012): 28–29; Joanne Shattock, "Contexts and Conditions of Criticism 1830–1914," in *The Cambridge History of Literary Criticism*, vol. 6, *The Nineteenth Century, c. 1830–1914* (New York: Cambridge University Press, 2013), 22; Laurel Brake, *Subjugated Knowledges: Journalism, Gender & Literature in the Nineteenth Century* (New York: New York University Press, 1994), 1–35.

16. Though the poststructuralist critique of the constructed-ness of historical narrative is now commonplace, for two influential works, the first theoretical, the second applied, see Michel Foucault, *The Archeology of Knowledge and the Discourse on Language,* trans. A. M. Sheridan Smith (New York: Pantheon Books, 1982) and Hayden White, *Metahistory: The Historical Imagination in the Nineteenth-Century Europe* (Baltimore: Johns Hopkins University Press, 1975). For a strong articulation of the contingency of critical value, see Barbara Herrnstein Smith, *Contingencies of Value: Alternative Perspectives for Critical Theory* (Cambridge, MA: Harvard University Press, 1988).

17. For key texts of the post-critical turn, see Rita Felski, *The Limits of Critique* (Chicago: University of Chicago Press, 2015); the essays collected in Elizabeth S. Anker and Rita Felski, eds., *Critique and Postcritique* (Durham, NC: Duke University Press, 2017); Bruno Latour, "Why Has Critique Run Out of Steam?" *Critical Inquiry* 30, no. 2 (Winter 2004): 225–48; and Christopher Castiglia, *The Practices of Hope: Literary Criticism in Disenchanted Times* (New York: New York University Press, 2017).

18. For Bourdieu's account of "position-takings," and the negotiation of positions and dispositions by artists within the cultural field, see Pierre Bourdieu, *The Field of Cultural Production: Essays on Art and Literature*, ed. Randal Johnson (New York: Columbia University Press, 1993), 61–64. Smith, *Contingencies of Value*, 14–16; Felski, *The Limits of Critique*, 12.

19. Edward T. Channing, "Forms of Criticism," *Lectures Read to the Seniors of Harvard College* (Boston: Ticknor and Fields, 1856), 179–82.

20. W. A. Jones, "Criticism in America," *United States Magazine and Democratic Review* 15, no. 75 (September 1844): 241. For the first installment, see W. A. Jones, "Critics and Criticism," *United States Magazine and Democratic Review* 15, no. 74 (August 1844): 153–62.

21. Jerome McGann, *A New Republic of Letters: Memory and Scholarship in the Age of Digital Reproduction* (Cambridge, MA: Harvard University Press, 2014), 19.

22. Miller, *The Raven and the Whale*, 15.

23. Shattock, "Contexts and Conditions for Criticism," 22.

24. In Baym's *Novels, Readers, and Reviewers,* for instance, the author opens her preface by noting that, "I have used as my sources original reviews of novels—any and all novels—appearing in the most widely read periodicals of the antebellum period," specifying that of the twenty-one periodicals that make up her sources, none fall below five thousand paid subscribers (7, 14).

25. Ford, *The Origins of Criticism*, ix–xi, 21–22; Derek Roper, *Reviewing Before the Edinburgh, 1788–1802* (Newark: University of Delaware Press, 1978), 19–20. For a study of satires of criticism in eighteenth-century England, see Philip Smallwood and Min Wild, eds., *Ridiculous Critics: Augustan Mockery of Critical Judgment* (Lewisburg, PA: Bucknell University Press, 2014).

26. Michael T. Gilmore, "The Literature of the Revolutionary and Early National Periods," in *The Cambridge History of American Literature,* vol. I, *1590–1820,* ed. Sacvan Bercovitch (New York: Cambridge University Press, 1994), 542–43, 563; Lewis P. Simpson, "Joseph Stevens Buckminster: The Rise of the New England Clerisy," in *The Man of Letters in New England and the South* (Baton Rouge: Louisiana State University Press, 1973), 3–31.

27. Frank Luther Mott, *A History of American Magazines, 1741–1850* (New York: D. Appleton and Company, 1930), 13–21.

28. For two early accounts of critical culture in the national period, see Charvat, *Origins of American Critical Thought* and Lewis P. Simpson, ed., *The Federalist Literary Mind: Selections from the* Monthly Anthology and Boston Review, *1803–1811* (Baton Rouge: Louisiana State University Press, 1962), 1–41. For more recent treatments of critical culture of the republican and national periods, particularly in early American magazines, see Catherine O'Donnell Kaplan, *Men of Letters in the Early Republic: Cultivating Forums of Citizenship* (Chapel Hill: University of North Carolina Press, 2008); Jared Gardner, *The Rise and Fall of Early American Magazine Culture* (Urbana: University of Illinois Press, 2012); and Cahill, *Liberty of the Imagination.* For a useful, wide ranging survey of the field, see Gilmore, "The Literature of the Revolutionary and Early National Periods," 541–72. Also, see Waterman, *Republic of Intellect.*

29. David S. Shields, *Civil Tongues and Polite Letters in British America* (Chapel Hill: University of North Carolina Press, 1997); Cahill, *Liberty of the Imagination;* Jay Fliegelman, *Declaring Independence: Jefferson, Natural Language, & the Culture of Performance* (Stanford, CA: Stanford University Press, 1993); Robert Ferguson, *The American Enlightenment, 1750–1820* (Cambridge, MA: Harvard University Press, 1997).

30. Discussions of the transformation of print during the antebellum period

are easily found. For several particularly good accounts, see Paul Starr, *The Creation of the Media: Political Origins of Modern Communications* (New York: Basic Books, 2004); Daniel Walker Howe, *What Hath God Wrought: The Transformation of America, 1815–1848* (New York: Oxford University Press, 2007); Scott E. Casper, Jeffrey D. Groves, Stephen W. Nissenbaum, and Michael Winship, eds. *A History of the Book in America*, vol. 3, *The Industrial Book, 1840–1880* (Chapel Hill: Published in association with the American Antiquarian Society by the University of North Carolina Press, 2007); and William Charvat, *Literary Publishing in America, 1790–1850* (Philadelphia: University of Pennsylvania Press, 1959).

31. Ronald J. Zboray, *A Fictive People: Antebellum Economic Development and the American Reading Republic* (New York: Oxford University Press, 1993), xv–xxi, 1–14; Loughran, *The Republic in Print*, 1–29.
32. Martyn Lyons, "New Readers in the Nineteenth Century: Women, Children, Workers," in *A History of Reading in the West*, ed. Guglielmo Cavallo and Roger Chartier, trans. Lydia G. Cochrane (Amherst: University of Massachusetts Press, 2003), 313; William Gilmore, *Reading Becomes a Necessity of Life: Material and Cultural Life in Rural New England, 1780–1835* (Knoxville: University of Tennessee Press, 1989).
33. For the impact of developing eyeglass and lighting technology, see Zboray, *A Fictive People*, 14–5. Machor, *Reading Fiction in Antebellum America*, 3, 18–29.
34. Mott, *A History of American Magazines*, 341–42.
35. J. Inman, "Magazine Literature," *Columbian Lady's and Gentleman's Magazine* 1, no. 1 (January 1844): 1.
36. Frank Luther Mott, *American Journalism: A History of Newspapers in the United States through 250 Years, 1690–1940* (New York: Macmillan, 1941), 216.
37. Charvat, *The Origins of American Critical Thought*, 5–6.
38. Washington Irving, *The Sketch Book*, in *History, Tales, and Sketches*, ed. James W. Tuttleton (New York: Library of America, 1983), 860–61.
39. Ibid., 861.
40. Robert Darnton, *George Washington's False Teeth* (New York: W. W. Norton and Co., 2003), 25; Ann M. Blair, *Too Much to Know: Managing Scholarly Information before the Modern Age* (New Haven: Yale University Press, 2010); James Gleick, *The Information: A History, a Theory, a Flood* (New York: Vintage Books, 2011); Alex Wright, *Glut: Mastering Information Through the Ages* (Washington, DC: Joseph Henry Press, 2007).
41. Roper, *Reviewing before the* Edinburgh, 19–20.
42. Jacques Rancière, *Mute Speech: Literature, Critical Theory, and Politics*, trans. James Swenson (New York: Columbia University Press, 2011). Also, see Jonathan Culler, "Introduction: Critical Paradigms," *PMLA* 125, no. 4 (October 2010): 905–15. M. H. Abrams, *The Mirror and the Lamp: Romantic Theory and the Critical Tradition* (New York: Oxford University Press, 1953).
43. John Guillory, *Cultural Capital: The Problem of Literary Canon Formation* (Chicago: University of Chicago Press, 1993).
44. James Russell Lowell, "Our Contributors.—No. XVII. Edgar Allan Poe," *Graham's Magazine* 27, no. 2 (February 1845): 49.

45. Cohen, *The Fabrication of American Literature*, 23–64.
46. Ian Small, *Conditions for Criticism: Authority, Knowledge, and Literature in the Late Nineteenth Century* (Oxford, UK: Clarendon Press, 1991); Jon Klancher, "The Vocation of Criticism and the Crisis of the Republic of Letters," in *The Cambridge History of Literary Criticism*, vol. 5, *Romanticism*, ed. Marshall Brown (New York: Cambridge University Press, 2000), 296–320; Shattock, "Contexts and Conditions of Criticism," 21–45.
47. Roper, *Reviewing before the* Edinburgh, 30–32.
48. Many books treat the rise of professionalization over the course of the nineteenth century produced as part of the social reconfiguration, class stratification, and vocational upheaval corollary to the shift from an agrarian to an industrial socio-economic system. The most well-known study is Harold Perkins's *The Rise of Professional Society: England since 1880* (New York: Routledge, 1989). For a work that treats the United States specifically, see Burton J. Bledstein, *The Culture of Professionalism: The Middle Class and the Development of Higher Education in America* (New York: W. W. Norton and Co., 1978). Also, see Thomas Bender, *Intellect and Public Life: Essays on the Social History of Academic Intellectuals in the United States* (Baltimore: The Johns Hopkins University Press, 1993). Paul Starr's examination of the development of the American medical profession in *The Social Transformation of American Medicine* (New York: Basic Books, 1982), 1–29, provides a useful context of the broader cultural forces driving the push toward professionalization in the United States. For a consideration of authority in relation to US literary culture specifically, see the essays collected in Günter Leypoldt, ed., *Intellectual Authority and Literary Culture in the US, 1790–1900* (Heidelberg: Universitätsverlag Winter, 2013).
49. "Motley Manners" [A. J. Duganne], "A Mirror for Authors," *Holden's Dollar Magazine* (January 1849): 22.
50. For more on Hicks's image and on the construction of the idea of a collective authorial enterprise in antebellum America, see J. Gerald Kennedy, "Inventing the Literati: Poe's Remapping of Antebellum Print Culture," in *Poe and the Remapping of Antebellum Print Culture*, ed. J. Gerald Kennedy and Jerome McGann (Baton Rouge: Louisiana State University Press, 2012), 13–36.
51. Sandra Tomc, *Industry and the Creative Mind: The Eccentric Writer in American Literature and Entertainment, 1790–1860* (Ann Arbor: University of Michigan Press, 2012).
52. For two strong examples of recent scholarship that explores non-print expressions of the antebellum critical impulse, in personal responses to literature and literary societies respectively, see Thomas Augst, *The Clerk's Tale: Young Men and Moral Life in Nineteenth-Century America* (Chicago: University of Chicago Press, 2003) and Elizabeth McHenry, *Forgotten Readers: Recovering the Lost History of African American Literary Societies* (Durham, NC: Duke University Press, 2002).

CHAPTER 1: CUTTING CORNERS WITH EMERSON

1. Jay Fliegelman, *Declaring Independence: Jefferson, Natural Language, & the Culture of Performance* (Stanford, CA: Stanford University Press, 1993), 166.

2. Michael Warner, *The Letters of the Republic: Publication and the Public Sphere in Eighteenth-Century America* (Cambridge, MA: Harvard University Press, 1990), 61.

3. David S. Shields, *Civil Tongues and Polite Letters in British America* (Chapel Hill: University of North Carolina Press, 1997).

4. For Buckminster's relation to the *Monthly Anthology*, see Lewis P. Simpson, *The Man of Letters in New England and the South* (Baton Rouge: Louisiana State University Press, 1973).

5. [William Emerson], "Preface," *Monthly Anthology, and Boston Review* 1 (1804): i–iii. See also Lewis P. Simpson, ed., *The Federalist Literary Mind: Selections from the* Monthly Anthology and Boston Review, *1803–1811* (Baton Rouge: Louisiana State University Press, 1962) and Catherine O'Donnell Kaplan, *Men of Letters in the Early Republic: Cultivating Forums of Citizenship* (Chapel Hill: University of North Carolina Press, 2008).

6. Frank Luther Mott, *A History of American Magazines, 1741–1850* (New York: D. Appleton and Company, 1930), 253–59.

7. Barbara Packer, *The Transcendentalists* (Athens: University of Georgia Press, 2007), 32–33.

8. Packer, *Transcendentalists*, 16. Buckminster published eight papers in the *Monthly Anthology* between 1805 and 1812, as well as several more for the *General Repository*. The articles responsible for spreading the tenets of biblical criticism to a wider audience are as follows: [J. S. Buckminster], "Notice of the Griesbach's Edition of the New Testament, Now Printing at Cambridge," *Monthly Anthology, and Boston Review* 5, no. 1 (January 1, 1808): 18–21; [J. S. Buckminster], "Greek Testament," *Monthly Anthology, and Boston Review* 6, no. 5 (May 1, 1809): 349; [J. S. Buckminster], "Article 18—Rev. of Griesbach's New Testament," *Monthly Anthology, and Boston Review* 10, no. 2 (February 1811): 107–14; [J. S. Buckminster], "Article 28—Rev. of Griesbach's New Testament," *Monthly Anthology, and Boston Review* 10, no. 6 (June 1811): 303–21; [J. S. Buckminster], "On the Accuracy and Fidelity of Griesbach," *General Repository and Review* (January 1, 1812): 89–101; [J. S. Buckminster], "To the Editor—Schleusner's Lexicon," *General Repository and Review* (April 1, 1812): 296. For the Harvard edition, see Johann Jakob Griesbach, *Novum Testamentum Graece* (Cambridge, MA: W. Wells and W. Hilliard, 1809).

9. [Elizabeth Palmer Peabody], "Art. III.—Spirit of the Hebrew Scriptures," *Christian Examiner and General Review* 16, no. 2 (May 1834): 174–203; [Elizabeth Palmer Peabody], "Art. II.–Spirit of the Hebrew Scriptures–No. II. Temptation, Sin, and Punishment," *Christian Examiner and General Review* 16, no. 3 (July 1834): 305–21; [Elizabeth Palmer Peabody], "Art. IV.—Spirit of Hebrew Scriptures–No. III," *Christian Examiner and General Review* 17, no. 1 (September 1834): 78–93; [George Ripley], "Art. III.—Spirit of Hebrew Poetry. Part 1," *Christian Examiner and General Review* 18, no. 2 (May 1835): 167–90; [George Ripley], "Art. III.—Spirit of Hebrew Poetry. Part 2," *Christian*

Examiner and General Review 18, no. 2 (May 1835): 190–214; [George Ripley], "Art. III.—Spirit of Hebrew Poetry. Part 3," *Christian Examiner and General Review* 18, no. 2 (May 1835): 214–22.

10. Packer, *Transcendentalists*, 16–17, 44–45.

11. Peabody, "Spirit of Hebrew Scriptures.—No. III," 93.

12. William Ellery Channing, "Remarks on a National Literature," vol. 1 of *The Works of William E. Channing* (Boston: James Munroe and Company, 1841), 245.

13. Quoted in Edward E. Chielens, *American Literary Magazines: The Eighteenth and Nineteenth Centuries* (Westport, CT: Greenwood Press, 1986), 104. The original article is "Notice of Recent Publications," *Christian Examiner and Religious Miscellany* 60, no. 1 (January 1856): 136.

14. Packer, *Transcendentalists*, 28.

15. Kenneth Walter Cameron, *Ralph Waldo Emerson's Reading* (Raleigh, NC: The Thistle Press, 1941).

16. Walter Harding, *Emerson's Library* (Charlottesville: University Press of Virginia, 1967).

17. Following his career as minister, Emerson delivered his first secular lecture on November 5, 1833, as the first in a series of four talks on the subject of natural history. He followed these up the following year with a series on biography and the year after with a series on English literature, both delivered at the Boston Masonic Temple to the Society for the Diffusion of Useful Knowledge. The Milton lecture that served as the basis for his essay in the *North American Review* was the fourth lecture in his series on biography, delivered on February 19, 1835, following an introductory lecture and lectures on Michelangelo and Martin Luther. For the text of the Milton lecture, see Ralph Waldo Emerson, "John Milton," *The Early Lectures of Ralph Waldo Emerson, vol. 1, 1833–1836*, ed. Stephen E. Whicher and Robert E. Spiller (Cambridge, MA: Harvard University Press, 1959), 144–63.

18. Robert D. Richardson Jr., *Emerson: The Mind on Fire* (Berkeley: University of California Press, 1995), 110.

19. Andrews Norton, *A Discourse on the Latest Form of Infidelity; delivered at the request of the "Association of the Alumni of the Cambridge Theological School," on the 19th of July, 1839* (Cambridge: John Owen, 1839).

20. [Ralph Waldo Emerson], "The Poetical Works of John Milton," *North American Review* 47, no. 100 (July 1838): 56–57. The essay was not reprinted in any collection of Emerson's writings for over a half century, finally appearing in Ralph Waldo Emerson, "Milton," *Natural History of the Intellect*, vol. 12 of *The Works of Ralph Waldo Emerson*, ed. James Elliott Cabot (Boston: Houghton, Mifflin and Company, 1893).

21. Richardson, *Emerson*, 196. Richard C. Pettigrew in "Emerson and Milton," *American Literature* 3, no. 1 (March 1931): 45–59, by contrast, identifies more accurately the fact that Emerson's criticism of Milton "tends to emphasize unduly the ethical and didactic excellences in Milton" and that in the Milton essay in particular "Emerson is interested primarily in Milton the man" (58).

22. Emerson, "The Poetical Works of John Milton," 60.

23. Oliver Wendell Holmes, *Ralph Waldo Emerson* (Boston: Houghton, Mifflin and Company, 1885), 112.

24. Orestes A. Brownson, "American Literature," *The Works of Orestes A. Brownson*, vol. 19, *Writings on Literature*, ed. Henry F. Brownson (Detroit: Thorndike Nourse, 1885), 3.

25. Ralph Waldo Emerson, *The Journals and Miscellaneous Notebooks of Ralph Waldo Emerson*, vol. 7, *1838–1842*, ed. A. W. Plumstead and Harrison Hayford (Cambridge, MA: Harvard University Press, 1969), 18.

26. Julie Ellison, *Emerson's Romantic Style* (Princeton, NJ: Princeton University Press, 1984); David Robinson, *Apostle of Culture: Emerson as Preacher and Lecturer* (Philadelphia: University of Pennsylvania Press, 1982).

27. Ralph Waldo Emerson, *The Journals and Miscellaneous Notebooks of Ralph Waldo Emerson*, ed. Alfred R. Ferguson, vol. 4 (Cambridge, MA: Harvard University Press, 1964), 335 (hereafter abbreviated as *JMN*). For similar remarks on the need to assert one's own thoughts and not minister to the occasion, also see *JMN* 4:348–49 and5:46. For a more general discussion of the Emerson's vocational anxieties as scholar, see Merton M. Sealts Jr., "Emerson on the Scholar, 1833–1837," *PMLA* 85, no. 2 (March 1970): 186, as well as his book length treatment *Emerson on the Scholar* (Columbia: University of Missouri Press, 1992).

28. Ralph Waldo Emerson to William Emerson, Concord, May 7, 1838, *The Letters of Ralph Waldo Emerson*, vol. 2, *1836–1841*, ed. Ralph L. Rusk (New York: Columbia University Press, 1939), 130.

29. Ralph Waldo Emerson, *An Oration, Delivered before the Literary Societies of Dartmouth College, July 24, 1838* (Boston: Charles C. Little and James Brown, 1838), 7–8.

30. For more of Cranch's caricatures, see Frederick DeWolfe Miller, *Christopher Pearse Cranch and His Caricatures of New England Transcendentalism* (Cambridge, MA: Harvard University Press, 1951).

31. Emerson, *An Oration, Delivered before the Literary Societies of Dartmouth*, 8, 14–15.

32. Ibid., 19, 25–26.

33. Ellison, *Emerson's Romantic Style*; Robinson, *Apostle of Culture*; Robert E. Spiller, "From Lecture into Essay: Emerson's Method of Composition," *Literary Criterion* 5 (Winter 1962): 28–38; Peter S. Field, "'The Transformation of Genius into Practical Power': Ralph Waldo Emerson and the Public Lecture," *Journal of the Early Republic* 21, no. 3 (Autumn 2001): 467–93.

34. Emerson, "The Poetical Works of John Milton," 56.

35. Gustaaf Van Cromphout in "Emerson and the Dialectics of History," *PMLA* 91, no. 1 (January 1976): 54–65, argues that Emerson's contradictions are part of a Hegelian dialectical view of history that expressed itself especially in his lectures and essays on biography. Richard P. Adams in "The Basic Contradiction in Emerson," *ESQ* 55 (1969): 106–10, traces Emerson's contradictions back to his concept of organicism.

36. Emerson, "Intellect," *The Collected Works of Ralph Waldo Emerson*, ed. Alfred R. Ferguson, Joseph Slater et al., 10 vols. to date (Cambridge, MA: Belknap

Press of Harvard University Press, 1971–2013) 2:198. Hereafter abbreviated *CW* with volume and page number.

37. Leonora Cranch Scott, *The Life and Letters of Christopher Pearse Cranch* (Boston: Houghton Mifflin Co., 1917), 64–65; John Q. Anderson, *The Liberating Gods: Emerson on Poets and Poetry* (Coral Gables, FL: University of Miami Press, 1971), 11.

38. Margaret Fuller, "A Short Essay on Critics," *Dial* 1, no. 1 (July 1840): 5.

39. The "Record of the Months" section, which included as a subsection the "Select List of Recent Publications," began with the second issue of the *Dial* 1, no. 2 (October 1840). The other articles referenced appeared as follows: Ralph Waldo Emerson, "The Editors to the Reader," *Dial* 1, no. 1 (July 1840): 1–4; C. C. Emerson, "Notes from the Journal of a Scholar," *Dial* 1, no. 1 (July 1840): 13–16; Margaret Fuller, "A Record of Impressions Produced by the Exhibition of Mr. Allston's Pictures in the Summer of 1839," *Dial* 1, no. 1 (July 1840): 73–83; George Ripley, "Brownson's Writings," *Dial* 1, no. 1 (July 1840): 22–46; Henry David Thoreau, "Aulus Persius Flaccus," *Dial* 1, no. 1 (July 1840): 117–21; Ralph Waldo Emerson, "Thoughts on Modern Literature," *Dial* 1, no. 2 (October 1840): 137–58.

40. There are numerous dimensions, both vocational and material, through which studies engage Emerson. For Emerson as preacher, see Susan L. Roberson, *Emerson in His Sermons: A Man-Made Self* (Columbia: University of Missouri Press, 1995). For his career as orator more generally, both as preacher and lay lecturer, see Robinson, *Apostle of Culture*. For Emerson's lifelong commitment to his journal, see Lawrence Rosenwald, *Emerson and the Art of the Diary* (New York: Oxford University Press, 1988). For Emerson's editorial endeavors, see Robert Richardson Jr., "Emerson as Editor," in *Emersonian Circles: Essays in Honor of Joel Myerson*, ed. Wesley T. Mott and Robert E. Burkholder (Rochester, NY: University of Rochester Press, 1997), 105–13.

41. Emerson, "Thoughts on Modern Literature," 141–42.

42. Ibid., 141, 143.

43. For Emerson's vocational anxieties, see Sealts, "Emerson on the Scholar," and Henry Nash Smith, "Emerson's Problem of Vocation: A Note on 'The American Scholar," *New England Quarterly* 12 (March 1939): 52–67.

44. Marilyn Butler, "Culture's Medium: The Role of the Review," in *The Cambridge Companion to British Romanticism*, ed. Stuart Curran (Cambridge, UK: Cambridge University Press, 1993), 123.

45. Lawrence Buell, *Emerson* (Cambridge, MA: Belknap Press of Harvard University Press, 2003), 39–40.

46. For an extensive treatment of Emerson's relationship to Goethe and especially his sense of Goethe as representative modern man, see Gustaaf Van Cromphout, *Emerson's Modernity and the Example of Goethe* (Columbia: University of Missouri Press, 1990).

47. Emerson, "Goethe, or the Writer," *CW* 4:156–57.

48. Ralph Waldo Emerson, "Literature," *The Early Lectures of Ralph Waldo Emerson*, vol. 2, *1836–1838*, ed. Stephen E. Whicher, Robert E. Spiller, and Wallace E. Williams (Cambridge, MA: Harvard University Press, 1964), 68.

49. Emerson, "Goethe," 4:157–59, 4:166.
50. Ralph Waldo Emerson, "Literary Ethics," *CW* 1:114.
51. Ralph Waldo Emerson, "Books," *CW* 7:99, 7:95–96.
52. Ibid., 7:97
53. Ibid., 7:96–97.
54. Thomas Jefferson to Robert Skipwith, with "A list of Books for a Private Library," Monticello, 3 August 1771, in Thomas Jefferson, *Writings*, ed. Merrill D. Peterson (New York: Library of America, 1884), 740–45.
55. Emerson, "Books," 7:103.
56. Ibid., 7:101, 7:104.
57. Ann M. Blair, *Too Much to Know: Managing Scholarly Information before the Modern Age* (New Haven: Yale University Press, 2010).

CHAPTER 2: ANTHOLOGY WARS

1. Rufus Wilmot Griswold, "The Intellectual History, Condition and Prospects of the Country," in *The Prose Writers of America* (Philadelphia: Carey and Hart, 1847), 50.
2. Griswold, *Prose Writers*, 50, 10.
3. Paul Starr, *The Creation of the Media: Political Origins of Modern Communications* (New York: Basic Books, 2004), 1.
4. Griswold, *Prose Writers*, 13–15.
5. Ibid., 49.
6. For an expansive treatment of this theme, see Trish Loughran, *The Republic in Print: Print Culture in the Age of U.S. Nation Building, 1770–1870* (New York: Columbia University Press, 2007).
7. For Griswold's designation as America's "first professional anthologist," see Alan Golding, "A History of American Poetry Anthologies," *From Outlaw to Classic: Canons in American Poetry* (Madison: University of Wisconsin Press, 1995), 13.
8. William Charvat provides the classic account of these changes in *Literary Publishing in America, 1790–1850* (Philadelphia: University of Pennsylvania Press, 1959).
9. The majority of my biographical material is drawn from the one full-length biography of Griswold, Joy Bayless's *Rufus Wilmot Griswold: Poe's Literary Executor* (Nashville, TN: Vanderbilt University Press, 1943). To Bayless's thorough and unbiased account of Griswold's life I am greatly indebted. Most factual material related to the events of Griswold's life is drawn from Bayless's study unless otherwise noted. For all points relating to my larger arguments, however, I return to the original sources so as to form independent conclusions.
10. For an account of the mammoths *Brother Jonathan* and the *New World*, see James J. Barnes, *Authors, Publishers and Politicians: The Quest for an Anglo-American Copyright Agreement, 1815–1854* (Columbus: Ohio State University Press, 1974), 1–29.
11. Starr, *The Creation of the Media*, 83–150.
12. Hellmut Lehmann-Haupt, *The Book in America: A History of the Making and Selling of Books in the United States* (New York: Bowker, 1951).

13. Barnes, *Authors, Publishers and Politicians*, 24.

14. Anon., *Lessons in Elocution: or, A selection of pieces in prose and verse* (Philadelphia: Printed by W. Young, 1788).

15. Library Company of Philadelphia, *A catalogue of the books, belonging to the Library Company of Philadelphia* (Philadelphia: Zachariah Poulson, Jr., 1789).

16. [Elihu Hubbard Smith, ed.], *American Poems: Selected and Original*, vol. 1 (Litchfield: Collier and Buel, 1793), iii–v. For the view of Smith's *American Poems* as the first American anthology, see Michael Gilmore, "The Literature of the Revolutionary and Early National Periods," in *The Cambridge History of American Literature*, vol. I, *1590–1820*, ed. Sacvan Bercovitch (New York: Cambridge University Press, 1994), 615.

17. Mathew Carey, "Advertisement," *The Beauties of Poetry, British and American* (Philadelphia: M. Carey, 1791).

18. The price and publication history of Smith's *American Poems* is noted by William K. Bottorff in the introduction to the facsimile reproduction of *American Poems (1793)*, ed. Elihu Hubbard Smith (Gainesville, FL: Scholars' Facsimiles & Reprints, 1966), vi.

19. Gilmore, "Literature of the Revolutionary and Early National Periods," 616.

20. Samuel Kettell, ed., *Specimens of American Poetry with Critical and Biographical Notices*, 3 vols. (Boston: S. G. Goodrich and Co., 1829), iii–iv.

21. For a capsule history of the origins of the anthology in antiquity and its evolution in the Renaissance, see Anne Ferry, *Tradition and the Individual Poem: An Inquiry into Anthologies* (Stanford, CA: Stanford University Press, 2001).

22. David Perkins, "Literary History and Historicism," in *The Cambridge History of Literary Criticism*, vol. 5, *Romanticism*, ed. Marshall Brown (New York: Cambridge University Press, 2000), 338.

23. René Wellek, *The Rise of English Literary History* (Chapel Hill: University of North Carolina Press, 1941), 1.

24. Barbara M. Benedict, *Making the Modern Reader: Cultural Mediation in Early Modern Literary Anthologies* (Princeton, NJ: Princeton University Press, 1996), 9.

25. Julia M. Wright, "'The Order of Time': Nationalism and Literary Anthologies, 1774–1831," *Papers on Language & Literature* 33, no. 4 (Fall 1997): 341n4.

26. Kettell, *Specimens of American Poetry*, iii.

27. Unsigned review of *Specimens of American Poetry*, by Samuel Kettell, *North American Review* 20, no. 65 (October 1829): 487.

28. Ibid., 489–90.

29. Elisa Tamarkin, *Anglophilia: Deference, Devotion, and Antebellum America* (Chicago: University of Chicago Press, 2008); Leonard Tennenhouse, *The Importance of Feeling English: American Literature and the British Diaspora, 1750–1850* (Princeton, NJ: Princeton University Press, 2007).

30. Benedict, *Making the Modern Reader*, 9; Wright, "'The Order of Time,'" 339–65, 341; Griswold's will is reprinted under the heading "Miscellany" in *Historical Magazine* 1, no. 12 (December 1857): 379. Rufus W. Griswold, *Catalogue of the Entire Private Library of the Late Rev. Rufus W. Griswold . . . To be sold at auction . . . May 23d 1859 . . . by Bangs, Merwin & Co.* (New York, 1859), 21.

31. Rufus Griswold, "Historical Introduction," *The Poets and Poetry of America* (Philadelphia: Carey and Hart, 1847), 17.

32. Rufus Griswold, "Preface to the First Edition," *The Poets and Poetry of America,* 7.

33. [Edwin Percy Whipple], review of *The Poets and Poetry of America,* by Rufus Griswold, *North American Review* 58, no. 82 (January 1844): 1.

34. Rufus Griswold, "To the Reader," *The Poets and Poetry of America,* v.

35. Unsigned review of *The Poets and Poetry of America,* by Rufus Griswold, *United States Magazine and Democratic Review* 11, no. 50 (August 1842): 177.

36. Unsigned review of *The Poets and Poetry of America,* by Rufus Griswold, *Southern Quarterly Review* 2, no. 3 (July 1842): 269–70.

37. Pierre Bourdieu, *Distinction: A Social Critique of the Judgement of Taste,* trans. Richard Nice (Cambridge, MA: Harvard University Press, 1984); Lawrence Levine, *Highbrow/Lowbrow: The Emergence of Cultural Hierarchy in America* (Cambridge, MA: Harvard University Press, 1999).

38. Unsigned review of *The Poets and Poetry of America,* by Rufus Griswold, *Graham's Lady's and Gentleman's Magazine* 21, no. 6 (December 1842): 342.

39. Frank Luther Mott, *Golden Multitudes: The Story of Best Sellers in the United States* (New York: Macmillan, 1947), 109.

40. Bayless, *Rufus Wilmot Griswold,* 41–50, 242–43.

41. Griswold, *Prose Writers,* 45.

42. "Recent Publications for Sale by Charles S. Francis & Co.," *Christian Inquirer* 1, no. 23 (March 20, 1847): 91.

43. While written specifically for the volume, the introductory survey had previously appeared in seven installments in the Washington *Daily National Intelligencer* from June to September 1845, later to be republished in the *Saturday Evening Post.*

44. Leah Price, *The Anthology and the Rise of the Novel: From Richardson to George Eliot* (New York: Cambridge University Press, 2000).

45. Washington Allston, quoted in Griswold, *Prose Writers,* 137.

46. This distinction Griswold bestowed upon Washington Irving and Judge Joseph Story in the frontispiece and vignette respectively and upon Jonathan Edwards, John James Audubon, James Fenimore Cooper, J. P. Kennedy, William Prescott, Ralph Waldo Emerson, and Charles Fenno Hoffman in the body of the book.

47. Griswold, "Intellectual History, Conditions, and Prospects," *Prose Writers,* 18.

48. Jared Sparks, "American History," in *Prose Writers,* 308.

49. William Ellery Channing, "The Present Age," in *Prose Writers,* 167.

50. For a good example of positive reactions to *The Prose Writers,* see the unsigned review of *The Prose Writers of America,* by Rufus Griswold, *Christian Parlor Magazine* (May 1, 1847): 32.

51. [Horace Binney Wallace], review of *The Prose Writers of America,* by Rufus Griswold, *Knickerbocker, or New York Monthly Magazine* 30, no. 4 (October 1847): 342–43. The complete review, continued in the next issue, 30, no. 5 (November 1847): 441–45, was posthumously reprinted in Wallace's *Literary Criticisms and Other Papers* (Philadelphia: Parry & McMillan, 1856), 3–55.

52. Review of *The Prose Writers of America*, by Rufus Griswold, *Godey's Magazine and Lady's Book* 34 (May 1847): 271–72.

53. [Evert Duyckinck], review of *The Prose Writers of America*, by Rufus Griswold, *Literary World* 1, no. 7 (March 20, 1847): 149.

54. Ibid., 149–51.

55. David Perkins, *Is Literary History Possible?* (Baltimore: Johns Hopkins University Press, 1993), 53–56.

56. Duyckinck, review of *Prose Writers of America*, 149.

57. William A. Jones, review of *The Prose Writers of America*, by Rufus W. Griswold, *United States Magazine, and Democratic Review* 20, no. 107 (May 1847): 384–86.

58. Ibid., 386.

59. For a survey of eighteenth-century literary historiography, see Wellek, *The Rise of English Literary History*. For a discussion of the eighteenth-century historiography more generally, see Ernst Breisach, *Historiography: Ancient, Medieval, & Modern* (Chicago: University of Chicago Press, 1983).

60. Jones, review of *The Prose Writers of America*, 390–91.

61. For an example of this sort of critique of New Historicism's flattening use of context, see Rita Felski, "Context Stinks!" *New Literary History* 42, no. 4 (Autumn 2011): 573–91. For a second interrogation of historicism, see Jonathan Rée, "The Vanity of Historicism," *New Literary History* 22, no. 4 (Autumn 1991): 961–83.

62. Jones, review of *The Prose Writers of America*, 389.

63. Griswold, *Prose Writers*, 5.

64. Jones, review of *The Prose Writers of America*, 388–89.

65. Evert and George Duyckinck, "Preface," *The Cyclopaedia of American Literature*, 2 vols. (New York: Charles Scribner, 1855), v. Though entered for copyright in 1855, the work first appeared in bookstores in the early months of 1856.

66. Evert and George Duyckinck, *Cyclopaedia of American Literature*, 533.

67. Unsigned review of *The Prose Writers of America*, by Rufus Griswold, *Knickerbocker; or New York Monthly Magazine* 29, no. 4 (April 1847): 364.

68. Evert and George Duyckinck, *Cyclopaedia of American Literature*, v–vii.

69. Ibid., vii.

70. For an in depth discussion of eighteenth-century literary compilations and series by the likes of John Bell and Samuel Johnson, see Thomas F. Bonnell, *The Most Disreputable Trade: Publishing the Classics of English Poetry, 1765–1810* (New York: Oxford University Press, 2008).

71. Wright, "'The Order of Time,'" 339–41.

72. As Philip Gaskell notes in *A New Introduction to Bibliography* (New York: Oxford University Press, 1972), in the nineteenth century, though the folio format still occasionally appeared, "the predominance of octavo [became] steadily more marked" (196). This shift was even more pronounced with books aiming for a large popular audience since to achieve high sales, a book needed to be affordable, thereby imposing restrictions on size.

73. Evert and George Duyckinck, *Cyclopaedia of American Literature*, vii–viii.

74. Perry Miller, *The Raven and the Whale: Poe, Melville, and the New York Literary Scene* (Baltimore: Johns Hopkins University Press, 1997), 329.

75. Herman Hooker to Griswold, February 21, 1856, in *Passages from the Correspondence and Other Papers of Rufus W. Griswold*, ed. William Griswold (Cambridge, MA: Wm Griswold, 1898), 306; C. F. Briggs to Griswold, Feb 13, 1856, *Passages from the Correspondence*, 305–6.

76. Rufus W. Griswold, review of *The Cyclopedia of American Literature*, by Evart A. Duyckinck [*sic*] and George L. Duyckinck (New York: Baker & Godwin, Book and Job Printers, 1856), 4, 9–10.

77. Ibid., 17.

78. Ibid., 30.

CHAPTER 3: REVIEWERS REVIEWED

1. Edgar Allan Poe, "Rufus W. Griswold," *Essays and Reviews*, ed. G. R. Thompson (New York: Library of America, 1984), 555–56.

2. Rufus Griswold, "Edgar A. Poe," *The Prose Writers of America*, 4th ed. (Philadelphia: Parry and McMillan, 1855), 524. Hereafter references are to the expanded 4th edition (1855) since it includes more authors as well as revisions by Griswold in the last years before his death in 1857.

3. Poe to Susan V. C. Ingram, Norfolk, 10 September 1849, *The Letters of Edgar Allan Poe*, ed. John Ward Ostrom, 2 vols. (New York: Gordian Press, 1966), 2:460.

4. Until recently, the specific site of the Johnson quote remained undiscovered, but in 2001, while working on an updated version of John Ward Ostrom's 1966 edition of Poe's letters, Burton Pollin solved the matter when he finally managed to identify the source as Johnson's "Plan to an English Dictionary," located in the "Miscellaneous Pieces" volume of his collected works, and probably becoming known to Poe when he wrote a review of Charles Richardson's *New Dictionary* in the August 1836 issue of the *Southern Literary Messenger*. For the full history of the allusion, see Burton Pollin, "Letter to the Editor" *Edgar Allan Poe Review* 2, no. 1 (Spring 2001): 95–96.

5. Poe, "Marginalia," *Essays and Reviews*, 1464.

6. Poe, "The Philosophy of Composition," *Essays and Reviews*, 14.

7. Poe, "Marginalia," *Essays and Reviews*, 1466.

8. For a range of views on the hoax versus poetics reading of "The Philosophy of Composition," see T. S. Eliot, "From Poe to Valéry," in *The Recognition of Edgar Allan Poe*, ed. Eric W. Carlson (Ann Arbor: University of Michigan Press, 1966), 211. Remy de Gourmont, "Marginalia on 'The Philosophy of Composition,'" in *Critical Essays on Edgar Allan Poe*, ed. Eric W. Carlson (Boston: G. K. Hall & Co., 1987), 85; Daniel Hoffman, in *Critical Essays on Edgar Allan Poe*, 95; Kent Ljungquist, "The Poet as Critic," in *The Cambridge Companion to Edgar Allan Poe*, ed. Kevin J. Hayes (New York: Cambridge University Press, 2002), 18–19.

9. For Poe's decision to leave *Graham's* on account of the "namby-pamby character of the Magazine" see his letter to Frederick Thomas. Poe to Frederick W. Thomas, Philadelphia, 25 May 1842, *Letters of Edgar Allan Poe*, 1:197–98.

10. Thomas Bender, *New York Intellect* (Baltimore: Johns Hopkins University Press, 1987), 157–58.

11. Kevin J. Hayes, *Poe and the Printed Word* (New York: Cambridge University Press, 2000), 93–97. The best account of American magazines is still to be found in Frank Luther Mott's *A History of American Magazines, 1741–1850* (New York: D. Appleton and Company, 1930), 498, from which I draw the following synopsis of the growth of monthly magazines.

12. Mott, *A History of American Magazines,* 342–54.

13. Ibid., 494–513.

14. Ibid., 513–25.

15. Ibid., 503.

16. For older marketplace approaches, see William Charvat, *The Profession of Authorship in America, 1800–1870,* ed. Matthew J. Bruccoli (Columbus: Ohio State University Press, 1968) as well as Michael T. Gilmore, *American Romanticism and the Marketplace* (Chicago: University of Chicago Press, 1985). For more recent, revisionist accounts of the antebellum marketplace, see Leon Jackson, *The Business of Letters: Authorial Economies in Antebellum America* (Stanford, CA: Stanford University Press, 2008); Terence Whalen, *Edgar Allan Poe and the Masses: The Political Economy of Literature in Antebellum America* (Princeton, NJ: Princeton University Press, 1999); Jonathan Elmer, *Reading at the Social Limit: Affect, Mass Culture, and Edgar Allan Poe* (Stanford, CA: Stanford University Press, 1995); and Sandra Tomc, *Industry and the Creative Mind: The Eccentric Writer in American Literature and Entertainment, 1790–1860* (Ann Arbor: University of Michigan Press, 2012). For the recent print culture turn in Poe studies, see the essays collected in J. Gerald Kennedy and Jerome McGann, eds., *Poe and the Remapping of Antebellum Print Culture* (Baton Rouge: Louisiana State University Press, 2012); Meredith McGill, *American Literature and the Culture of Reprinting, 1834–1853* (Philadelphia: University of Pennsylvania Press, 2003), 141–217; Hayes, *Poe and the Printed Word*; and Eliza Richards, *Gender and the Poetics of Reception in Poe's Circle* (New York: Cambridge University Press, 2004).

17. Kennedy and McGann, eds., *Poe and the Remapping of Antebellum Print Culture,* 9.

18. Michael Allen, *Poe and the British Magazine Tradition* (New York: Oxford University Press, 1969), 16–17.

19. Arthur Hobson Quinn, *Edgar Allan Poe: A Critical Biography* (Baltimore: Johns Hopkins University Press, 1998), 246–47.

20. Subsequent citations to Poe's reviews refer to Edgar Allan Poe, *Essays and Reviews,* ed. G. R. Thompson (New York: Library of America, 1984) and will be included parenthetically.

21. For a discussion of this principle, see Lewis P. Simpson, "Poe's Vision of His Ideal Magazine," in *The Man of Letters in New England and the South* (Baton Rouge: Louisiana State University Press, 1973), 131–49. Simpson's essay is particularly astute at articulating the antithetical motives—some high, others low—that permeate Poe's sense of the vocation of criticism. James Russell Lowell, "Our Contributors.—No. XVII. Edgar Allan Poe," *Graham's Magazine* 27, no. 2 (February 1845): 49.

22. Poe for his own part liked to draw more refined comparisons for his severe style of reviewing. As he wrote in a segment called "Literary Small Talk" in 1839: "I have had no little to do, in my day, with the trade of Aristarchus, and have even been accused of playing the Zoilus. Yet I cannot bring myself to feel any goadings of conscience for undue severity" (E&R 1061). Here Poe aligns himself with the severe Greek grammarian and classical literary scholar, Zoilus, known for his commentary on Homer, as opposed to the gentler Aristarchus.

23. Poe to Thomas W. White, Baltimore, 30 April 1835, Letters of Edgar Allan Poe, 1:56.

24. Poe to Harrison Hall, 2 September 1836, Letters of Edgar Allan Poe, 1:103–4.

25. Edgar Allan Poe, "Tales of the Folio Club," in Poetry and Tales, ed. Patrick F. Quinn (New York: Library of America, 1984), 131–33.

26. Thomas Ollive Mabbott, ed., The Collected Works of Edgar Allan Poe, by Edgar Allan Poe, vol. 1, Tales & Sketches (Chicago: University of Illinois Press, 2000), 201.

27. James Russell Lowell, A Fable for Critics (New York: G.P. Putnam, 1848), 59.

28. Poe to Joseph Evans Snodgrass, Philadelphia, 12 July 1841, Letters of Edgar Allan Poe, 1:175.

29. Lara Langer Cohen, The Fabrication of American Literature: Fraudulence and Antebellum Print Culture (Philadelphia: University of Pennsylvania Press, 2012), 23–64.

30. Poe to Philip P. Cooke, New York, 9 August 1846, Letters of Edgar Allan Poe, 2:329.

31. Elmer, Reading at the Social Limit; Whalen, Edgar Allan Poe and the Masses.

32. Mabbott, The Collected Works of Edgar Allan Poe, 2:1377.

33. Yvor Winters, "Edgar Allan Poe: A Crisis in the History of American Obscurantism," in Carlson, The Recognition of Edgar Allan Poe, 176–202.

34. Perry Miller, The Raven and the Whale: Poe, Melville, and the New York Literary Scene (Baltimore: Johns Hopkins University Press, 1997), 15.

35. Edgar Allan Poe, The Poe Log: A Documentary Life of Edgar Allan Poe, 1809–1849, ed. Dwight Thomas and David K. Jackson (Boston: G. K. Hall & Co., 1987), 638.

36. Poe to George W. Eveleth, 15 December 1846, Letters of Edgar Allan Poe, 2:331–33.

37. Michael Warner, The Letters of the Republic: Publication and the Public Sphere in Eighteenth-Century America (Cambridge, MA: Harvard University Press, 1990).

38. Edward Said, Representations of the Intellectual (New York: Vintage Books, 1996), 13.

39. For a particularly good discussion of Poe's carefully calculated theatricality in both his life and his writings, specifically emphasizing Poe's roots in the theater, see N. Bryllion Fagin, The Histrionic Mr. Poe (Baltimore: Johns Hopkins University Press, 1949).

40. For Hoffman and Bristed's debate over the propriety of personality criticism, see their lively exchange: Charles Fenno Hoffman, "A Spicy Cut-Up of an Author," Literary World 3, no. 3 (February 19, 1848): 41–42, and Charles

Astor Bristed, "Home Correspondence. Criticism," *Literary World* (March 18, 1848): 125–26.

41. Poe to Philip P. Cooke, New York, 9 August 1846, *Letters of Edgar Allan Poe*, 2:328.

42. Poe to George Lippard, Philadelphia, 18 February 1844, *Letters of Edgar Allan Poe*, 1:243

43. Poe to Thomas W. White, Baltimore, 30 April 1835, *Letters of Edgar Allan Poe*, 1:57–58.

44. Poe to George Eveleth, New York, 4 January 1848, *Letters of Edgar Allan Poe*, 2:355.

45. G. R. Thompson, *Poe's Fiction: Romantic Irony in the Gothic Tales* (Madison: University of Wisconsin Press, 1973).

46. Neil Harris, *Humbug: The Art of P. T. Barnum* (Chicago: University of Chicago Press, 1973), 61–89.

47. Denise Gigante, introduction to *The Great Age of the English Essay: An Anthology*, ed. Denise Gigante (New Haven, CT: Yale University Press, 2008), xv–xvi.

48. Poe to James Russell Lowell, New York, 18 August 1844, *Letters of Edgar Allan Poe*, 1:261.

49. Poe to George Eveleth, New York, 15 December 1846, *Letters of Edgar Allan Poe*, 2:332–33.

50. Ibid, 2:332–33.

51. Quinn, *Edgar Allan Poe*, 560–61.

CHAPTER 4: BLACK, WHITE, AND READ ALL OVER

1. Edgar A. Poe, "The Literati of New York City.–No. IV.–Sarah Margaret Fuller," *Godey's Lady's Book* 33 (August 1846): 72.

2. Margaret Fuller, review of *Tales*, by Edgar Allan Poe, *New-York Daily Tribune*, July 11, 1845 (*MFC* 153); Fuller, review of *The Raven and Other Poems*, by Edgar Allan Poe, *New-York Daily Tribune*, November 26, 1845 (*MFC* 271–76). In citing Fuller's *Tribune* reviews in this chapter, I will provide citations to their initial publication date in the *New-York Daily Tribune* (*NYDT* hereafter) since I argue that this original publication context mattered to the way her reviews were understood. These *Tribune* issues are accessible through the Chronicling America website (https://chroniclingamerica.loc.gov/), which, as a joint venture of the National Endowment for the Humanities and the Library of Congress, is free to use, unrestricted by institutional paywalls. The *New-York Weekly Tribune* (hereafter *NYWT*) is not available there, however, and is harder to access in general. For convenience, I will also include page numbers to Judith Mattson Bean and Joel Myerson's edited collection, *Margaret Fuller, Critic: Writings from the New-York Tribune, 1844–1846* (New York: Columbia University Press, 2000), abbreviated *MFC* hereafter if the piece is one of the eighty-eight reviews printed in the book edition and abbreviated *MFCD* (along with its numbering) if the piece is only included in the accompanying CD-ROM. I encourage readers to consult the original *Tribune* versions and the reprinted versions in *Margaret Fuller, Critic* as

well as in other edited collections to see for themselves the difference that these contexts make in shaping the experience of reading Fuller's reviews and of antebellum literary criticism more generally. The differences can be startling.

3. Charles Capper, *Margaret Fuller: An American Romantic Life*, vol. 2, *The Public Years* (New York: Oxford University Press, 2007), 198. For Fuller's view of her star as an assertion of ownership of the opinions expressed, see Fuller, "A Few Words in Reply to Mr. U. C. Hill," *NYDT*, supplement, May 16, 1846 (*MFCD*, C285).

4. Thomas Bender, *New York Intellect* (Baltimore: Johns Hopkins University Press, 1987), 157–61.

5. Even forty years ago Joel Myerson observed that scholarship on Fuller's criticism is "the most worked-over area of Fuller scholarship" (xv). For a good starting place on early treatments of Fuller's criticism see Joel Myerson, introduction to *Critical Essays on Margaret Fuller*, ed. Joel Myerson (Boston: G. K. Hall & Co., 1980), xiv–xvi. Also, see Larry J. Reynolds, "Prospects for the Study of Margaret Fuller," *Resources for American Literary Study* 26, no. 2 (2000): 139–58, as well as the "Archives" page of the Margaret Fuller Society website, which maintains a comprehensive up-to-date bibliography: https://margaretfullersociety.files.word press.com/2018/02/bibliography-on -fuller-new.pdf

6. While numerous collections of Fuller's writings offer samplings of Fuller's *Tribune* pieces, from Arthur Buckminster Fuller's posthumous volumes in the 1850s, to mid-twentieth-century collections by Mason Wade and Perry Miller, to late twentieth century collections by Bell Gale Chevigny, Joel Myerson, Jeffrey Steele, and Mary Kelley, it was primarily three collections, alongside of new biographies by Charles Capper and the completed six volume *Letters of Margaret Fuller* edited by Robert Hudspeth, that made a new generation of scholarship on Fuller's *Tribune* writings possible. For these volumes, see Larry J. Reynolds and Susan Belasco Smith, eds., *"These Sad But Glorious Days": Dispatches from Europe, 1846–1850* (New Haven: Yale University Press, 1991); Catherine C. Mitchell, ed., *Margaret Fuller's New York Journalism* (Knoxville: University of Tennessee Press, 1995); and Bean and Myerson, eds., *Margaret Fuller, Critic* (2000). For several of the best studies of Fuller's New York period *Tribune* pieces, see Bean and Myerson, introduction to *Margaret Fuller, Critic*, xv–xl; Capper, *Margaret Fuller: An American Romantic Life*, 2:194–277. Christina Zwarg, "Reading before Marx: Margaret Fuller and the *New-York Daily Tribune*," in *Readers in History: Nineteenth-Century Literature and the Contexts of Response*, ed. James L. Machor (Baltimore: Johns Hopkins University Press, 1993), 228–58; and Paula Kopacz, "Feminist at the *Tribune*: Margaret Fuller as Professional Writer," *Studies in the American Renaissance* (1991): 119–39. Since the appearance of these collections and formative studies, a steady stream of articles and book chapters on Fuller's New York journalism have appeared.

7. Susan Belasco Smith, "Margaret Fuller in New York: Private Letters, Public Texts," *Documentary Editing* 18, no. 3 (September 1996): 63–64.

8. For a recent discussion of the shifting ground of professionalization and

intellectual authority from a number of perspectives, see the essays collected in Günter Leypoldt, ed., *Intellectual Authority and Literary Culture in the US, 1790–1900* (Heidelberg: Universitätsverlag Winter, 2013).

9. For just a few of the many works that treat the emergence of institutionalized literary studies in the late nineteenth and early twentieth centuries, see Gerald Graff, *Professing Literature: An Institutional History* (Chicago: University of Chicago Press, 2007); Bruce Robbins, *Secular Vocations: Intellectuals, Professionalism, Culture* (New York: Verso, 1993); Kermit Vanderbilt, *American Literature and the Academy: The Roots, Growth, and Maturity of a Profession* (Philadelphia: University of Pennsylvania Press, 1986); David R. Shumway, *Creating American Civilization: A Genealogy of American Literature as an Academic Discipline* (Minneapolis: University of Minnesota Press, 1994); and Robert Scholes, *The Rise and Fall of English* (New Haven: Yale University Press, 1998), 1–28.

10. Horace Greeley, "The Dial. No. II," *New-Yorker* 10, no. 5 (October 17, 1840): 78; Capper, *Margaret Fuller: An American Romantic Life*, 2:122.

11. Jeffrey Steele, "Reconfiguring 'public attention': Margaret Fuller in New York City," *Nineteenth-Century Prose* 42, no. 2 (Fall 2015): 130. Also, Edwin G. Burrows and Mike Wallace, *Gotham: A History of New York City to 1898* (New York: Oxford University Press, 1999), 674–81.

12. Mitchell, *Margaret Fuller's New York Journalism*, 14.

13. Thomas Wentworth Higginson, *Margaret Fuller Ossoli* (Boston: Houghton, Mifflin and Company, 1884), 216–17.

14. For two descriptions of Fuller's canonization in the late twentieth century, see Bell Gale Chevigny's foreword to the revised edition of *The Woman and the Myth: Margaret Fuller's Life and Writings*, ed. Bell Gale Chevigny (Boston: Northeastern University Press, 1994), xv–xlii, in which Chevigny surveys the rise in Fuller's status since the publication of the first edition of her collection in 1976. Also, see Joel Myerson's review of four new collections of Fuller's writings, "The Canonization of Margaret Fuller," *Review* vol. 18 (1996), ed. James O. Hoge (Charlottesville: University Press of Virginia, 1996): 31–43. For a more popular account, see Judith Thurman, "An Unfinished Woman: The Desires of Margaret Fuller," *New Yorker* 89, no.7 (April 1,2013): 75–81.

15. Bell Gale Chevigny, "The Long Arm of Censorship: Myth-Making in Margaret Fuller's Time and Our Own," *Signs* 2, no. 2 (Winter 1976): 450–60. For the shifting status of Fuller's reputation in the late nineteenth century, see Thomas R. Mitchell, "Julian Hawthorne and the 'Scandal' of Margaret Fuller," *American Literary History* 7, no. 2 (Summer 1995): 210–33.

16. Fuller, "New Year's Day," *NYDT*, January 1, 1845 (*MFC* 15).

17. Benedict Anderson, *Imagined Communities: Reflections on the Origin and Spread of Nationalism* (New York: Verso, 2006), 24–36. For revisionist responses that complicate Anderson's print-capitalist account of imagined communities, see Ronald J. Zboray, *A Fictive People: Antebellum Economic Development and the American Reading Republic* (New York: Oxford University Press, 1993); Lara Langer Cohen, *The Fabrication of American Literature: Fraudulence and Antebellum Print Culture* (Philadelphia: University of Pennsylvania Press, 2012); and Trish Loughran, *The Republic in Print: Print Culture in the Age of*

U.S. Nation Building, 1770–1870 (New York: Columbia University Press, 2007).

18. Fuller to [?], [1845], in *The Letters of Margaret Fuller*, ed. Robert N. Hudspeth, 6 vols. (Ithaca, NY: Cornell University Press, 1983–1994), 4:39–40 (hereafter *Letters*).

19. Christopher B. Daly, *Covering America: A Narrative History of a Nation's Journalism* (Amherst: University of Massachusetts Press, 2012), 56. For Alexis De Tocqueville's famous description of the American press, see *Democracy in America*, trans. Gerald E. Bevan (New York: Penguin, 2003), 209–19, 600–604. For other accounts of the development of the antebellum press, see Frank Luther Mott, *American Journalism: A History of Newspapers in the United States through 250 Years, 1690–1940* (New York: Macmillan, 1941), 215–326; Michael Schudson, *Discovering the News: A Social History of American Newspapers* (New York: Basic Books, 1978); Paul Starr, *The Creation of the Media: Political Origins of Modern Communications* (New York: Basic Books, 2004); David Paul Nord, *Communities of Journalism: A History of American Newspapers and Their Readers* (Urbana: University of Illinois Press, 2001); and Dan Schiller, *Objectivity and the News: The Public and the Rise of Commercial Journalism* (Philadelphia: University of Pennsylvania Press, 1981).

20. Andie Tucher, "Newspapers and Periodicals," in *A History of the Book in America*, ed. Robert A. Gross and Mary Kelley, vol. 2, *An Extensive Republic* (Chapel Hill: Published in association with the American Antiquarian Society by the University of North Carolina Press, 2010), 390.

21. Schudson, *Discovering the News*, 14–31.

22. Ibid., 25.

23. Ibid., 31–33.

24. Ibid., 13.

25. Jeffrey D. Groves, "Introduction. Periodicals and Serial Publication," in *A History of the Book in America*, ed. Scott E. Csper, Jeffrey D. Groves, Stephen W. Nissenbaum, and Michael Winship, vol. 3, *The Industrial Book* (Chapel Hill: University of North Carolina Press, 2007), 224–30.

26. Megan Marshall, *Margaret Fuller: A New American Life* (Boston: Mariner Books, 2014), 239.

27. John Nerone, "Newspapers and the Public Sphere," in *A History of the Book in America*, vol. 3, *The Industrial Book*, 230–48.

28. Mark Canada, *Literature and Journalism in Antebellum America* (New York: Palgrave Macmillan, 2011), 4–5. Canada provides a useful summary of scholarly tendencies in treatments of the intersecting trajectories of American literature and journalism. For a good example of the apprenticeship model of literary journalism, see Shelley Fisher Fishkin, *From Fact to Fiction: Journalism and Imaginative Writing in America* (Baltimore: Johns Hopkins University Press, 1985).

29. For one particularly notable collection treating periodical studies in America, see Kenneth M. Price and Susan Belasco Smith, *Periodical Literature in Nineteenth-Century America* (Charlottesville: University Press of Virginia, 1996). The Research Society of American Periodicals (RSAP), founded in 1991, currently sponsors a yearly session at the American Literature

Association (ALA) as well as the journal *American Periodicals*, devoted to scholarship relating to American periodicals and newspapers. Also, see Sean Latham and Robert Scholes, "The Rise of Periodical Studies," *PMLA* 121, no. 2 (March 2006): 517–31.

30. "Newspaper Criticism—Degeneracy of the Press," *New-York Mirror* (August 10, 1833): 47.

31. For more on the cultivation of the new form of literary journalism in Charles Greene's Boston *Post*, see Robert J. Scholnick, "'The Ultraism of the Day': Greene's *Boston Post*, Hawthorne, Fuller, Melville, Stowe, and Literary Journalism in Antebellum America," *American Periodicals* 18, no. 2 (2008): 163–91, and Joan Shelley Rubin, *The Making of Middlebrow Culture* (Chapel Hill: The University of North Carolina Press, 1992), 35–36.

32. W. A. Jones, "Critics and Criticism of the Nineteenth Century," *United States Magazine and Democratic Review* 15, no. 74 (August 1844): 161–62.

33. W. A. Jones, "Criticism in America," *United States Magazine and Democratic Review* 15, no. 75 (September 1844): 248–9; William Charvat, *The Origins of American Critical Thought, 1810–1835* (New York: A.S. Barnes and Co., 1961), 4–6.

34. Jones, "Criticism in America," 248–49.

35. T. W. M., "Publishers, Critics and Criticism," *American Publishers' Circular* 2, no. 1 (January 5, 1856): 1–2.

36. T. W. M., "Publishers, Critics and Criticism," 2–3.

37. "Newspaper Criticism," *New York Daily Times*, January 9, 1856.

38. T. W. M., "Newspaper Criticism," *American Publishers' Circular*, 2, no. 3 (January 19, 1856): 29–31.

39. "Journalism," *United States Magazine and Democratic Review* 10, no. 43 (January 1842): 52–53, 54–56.

40. Ibid., 58, 61–62.

41. For a few of the many articles on the decline of newspaper book review sections in the twenty-first century, see Mokoto Rich, "Are Book Reviews Out of Print?" *New York Times*, May 2, 2007; Mokoto Rich, "Washington Post's Book World Goes Out of Print as a Separate Section," *New York Times*, January 28, 2009; John Palattella, "The Death and Life of the Book Review," *Nation*, June 3, 2010, https://www.thenation.com/article/death-and-life-book-review/; Garth Risk Hallberg, "The Future of Book Coverage: Pt. I: R.I.P., NYT?" *The Millions*, April 22, 2009, https://themillions.com/2009/04/future-of-book-coverage-part-i-rip-nyt_22.html.

42. Mott, *American Journalism*, 270; Rubin, *The Making of Middlebrow Culture*, 35–36.

43. Scholnick, "'The Ultraism of the Day,'" 163–64; Capper, *Margaret Fuller: An American Romantic Life*, 2:198.

44. Fuller to Maria Rotch, September 25, 1844, *Letters*, 3:230

45. Horace Greeley, quoted in Marshall, *Margaret Fuller*, 219.

46. Bell Gale Chevigny, "To the Edges of Ideology: Margaret Fuller's Centrifugal Evolution," *American Quarterly* 38, no. 2 (Summer 1986): 173–201.

47. For many of the same reasons she was neglected in the early twentieth century, Fuller is celebrated now: her status as a pioneering women's rights advocate made her a central figure since the rise of feminist literary studies

in the 1970s. Her work as a reviewer and critical theorist made her a key figure for reader response criticism/reception studies in the 1980s. Her work as a foreign correspondent during the revolutionary fervor of 1848 made her a natural fit for first Marxist criticism—indeed, Karl Marx himself contributed to the *Tribune* after her death—and more recently for transnational, hemispheric, and post-national approaches to literature. One indication of this latter interest is the launch of the *Margaret Fuller Transnational Archive*, a digital humanities initiative housed at Northeastern University's Lab for Texts, Maps, and Networks that uses Fuller as a case study for "mapping topographies of revolution," tracing overlapping pathways of print and politics across the porous national boundaries of the nineteenth-century Atlantic (http://margaretfullerarchive.neu.edu/about). For a survey of evolving critical approaches to Fuller see Chevigny's foreword to the revised edition of *The Woman and the Myth*, xv–xlii. For a discussion of the ways in which Fuller anticipated twentieth-century critical concerns, see Bell Gale Chevigny, "'Cheat Me [On] by No Illusion': Margaret Fuller's Cultural Critique and Its Legacies," in *Margaret Fuller's Cultural Critique: Her Age and Legacy*, ed. Fritz Fleischmann (New York: Peter Lang, 2000), 27–41.

48. Ralph Waldo Emerson to Samuel Ward, December 2, 1844, *The Letters of Ralph Waldo Emerson*, ed. Eleanor M. Tilton, vol. 7 (New York: Columbia University Press, 1990), 618.

49. Emerson to Frederick Henry Hedge, April 12, 1838, in *Letters of Ralph Waldo Emerson*, 7:302–3.

50. Fuller to James F. Clarke, [August 14, 1845], *Letters*, 6:359–60.

51. Fuller to Eugene Fuller, March 9, 1845, *Letters*, 4:56–57; Fuller to Richard F. Fuller, March 2, 1845, *Letters*, 4:53–54.

52. Fuller to Samuel G. and Anna B. Ward, March 3, 1846, *Letters*, 4:192–93.

53. Fuller, "A Short Essay on Critics," *Dial* 1, no. 1 (July 1840): 8–9.

54. [Ralph Waldo Emerson,] "Editors to the Reader," *Dial* 1, no. 1 (July 1840): 3; Fuller, "A Short Essay on Critics," 7, 5. For a treatment of Fuller's development as a professional writer, see Steven Fink, "Margaret Fuller: The Evolution of a Woman of Letters," in *Reciprocal Influences: Literary Production, Distribution, and Consumption in America*, ed. Steven Fink and Susan S. Williams (Columbus: Ohio State University Press, 1999), 55–74.

55. Fuller to Samuel G. Ward, December 29, 1844, *Letters*, 3:256.

56. Fuller to [?], [1845], *Letters*, 4:40; Fuller to Eugene Fuller, March 9, 1845, *Letters*, 4:56.

57. Steele, "Reconfiguring 'public attention,'" 131.

58. Kevin G. Barnhurst and John Nerone, *The Form of the News: A History* (New York: The Guilford Press, 2001), 6–7.

59. For a detailed description of the *Tribune* at the time of Fuller's employment, see Mitchell, *Margaret Fuller's New York Journalism*, 3–48.

60. Fuller, "Browning's Poems," *NYDT*, April 1, 1846; *NYWT*, April 4, 1846 (*MFC* 399).

61. Ironically, Arthur Buckminster Fuller, the earliest editor of Fuller's writings after Fuller herself, remained most faithful to Fuller's original *Tribune* essays in those he included in *Life Without and Life Within* (Boston: Brown, Taggard

and Chase, 1860) and *Woman in the Nineteenth-Century and Kindred Papers* (Boston: John P. Jewett and Company, 1855), including excerpted passages in full and altering the pieces as little as possible. Twentieth-century editors weren't as scrupulous, however, cutting liberally from both critical and excerpted content in Fuller's reviews. In the mid-twentieth century, while Perry Miller cuts extensively in his *Margaret Fuller: American Romantic* (Garden City, NY: Anchor, 1963), often selecting just a paragraph or two that highlights some particular theme, Mason Wade in *The Writings of Margaret Fuller* (New York: The Viking Press, 1941) prefers to select fewer reviews but to include them in full, including excerpted passages. Despite the importance of Chevigny's volume *The Woman and the Myth* to the recovery of Fuller's reputation, surprisingly, she is one of the worst offenders when it comes to tampering with extracts, often leaving out excerpts entirely, as in Fuller's review of Frederick Douglass's *Narrative*, and even more problematically, often excising key portions of critical commentary in such a way as to distort Fuller's argument, as with Fuller's disparaging remarks on Elizabeth Barrett Browning, which Chevigny removes in her attempt to show Fuller's feminist solidarity with a fellow female writer.

In more recent collections, Jeffrey Steele in *The Essential Margaret Fuller* (New Brunswick: Rutgers University Press, 1992) includes only six *Tribune* pieces from the New York period in his collection, of which five are editorials rather than literary reviews (the one review is of Emerson). Mary Kelley, in *The Portable Margaret Fuller* (New York: Penguin, 1994) includes six pieces, four of them editorials and two literary reviews (Emerson and Douglass), omitting excerpts in Fuller's review of Douglass. Eve Kornfeld, in *Margaret Fuller: A Brief Biography with Documents* (Boston: Bedford Books, 1997) includes six pieces, four editorials and two literary reviews (Emerson and George Sand), omitting excerpts. Catherine Mitchell focuses primarily on editorials and journalism rather than literary reviews in *Margaret Fuller's New York Journalism* (1995).

Interestingly, Bean and Myerson in *Margaret Fuller, Critic* (2000) include excerpts embedded within Fuller's critical commentary but omit passages that follow immediately after the close of the review, even when Fuller sets them up explicitly, as when they omit the excerpted poem "Israfel" from her review of Poe's *The Raven and Other Poems* or omit the entirety of her lengthy excerpt from Frederick Douglass's *Narrative*, a practice we see in Myerson's earlier collection *Margaret Fuller: Essays on American Life and Letters* as well (New Haven, CT: College and University Press, 1978). In the more recent volume, Bean and Myerson omit these excerpts not just in the reviews included in the book but also on the CD-ROM where space constraints are ostensibly no longer a concern. It's safe to say that in modern editions, readers are not getting the full reviews as they appeared in the *Tribune*, while these alterations and excisions can range from trifling to deeply significant. More generally, when it comes to excerpted material, an area of significant concern when it comes to collections of literary criticism, modern anthologies continue to grapple with a significant problem that current editorial practice hasn't yet figured out an effective way to overcome.

62. Meredith McGill, *American Literature and the Culture of Reprinting, 1834–1853* (Philadelphia: University of Pennsylvania Press, 2003).

63. Fuller, review of *Narrative of the Life of Frederick Douglass*, by Frederick Douglass, *NYDT* (June 10, 1845) (*MFC* 131–33). Steven Mailloux, "Reading as a Historical Act: Cultural Rhetoric, Bible Politics, and Fuller's Review of Douglass's *Narrative*," in *Readers in History*, 3–31. Ironically, while Mailloux makes Fuller's review of Douglass's *Narrative* a case study in historical hermeneutics, exemplifying the principle of the historical contingency of interpretation and reviews as a rhetorical act embedded in contemporaneous discourses and debates, putting special weight on Douglass's own words as excerpted in the review, almost all collections, including *Margaret Fuller, Critic*, omit the long passage from Douglass's *Narrative*.

64. Gottfried Kinkel, "Popular Literature in Germany," *NYDT*, January 27, 1845 (*MFCD* C92); "The Social Movement in Europe," *NYDT*, August 5, 1845 (*MFCD* C171); Christina Zwarg, *Feminist Conversations: Fuller, Emerson, and the Play of Reading* (Ithaca, NY: Cornell University Press, 1995), 1–10, 201.

65. Fuller, "Critics and Essayists," supplement, *NYDT*, June 10, 1846 (*MFC* 446).

66. Anderson, *Imagined Communities*, 25.

67. Fuller, "United States Exploring Expedition," *NYDT*, June 28, 1845 (*MFC* 143–4); Fuller, "The Irish Character," *NYDT*, June 28, 1845 (*MFC* 146–48).

68. Fuller, "Critics and Essayists" (*MFC* 439).

69. Robert N. Hudspeth, "'A Higher Standard in Thought and Action': Margaret Fuller and the Idea of Criticism," *American Unitarianism: 1805–1856*, ed. Conrad Edick Wright (Boston: The Massachusetts Historical Society and Northeastern University Press, 1989), 149.

70. Fuller, "Emerson's Essays," *NYDT*, December 7, 1844 (*MFC* 7).

71. William Gilmore, *Reading Becomes a Necessity of Life: Material and Cultural Life in Rural New England, 1780–1835* (Knoxville: University of Tennessee Press, 1989); James Machor, *Reading Fiction in Antebellum America: Informed Response and Reception History, 1820–1865* (Baltimore: Johns Hopkins University Press, 2011), 7, 14–15.

72. See in particular Zwarg, "Reading Before Marx"; Kopacz, "Feminist at the *Tribune*"; and Bean and Myerson, introduction to *Margaret Fuller, Critic*.

73. Fuller, review of *Memoirs and Essays*, by Anna Jameson, *NYDT*, July 24, 1846; *NYWT*, August 1, 1846 (*MFC* 476); Fuller, "Thanksgiving," *NYDT*, December 12, 1844 (*MFC* 9–10); Fuller, "Thom's Poems," *NYDT*, August 22, 1845 (*MFCD* C175).

74. Fuller, "Asylum for Discharged Female Convicts," *NYDT*, June 19, 1845 (*MFC* 136).

75. Zwarg, "Reading Before Marx," 231–32.

76. Fuller, "Asylum for Discharged Female Convicts" (*MFC* 136–37); Fuller, "Thom's Poems."

77. Fuller, "Cassius M. Clay," *NYWT*, January 17, 1846 (*MFC* 338–41); Fuller, "Methodism at the Fountain," *NYWT*, January 24, 1846 (*MFCD* C239); Fuller, review of *Twenty-Fifth Annual Report of the Bloomingdale Asylum for the Insane*, by Pliny Earle, *NYWT*, February 14, 1846 (*MFCD* C244); Fuller, "Prison Discipline," *NYWT*, February 28, 1846 (*MFCD* C253); Fuller,

"Darkness Visible," *NYWT,* March 7, 1846 (*MFCD* C253); Fuller, review of *Twenty-Seventh Annual Report and Documents of the New York Institution of the Deaf and Dumb to the Legislator of the State of New York for 1845, NYWT,* March 21, 1846 (*MFCD* C257).

78. John Evelev, "Alternatives to Professional Autonomy: N.P. Willis and Margaret Fuller in the Antebellum Literary Field," in *Intellectual Authority and Literary Culture in the US,* ed. Leypoldt, 133. For Evelev, public intellectuals are defined primarily by their "refusal to specialize, their commitment to a market-based (heteronomous, not autonomous) intellectual engagement with the fields of cultural production and social production," and in seeking "to break down distinctions between literary and cultural fields" (118), characteristics that match Fuller's role at the *Tribune* precisely. For Lawrence Buell's characterization of Emerson as public intellectual, see Lawrence Buell, *Emerson* (Cambridge, MA: Belknap Press of Harvard University Press, 1993).

79. Fuller, "1st January 1846," *NYDT,* January 1, 1846; *NYWT,* January 3, 1846 (*MFC* 323–42).

80. Horace Greeley, quoted in *Memoirs of Margaret Fuller Ossoli,* ed. W. H. Channing, J. F. Clarke, and R. W. Emerson (Boston: Phillips, Sampson and Company, 1852), 2:158.

81. Fuller, review of *Ellen; or Forgive and Forget,* by Schoolcraft Jones, *NYDT,* January 10, 1846 (*MFC* 336).

82. Horace Greeley, quoted in *Memoirs of Margaret Fuller Ossoli,* 2:154–55.

83. Wilma R. Ebbitt, "Margaret Fuller's Ideas on Criticism," in *Critical Essays on Margaret Fuller,* ed. Joel Myerson (Boston: G. K. Hall & Co., 1980), 216.

84. Margaret Fuller, "American Literature; Its Position in the Present Time, and Prospects for the Future," in *Papers on Literature and Art* (New York: Wiley and Putnam, 1946), 137–39.

85. Ibid., 140.

86. Fuller, preface to *Papers on Literature and Art,* viii.

87. Fuller, "Farewell," *NYDT,* August 1, 1846 (*MFCD* C316) .

88. Fuller to Evert A. Duyckinck, February 2, 1846, *Letters,* 4:183–84; Fuller to Richard F. Fuller, ca. March 10, 1846, *Letters,* 4:197–98.

89. Fuller to Evert A. Duyckinck, October 30, 1846, *Letters,* 4:234–35; Fuller to Evert A. Duyckinck, June 28, 1846, *Letters,* 4:212; S. Margaret Fuller, preface to *Papers on Literature and Art* (New York: Wiley and Putnam, 1846), v–vi. For a discussion of Fuller's original conception for her critical volume, see Judith Mattson Bean, "Margaret Fuller's (Unsuccessful) Plan for *Papers on Literature and Art,*" *ANQ* 14, no. 2 (Spring 2001): 26–31.

90. Fuller, *Papers on Literature and Art,* vi.

91. Bean and Myerson, introduction to *Margaret Fuller, Critic,* xli.

CHAPTER 5: SLAVERY REVIEWED

1. Maria J. McIntosh, *Two Pictures; or What We Think of Ourselves, and What the World Thinks of Us* (New York: D. Appleton and Company, 1863), 474–75. For more on McIntosh's novel, see Cindy Weinstein, "*Uncle Tom's Cabin* and

the South," in *The Cambridge Companion to Harriet Beecher Stowe* (New York: Cambridge University Press, 2004), 39–57.

2. For more on McIntosh and anti-Tom novels by Southern women, see Joy Jordan-Lake, *Whitewashing Uncle Tom's Cabin: Nineteenth-Century Women Novelists Respond to Stowe* (Nashville, TN: Vanderbilt University Press, 2005).

3. Claire Parfait, *The Publishing History of Uncle Tom's Cabin, 1852–2002* (Burlington, VT: Ashgate, 2004), 6, chap. 5. Michael Winship reiterates this point in "'The Greatest Book of Its Kind': A Publishing History of 'Uncle Tom's Cabin,'" *Proceedings of the American Antiquarian Society* 109, no. 2 (October 1999): 323–24. For an account of the sources for Lincoln's famous statement about Stowe, see David S. Reynolds, *Mightier Than the Sword: Uncle Tom's Cabin and the Battle for America* (New York: W. W. Norton & Company, 2011), ix–x, 277.

4. Unsigned review of *The Literature of the Rebellion*, by John Russell Bartlett, *North American Review* 104, no. 214 (January 1867): 305–6.

5. This argument has been commonly asserted in relation to the slave narrative's impact on the development of American fiction. See, for example, Augusta Rohrbach, *Truth Stranger Than Fiction: Race, Realism, and the U.S. Literary Marketplace* (New York: Palgrave Macmillan, 2002).

6. For the recent attention to Stowe within a transatlantic context, see Denise Kohn, Sarah Meer, and Emily B. Todd, eds., *Transatlantic Stowe: Harriet Beecher Stowe and European Culture* (Iowa City: University of Iowa Press, 2006). Sarah Meer, *Uncle Tom Mania: Slavery, Minstrelsy, and Transatlantic Culture in the 1850s* (Athens: University of Georgia Press, 2005). Also, see Audrey Fisch, *American Slaves in Victorian England: Abolitionist Politics in Popular Literature and Culture* (New York: Cambridge University Press, 2000).

7. For an excellent treatment of anti-Tom novels, see Meer, *Uncle Tom Mania*, chap. 3.

8. For the political implications of the novel's serialization, both in terms of its antislavery message and the status of fiction, see Barbara Hochman, *Uncle Tom's Cabin and the Reading Revolution* (Amherst: University of Massachusetts Press, 2011), 27–50. Also, see Susan Belasco Smith, "Serialization and the Nature of *Uncle Tom's Cabin*," in *Periodical Literature in Nineteenth-Century America*, ed. Kenneth M. Price and Susan Belasco Smith (Charlottesville: University Press of Virginia, 1996), 69–89.

9. For an account of *Uncle Tom's Cabin's* publishing history, see Winship, "'The Greatest Book of Its Kind.'"

10. Tom Standage fleshes out this technological comparison in *Writing on the Wall: Social Media the First 2,000 Years* (New York: Bloomsbury, 2013).

11. [George Frederick Holmes], review of *Uncle Tom's Cabin*, by Harriet Beecher Stowe, *Southern Literary Messenger* 18, no. 12 (December 1852): 725–26.

12. Ibid., 725.

13. See the essays collected in Thomas Nelson Page's *Old South* (Chautauqua, NY: The Chautauqua Press, 1919), particularly "The Want of a History of the Southern People," 253–73.

14. Unsigned review of *Uncle Tom's Cabin*, by Harriet Beecher Stowe, *Christian Examiner and Religious Miscellany* 52, no. 3 (May 1852): 451.

15. "Uncle Tomitudes," *Putnam's Monthly Magazine* 1, no. 1 (January 1853): 97.
16. Ibid., 100.
17. [John R. Thompson], "Notices of New Works: *Uncle Tom's Cabin*," *Southern Literary Messenger* 18, no. 10 (October 1852): 630–31.
18. [Holmes], review of *Uncle Tom's Cabin*, 722.
19. "L S M" [Louisa McCord], review of *Uncle Tom's Cabin*, by Harriet Beecher Stowe, *Southern Quarterly Review* 7, no. 13 (January 1853): 81–120.
20. Ibid., 92, 101, 118.
21. Ibid., 110, 81.
22. Ibid., 81, 104, 112, 115.
23. Walpole, "Southern Slavery. A Glance at Uncle Tom's Cabin. By a Southerner," *New York Daily Times*, first paper, June 22, 1853; second paper, June 28, 1853; third paper, July 9 1853; fourth paper, July 16, 1853.
24. "C.," review of *Uncle Tom's Cabin*, by Harriet Beecher Stowe, *Mercersburg Review* (July 1852).
25. "W. B. S.," review of *Uncle Tom's Cabin*, by Harriet Beecher Stowe, *Morning Post* [Boston], May 3, 1852.
26. "Uncle Tomitudes," 102.
27. Unsigned review of *Uncle Tom's Cabin*, by Harriet Beecher Stowe, *Southern Press Review* (1852). Stephen Railton, *Uncle Tom's Cabin and American Culture* (University of Virginia, 1998–2012), http://utc.iath.virginia.edu/reviews/rere 27at.html.
28. [Holmes], review of *Uncle Tom's Cabin*, 721.
29. James Baldwin, "Everybody's Protest Novel," in *Notes of a Native Son* (Boston: Beacon Press, 1984), 14–15.
30. [Armistead Wilson], "Issue of Half a Million Anti-Slavery Tracts. 'Strike While the Iron Is Hot," *Frederick Douglass' Paper*, May 6, 1853.
31. *Uncle Tom in England. The London Times on Uncle Tom's Cabin. A Review* (New York: Bunce and Brother, 1852), 1–2, 5.
32. A Carolinian [Edward J. Pringle], *Slavery in the Southern States* (Cambridge: John Bartlett, 1852), 3, 8.
33. Laurel Brake, "Pamphlets and the Economy of Print in the Nineteenth Century: A Taster," *19th Century British Pamphlets Online* (March 20, 2009), 2–4. http://www.britishpamphlets.org/uk.
34. Pringle appears, for instance, in the footnotes of Elizabeth Fox-Genovese and Eugene D. Genovese, *Slavery in White and Black: Class and Race in the Southern Slaveholders' New World Order* (New York: Cambridge University Press, 2008), 53, 234. Also, see Bertram Wyatt-Brown, *The Shaping of Southern Culture: Honor, Grace, and War, 1760s–1880s* (Chapel Hill: University of North Carolina Press, 2001), 353n12.
35. "Pro-Slavery Literature," *Liberator* 22, no. 45 (November 5, 1852): 179.
36. Arthur Helps, *A Letter on "Uncle Tom's Cabin"* (Cambridge, MA: John Bartlett, 1852); Nassau William Senior, *American Slavery: A Reprint of an Article on "Uncle Tom's Cabin," of which a Portion Was Inserted in the 206th Number of the "Edinburgh Review;" and of Mr. Sumner's Speech of the 19th and 20th of May, 1856. With a Notice of the Events which Followed that Speech* (London: Longman, Brown, Green, Longmans, & Roberts, 1856); Joel Parker and A. Rood,

The Discussion Between Rev. Joel Parker, and Rev. A. Rood, on the Question "What Are the Evils Inseparable from Slavery," Which Was Referred to By Mrs. Stowe, in "Uncle Tom's Cabin." Reprinted from the Philadelphia Christian Observer of 1846 (New York: S. W. Benedict, 1852).

37. Though no studies, to my knowledge, treat the subgenre of book reviews reprinted as pamphlets, there is a small but significant body of scholarships on pamphlets themselves. For two classic accounts of pamphlets, see George Orwell, introduction to *British Pamphleteers*, ed. George Orwell and Reginald Reynolds, 2 vols. (London: A. Wingate, 1948–1951), 1:15, and Samuel Johnson, "Introduction to the *Harleian Miscellany* (On the Origin and Importance of Small Tracts and Fugitive Pieces)," *The Major Works*, ed. Donald Greene (New York: Oxford University Press, 2008), 122–27. For treatments of the pamphlet form as formative to the political culture of Early Modern England and the American Revolutionary period, respectively, see Joad Raymond, *Pamphlets and Pamphleteering in Early Modern Britain* (New York: Cambridge University Press, 2003), and Bernard Bailyn, *The Ideological Origins of the American Revolution* (Cambridge, MA: The Belknap Press of Harvard University Press, 1992). For accounts of the pamphlet in the nineteenth century in regard to the black political protest movement and the spread of evangelical religion, see Marcy Dinius, "'Look!! Look!!! at This!!!!': The Radical Typography of David Walker's *Appeal*," *PMLA* 126, no. 1 (January 2011): 55–72; Richard Newman, Patrick Rael, and Phillip Lapsansky, eds., *Pamphlets of Protest: An Anthology of Early African American Protest Literature, 1790–1860* (New York: Routledge, 2001); and David Paul Nord, "Free Grace, Free Books, Free Riders: The Economics of Religious Publishing in Early Nineteenth-Century America," *Proceedings of the American Antiquarian Society* 106 (1997): 241–72.

38. Nord, "Free Grace, Free Books, Free Riders," 241–72. Also see David Paul Nord, *Faith in Reading: Religious Publishing and the Birth of Mass Media in America* (New York: Oxford University Press, 2004).

39. Newman, Rael, and Lapsansky, introduction to *Pamphlets of Protest*, 2, 7.

40. A. Woodward, *A Review of Uncle Tom's Cabin; or, An Essay on Slavery* (Cincinnati, OH: Applegate & Co., 1853); F. C. Adams, *Uncle Tom at Home. A Review of the Reviewers and Repudiators of Uncle Tom's Cabin* (Philadelphia: Willis P. Hazard, 1853); E. J. Sterns, *Notes on Uncle Tom's Cabin: Being a Logical Answer to Its Allegations and Inferences Against Slavery as an Institution. With a Supplementary Note on The Key, and An Appendix of Authorities* (Philadelphia: Lippincott, Grambo & Co., 1853).

41. Nicholas Brimblecomb [pseud.], *Uncle Tom's Cabin in Ruins! Triumphant Defence of Slavery! in a Series of Letters to Harriet Beecher Stowe* (Boston: Charles Waite, 1853). For the review in *Frederick Douglass' Paper*, unsigned, though possibly by Julia Griffiths, see "Uncle Tom's Cabin in Ruins," *Frederick Douglass' Paper*, January 21, 1853.

42. Weinstein, "*Uncle Tom's Cabin* and the South," 39–57.

43. Harriet Beecher Stowe, *A Key to Uncle Tom's Cabin* (Boston: John P. Jewett & Co., 1853), iii.

44. Ibid., 5.

45. Ibid., 5.

46. Ibid., 47.

47. Weinstein, "*Uncle Tom's Cabin* and the South," 50–51.

48. Stowe, *A Key*, 46.

49. Ibid., 88, 114–15.

50. Ibid., 75.

51. Frederick Douglass, "Letter from the Editor," *Frederick Douglass' Paper*, July 30, 1852 (hereafter *FDP*).

52. Delany and Douglass, "Letter from M. R. Delany" and "Remarks," *FDP*, April 1, 1853.

53. Robert S. Levine, "*Uncle Tom's Cabin* in *Frederick Douglass' Paper*: An Analysis of Reception," *American Literature* 64, no. 1 (March 1992): 74. For Jane Tompkins's notion of "cultural work," see *Sensational Designs: The Cultural Work of American Fiction, 1790–1860* (New York: Oxford University Press, 1985).

54. Frederick Douglass, "Mrs. Stowe's Visit to England," *FDP*, April 15, 1853.

55. O. A. Bowe, "A Word from Old Herkimer," *FDP*, July 30, 1852.

56. Meredith McGill, *American Literature and the Culture of Reprinting, 1834–1853* (Philadelphia: University of Pennsylvania Press, 2003); Ryan Cordell, "Reprinting, Circulation, and the Network Author in Antebellum Newspapers," *American Literary History* 27, no. 3 (Fall 2015): 418.

57. Ellen Gruber Garvey, *Writing with Scissors: American Scrapbooks from the Civil War to the Harlem Renaissance* (New York: Oxford University Press, 2012), 30–31; Frances Smith Foster, "A Narrative of the Interesting Origins and (Somewhat) Surprising Developments of African-American Print Culture," *American Literary History* 17, no. 4 (Winter 2005): 727–28.

58. Ellen Gruber Garvey, "'facts and FACTS': Abolitionists' Database Innovations," in *"Raw Data" Is an Oxymoron*, ed. Lisa Gitelman (Cambridge, MA: MIT Press, 2013), 89–102.

59. John Ernest, "Beyond Douglass and Jacobs," in *The Cambridge Companion to the African American Slave Narrative*, ed. Audrey Fisch (New York: Cambridge University Press, 2007), 218–31. Eric Gardner, *Unexpected Places: Relocating Nineteenth-Century African American Literature* (Jackson: University Press of Mississippi, 2009), 6–10, and Eric Gardner, *Black Print Unbound: The Christian Recorder, African American Literature, and Periodical Culture* (New York: Oxford University Press, 2015), 9–14.

60. Robert S. Levine, *Martin Delany, Frederick Douglass, and the Politics of Representative Identity* (Chapel Hill: University of North Carolina Press, 1997).

61. Elizabeth McHenry, *Forgotten Readers: Recovering the Lost History of African American Literary Societies* (Durham, NC: Duke University Press, 2002), 114–29.

62. Hochman, *Uncle Tom's Cabin and the Reading Revolution*, 78–103.

63. "Poems by Phillis Wheatley," *FDP*, August 31, 1855; "The Garies and Their Friends," *FDP*, December 4, 1857; "The White Slave; or Memoirs of a Fugitive," *FDP*, August 6, 1852; "Ida May—A Story of Things Actual and Possible," *FDP*, November 17, 1854; "Minnie Hermon," *FDP*, June 16, 1854; "Aunt Phillis' Cabin, or Southern Life As It Is," *FDP*, September 3, 1852; "Life at the South; or Uncle Tom's Cabin As It Is," *FDP*, August 13, 1852; Laura J. Curtis, "Christine, or, Woman's Trials and Triumphs," *FDP*, January 18, 1856, and

February 1, 1856; Elizabeth Livermore, "Zoe, or The Quadroon's Triumph," *FDP*, October 5, 1855; William J. Wilson, "An Original Story. Terrance Ludlam," *FDP*, August 11, 1854, and August 18, 1854.

64. McHenry, *Forgotten Readers*, 123–25.

65. Fanny Fern, "A Street Scene," *FDP*, July 21, 1854. Griffiths also reviewed *Fern Leaves*: "Fern Leaves," *FDP*, June 16, 1854, and "Ruth Hall," *FDP*, December 29, 1854. In turn, Griffiths reprinted Fanny Fern's review of *My Bondage and My Freedom*, *FDP*, September 14, 1855. "This, That, and the Other," *FDP* September 1, 1854. "The Author of 'Jane Eyre,'" *FDP*, August 31, 1855. "A Few Personal Recollections on Christopher North," *FDP*, February 22, 1855. "Anecdotes of Milton," *FDP*, November 30, 1855. Harriet Beecher Stowe, "Sunny Memories of Foreign Lands," *FDP*, August 4, 1854. Charles Dickens, "A Night in London," *FDP*, February 2, 1855. Henry Ward Beecher, "The Duty of Owning Books," *FDP*, March 4, 1859. "New Publications. My Bondage and My Freedom," *FDP*, September 21, 1855.

66. Perhaps the most glaring of these instances is Julia Griffiths's signed response to George Graham's "Black Letters" ["Literary Notices. Graham," (February 25, 1853)], which Railton attributes to Douglass. (http://utc.iath.virginia.edu/africam/afaro3jt.html). Indeed, for as valuable as the database is, it should be noted that Railton's dating of pieces, as with his attribution, is often unreliable. McHenry, for her part, buries the problem of uncertain editorial attribution in a footnote, referring to Douglass as author in the body of the text while pointing out in a footnote that, "It should be noted that the entries in the 'Literary Notices' column of the paper during this time may have been written by Douglass but are more likely the work of Julia Griffiths, Douglass's English comrade, financial supporter, and literary editor." Like Levine, McHenry resolves the issue by reference to the eponymous name of the paper and Benjamin Quarles's assertion that *Frederick Douglass' Paper* was "to an unusual degree the product of one man's thinking" (347–48n94). As this chapter suggests, I am less convinced by this argument or by Quarles's notion of the paper's homogenous intellectual cast. For the original assertion, see Benjamin Quarles, *Frederick Douglass* (New York: Atheneum, 1968), 83–84, first published 1948.

67. Perhaps the clearest indication of the privileged status of the responses by Allen and Wilson specifically are their inclusion within the Norton Critical Edition of Stowe's *Uncle Tom's Cabin*, ed. Elizabeth Ammons, 2nd ed. (New York: W. W. Norton & Company, 2010), 499–503.

68. The critical responses most frequently discussed are the following: "Literary Notices. Uncle Tom's Cabin," *FDP*, April 8, 1852; William G. Allen, "Communications. Letter from Wm. G. Allen," *FDP*, May 20, 1852; Ethiop [William J. Wilson], "From Our Brooklyn Correspondent," *FDP*, June 17, 1852; and Frederick Douglass, "A Day and a Night in 'Uncle Tom's Cabin,'" *FDP*, March 4, 1853. For the debate between Douglass and Delany, see Martin Delany and Frederick Douglass, "Letter from M. R. Delany" [1] and "Remarks," *FDP*, April 1, 1853; Martin Delany, "Uncle Tom" [2], *FDP*, April 29, 1853; Frederick Douglass, "The Letter of M. R. Delany," *FDP*, May 6, 1853; Martin R. Delany, "Mrs. Stowe's Position" [3], *FDP*, May 6, 1853.

69. The best account of the reception to *Uncle Tom's Cabin* in *Frederick Douglass' Paper* is Levine's "*Uncle Tom's Cabin* in *Frederick Douglass' Paper*," 71–93. Levine gives an expanded treatment with a focus on the Douglass and Delany as representative figures for competing visions of racial progress in *Martin Delany, Frederick Douglass, and the Politics of Representative Identity*, 58–98. For other accounts of the antebellum black reception to Stowe's novel, see Marva Banks, "*Uncle Tom's Cabin* and Antebellum Black Response," in *Readers in History: Nineteenth-Century Literature and the Contexts of Response*, ed. James L. Machor (Baltimore: Johns Hopkins University Press, 1993), 209–27; Lydia Willsky, "Countering the Rhetoric of Slavery: The Critical Roots and Critical Reception of *Uncle Tom's Cabin*," in *Critical Insights: Literature of Protest*, ed. Kimberly Drake (Ipswich, MA: Salem Press, 2013), 27–43. McHenry, *Forgotten Readers*, 125–29. Also, see Lois Brown, "African American Responses to *Uncle Tom's Cabin*," *Uncle Tom's Cabin and American Culture*, Stephen Railton & the University of Virginia. http://utc.iath.virginia.edu/interpret/interframe.html.

70. Levine, "*Uncle Tom's Cabin* in *Frederick Douglass' Paper*," 75–77.

71. Levine, "*Uncle Tom's Cabin* in *Frederick Douglass' Paper*," 73; McHenry, *Forgotten Readers*, 347–48n94; Quarles, *Frederick Douglass*, 83–84.

72. Frederick Douglass, "The Letter of Mr. Delany," *North Star*, June 27, 1850.

73. Frederick Douglass, "George Thompson, R. D. Webb and the Liberty Party Again," *FDP*, November 6, 1851.

74. Lara Langer Cohen and Jordan Alexander Stein, introduction to *Early African American Print Culture*, ed. Lara Langer Cohen and Jordan Alexander Stein (Philadelphia: University of Pennsylvania Press, 2012), 14. For Cohen's notion of the "patchwork aesthetic," see in the above volume "Notes from the State of Saint Domingue: The Practice of Citation in *Clotel*," 164. For a similar intervention into the principles by which African American literary history is ordered, including the overemphasis on authorship, see John Ernest, *Chaotic Justice: Rethinking African American Literary History* (Chapel Hill: University of North Carolina Press, 2009).

75. In her account of the antebellum black reception of *Uncle Tom's Cabin*, for instance, Marva Banks notes that, while "initially, blacks eagerly heralded it and were optimistic about the impetus it would give to the abolitionist cause," nonetheless, "as blacks became increasingly aware that Stowe's novel had an equivalent power to foster certain images of black inferiority and could therefore be used to bolster the proslavery argument, their early enthusiasm often changed to skepticism and then to anger." To be sure, the black response to *Uncle Tom's Cabin* was mixed, but it didn't *become* so over time. Rather that skepticism was there from the outset. Banks, "*Uncle Tom's Cabin* and Antebellum Black Response," 225.

76. Sarah Meer, "Douglass as Orator and Editor," in *The Cambridge Companion to Frederick Douglass*, ed. Maurice S. Lee (New York: Cambridge University Press, 2009), 46–59; Sarah Meer, "Public and Personal Letters: Julia Griffiths and *Frederick Douglass' Paper*," *Slavery & Abolition* 33, no. 2 (June 2012): 251–64.

77. Levine, "*Uncle Tom's Cabin* in *Frederick Douglass' Paper*," 78–79.

78. "American and Foreign Anti-Slavery Society," *FDP*, May 27, 1852. For

Theodore Parker's famous assertion that "all of the original romance of Americans" is to be found in slave narratives, "not in the white man's novel," see his August 8, 1849, address, "The American Scholar," in George Willis Cooke, ed., *The American Scholar*, vol. 8 of *Centenary Edition of Theodore Parker's Writings* (Boston: American Unitarian Association, 1907), 37.

79. For remarks on *Uncle Tom's Cabin* appearing within the minutes of an antislavery meeting, see "American and Foreign Anti-Slavery Society," *FDP*, May 27, 1852; for a report of the novel's discussion in Congress, see "Uncle Tom in the Senate," *FDP*, April 1, 1853. For addresses and minutes from fundraising celebrations in Stowe's honor, see the account of the Glasgow Emancipation Society celebration, "From the Glasgow Saturday Post. 'Uncle Tom's Cabin'—Public Meeting at the City Hall," *FDP*, December 24, 1852, and "Anti-Slavery Meeting in Belfast," *FDP*, January 21, 1853. For Southern testimonials as to the accuracy of Stowe's depictions, see "A Slaveholder, writing from New Orleans," *FDP*, July 16, 1852; John, "Uncle Tom's Cabin," *FDP*, October 22, 1852, and Republican, "Light in the South," *FDP*, August 13, 1852, and "Uncle Tom's Cabin," *FDP*, October 22, 1852. For real life incidents contrasted to *UTC*, see "Another Incident for 'Uncle Tom's Cabin,'" *FDP*, January 28, 1853, and "'Uncle Tom's Cabin' Outdone," *FDP*, November 23, 1855.

80. Henry Ward Beecher, "Reply of Henry Ward Beecher" [1], *FDP*, November 5, 1852, and [2] *FDP*, November 12, 1852.

81. For one of the many reports on sales of *UTC*, see "Uncle Tom's Cabin," *FDP*, November 5, 1852. For *UTC* in German, see "'Uncle Tom's Cabin' in German," *FDP*, October 22, 1852. For *UTC* in France and Hawaii, see "Uncle Tom's Cabin," *FDP*, February 4, 1853. Also, see George Sand's review: George Sand, "A French Author's Criticism of Uncle Tom's Cabin," *FDP*, February 18, 1853. For the account of a man who hadn't yet read this book, see "The man who has not read *Uncle Tom's Cabin*," *FDP*, August 5, 1853. The latter is incorrectly dated June 22, 1853 in Railton's database.

82. For the biographical sketch of Stowe, see "Some Account of Mrs. Beecher Stowe's Family, by an Alabama Man," *FDP*, December 17, 1852. For two of the many accounts of dramatizations, see "Uncle Tom's Cabin on the Stage," *FDP*, August 20, 1852, and "Uncle Tom's Cabin at the National Theater," *FDP*, October 8, 1852. For an account of a diorama representation of the story, see J. N. Still, "Exhibitions and Lectures. Diorama of Uncle Tom's Cabin," *FDP*, May 4, 1855. For reviews of anti-Tom novels, see "Stolen Thunder," *FDP*, October 22, 1852; "Literary Notices. Life at the South. By W. L. G. Smith," *FDP*, August 13, 1852, and Julia Griffiths, "Literary Notices. Aunt Phillis' Cabin," *FDP*, September 3, 1852, and "Anti-Tom. Uncle Tom's Cabin contrasted with Buckingham Hall," *FDP*, December 17, 1852. For the reception of *UTC* in England, see A. H. [Arthur Helps], "Uncle Tom's Cabin," *FDP*, October 8, 1852; Earl of Carlisle, "Introduction to Uncle Tom's Cabin.—By the Earl of Carlisle, for the English Edition," *FDP*, December 24, 1852; "Uncle Tom in England," *FDP*, October 15, 1852; and "Uncle Tom in England," *FDP*, December 17, 1852.

83. For celebrations for Stowe in Glasgow and Belfast, see "From the Glasgow Saturday Post. 'Uncle Tom's Cabin'—Public Meeting at the City Hall," *FDP*,

December 24, 1852; and "Address to Mrs. Beecher Stowe ... Belfast, Ireland," *FDP*, January 21, 1853. For reviews of reviews, see the New York *Independent*'s rejoinder to M. Emile Montegut's review in *Revue des Deux Mondes*, reprinted in *FDP*: "Uncle Tom's Cabin," *FDP*, November 19, 1852. Also, see the English correspondent for the *Independent*'s response to a review from the *London Times*: "Uncle Tom's Cabin in England," *FDP*, December 17, 1852. For Douglass's printing of an apologist attack on the novel, see "Uncle Tom's Cabin at the National Theater." For the response to George Graham's infamous review, see Julia Griffiths, "Literary Notices. Graham's Magazine" [1], *FDP*, January 21, 1853; "Literary Notices. Graham" [2], *FDP*, February 25, 1853; "Graham vs. Uncle Tom" [3], *FDP*, March 4, 1853.

84. Frederick Douglass, editorial note for William Wells Brown, "Letter from William W. Brown" *FDP*, June 10, 1853.

85. E., "Negro Intellect.—Ellis and Douglass, and Uncle Tom," *FDP*, July 15, 1853.

86. As Stowe wrote in her famous letter to Douglass, "I have noticed with regret, your sentiments on two subjects,—the church—& African Colonization—& with the more regret, because I think you have a considerable share of reason for your feelings on both these subjects—*but* I would willingly if I could modify your view on both points." Harriet Beecher Stowe to Frederick Douglass, July 9, 1851, in Joan D. Hedrick, ed., *The Oxford Harriet Beecher Stowe Reader* (New York: Oxford University Press, 1999), 59.

87. Sans Nom [pseud.], "Little Sodus," *FDP*, Aug 6, 1852.

88. Robert B. Stepto, "Sharing the Thunder: The Literary Exchanges of Harriet Beecher Stowe, Henry Bibb, and Frederick Douglass," in *New Essays on Uncle Tom's Cabin*, ed. Eric J. Sundquist (New York: Cambridge University Press, 1986), 135–53. Douglass serialized "The Heroic Slave" in *FDP* in four parts: [1] March 4, 1853; [2] March 11, 1853; [3] March 18, 1853; [4] March 25, 1853.

89. Sarah Meer, "Public and Personal Letters: Julia Griffiths and *Frederick Douglass' Paper*," *Slavery & Abolition* 33, no. 2 (June 2012): 251–64.

90. Robert Fanuzzi, *Abolition's Public Sphere* (Minneapolis: University of Minnesota Press, 2003).

91. For instance, for Robert Fanuzzi, the cultural emphasis on Douglass's "manliness" and his embodied form exposed the limits of the public sphere model emphasized by Garrison. Fanuzzi, *Abolition's Public Sphere*, esp. chap. 3, "Frederick Douglass's Public Body," 83–128.

92. For these frequently cited responses, see previous citation, chap. 5, n. 68.

93. Meredith L. McGill and Andrew Parker, "The Future of the Literary Past," *PMLA* 125, no. 4 (October 2010): 959–67.

94. Maurice S. Lee, "Falsifiability, Confirmation Bias, and Textual Promiscuity," *J19* 2, no. 1 (Spring 2014): 164; James Mussell, *The Nineteenth-Century Press in the Digital Age* (New York: Palgrave Macmillan, 2012), 20–21.

CODA: FROM THE STEAM PRESS TO AMAZON.COM

1. Jay Greene, "Amazon opening its first real bookstore—at U-Village," *Seattle Times*, November 2, 2015, http://www.seattletimes.com/business/amazon/amazon

-opens-first-bricks-and-mortar-bookstore-at-u-village/.Rich Duprey,"Retailers Should Be Wary—Amazom.com Is Closing All Its Pop-Up Stores," *Motley Fool,* March 17, 2019, https://www.fool.com/investing/2019/03/17/maybe amazon-should-stick-with-being-an-online-ret-aspx. George Packer "Cheap Words," *New Yorker,* February 17 & 24, 2014, http://www.newyorker.com /magazine/2014/02/17/cheap-words.

2. Christian Lorentzen, "Samuel L. Jackson, *Mad Max,* and Susan Sontag: My Road Trip with A.O. Scott," *Vulture,* February 5, 2016, http://www.vulture .com/2016/02/ on-criticism-my-road-trip-with-ao-scott.html.

3. A. O. Scott, *Better Living Through Criticism: How to Think About Art, Pleasure, Beauty, and Truth* (New York: Penguin Press, 2016), 11–12.

4. Ibid., 172, 211–12.

5. Calum Marsh, "A. O. Scott, Last of the Power Critics," review of *Better Living Through Criticism,* by A. O. Scott, *New Republic,* February 10, 2016, https:// newrepublic.com/article/129621/a-o-scott-last-power-critics.

6. Laura Miller, "The Critic as Artist. A.O. Scott defends criticism—but against whom?" review of *Better Living Though Criticism,* by A. O. Scott, *Slate,* January 31, 2016, http://www.slate.com/articles/arts/books/2016/01/a _o_scott_s_better_living_through_criticism_reviewed.html. For two highly critical reviews of Scott's book, attacking him for lacking both an argument and critical conviction, see Leon Wieseltier, "A. O. Scott, Critic Without a Cause," review of *Better Living Though Criticism,* by A. O. Scott, *Atlantic,* February 26, 2016, http://www.theatlantic.com/magazine/archive/2016/03/ao -scott-critic-without-a-cause/426828/, and Nathan Heller, "Says You: How to Be a Critic in an Age of Opinion," review of *Better Living Though Criticism,* by A. O. Scott, *New Yorker,* March 7, 2016, http://www.newyorker.com/ magazine/2016/03/07/critics-in-the-age-of-opinion. For more positive reviews, see Laura Kipnis, "Critical Condition," review of *Better Living Though Criticism,* by A. O. Scott, *Bookforum* (February/March 2016): 31, and Michael Wood, "In 'Better Living Through Criticism,' A.O. Scott Defends His Job," review of *Better Living Though Criticism,* by A. O. Scott, *New York Times,* February 3, 2016, http://www.nytimes.com/2016/02/04/books/review-in-better living-through-criticism-ao-scott-offers-insight.html.

7. Scott, *Better Living Through Criticism,* 213–14.

8. Wieseltier, "A. O. Scott, Critic Without a Cause."

9. Isaac Chotiner, "A Conversation with the *New York Times'* A.O. Scott," *Slate,* 4 February 2016, http://www.slate.com/articles/arts/books/2016/02/an _interview_with_a_o_scott_about_oscarssowhite_better_living_through_cr iticism.html.

10. Rick Moody, *Hotels of North America: A Novel* (New York: Little, Brown and Company, 2015), 194–95.

11. Ibid., 149.

12. Ibid., 198.

INDEX

Page numbers in italics indicate figures.